MIDWESTERN NATIVE
SHRUBS AND TREES

MIDWESTERN NATIVE SHRUBS AND TREES

gardening alternatives
to nonnative species

ぎゝ

AN ILLUSTRATED GUIDE

ぎゝ

Charlotte Adelman
and
Bernard L. Schwartz

OHIO UNIVERSITY PRESS

ATHENS

Other Books by Charlotte Adelman and Bernard Schwartz

The Midwestern Native Garden: Native Alternatives
to Nonnative Flowers and Plants
An Illustrated Guide

Flowering Prairie Plants

Louis Agassiz Fuertes: A Retrospective Sampling of
His Bird Drawings and Paintings, by Bernard L. Schwartz

Prairie Directory of North America—The United States and Canada
Prairie Directory of North America—The United States,
Canada and Mexico (Second Edition)

WBAI—The First 75 Years, by Charlotte Adelman

Ohio University Press, Athens, Ohio 45701
ohioswallow.com
© 2016 by Ohio University Press
All rights reserved

To obtain permission to quote, reprint, or otherwise reproduce or distribute
material from Ohio University Press publications, please contact our rights and
permissions department at (740) 593-1154 or (740) 593-4536 (fax).

Printed in the United States of America
Ohio University Press books are printed on acid-free paper ∞™

27 26 25 24 23 22 21 20 19 18 17   5 4 3 2 1

Library of Congress Cataloging-in-Publication Data

Names: Adelman, Charlotte, 1937– author. | Schwartz, Bernard L., 1933– author.
Title: Midwestern native shrubs and trees : gardening alternatives to
  nonnative species : an illustrated guide / Charlotte Adelman and Bernard
  L. Schwartz.
Description: Athens, Ohio : Ohio University Press, [2017] | Includes
  bibliographical references and index.
Identifiers: LCCN 2016051637| ISBN 9780821421666 (hc : alk. paper) | ISBN
  9780821421642 (pb : alk. paper) | ISBN 9780821445303 (pdf)
Subjects: LCSH: Endemic plants—Middle West. | Woody plants—Middle West. |
  Shrubs—Middle West. | Trees—Middle West.
Classification: LCC QK128 .A34 2017 | DDC 582.160977—dc23
LC record available at https://lccn.loc.gov/2016051637

CONTENTS

Preface   vii

Acknowledgments   ix

How to Use This Book   xi

Abbreviations Used   xv

Introduction   1

Chapter 1 Spring   11

Chapter 2 Summer   121

Chapter 3 Fall   225

Chapter 4 Winter   303

Notes   357

Glossary   381

Selected Bibliography and Resources   387

Illustration and Photography Credits   397

Index   411

PREFACE

Having a yard or garden enables almost every homeowner, gardener, and landscaper to create a beautiful, low-maintenance native plant sanctuary that sustains native wildlife. Midwestern native plants and birds, butterflies, and bees co-evolved and need each other for a healthy future. *The Midwestern Native Garden: Native Alternatives to Nonnative Flowers and Plants* discussed native herbaceous plant alternatives to Eurasian introductions and nativars (cultivars of native plants). Remembering landscaping mistakes we had made, we noted in the preface to that volume, "Because we love birds, we lined our borders with berry- and fruit-producing trees and shrubs. Later, to our horror, we discovered that most of our well-meaning plant choices were not native to North America and that some were invasive pests. We realized we had made choices without first getting good information." This book continues the work of the first volume by providing reliable information for midwestern native alternatives to nonnative trees and shrubs.

When we speak of butterflies, flowers usually come to mind, but "woody plants support more butterfly caterpillars than herbaceous plants."[1] As a group, native trees and shrubs excel as host plants for butterflies and moths, whose larvae or caterpillars "are disproportionately valuable sources of food for many terrestrial birds, particularly warblers and neotropical migrants of conservation concern."[2] What makes native woody plants invaluable to wildlife? "Plants have evolved over time alongside the insect and animal populations that feed and reproduce on them, so planting a variety of plants native to your area is one of the simplest ways of helping out your local wildlife. But . . . on the whole, woody plants like trees and shrubs provide food and shelter to the greatest variety of wildlife. So when choosing where you can have the most impact for your local wildlife, shrubs and trees can be a better bet than perennials and small flowers."[3]

As someone who likes to walk and look, I often wander around my neighborhood, observing the local landscaping. Large trees have been replaced by new homes and large garages. Eurasian burning bush, saucer magnolia, dwarf Korean lilac, Japanese lilac tree, winter creeper, and common boxwood are ubiquitous, but they don't attract butterflies, bees, or birds. Butterflies are rare, goldfinches are scarce, and migrating birds have become uncommon. Scientific data substantiate the decrease of these once abundant wild creatures.[4] "The songbirds that brighten spring mornings have been in decline since the 1960s, having lost 40 percent of their numbers so far," writes entomologist and ecologist Douglas Tallamy. These losses are due "to a host of factors but mainly to habitat loss, which includes displacement of native plants by aliens. The worst invaders are Asian and European."[5]

"Homeowners and developers alike are beginning to appreciate the environmental, economic and aesthetic benefits of natural landscaping," according to the US Environmental Protection Agency.[6] Horticulturists and naturalists provide an explanation for this trend: "Today, there is renewed interest in 'going native' and restoring diversity to our landscapes by choosing native plants. The reasons for this are many and varied. Planting a native plant provides habitat for a variety of native wildlife species such as songbirds and butterflies. Including native species provides a historical sense of pride to a gardener who grows a plant that Native Americans or early pioneers valued. Furthermore, regionally-adapted native plants have developed a natural resistance to regional pests, and a tolerance to drought, ice storms and other environmental extremes common to the area."[7] Midwesterners with questions about native plants can readily find answers. Typing words like "native plant" into an Internet browser produces helpful information. Organizations and books devoted to birds, butterflies, pollinators, gardening with native plants, native plant nursery catalogs, and our own observations provide information and inspiration to advance the trend toward "natural landscaping." For more information, please see Selected Bibliography and Resources.

"Now is the time to get started because time is not on our side as more of our native habitats disappear."[8] Regardless of the location or the size of our property, native plants create habitats and migration corridors for wildlife. Even small urban patches can be lifesavers for pollinators (butterflies, moths, bees, beetles, bats, ruby-throated hummingbirds), insect-eating migrating warblers, and other birds that fly from place to place.[9] Plantings of thoughtfully chosen and responsibly cared-for native woody and herbaceous species help prevent harm and ensure maximum benefits.

"Planting natives in small landscapes will not recreate ancient ecosystems, but it does create biodiversity to support what's left of our wildlife," states Douglas Tallamy, who suggests keeping lawn for where we walk or use it for recreation. "The rest of the landscape would consist of bunching grasses, shrubs, understory trees and canopy trees."[10] Simply by replacing portions of our lawns with native trees, shrubs, and herbaceous species, we can greatly improve home and neighborhood ecosystems.[11] Sharing information about the importance of natives and how to choose and purchase them helps create change. Whether by small incremental steps or by big landscaping projects, each of us can decide to help ensure a future for butterflies and birds by choosing life-giving native shrubs and trees.

Homeowners, gardeners, and landscapers have the ability and opportunity to make good environmental choices and to create beautiful landscapes and gardens. And that is something to celebrate. We wrote this book to bring wider attention to the age-old connection between native woody plants and native wildlife. We hope the information we share will intrigue and inspire readers to protect this delicate balance by emphasizing native midwestern woody plants when landscaping and gardening.

ACKNOWLEDGMENTS

THE AUTHORS gratefully acknowledge the many people and organizations that helped make this book possible.

The people and organizations are listed in no particular order:

We thank Gillian Berchowitz, director of Ohio University Press, for her support, counsel, and recognition of the environmental importance of regionally native plants for our gardens and landscapes.

We also thank:

The United States Department of Agriculture—USDA PLANTS Database (http://plants.usda.gov/java/) and all the individuals from the USDA who contributed photographs for this book

Jeffrey S. Pippen (www.duke.edu/~jspippen/nature.htm), who contributed a wondrous supply of butterfly photographs

Rob's Plants at www.robsplants.com

The Missouri Botanical Garden Plant Finder (http://www.missouribotanicalgarden.org/plantfinder/plantfindersearch.aspx)

The many photographers who released their photographs into the public domain

Mary Vaux Walcott, *North American Wild Flowers* (1925)

Alice Lounsberry (author, 1872–1949), Ellis Rowan (artist, 1847–1922)

Harriet L. Keeler (author, 1846–1921)

Lady Bird Johnson Wildflower Center

The illustrations by Louis Agassiz Fuertes and the many artists from the books used in this book:

Otto Wilhelm Thomé, *Flora von Deutschland, Österreich und der Schweiz* (1885–1905)

Carl Axel Magnus Lindman, *Bilder ur Nordens Flora* (1901–5)

Franz Köhler, *Köhler's Medizinal-Pflanzen* (1887)

Johann Georg Sturm, *Deutschlands Flora in Abbildungen* (1796)

William Curtis (1746–1799), *Curtis's Botanical Magazine*

Forestry Images, http://www.forestryimages.org/

Illustrations by Allan Brooks

Darrell Kromm of Reeseville Ridge Nursery, Reeseville, Wisconsin

Paul L. Redfearn Jr. from the Missouri State University Herbarium

Dr. John Hilty, whose website (http://www.illinoiswildflowers.info/) provides unique data on plants, birds, plant pollinators, butterflies, and other insects

Douglas W. Tallamy (entomologist, ecologist, author) for his vast knowledge and
     inspiration
We also thank the other authors, illustrators, and photographers who contributed
     to this book.
Finally, we are grateful to all our friends, native plant enthusiasts, and envi-
ronmentally minded acquaintances who encouraged us in our endeavors to finish
this book.

HOW TO USE THIS BOOK

M IDWESTERN GARDENING and landscaping take into account the changing seasons, so we present our book on woody species in sections entitled Spring, Summer, Fall, and Winter. Spring focuses on spring flowers. Summer looks at summer flowers and shade. Fall features leaf color. In winter, bark, decorative shapes, and evergreens become the focus. Each season is subdivided into shrubs and trees (species sometimes overlap) and contains a selection of alphabetically listed (in red) nonnative (introduced, alien, exotic) woody plants that are popular in the Midwest (each followed by one or more native species, listed in green). For maximum accessibility, we list the plants by their common names. Later references to the plant use only the first common name listed. Following a plant's common name or names, we list its family, genus, and, in parentheses, species. When we repeat the genus name, it is abbreviated, as in this example: *H. cinerea* instead of *Hydrangea cinerea*. We provide the nonnative plant's origin (not shown in USDA PLANTS), frequently Asia or Europe. Next we present the plant's height, notable ornamental features (flowers, fruit, fall color), and cultivation requirements. We provide Ecological Threat notes, based on USDA PLANTS maps designating nonnative plants naturalized in the Midwest (eastern half of the United States). USDA PLANTS maps reveal the great extent to which nonnative woody and herbaceous species have moved into our midwestern ecosystems. Using "I" for "Introduced" and defining the term as "naturalized," USDA PLANTS states, "In general, introduced plants are likely to invade or become noxious since they lack co-evolved competitors and natural enemies to control their populations."[1] No single clear controlling entity defines the term invasive, or designates a species as being invasive or not. To determine if a nonnative plant is invasive, we relied on data from a variety of invasive plant organizations and governmental resources that evaluate plant species for invasiveness. For information on these resources, please see Selected Bibliography and Resources.

Following each nonnative plant entry is at least one midwestern native woody species (listed in green) that resembles the nonnative plant in height, notable ornamental features (flowers, fruit, fall color), and cultivation requirements. An entry in, say, Spring may mention summer fruit, fall color, or overwintering leaves or berries, so we cross-reference to identify native woody species that have multiple seasons of interest. The US National Arboretum defines a native plant as "one that occurs naturally in a particular region, ecosystem, or habitat without direct or indirect human intervention. We consider the flora present at the time Europeans arrived in North

America as the species native to the eastern United States."[2] "Even though their off-spring reproduce and spread naturally (without human help), naturalized plants do not, over time, become native members of the local plant community."[3] We verified that a plant is native, "N," through USDA PLANTS, and checked its subordinate taxa (varieties) and maps for distribution. A Nature Note following each native plant entry references some of the vital connections between the native plant and wildlife, especially butterflies, other native insects, and birds. Because most native insects (including butterflies) lay their eggs on native plants, and require them for successful reproduction, and most birds feed caterpillars (larval stage of Lepidoptera—butter-flies/moths) and other insects to their offspring, we provide the number of Lepidoptera species hosted by many of the native woody species, based on Douglas Tallamy's studies on butterfly and moth productivity. (Please see Selected Bibliography and Resources for Native Woody Species and Native Herbaceous Species in Descending Order of Lepidoptera Productivity.) We note when a plant has become rare, threatened, endangered, or extirpated in the region, according to information provided by USDA PLANTS. Our sources include the Morton Arboretum's "Not recommended" species, and "Plants Tolerant to Black Walnut;"[4] Christopher Starbuck's "unusual trees" for specimen planting;[5] and data from "Average and Maximum Lifespan of Virginia Trees."[6]

Selecting popular nonnative shrubs and trees was an eye-opener. The choices offered by most mail order catalogs, big-box stores, generalist nurseries, and garden centers are between one nonnative and another nonnative plant. Nonnative plants commercially offered are often invasive species and their hybrids and cultivars. Because popular nonnative plant cultivars sold as "safe" to natural areas reduce—but do not eliminate—viable seeds, at this time all cultivars of nonnative invasive plants remain invasive.[7]

Evaluating popular native woody species was also revealing. "Nearly every plant currently available is a cultivar of a native."[8] To determine a plant's true identity, read its label; its Latin name should be listed. If you have questions, have the proprietor provide a USDA PLANTS printout. Enter into a computer search screen the plant's name(s) as shown on the label followed by USDA PLANTS. "I" for "introduced" is a nonnative plant that has naturalized. "N" is for "native." Maps show the plant's distribution. USDA PLANTS does not provide cultivar/nativar information. However, the plant's label should. (See Introduction, p. 9). Have the seller verify that a native plant is not a cultivar/nativar.

Our focus on native plants in the Midwest, an admittedly broad and imprecise region, is complicated by the existence of varying definitions, categories, and climate zones. We include locations with similar native plant gardening conditions: Arkansas, Illinois, Indiana, Iowa, Kansas, Kentucky, Michigan, Minnesota, Missouri, Ohio, Wisconsin, and Ontario, Canada. Our suggestions for native shrubs and trees apply to most adjacent states and the states within the eastern broadleaf forest province (see below).

USDA Hardiness Zones Maps show ten different zones, each of which represents an area of winter hardiness for the plants in our landscape. This book provides information on each entry's zones, but some are changing. For example, the U.S. Department of Agriculture puts Chicago into Plant Hardiness Zone 5b, with the outlying areas falling into the slightly colder Zone 5a. The Arbor Day Foundation's updated hardiness map places the Chicago lakefront and southern suburbs into the upper reaches of Zone 6.[9] For the most current guidance in choosing plants that do well in specific parts of the region, refer to the USDA Hardiness Zone map. Plants that share midwestern hardiness zones but are native to entirely different geographical locations and ecosystems are poor choices for midwestern landscapes. "Hardiness ratings alone are inadequate to guide landscapers in selecting the most successful plants," states the US National Arboretum.[10] Another way of analyzing the region to which a plant is native is by its plant province or regional vegetation type. Most midwestern states we reference fall within the eastern broadleaf forest province or vegetation type.[11]

Many homeowners, gardeners, and landscapers seek to benefit the greatest number of Lepidoptera (butterflies/moths) and the birds that eat and feed the caterpillars to their offspring, by planting their host plants. To determine if a butterfly is local in your area, Jeffrey S. Pippen, of Duke University's Nicholas School of the Environment, recommends accessing Butterflies and Moths of North America. (Please see Butterflies, Moths, and Other Insects in Selected Bibliography and Resources.) We show the number of caterpillar species produced by many of the native host plants. For a consolidated listing, please see Selected Bibliography and Resources for both Native Woody Species and Native Herbaceous Species in Descending Order of Lepidoptera Productivity.

Some plants in this book may be familiar under other names, both common and Latin. Because a plant's botanical name is its only positive identification, its botanical name should be verified before making a purchase or before incorporating plants even when they have been provided by a neighbor or friend. Occasionally botanical names change, so if one doesn't ring a bell, check its current status. This is also true of animal names, especially butterflies, whose common and scientific names have changed significantly, some quite recently, over the past century.

Shrub and tree heights, blooming and fruiting times, and cultivation requirements can vary with a plant's geographical location and because of light and soil differences and other environmental factors. These variations can give rise to different information from different sources. For the best results, before you purchase a shrub or tree discuss its specific requirements with the purveyor or landscaper. We do not delve deeply into the many diseases and disorders that affect woody plants or the toxicity of various species to humans and animals. As one midwestern state extension agency points out, "Despite providing our trees and shrubs with all their necessities, diseases and insects can still cause problems. In most cases, however, healthy mature trees and shrubs are able to defend themselves against minor insect and fungal disease exposure without intervention by us."[12] "If you can minimize environmental stress by choosing plants suitable for your light, soil, and temperature conditions, most of them should grow reasonably well, and if not, try them in another spot or get something else," writes William Cullina, adding, "I firmly believe that there is no plant worth growing if it must be maintained by applications of poisons."[13] Hybrids and cultivars bred for disease resistance may be less susceptible to a particular disease but not to all diseases and problems. A study notes, "It is important to note that the term disease resistance does not mean that the plant is completely immune to disease but instead refers to a plant's ability to minimize infection by the pathogen. Unfortunately, no cultivar is resistant to all diseases."[14] In fact, like the Irish potato, because cultivars and nativars are genetically deprived of a variety of the "tools" necessary to adapt to change, "They could be considered more vulnerable by virtue of their sameness," writes Wild Ones.[15]

Native woody species play an indispensable aesthetic and environmental role in midwestern urban, suburban, and rural landscaping. We encourage consumers to patronize native plant nurseries and when hiring landscapers or visiting general nurseries, to insist that these establishments provide you only with true native species.

ABBREVIATIONS USED

NABA	North American Butterfly Association
NBII	National Biological Information Infrastructure
NRCS	National Resource Conservation Service
spp.	species as a plural
syn.	synonym
US	United States
USDA	United States Department of Agriculture
USDA PLANTS	USDA NRCS PLANTS Database
US EPA	United States Environmental Protection Agency
USFWS	United States Fish and Wildlife Services
var.	variety

MIDWESTERN NATIVE
SHRUBS AND TREES

INTRODUCTION

T HIS BOOK ABOUT shrubs and trees is a companion to *The Midwestern Native Garden: Native Alternatives to Nonnative Flowers and Plants, An Illustrated Guide.* Its purpose is to serve as a useful resource for homeowners, gardeners, and landscapers seeking to evaluate prospective woody plantings. The book covers the plant qualities that the typical gardener wants to know, such as height, color, and bloom time of the nonnative plants, and their native alternatives. To incorporate a deeper level, it explores profound connections between native midwestern woody plants and the region's ecological community. The lives of butterflies, bees, and birds are central to the discussion. The goal is to choose the trees and shrubs that make the best use of available space. The multiple objectives of visual beauty, adaptation to the local climate and soil, and maximum contribution to native wildlife can be best achieved by choosing native species for our gardens and landscapes.

Professional landscape designers call trees and shrubs the bones of the garden. "Trees are the most permanent elements in any planting plan," notes the American Horticultural Society. "Since a tree is probably the most expensive of garden plants and usually the most prominent, selection and siting are the most important decisions. Shrubs can form the backbone of your garden design, and with their variety of foliage, flowers, fruits, and stems, they also provide interest through the seasons."[1] The natives tend to be hardier, longer-lived, and easier to maintain and grow than introductions from faraway places. When it comes to aesthetics, the native trees and shrubs growing in a midwestern backyard, garden, or landscape, regardless of their size, produce four seasons of beauty and visual impact. Midwesterners desiring an aesthetically pleasing, ever-changing tapestry of hardy plants will choose native species instead of the usual nonnative fare offered at most nurseries.

Midwestern Lepidoptera (butterflies, moths), birds, and bees evolved with midwestern plants. They need each other to complete their life cycles. Each native tree and shrub in the backyard is a life-giving force. The huge benefits to wildlife in terms of reproduction, food, and habitat that each native plant provides cannot be duplicated by nonnative species. "Planting nonnative plants, like butterfly bush, in your yard is actually making it harder for the butterflies and birds in your neighborhood to survive."[2] Though it isn't well known, "more than 90 percent" of our native butterflies and moths can feed only on particular native host plants during their larval caterpillar stage.[3] "A butterfly's most important relationship is with the plants eaten by its caterpillars."[4] Perpetuation of a butterfly species requires a habitat that will support the full life cycle of the butterfly, not just the adult stage.[5] Importantly, many native trees and shrubs excel as host plants that benefit butterfly and moth populations as well as the birds that eat the caterpillars and feed them to their offspring.

Gardeners and landscapers can choose plants on the basis of their roles in the local ecosystem. Nonnative shrubs and trees occupy spaces in our yards, gardens, and landscapes that would be better filled by native woody species that increase biodiversity. The online USDA PLANTS Database enables us to access individual plant species, determine if they are native or introduced, and check the maps. Plants shown as introduced ("I") are defined as naturalized, not native to the area, and, in general, "likely to invade or become noxious since they lack co-evolved competitors and natural enemies to control their populations."[6] Plants shown as native ("N") can be checked for their distribution in the United States and Canada, classification, synonyms, legal status, data sources and documentation, and related links. Reliable information takes the uncertainty out of shopping. When we choose midwestern native plants, we attract birds, butterflies, and other wildlife that add an additional layer of beauty to our yards and gardens.

Whether used as a sanctuary, a miniature nature preserve, or a playground for children, yards, landscapes, and gardens of native plants are a sound investment and provide peace of mind. Midwestern native plants have been here since the last Ice Age. For more than 10,000 years, these plants adapted to the region's soils, seasons, rainfall, and wildlife. Native woody and herbaceous plants are beautiful and hardy, and once established they require less maintenance than conventional lawns and nonnative ornamentals. Because native plants have adapted to local conditions, they are more resistant to pest problems. Synthetic pesticides, herbicides, and fertilizers have no place in the native garden, as they kill butterflies, other pollinators, and the plants themselves and harm human health. (If problems arise, we can employ other ways to control them.) Natives rarely need watering. They improve water quality and reduce flooding, serve as carbon sinks, and reduce the demand for nonrenewable resources. The US Environmental Protection Agency (EPA) explains that "native landscaping practices can help improve air quality on a local, regional and global level. Locally, smog (ground level ozone) and air toxics can be drastically reduced by the virtual elimination of the need for lawn maintenance equipment (lawn mowers, weed edgers, leaf blowers, etc.) which is fueled by gasoline, electricity or batteries. All of these fuel types are associated with the emissions of [many] air pollutants."[7] Reduced lawn and expanded native plantings produce healthier environments, and the absence of loud machinery brings peace and quiet. Regionally native plants create an authentic sense of place in the landscaping at home, in parks, and in other public places throughout our communities. While creating a future for the regional ecosystem, native gardens with diverse plants that attract a host of birds, butterflies, and beneficial insects also serve as convenient places to learn about plants and wildlife and simply enjoy nature.

There are other benefits. Gardens of native plants reduce opportunities for nonnative plants to overrun the landscape. Seed from native plants that is carried by wind and birds from our garden into natural areas does not degrade the environment. "Nonnative plant species pose a significant threat to the natural ecosystems of the United States. Many of these invasive plants are escapees from gardens and landscapes where they were originally planted. Purchased at local nurseries, wholesale suppliers and elsewhere, these plants have the potential of taking over large areas, affecting native plants and animals and negatively changing the ecosystem."[8]

The statistics are alarming. In the United States, more than 100 million acres of land have been taken over by invasive plants and the annual increase has been estimated to be 14 percent.[9] "The impact of all of these nonnative plants is creating novel ecosystems that are not supporting food webs, therefore not supporting biodiversity."[10] The huge numbers of nonnative plant species that have naturalized and flourish without human assistance can be seen by looking at the maps on the USDA PLANTS Database. Native plants once grew in the spaces now holding naturalized nonnative plants, and their absence deprives birds and butterflies of reproduction sites, shelter, and food. History also shows that many seemingly benign nonnative plants become invasive. Eliminating this possibility from our own gardens and landscapes is a significant advantage of going native.

Research of interest from an ecological perspective also serves to scientifically document the potential negative impacts an invasive plant can have on human health. Studies reveal that the exotic invasive shrub Japanese barberry provides habitat favorable to the blacklegged tick, exposing people to tick bites and the associated Lyme disease threat.[11] Another study looked at how leaf litter in water influences the abundance of mosquitoes, which can transmit West Nile virus to humans and wildlife, and found that two of the most widespread nonnative, invasive plants, Amur honeysuckle and autumn olive, yielded significantly higher numbers of adult mosquitoes than the other leaf species. Nonnative invasive plants "are having very significant ecological impacts, displacing a lot of native species. And now we're seeing that some of them also enhance the transmission of a dangerous disease," said the researchers.[12] Choosing native species is the ounce of prevention that is worth a pound of cure.

A plant's origin is the key to its beneficial ecological role. Is the tree or shrub native to the Midwest, or an introduction from Eurasia? Is the plant a true native, or is it a nativar (a recent term combining the words "native" and "cultivar")? People making gardening and landscaping decisions may feel too busy or distracted by other concerns to pay attention to the origins of their woody plants. This book aims to lighten that burden by providing this information. Awareness of the key environmental role played by native plants encourages landscaping that benefits birds and butterflies rather than a nursery's preferences or the landscaper's convenience. A plant's origin is relevant when the town or city where you live conducts an annual tree sale for its parkways, or a local organization sells plants to raise revenue for a good cause.

It seems counterintuitive, but the majority of plants used in agriculture, forestry, and horticulture in North America are not native to the continent.[13] One of the biggest —yet least recognized—impacts humans are having on urban habitats is a change in vegetation from predominantly native to nonnative species. "As the nursery industry evolved in the 1800s, exotic plants were imported from foreign lands. As a result, approximately 80 percent of the plants in the nursery trade today are non-native exotics."[14] And, about 80 percent of suburbia is landscaped with plants from Asia.[15] The majority of woody plants in the United States that became invasive were introduced into this country for horticultural purposes.[16]

Studies indicate that a plant that is invasive in one region might be problematic in another region, particularly if the two regions have similar climates. For woody ornamental species, for example, being invasive elsewhere was the single best predictor of potential invasiveness in a new region of introduction.[17] Unfortunately, there is no screening method to determine if newly introduced plants are going to become invasive. Estimates have put the economic cost of invasive plants in natural areas, agriculture, and gardens at $125 billion per year, and deem it to be "rising quickly."[18] Laws to prevent the sale of invasive plants are created only after the plants have already become a problem. Even then, outlawing nonnative invasive ornamental species is sometimes opposed because their sale is economically beneficial to the nursery industry and to the state.[19]

Decades can pass before a seemingly inoffensive nonnative ornamental plant becomes invasive. "In general, introduced plants [defined as not native to the area that have naturalized] are likely to invade or become noxious since they lack co-evolved competitors and natural enemies to control their populations," states USDA PLANTS.[20] The marketing period—the number of years nonnative horticultural plants are sold —has profound influence on their naturalization and invasion. As long as they are sold, nonnative plants will continue to naturalize and invade, notes a federal study.[21] This pattern also applies to cultivars of nonnative plants.[22] Even "sterile" nonnative invasive cultivars, though less fecund, eventually produce enough pollen and seed to reproduce, so cultivars of invasive plants remain invasive and are not "safe" for the environment.[23]

Plant choices, like clothing styles, have gone in and out of fashion. Plantings reveal information about the landscaping time period of a home or neighborhood, but there is usually a common denominator in the plants' origins—Europe or Asia. Studies verify our personal observations. "Most of the ornamental species in parks and gardens are alien, e.g., lawn grasses, rose bushes, lilacs." Introduced flora dominates "the visual impact of the flora in much of middle North America."[24] The persistence of consumers' habits in choosing introduced species is revealed in popular garden catalogs that continue to advertise nonnative ornamental plants.[25]

Creating environmental benefits that never go out of fashion is a byproduct of choosing native species. Arguing that "for the first time in its history, gardening has taken on a role that transcends the needs of the gardener," Douglas Tallamy, author, researcher, and professor and chair of the department of entomology and wildlife ecology at the University of Delaware, writes that gardeners have become "important players in the management of our nation's wildlife." "Gardening with natives is no longer just a peripheral option" but one that "mainstream gardeners can no longer afford to ignore." "It is now within the power of individual gardeners to do something that we all dream of doing: to make a difference. In this case, the 'difference' will be to the future of biodiversity, to the native plants and animals of North America and the ecosystems that sustain them. . . . My argument for using native plant species moves beyond debatable values and ethics into the world of scientific fact," he writes.[26] "As quickly as possible, we need to triple the number of native trees in our lawns and underplant them with the understory and shrub layers absent from most managed landscapes."[27]

The prospect of planting native species is ethically, morally, aesthetically, and scientifically appealing. But the fear that plantings of native species look messy, weedy, disorganized, or unplanned can be a deterrent. These fears, though understandable, are misplaced. "There is no inherent conflict between creating a beautiful garden and establishing a functioning, sustainable garden ecosystem."[28] Whether the plant is native or introduced from Eurasia makes no difference to its appearance (though many introductions and cultivars are high maintenance). Many native species resemble or look exactly like popular nonnative species and share cultivation requirements. A plant's origin does not determine its ornamental role. "Basic design concepts using natives are exactly the same as those used when landscaping with aliens. Small plants in front, tall ones in back, and so on," writes Douglas Tallamy. "Along with a beautiful garden," we are trying "to create new habitat for our animal friends," so "native border gardens should be as wide as possible and as densely planted as possible."[29] The factors that will determine a purposeful and neat-looking planting are selecting plants that fit the site, the garden and landscape design, the style and layout, and maintenance. When we choose native species that fulfill our aesthetic requirements, select the best locations for their well-being and our sensibilities, and provide them with maintenance that ensures their health and the desired well-groomed appearance, we take meaningful steps to reverse the region's declines in birds, bees, and butterflies. Plantings and gardens of native species are eternally fashionable.

Birds and butterflies are a big reason for gardening. These beautiful creatures bring a lot of pleasure to adults and children. Birds and butterflies are naturally more attracted to native plants than to most exotic plants, because over thousands of years our local insects and birds have evolved to depend on indigenous plants for their food, reproduction, and shelter.[30] Eurasian plants evolved in faraway places where they developed cycles of bloom times that can be too early or too late to provide midwestern pollinators with pollen and nectar, and cycles of fruit production that don't meet the needs of native birds. "Native plants, which have co-evolved with native wild birds, are more likely to provide a mix of foods—just the right size, and with just the right kind of nutrition—and just when the birds need them."[31] To survive freezing nights, small songbirds like black-capped chickadees must sustain themselves with berries rich in fats and antioxidants. Yards and gardens with abundant native shrubs and trees enable birds to spend less energy foraging.[32] Some migrating warblers time their spring return to the Midwest to coincide with the emergence of little-noticed and beneficial insects that, in turn, time their emergence to coincide with the new growth of native oak leaves.[33] When required native host plants are too hard to find or unavailable, Lepidoptera will not reproduce. When native plants are readily available, more species, greater numbers, and healthier butterfly and moth populations occur. Reproduction rates corroborate this. On average, native plants support 13 times more caterpillars (larval stage of butterflies/moths) than nonnative plants.[34] "Adaptation by our native insect fauna to plant species that evolved elsewhere is a slow process indeed."[35] To enjoy birds and butterflies within our lifetimes, we must plant natives.

For nesting birds, the importance of native woody plants cannot be overstated. Birds nesting in nonnatives such as buckthorn and honeysuckle are more likely to fall victim to predators such as cats and raccoons. This is due to characteristics like sturdier lower branches.[36] Bird reproduction is controlled by food availability. Contrary to what many people believe, most "birds do not reproduce on berries and seeds," Tallamy says, noting, "Ninety-six percent of terrestrial birds rear their young on insects." For insects, including butterflies, to exist, they must lay their eggs on "host plants." Butterfly caterpillars don't eat most nonnative plants, which they find toxic, bad tasting, or tough, so butterflies rarely lay their eggs on them.[37] Most butterfly caterpillars eat native host plants, and that is where the birds go to find them. "If you have a lot of trees that are not native, to the birds, it's almost as if there are no trees at all."[38] Planting natives makes life easier for nesting birds to feed their nestlings. Comparisons done of production of the butterfly and moth caterpillar stage eaten by insectivorous birds demonstrate that Asian woody species produce a significant loss in breeding bird species and abundance.[39] Don't worry about birds eating all the caterpillars. When we create a diversity and abundance of native host plants, the resulting populations of caterpillars are more than adequate to sustain healthy populations of both butterflies and birds.

We associate hummingbirds with flower nectar, but they feed insects to their rapidly growing young, and the adult birds eat them too.[40] Sunflower seeds entice cardinals to bird feeders, but they eat and feed insects to their nestlings.[41] Chickadees, another popular visitor, almost exclusively feed their babies Lepidoptera caterpillars.[42] "Regardless of the size of your yard, you can help reverse the loss of bird habitat. By planting the native plants upon which our birds depend, you'll be rewarded with a bounty of birds and natural beauty just beyond your doorstep."[43] "Studies have shown that even modest increases in the native plant cover on suburban properties raise the number and species of breeding birds, including birds of conservation concern. As gardeners and stewards of our land, we have never been so empowered to help save biodiversity from extinction, and the need to do so has never been so great. All we need to do is plant native plants!"[44] (For information on caterpillar productiveness of some important woody and herbaceous species see Selected Bibliography and Resources for Native Woody Species and Native Herbaceous Species in Descending Order of Lepidoptera Productivity.)

Modern landscapes are heavily loaded with male-only trees and shrubs, favored by landscapers because they are "litter-free." Because male plants don't produce fruits or seeds, they have long been considered to be desirable landscape plants. For allergy and hay fever sufferers, there is an unintended and unpleasant consequence. The very abundant, lightweight pollen produced by many male conifers and broadleaved trees is intended to pollinate the flowers of their female counterparts, but a lot is blown by the wind into people's noses. "In contrast, a flower, tree or shrub pollinated solely by insects can be ruled out as an important cause of hay fever."[45] To prevent unneeded suffering, here is a tip. Don't purposely plant male (pollen-producing) plants. Commonsense landscaping includes a good mix of naturally sexed native shrubs and trees. It also benefits wildlife because the buds, fruits, nuts, and seeds found on female trees are their food.

"As people learn the importance of native plants, they begin shopping for them. However, straight species are hard to find. Nearly every plant currently available is a cultivar of a native."[46] "'Nativar' is one term for a cultivar of a native species," states the Wild Ones website. "Like all cultivars, nativars are the result of artificial selections made by humans from the natural variation found in species. Nativars are almost always propagated vegetatively to preserve their selected trait, which means they no longer participate in natural reproduction patterns that would maintain genetic diversity."[47] Traits they are bred or selected for include showiness, compactness, or resistance to a specific problem — but not all problems—as gardeners know who complain about poor performance.

Gardening with nativars is a risky experiment. Studies are under way, but the science is still in its infancy.[48] "The biggest danger is that the nativar may interbreed with a local genotype, destroying and replacing the local genotype," warns naturalist Sue Sweeney. "Interbreeding might turn a local genotype into a plant that the local fauna can not recognize as food, or, worse yet, into an invasive."[49] How nativars meet wildlife's fundamental needs is an important subject that has not been widely explored. Some shortcomings are apparent. When scientific breeding changes leaf color (green leaf becoming purple or variegated), the leaf chemistry is undoubtedly changed. Variegated leaves in cultivars have less chlorophyll than solid green leaves and so are less nutritious for insects. Purple leaves are loaded with chemicals that deter insect feeding.[50] A result is less insect food for nesting birds. An example is ninebark (see Spring Shrubs, p. 44). Selecting for height produces more lost food for birds. An example is 'Gro-Low' Fragrant Sumac (see Fall Shrubs, p. 242). Advertised for ornamental fruit, not all serviceberry nativars produce (see Spring Trees, Serviceberry Cultivar/Nativar Note, p. 78). At this time, only female inkberry nativars are commercially available.[51] The female shrubs need a male to produce fruit, so birds go hungry. Sterile nativars are "bad news for goldfinches, who want the seed," and doubled flowers are "bad news for pollinators, who can't effectively reach the pollen and nectar."[52] An insect's mouthparts can only pollinate plants with "a particular morphology" [form and structure of an organism or any of its parts], so "altering a flower's shape might make it incompatible with pollinators."[53]

Nursery industry marketing strategies call for frequently offering new, trendy nativars featuring different colors and shapes. What can a consumer do when nearly every plant currently available is a nativar?[54] Patronizing native plant landscapers, nurseries, and plant sales, and being selective when visiting generalist purveyors, are ways to overcome these challenges. Midwesterners *can* create gardens, yards, and communities composed of true native plants.

The idea of restoring all of North America's ecosystems to a pure, pre–European immigrant state is unrealistic. But perfection is not required. Recognition of the fundamental connection between native plant species and wildlife is essential. This insight leads to pitching in and planting native species in areas over which we have unique control (yards, gardens, condominium balconies). Choosing natives is a practical, direct, and enjoyable way to help wildlife and achieve immense good. To our readers we say, before planting a shrub or tree, think about the beauty and the environmental benefits provided by our true native midwestern woody species.

Each gardener and landscaper should decide on the pace at which to convert to native shrubs and trees. Substituting natives for nonnative species need not require a drastic overhaul of a garden. Homeowners may choose to proceed gradually, adding or replacing nonnative shrubs and trees as they decline or die. Some may opt to do it themselves, others to employ a professional native plant landscaper, or some combination of these approaches. Going at one's own pace is essential to achieve the most joyful and ultimately successful results. Before you start planting and rearranging, consider the essential items (cover, food, water, reproduction) for birds and butterflies, and plan so that you use the space you have in the most effective manner. To maximize space, create layers of taller trees, shorter trees/shrubs, and herbaceous plants. While you are planning your yard, remember to plan places for yourself. Place birdbaths and wildlife-attracting native plants within window view. Keep bird, butterfly, caterpillar, and plant identification guides at the ready. Put a bench in a quiet place and enjoy.

We've examined a range of well-documented reasons that inspire midwestern gardeners to choose true native shrubs and trees. Regardless of the concepts that resonate most with you, we offer some great choices. For the best results, take your time. Go beyond our suggestions. Develop your own ideas based on observation and your own research. Enjoy the aesthetic—and bird and butterfly results—with friends and neighbors. Share the seedlings, root sprouts, seeds, nuts, and acorns that can grow into treasured trees and shrubs. Include native flowers, grasses, and sedges in your yard or garden and create an even more varied, beautiful, and welcoming natural habitat. Collect native plant nursery catalogs and spend time marveling at images of beautiful native trees and shrubs. Ask your local nursery or garden center to stock true native species.

For yards, gardens, and landscapes, large and small, our book can serve as a handy guide for choosing true native midwestern shrubs and trees.

Purveyor Note

Locating purveyors of native plants can seem challenging, but native plants can be obtained from a variety of sources. (Please see Selected Resources in the bibliography.) Check local newspapers for native plant sales held by park districts, forest preserves, municipalities, local environmental and native plant organizations, and individuals seeking to share the bounty produced by their beautiful native gardens. Ask these entities to suggest nurseries, retailers, wholesalers, and landscaping services that specialize in native plants. For a wide variety of native midwestern species, access online native plant sellers. Obtain catalogs to peruse at leisure; they are informative and sometimes suggest garden layouts. Their large inventories, the ease of ordering, and the convenience of deliveries right to one's door are attractive features. If a local retail nursery, "big box" garden center, or all-purpose online plant seller offers some native selections, be sure the listing or the label substantiates that the plants are true native species. "In scientific names, cultivars are mentioned within single quotes, as in *Juniperus virginiana* 'Taylor' for Eastern redcedar. But in commercial names (common and scientific), quotes are sometimes missing."[55] Even without quotes, names like Taylor put one on notice. Purchasing true native plants will become easier as customers let sellers know they want the true or straight midwestern native species.

Environmental Reminder

Removing native plants from their natural environments increases their vulnerability. Removal also decreases survival chances for the beneficial insects, including butterflies and specialist bees that depend on the native plants for survival. We urge you to patronize purveyors of native plants, shrubs, and trees (see the Selected Resources section in the bibliography) and to share native plant bounty among friends, relatives, and neighbors.

1

SPRING

The Midwest's long, cold winters inspire dreams of flowering shrubs and trees, musical birds, and colorful butterflies. Serviceberries, cherries and plums, and crab apples and roses are prized by homeowners and landscapers for their fragrance and beauty. In centuries past, Native American foragers esteemed these species for their fruits. They were eaten fresh or dried, in soups and stews, but the most common use was to add them to pemmican, an ancient mixture of pounded dried meat and fat. Archaeologists have discovered the pits from chokecherry, serviceberry, and American plum at prehistoric prairie Indian sites.[1] Early explorers, travelers, military expeditions, and settlers also enjoyed eating the wild fruits.

Nature captivated 1830s Illinois pioneer Eliza W. Farnham. "It is always pleasant to resume communication with the world around, when the icy fetters of winter are cast off. . . . The spring of '37 opened with delicious beauty on the prairie land!" She appreciated "a floral hedge six or eight feet in height" farmers planted. She felt "a thrill of gratitude" toward men she saw planting a tree. "Though set on private property," a tree "is a public blessing. . . . Its beauty may be seen, its glory appreciated by all. And the rapid growth which the locust, cotton-wood, aspen, and some other species have in the strong soil leaves no excuse for living long in a treeless and birdless home. Oh, I love nature. Living much with nature, makes me wiser, better, purer, and therefore, happier!"[2]

Walking through the woods in the spring of 1900, naturalist and writer Alice Lounsberry was struck by "the music passing through the tree-tops and quivering in the insects' wings, and . . . the subtle unfoldings of spring. There is no passing it by; it is one of the spirits of nature that the dullest eye must see and admire. . . . It is then that the knowing ones sigh as with relief and feel grateful that the spring is indeed on its way. The winter has passed."[3]

Most home landscapes are dominated by lawn and by Eurasian ornamentals, some of which Lounsberry identified as they were becoming popular. Most "native" plants are cultivars (nativars) of a native.[4] Gardeners occasionally remember once-abundant birds, butterflies, and fireflies, but rarely connect their declines to plant choices and landscaping practices that ignore the needs of wildlife. Human recognition of the mutualistic interactions between native plants and native wildlife is essential when we consider spring cleanup. Lepidoptera (butterflies and moths) need native host plants as places to lay eggs and as food for their caterpillars. Nesting birds need Lepidoptera caterpillars to feed their nestlings. A decline or absence of native host plants results in a decline or absence of caterpillars, butterflies, and birds. Red admiral (p. 192), green comma (p. 103), mourning cloak (p. 62), and question mark (p. 176) butterflies spend winters in bark and crevices in trees, woodpiles, snags, and logs. Eastern tailed-blue, frosted elfin (p. 329), gray hairstreak, Ozark swallowtail, and black swallowtail butterflies spend winters on or near their herbaceous host plants.[5] Leaf litter holds dormant insects, snails, bugs, and worms that support robins, native sparrows, brown thrashers, other hungry spring migrating birds and firefly/lightning bug larvae (glow worms). Spring cleanups that eliminate leaf litter unwittingly create firefly-free zones, depriving people of a magical aspect of summer evenings. Wholesale disposal of woody material, standing native flowers and grasses, and every errant leaf has the unintended consequence of a diminished future with fewer butterflies and birds. Spring is a good time to rethink routine gardening practices that prevent much of our desirable wildlife from surviving. Choosing native woody and herbaceous host plants, forgoing pesticides, and conducting suitably restrained cleanups are sustainable techniques for the many homeowners and gardeners who love birds, butterflies, and fireflies and want to help them prosper.

Native trees and shrubs furnish wildlife with the essential elements of life, including food, shelter, and the ability to reproduce. Although many trees and shrubs introduced from Asia and Europe are beautiful, they can never match the combination of beauty and benefits to birds and butterflies that the native species provide. Eurasian shrubs and trees spent thousands of years developing in parallel with the needs of European and Asian wildlife. In contrast, midwestern shrubs and trees spent thousands of years developing simultaneously with the needs of midwestern wildlife. This shared midwestern developmental history enables true midwestern shrubs and trees to provide midwestern butterflies, bees, fireflies, and birds with the food, shelter, and reproduction sites they need to in order to succeed.

When it comes to planting, spring is a window of opportunity. Will my new tree be one that everyone else has? Will my new shrub be the latest fad, trend, decorative novelty, or whatever happens to fit in with some landscaper's agenda? Or will I choose native shrubs and trees that thrive in the Midwest, provide fragrance and beauty, and also provide a future for midwestern bees, butterflies, fireflies, and birds? In the Spring chapter, we present a wide array of native woody alternatives, both shrubs and trees, to today's popular introductions.

Spring Shrubs

Nonnative:

ABELIA, FRAGRANT ABELIA, KOREAN ABELIA. **Family:** Honeysuckle (Caprifoliaceae). **Genus:** *Abelia* (*A. mosanensis*). **Origin:** Korea. **Height/Spread:** 4–6 feet. **Ornamental Attributes:** Twiggy shrub; fragrant, pinkish-white flowers in spring. **Cultivation:** Full sun to part shade, well-drained soil, winter shelter. **Zones:** 5–9.

Native Alternatives:

CHOKEBERRY. **Family:** Rose (Rosaceae). **Genus:** *Aronia, Photinia, Pyrus.* **Confusion Note:** It is easy to confuse chokeberry and chokecherry (p. 83). **Chokeberry Ornamental Attributes:** Showy, adaptable, trouble-free chokeberries provide all-season beauty. Clusters of long-lasting fragrant white, red anther-centered, five-petaled flowers in late April and May; shiny green leaves with brilliant fall color; colorful fruits that persist through winter; multiple stems. **Cultivation:** Sun or partial sun. "Chokeberries flower prolifically, especially when grown in full sun. In this setting, they usually produce a large quantity of fruit and develop beautiful fall color," write Weeks and Weeks.[6] Wet to dry soils, best in between; thrive in slightly acid soils. Do well in soggy, marshy soils with poor drainage. Adaptable and low maintenance. Most attractive, and best for wildlife massed and in colonies; good for shrub borders and rain gardens; BLACK CHOKEBERRY (*A., P. melanocarpa*). **Height/Spread:** 3–8 feet. **Ornamental Attributes:** White flowers, spectacular glossy red-orange fall color, edible black fruits on red pedicels, exfoliating bark. "The aesthetically pleasing *Aronia melanocarpa* is being heralded throughout the Midwest for its year-round interest," according to the Chicago Botanic Garden.[7] **Note:** Endangered in parts of the Midwest. **Zones:** 3–8; RED CHOKEBERRY (*A. arbutifolia, syn. Aronia prunifolia, Photinia pyrifolia*).[8] **Height:** 5–7 feet. **Spread:** 3–5 feet. **Ornamental Attributes:** White flowers. "The leaves of red

Abelia (*Abelia mosanensis*)

Black chokeberry (*Photinia melanocarpa*)
Also see pp. 264, 337

Red chokeberry (*Photinia pyrifolia*)
Also see p. 338

chokeberry turn fire engine-red with the onset of cool, autumn weather," Terry L. Ettinger notes. "In fact, they easily rival the insanely popular—and therefore way over-planted—burning bush for outstanding fall foliage color!"[9] Glossy bright red berries. **Zones:** 4–9; **PURPLE CHOKEBERRY** (*A. floribunda, Photinia floribunda, Pyrus floribunda*). **Height/Spread:** 3–10 feet. **Ornamental Attributes:** White flowers, purple fruit, deep red fall foliage. **Range Note:** Hybridization by red and black chokeberry due to overlapping ranges created the purple chokeberry that some taxonomists consider a distinct third species.[10] **Zones:** 4–7. **Chokeberry Nature Note:** Nectar and pollen attract the small native bees that are their primary pollinators and other small insects that draw in nesting birds seeking food for their babies. Chokeberries host 29 species of Lepidoptera (butterflies and moths), including red admiral (p. 192), striped hairstreak (p. 18), and coral hairstreak (p. 18), whose caterpillars serve as food for birds and their nestlings. At least 21 species of overwintering and early-arriving migrating birds use the persistent berries as emergency food, including American robin (p. 62), cedar waxwing (p. 36), eastern meadowlark, black-capped chickadee (p. 322), and northern cardinal (p. 61). The shrubs' multistemmed habit provides many birds with nesting habitat, and protective cover to ground-feeding birds, including eastern towhee (p. 235), wood thrush (p. 175), brown thrasher (p. 219), and northern flicker (p. 99).

More Native Alternatives:

ELDERBERRY SPP., p. 29; **FOTHERGILLA SPP.**, p. 27; **NINEBARK**, p. 44; **RHODODENDRON, AZALEA SPP.**, p. 56; **ROSE SPP.**, p. 60; **SERVICEBERRY SPP.**, p. 20.

See Summer Shrubs for **HYDRANGEA SPP.**, p. 143.

Red chokeberry flowers (*Photinia pyrifolia*)
Also see p. 270

Nonnative:

ALDER SPP. See Winter Trees, p. 316.

Nonnative:

AUTUMN OLIVE & RUSSIAN OLIVE. See Fall Shrubs, p. 229.

Nonnative:

AZALEA. See *RHODODENDRON,* p. 56.

Nonnative:

BEAUTYBUSH. **Family:** Honeysuckle (Caprifoliaceae). **Genus:** *Kolkwitzia* (*K. amabilis*). **Origin:** China. **Height/Spread:** 6–10 feet. **Ornamental Attributes:** Short-lived, pink flowers in late spring are its feature of interest. Its arching, leggy, weedy-looking branches frequently die and need pruning; poor to no fall color. **Cultivation:** Full sun, moist well-drained soil, regular watering, high-maintenance pruning. **Ecological Threat:** Naturalized in midwestern states. **Zones:** 5–8.

Beautybush (*Kolkwitzia amabilis*)

Native Alternatives:

AMERICAN BLADDERNUT, p. 41; AMERICAN SMOKETREE, p. 65; CHOKEBERRY SPP., p. 13; ELDERBERRY SPP., p. 29; FOTHERGILLA SPP., p. 27; NINEBARK, p. 44; SCENTLESS MOCK ORANGE, p. 46.

See Spring Trees for AMERICAN PLUM and other native plums, p. 78; FRINGE TREE, p. 105; SERVICEBERRY SPP., p. 77.

Nonnative:

BLADDERNUT, WHITE BLADDERNUT, EUROPEAN BLADDERNUT. **Family:** Bladdernut (Staphyleaceae). **Genus:** *Staphylea* (*S. pinnata*). **Origin:** Europe, Asia Minor. **Height/Spread:** 10–15 feet. **Ornamental Attributes:** Fragrant flowers in May to June, bladder-like seeds. **Cultivation:** Full to part sun, well-drained soil. Naturalizes. **Zones:** 6–8.

Bladdernut (*Staphylea pinnata*)

Native Alternatives:

AMERICAN BLADDERNUT, p. 41; FOTHERGILLA SPP., p. 27.
  See Spring Trees for AMERICAN PLUM and other native plums, p. 78; FRINGE TREE, p. 105; SERVICEBERRY SPP., p. 77; SNOWBELL, p. 116.

Nonnative:

CHERRY, PLUM, ALMOND. **Family:** Rose (Rosaceae). **Genus:** *Prunus.* **Problem Note:** Compared to other ornamentals, *Prunus* species live short lives (15–20 years). Only members of the genus *Prunus,* including cherries, plums, almonds, apricots, and peaches, are afflicted by the fungus called black knot; it occurs on Japanese, European, and American species. Applications of costly fertilizers, fungicides, herbicides, pesticides, and insecticides containing permethin aimed at the numerous insect pests, root rot, and the bacterial and fungal diseases that plague the ornamental species pose dangers to adults and children, as well as to butterflies, bees, and birds. The early blooms are susceptible to frost damage. **Cultivation:** Sun, regular pruning, watering, fertilizing, lack of crowding. Moist, well-drained acid to near neutral soils. **Cultivar Note:** Suckers from roots of purple-leaved grafted cultivars will be green, not purple; *FLOWERING ALMOND, CHINESE PLUM* (*P. glandulosa*). **Origin:** China, Japan. **Height/Spread:** 4–5 feet. **Ornamental Attributes:** Pink/white flowers in April, no fall color, unkempt appearance. "It has a suckering tendency and will sneak around the garden and the neighborhood, appearing in places it was never planted," writes Michael A. Dirr.[11] The life span of *P. glandulosa* 'Sinensis', the dwarf flowering almond cultivar, is less than 10 years. **Ecological Threat:** Naturalized in midwestern states and Canada. **Zones:** 4–8; *FLOWERING PLUM, FLOWERING ALMOND* (*Amygdalus triloba,* syn. *P. triloba*). **Height/**

Flowering almond
(*Prunus glandulosa*)

Spread: 10–15 feet. **Ornamental Attributes:** Multistemmed shrub/tree, pink flowers. **Ecological Threat:** Naturalized in midwestern states. **Zones:** 3–7; *NANKING CHERRY, DOWNY CHERRY* (*Cerasus tomentosa*, syn. *P. tomentosa*). **Origin:** China, Tibet. **Height/Spread:** 6–10 feet. **Ornamental Attributes:** Inconspicuous white/light pink flowers in April. **Ecological Threat:** Naturalized in midwestern states and Canada. **Zones:** 2–7; *PURPLELEAF CHERRY, PURPLE-LEAF SANDCHERRY* (*Prunus* × *cistena*). Hybrid of *P. pumila* and *P. cerasifera* 'Atropurpurea'. **Origin:** Asia and North America. **Height/Spread:** 8 feet. **Ornamental Attributes:** Pink flowers in mid- to late spring, sap-oozing stems, red-purple summer leaves. When top grafted on root stock with green leaves to form a small accent tree, suckers will produce green leaves. **Life Span:** 10–15 years; can die one branch at a time. **Zones:** 4–8.

Also see Spring Trees for *CHERRY, PLUM,* p. 81.

Native Alternatives:

SAND CHERRY, GREAT LAKES SANDCHERRY. **Family:** Rose (Rosaceae). **Genus:** *Prunus* (*P. pumila* var. *pumila*). **Height/Spread:** 3 feet. **Note:** Threatened in Arkansas, presumed extirpated in Ohio; CREEPING SAND CHERRY, EASTERN SAND CHERRY (*P. pumila* var. *depressa*). **Height:** 3–8 inches. **Ornamental Attributes:** Red-throated white flowers from April to June, large black cherries on bright red pedicels, deep red fall leaves. "It is almost a harbinger of spring . . . it is a beautiful sight to see when in flower described as having 'clouds of flowers.' Unfortunately, most nurseries sell only exotic varieties of *Prunus,* though none are more hardy or more beautiful than our natives," note Weeks, Weeks, and Parker.[12] Both make excellent groundcovers. **Cultivation:** Full sun, shade intolerant. Moist to dry, well-drained soil. Grow largest in moist, fertile soil.

Sand cherry (*Prunus pumila* var. *pumila*)

Eastern tiger swallowtail butterfly
(*Papilio glaucus*)

Red-spotted purple butterfly
(*Limenitis arthemis*)

Coral hairstreak butterfly (*Satyrium titus*)

Striped hairstreak butterfly
(*Satyrium liparops*)

Cecropia moth (*Hyalophora cecropia*)

Columbia silkmoth (*Hyalophora columbia*)

Prunus **Nature Note:** Native cherries and plums host 456 Lepidoptera species, a number surpassed only by our native oaks. These butterflies and moths include spring azure (p. 95), Henry's elfin (p. 93), viceroy (p. 54), eastern tiger swallowtail, coral hairstreak, striped hairstreak, red-spotted purple, promethea moth, cecropia moth, Columbia silkmoth and other giant silk moths, white-lined sphinx moth (p. 108), hummingbird clearwing moth (p. 72), banded tussock moth, and band-edged prominent moth. Birds eat the nutritious caterpillars and feed them to their nestlings. Ants, attracted to cherries' extrafloral nectaries (small glands on the stalks), protect the leaves from some leaf-chewing insects. Ruby-throated hummingbirds (p. 91), bumblebees (p. 61), honeybees, bee-mimicking flies, flower beetles, various small pollinating insects, and skipper and other adult butterflies visit for the early pollen and nectar. Birds eat the insects and feed them to their offspring. The plentiful fruits help sustain more than 84 species of birds, including northern cardinal (p. 61), gray catbird (p. 79), eastern kingbird (p. 55), American robin (p. 62), cedar waxwing (p. 36), red-headed woodpecker (p. 212), northern flicker (p. 99), northern mockingbird (p. 256), rose-breasted grosbeak (p. 200), white-throated sparrow (p. 108), Baltimore oriole (p. 167), eastern bluebird (p. 61), brown thrasher (p. 219), wood thrush (p. 175), vireos, and scarlet tanager; and mammals, including chipmunks (p. 94), squirrels, and foxes. The ornate box turtle, found in open sandy habitats, also eats them. Some mammals and shrub- and ground-nesting birds use the plants as cover. **Zones:** 3–6.

Honeybee (*Apis mellifera*)

See Spring Trees for *Prunus* spp.: AMERICAN PLUM and other native plums, p. 78; BLACK CHERRY, p. 82; CHOKECHERRY, p. 83; PIN CHERRY, p. 83.

More Native Alternatives:

SWEETSHRUB, EASTERN SWEETSHRUB, CAROLINA ALLSPICE. **Family:** Strawberry-shrub (Calycanthaceae). **Genus:** *Calycanthus* (*C. floridus* var. *glaucus*). **Height/ Spread:** 4–8 feet. Taller in shaded areas. **Ornamental Attributes:** Fragrant, long-lasting

Sweetshrub (*Calycanthus floridus*)

individual dark red or maroon flowers that ladies once tucked into their blouses to perfume themselves. Glossy, aromatic dark green foliage turns golden yellow in fall. Urn-shaped seed capsules persist through the winter. All parts of the plant, including the multiple stems, are fragrant. "If only for the purplish-red, pleasantly-scented flowers, this North American shrub is worthy of extensive culture. The hardiness, accommodating nature, and delicious perfume of its brightly-coloured flowers render this shrub one of the choicest subjects," wrote the English gardener, A. D. Webster, in 1893.[13] **Cultivation:** Easily grown. Full to part sun, moist to dry well-drained soil. Low maintenance, drought resistant, no known pests or diseases. **Note:** Endangered or presumed extirpated in parts of the Midwest. **Nature Note:** Birds seek its pollinating beetles to feed their babies. Sweetshrub hosts 2 Lepidoptera species. Birds and their nestlings eat the caterpillars. **Historical Note:** *Calycanthus* is one of many in the ancient line of beetle-pollinated magnolia relatives.[14] **Zones:** (4) 5–9.

SERVICEBERRY, JUNEBERRY, SHADBUSH. **Family:** Rose (Rosaceae). **Genus:** *Amelanchier.* **Genus Note:** Serviceberries freely hybridize, making it difficult to identify specimens. **Ornamental Attributes:** "Serviceberries are like harbingers of spring—their early, attractive, white flowers are a vision of spring for winter-weary eyes," write Weeks and Weeks. Showy, fragrant clusters of five-petaled white (sometimes pink-tinged) flowers in April or May bloom at the same time as the invasive Bradford pear. True to their name, the showy, sweet, edible purplish-black, blueberry-like fruits always ripen in June. The pretty green summer leaves turn showy orange, red, yellow in fall at exactly the same time as the leaves of the

Serviceberry spp. (*Amelanchier*)
Also see pp. 77, 271

invasive nonnative burning bush turn pinkish or red. The gracefully shaped shrubs and trees have silver-gray bark providing winter interest. The shrubs create nice groundcovers and hedges. **Cultivation:** Easily grown. Sun best for fruit and fall color. Wide range of moist, well-drained soils. Mulching is a good idea. Frost hardy, salt and black walnut tree toxicity tolerant. Self-pollinating flowers; RUNNING SERVICEBERRY, RUNNING JUNEBERRY, DWARF SERVICEBERRY, THICKET SERVICEBERRY (*A. stolonifera, A. spicata*). **Height:** 1–6 feet. **Spread:** 3–10 feet; LOW SERVICEBERRY, LOW JUNEBERRY (*A. humilis*). **Height/Spread:** 2–3 feet. **Note:** Endangered in parts of the Midwest; ROUNDLEAF SERVICEBERRY (*A. sanguinea* var. *sanguinea*). **Height/Spread:** 3–8 feet. **Note:** Threatened or endangered in parts of the Midwest. **Nature Note:** The berries are high in carbohydrates and protein and ripen early in the growing season when fruit availability is scarce. They are top favorites for more than 40 species of birds, including cedar waxwing (p. 36), American robin (p. 62), northern cardinal (p. 61), Baltimore oriole (p. 167), brown thrasher (p. 219), eastern bluebird (p. 61), northern mockingbird (p. 256), wood thrush (p. 175), rose-breasted grosbeak (p. 200), red-bellied woodpecker (p. 55), tufted titmouse (p. 169), scarlet tanager, pileated woodpecker, and gray catbird (p. 79), as well as chipmunks (p. 94) and squirrels. "Because they blossom as early as mid-April, serviceberries supply nectar for emerging insects when little else is available," writes naturalist and author Mariette Nowak.[15] Birds eat the insects and feed them to their nestlings. Serviceberries host 124 species of Lepidoptera (butterflies/moths), including the red-spotted purple (p. 18), striped hairstreak (p. 18), eastern tiger swallowtail (p. 18), and viceroy (p. 54). Ruby-throated hummingbirds (p. 91) and adult butterflies, such as spring azure (p. 95), visit for nectar. Serviceberry has special value to important pollinators, including native bees. **Zones:** 4–8.

See Spring Trees for more SERVICEBERRY SPP., p. 77.

More Native Alternatives:

BLUEBERRY SPP., p. 27; CHOKEBERRY SPP., p. 13; DOGWOOD SPP., p. 48; FOTHERGILLA SPP., p. 27; NATIVE HONEYSUCKLE ALTERNATIVES, p. 38; RED BUCKEYE, p. 33; RHODODENDRON, AZALEA SPP., p. 56; VIBURNUM SPP., p. 69; WAFER ASH, p. 45.

See Summer Shrubs for HYDRANGEA SPP., p. 143; ST. JOHN'S WORT SPP., p. 145.

See Spring Trees for AMERICAN PLUM and other native plums, p. 78; CAROLINA SILVERBELL, p. 80; CRAB APPLE SPP., p. 89; FRINGE TREE, p. 105; REDBUD, p. 92.

Nonnative:

CHINESE FRINGE TREE. See Spring Trees for *FRINGE TREE*, p. 103.

Nonnative:

CORNELIAN CHERRY, CORNELIAN CHERRY DOGWOOD. **Family:** Dogwood (Cornaceae). **Genus:** *Cornus* (*C. mas*). **Origin:** Europe, Asia. **Height/Spread:** 15–20 feet. **Ornamental Attributes:** Pale

Cornelian cherry flowers (*Cornus mas*)

Cornelian cherry (*Cornus mas*)

yellow flowers in April. Red fall fruits; reddish fall leaves. **Cultivation:** Full sun, moist well-drained soil. Dense shade beneath mature specimens prevents growth of other plants. **Zones:** 4–7.

Native Alternatives:

SPICEBUSH, NORTHERN SPICEBUSH, COMMON SPICEBUSH, ALLSPICE BUSH, FORSYTHIA OF THE WILDS. Family: Laurel (Lauraceae). **Genus:** *Lindera* (*L. benzoin*). **Height/Spread:** 6–12 feet. **Ornamental Attributes:** The tiny, bright yellow, very fragrant flowers bloom March to April. "In the North this plant is thought of as the 'forsythia of the wilds' as its early spring flowering gives a subtle yellow tinge to many lowland woods where it is common," notes the Lady Bird Johnson Wildflower Center.[16] "The combination of the yellow foliage and red berries really makes this shrub pop in the fall," writes Jason Sheets.[17] **Cultivation:** Fast-growing, moist woods, understory shrub. Partial sun to light shade; best in rich moist soil, takes wet to moderately dry soil. Needs male plant for berries on female plants. Deer resistant; tolerates black walnut tree toxicity. **Nature Note:** Preferred host of spicebush swallowtail butterfly; also hosts an additional 10 species of Lepidoptera, including the eastern tiger swallowtail butterfly (p. 18), giant leopard moth, and promethea silkmoth. Birds and their nestlings eat the caterpillars. Mammals seek the July to October fruits, as do 17 bird species, including eastern kingbird (p. 55), wood thrush (p. 175), northern mockingbird (p. 256), great crested flycatcher, red-eyed vireo

Spicebush swallowtail butterfly

(*Papilio troilus*)

Promethea silkworm caterpillar (*Callosamia promethea*)

Spicebush flowers (*Lindera benzoin*)

(p. 112), gray catbird (p. 79), American robin (p. 62), and white-throated sparrow (p. 108). The nutritious high-fat, protein-rich fruits enable migrating warblers to store a special, high-energy fat in their bodies to survive what might be several weeks without eating. The flowers attract small native bees, flies, and other tiny insects that warblers and other nesting birds feed to their young. Wood thrush (p. 175) and other mid-canopy species nest in the larger shrubs. **Zones:** 4–9.

For more yellow-flowering spring shrubs, see GOLDEN CURRANT, p. 35; NATIVE HONEYSUCKLE ALTERNATIVES, p. 38; OZARK WITCH HAZEL, p. 75; ROUGH-LEAF DOGWOOD, p. 49.

See Summer Shrubs for AMERICAN BLACK CURRANT, p. 138, BUTTERFLY SHRUB, p. 129.

See Fall Shrubs for LEATHERWOOD, p. 232, SILVER BUFFALOBERRY, p. 229.

See Spring Trees for SASSAFRAS (SHRUB FORM), p. 99.

More Native Alternatives:

CHOKEBERRY SPP., p. 63; DOGWOOD SPP., p. 48; FOTHERGILLA SPP., p. 27; OZARK WITCH HAZEL, p. 75; SERVICEBERRY SPP., p. 20; VIBURNUM SPP., p. 69.
See Winter Shrubs for DWARF CHINKAPIN OAK, p. 311.
See Spring Trees for AMERICAN PLUM and other native plums, p. 78; CAROLINA SILVERBELL, p. 80; CHERRY SPP., p. 82; COPENHAGEN HAWTHORN and other native hawthorns, p. 106; FLOWERING DOGWOOD, p. 94; SERVICEBERRY, p. 77.

Nonnative:

DAPHNE, MEZEREUM, SPURGE OLIVE, FEBRUARY DAPHNE. **Family:** Mezereum (Thymelaeaceae). **Genus:** *Daphne* (*D. mezereum*). **Origin:** Europe. **Height/Spread:** 3–4 feet. **Ornamental Attributes:** Short-lived plant with fragrant pink flowers in April to May. **Cultivation:** Part to full sun, well-drained dry, sandy soil. **Problems:** All daphne species, hybrids, and cultivars are highly poisonous if eaten and are known to inexplicably die; susceptible to disease, frost, and snow damage. Salt intolerant. **Ecological Threat:** Invasive in midwestern states. **Zones:** 5–8.

Daphne (*Daphne mezereum*)

Native Alternatives:

BLACK HUCKLEBERRY, p. 28; BLUEBERRY SPP., p. 27; CHOKEBERRY SPP., p. 13; CURRANT SPP., p. 35; FOTHERGILLA SPP., p. 27; RHODODENDRUM, AZALEA SPP., p. 56; SAND CHERRY, p. 17; SERVICEBERRY SPP., p. 20; SPICEBUSH, p. 22; SWEETSHRUB, p. 19.

See Summer Shrubs for FALSE INDIGO BUSH, p. 132; LEADPLANT, p. 133; NEW JERSEY TEA, p. 134.

See Fall Shrubs for LEATHERWOOD, p. 232.

See Spring Trees for FRINGE TREE, p. 105; SNOWBELL, p. 116.

Nonnative:

DEUTZIA. **Family:** Hydrangea (Hydrangeaceae). **Genus:** *Deutzia; SLENDER DEUTZIA, SLENDER PRIDE OF ROCHESTER* (*D. gracilis*); *FUZZY PRIDE-OF-ROCHESTER* (*D. scabra*). **Origin:** Japan. **Height/Spread:** 2–5 feet. **Ornamental Attributes:** Short-lived stems hold white flowers in April to May. **Cultivation:** Sun best for flowers; rich, moist well-drained soil; naturalizes, requires annual pruning, thinning. **Ecological Threat:** *D. scabra* is invasive and naturalized in midwestern states. **Zones:** 5–8.

Slender deutzia
(*Deutzia gracilis*)

Dwarf fothergilla
(*Fothergilla gardenii*)

Dwarf fothergilla flowers
(*Fothergilla gardenii*)

Native Alternatives:

FOTHERGILLA, DWARF FOTHERGILLA, DWARF WITCHALDER. **Family:** Witch hazel (Hamamelidaceae). **Genus:** *Fothergilla* (*F. gardenii*). **Height/Spread:** 2–3 feet. **Ornamental Attributes:** Fragrant, creamy-white tinged with green, early spring bottlebrush-like flowers. Each glaucous blue-green leaf spends a long time displaying its brilliant orange, yellow, and red fall colors. Twiggy, zigzag stems on this multistemmed shrub provide winter interest. Neat mounded appearance, praised as never needing pruning. "This is the perfect shrub for small gardens, particularly—though not exclusively—those that are naturally moist," writes Patricia A. Taylor.[18] **Cultivation:** Sun best for color, but tolerates light shade; moist to moderately wet, well-drained, organically rich, moist acidic soil. Avoid dry sites. Low maintenance. A southeastern native, fothergilla is recommended for the Midwest by the Morton Arboretum on the basis of ornamental value, proven hardiness, availability, and freedom from serious problems. **Note:** Threatened or endangered in parts of its native range. **Zones:** (4) 5–9; **LARGE FOTHERGILLA, MOUNTAIN WITCHALDER** (*F. major*). **Height/Spread:** 6–12 feet. Showier flowers, hardier and more drought tolerant than the dwarf species. **Zones:** 4–8. **Both Species:** Tremendously disease and insect resistant. "Classic, multi-season shrubs, fothergillas are tidy, exceptionally low-maintenance plants with fragrant white spring flowers and spectacularly colored fall foliage. Gardeners who find it difficult to select just one should consider the possibility of having both these shrubs in their gardens," writes Taylor.[19] **Nature Note:** Rich sources of nectar for bees, butterflies, and other insect pollinators that nesting birds feed to baby birds. Birds and mammals eat the inconspicuous black fruits.

BLUEBERRY. **Family:** Heath (Ericaceae). **Genus:** *Vaccinium;* **HIGHBUSH BLUEBERRY** (*V. corymbosum*). **Height/Spread:** 4–12 feet. **Ornamental Attributes:** Drooping clusters of white to pink-tinted bell-shaped flowers followed by edible, blue fruit. Green, or often red twigs. Reddish-green spring leaves turn blue-green in summer and fiery red, yellow, orange, and purple in fall. As it ages, this multistemmed shrub assumes an attractive gnarled shape, providing winter interest. "For pure ornamental value, the blueberry bush is hard to beat," writes the Chicago Botanic Garden.[20] "A good substitute for burning bush," writes Penelope O'Sullivan.[21] **Cultivation:** Full sun, moist to dry, acidic soil. Recycled Christmas tree

Highbush blueberry
(*Vaccinium
corymbosum*)

House wren (*Troglodytes aedon*)

branches make excellent acidic mulch. **Note:** Endangered in parts of the Midwest. **Zones:** 3–8; LOWBUSH BLUEBERRY (*V. angustifolium*). **Height:** 6 inches–2 feet. **Note:** Threatened in parts of the Midwest. **Zones:** 3–6; CRANBERRY (*V. macrocarpon*). **Height:** Less than 1-foot-tall mat. **Ornamental Attributes:** Flowers create pink hazes over bogs. Edible, red fruit. Leathery evergreen leaves turn a variety of fall colors. Use as groundcover. **Cultivation:** Sun best for fruit; wet to moist acidic soil. **Note:** Endangered in Illinois, threatened in Tennessee. **Zones:** 2–6; MOUNTAIN CRANBERRY, LINGONBERRY (*V. vitis-idaea*). **Ornamental Attributes:** Mat-forming groundcover. **Note:** Endangered in Michigan and Wisconsin. **Zones:** 3–6; BLACK HUCKLEBERRY, DANGLEBERRY. **Genus:** *Gaylussacia* (*G. baccata*). **Height:** 2 feet. **Spread:** 2–4 feet. **Ornamental Attributes:** Urn-shaped blueberry-like spring flowers, edible black fruit, red fall color. **Cultivation:** Sun, part shade, moist or dry well-drained soil. **Note:** Threatened in Iowa. **Zones:** 4–8. **Heath Family Nature Note:** Blueberries and cranberries (*Vaccinium* genus) host 294 species of butterflies and moths, including brown elfin, spring azure (p. 95), summer azure (p. 128), azalea sphinx, Edwards' hairstreak (p. 210), and striped hairstreak (p. 18). HUCKLEBERRY (*Gaylussacia* genus) hosts 44 species of butterflies and moths. Including heath family plants in addition to "rosids," a group that includes trees and shrubs like oaks, willows, beeches, maples, and elms, helps increase Lepidoptera (butterfly/moth) diversity because these plants host different insects such as the slender clearwing moth, that only lays her eggs on plants in the heath family. The plants provide shelter to many animals. Blue jay (p. 79), red-winged blackbird (p. 55), black-capped chickadee (p. 322), scarlet tanager, gray catbird (p. 79), eastern towhee (p. 235), red-headed and red-bellied woodpeckers (pp. 212, 55), house wren, and warblers seek the midsummer berries and use the stems to create nests.

For more heath family plants see BEARBERRY, p. 156; DEERBERRY, p. 138; SOURWOOD, p. 186.

More Native Alternatives:

CHOKEBERRY SPP., p. 13; SAND CHERRY, p. 17; SERVICEBERRY SPP., p. 20; VIBURNUM SPP., p. 69; WAFER ASH, p. 45.
See Summer Shrubs for HYDRANGEA SPP., p. 143; NEW JERSEY TEA, p. 134.
See Fall Shrubs for SUMAC SPP., p. 242.

Nonnative:

DOGWOOD. See Winter Shrubs, p. 309.

Native Alternatives:

DOGWOOD SPP., p. 48.
See Winter Shrubs for REDOSIER DOGWOOD, p. 310.

European elderberry
(*Sambucus nigra*)

Nonnative:

ELDERBERRY, EUROPEAN ELDERBERRY, BLACK ELDERBERRY. **Family:** Elderberry (Adoxaceae). **Genus:** *Sambucus* (*S. nigra*). **Origin:** Europe. **Height:** 10–20 feet. **Spread:** 8–12 feet. **Ornamental Attributes:** Showy flat white, ill-smelling flowers in late spring to early summer; dark purple, edible berries. **Cultivation:** Full sun best, moderately moist soil. **Zones:** 5–7.

Native Alternatives:

ELDERBERRY. **Family:** Elderberry (Adoxaceae). **Genus:** *Sambucus;* AMERICAN BLACK ELDERBERRY (*Sambucus nigra* L. subsp. *canadensis*). **Height/Spread:** 8–15 feet. **Ornamental Attributes:** Showy, flat, white long-blooming flower heads in June and July; showy, glistening clusters of edible dark purple fruits held on magenta pedicels in August to September; yellow fall leaves. The flowers have "a pure sweet scent. . . . We like the contrast of lacy flower heads against tropical green foliage . . . in most gardens of fragrance," wrote Wilson and Bell.[22] **Cultivation:** Adaptable, low maintenance, easy-to-grow shrub. Full sun best; takes shade. Best in moderately moist, well-drained soils; tolerates dry conditions. Suckers create thickets. To encourage vigorous regrowth, cut to the ground in March. **Food Note:** Quintessential American

American black elderberry
(*Sambucus canadensis*)
Also see p. 267

plant produces fruits and flowers used for centuries to make wine, jam, jelly, preserves, pies, and juice. **Nature Note:** Little carpenter and mason bees hollow out stems, creating nesting material and locations. They cause little damage and create future pollinators. Shrub may be used for conservation biological control. Fruits are rich in carbohydrates and protein and provide important food for migrating birds. Provides cover, nesting sites, and habitat for local and migrating birds and other wildlife. Supports bees, butterflies, and other pollinators; pollen is a honeybee favorite. Eastern chipmunk (p. 94), red squirrel, Franklin's ground squirrel, woodchuck, foxes, and rabbits and more than 120 species of birds seek the mid- to late summer fruits, including red-bellied woodpecker (p. 55), red-headed woodpecker (p. 212), pileated woodpecker, American crow (p. 244), scarlet tanager, gray catbird (p. 79), red-breasted nuthatch (p. 322), white-breasted nuthatch, American robin (p. 62), golden and ruby-crowned kinglets (p. 233), eastern bluebird (p. 61), wood thrush (p. 175), cedar waxwing (p. 36), brown thrasher (p. 219), red-eyed vireo (p. 112), and northern cardinal (p. 61). "Common Elderberry is an attractive shrub, but often ignored because of its ubiquitous occurrence. In fact, people often destroy this shrub along fences or waterways in residential areas, notwithstanding its outstanding value to wildlife, particularly to songbirds," writes John Hilty.[23] **Zones:** 3–8; RED ELDERBERRY, SCARLET ELDER (*S. racemosa*). **Height/Spread:** 10–12 feet. **Ornamental Attributes:** Common to the more northerly regions of the Midwest, cones of soft white flowers resemble white lilac flowers. Eye-popping, slightly toxic red summer berries; yellow fall leaves. Stems, bark, leaves, and roots contain cyanide-producing toxins, so most mammalian herbivores avoid the shrub. **Cultivation:** Full sun best, moderately moist soil. Can grow almost anywhere. **Note:** Threatened in Illinois. **Zones:** 4–6; **Elderberry Note:** Tolerate black walnut tree toxicity. **Elderberry Host Plant Note:** Native elderberries host 42 species of Lepidoptera (butterflies/moths), including Henry's elfin (p. 93). Birds eat and feed the caterpillars to their nestlings.

White-breasted nuthatch
(*Sitta carolinensis*)

More Native Alternatives:

CHOKEBERRY SPP., p. 13; CURRANT SPP., p. 35; NINEBARK, p. 44.
See Spring Trees for AMERICAN PLUM and other native plums, p. 78; AMERICAN SNOWBELL, p. 116; CHERRY SPP., p. 82; SERVICEBERRY SPP., pp. 20, 77.

Nonnative:

FLOWERING QUINCE. **Family:** Rose (Rosaceae). **Genus:** *Chaenomeles; COMMON FLOWERING QUINCE* (*C. speciosa*). **Origin:** China; *JAPANESE FLOWERING QUINCE* (*C. japonica*). **Origin:** Japan. **Height/Spread:** 6–10 feet. **Ornamental Attributes:** Spiny, stubby shrubs; red, sometimes white or pink flowers in March to April bloom for a short time. No fall color. "Not pretty except in bloom, this ungainly, deciduous shrub brings little to most home landscapes," writes Penelope O'Sullivan.[24] **Cultivation:** Full sun best, moist well-drained soil, naturalizes. **Ecological Threat:** Naturalized in midwestern states. **Zones:** 5–8.

Japanese flowering quince (*Chaenomeles japonica*)

Red buckeye (*Aesculus pavia* var. *pavia*)

Native Alternatives:

RED BUCKEYE. **Family:** Soapberry (Sapindaceae). **Genus:** *Aesculus* (*A. pavia* var. *pavia*). Large shrub/small tree. "Though buckeyes are the smaller, shrub members of the horse chestnut (*Aesculus*) genus, they are rather massive when compared with other shrubs," writes Penelope O'Sullivan, and "wonderfully pest free."[25] **Height/Spread:** 6–15 feet; can grow taller. **Ornamental Attributes:** Large, brilliant red flowers bloom for several weeks from mid-spring to early summer, attracting ruby-throated hummingbirds (p. 91). Specimens that have grown in full sun and have a dense crown have a blooming period that is "almost theatrical in brilliance." With flower panicles that are among "the most beautiful of any temperate-zone species" and its distinctive buckeye foliage (opposite, compound) appearing early, red buckeye is "among our most welcome harbingers of spring," write Sternberg and Wilson.[26] Coarse, open structure (especially when the branches are permitted to fully develop to the ground), and

Red buckeye flowers
(*Aesculus pavia*
var. *pavia*)

Common buckeye butterfly
(*Junonia coenia*)

light brown, flaky bark offer winter interest; seeds are encased in smooth orange-brown husks. One of Christopher J. Starbuck's "Uncommon Trees for Specimen Planting." **Cultivation:** Full sun best, takes part sun; moist well-drained soil. **Native American Note:** Toxic seeds used to drug fish, making them easier to catch. **Note:** Threatened in parts of North America, including Kentucky. **Nature Note:** See YELLOW BUCKEYE, p. 98. **Zones:** 4–8.

More Native Buckeye Alternatives:

See Summer Shrubs for BOTTLEBRUSH BUCK-EYE, p. 130.

See Summer Trees for OHIO BUCKEYE, p. 184.

More Native Alternatives:

CHOKEBERRY SPP., p. 13; FOTHERGILLA SPP., p. 27; NORTHERN BUSH HONEY-SUCKLE, p. 38; OZARK WITCH HAZEL, p. 75; RED CURRANT, p. 35; RHODODEN-DRON, AZALEA SPP., p. 56; ROSE SPP., p. 60; SAND CHERRY, p. 17; SWEETSHRUB, p. 19.

See Fall Shrubs for AMERICAN BARBERRY, p. 233; LEATHERWOOD, p. 232.

See Spring Trees for FRINGE TREE, p. 105; REDBUD, p. 92..

Forsythia flowers (*Forsythia*)

Nonnative:

FORSYTHIA. Family: Olive (Oleaceae). Genus: *Forsythia.* Origin: Asia. Height/Spread: 4–9 feet. Ornamental Attributes: Yellow flowers in April to May that rarely receive visits from birds or butterflies. Following bloom, forsythia shrubs have neither fall color nor other ornamental value. "Forsythia is a suburban landscape cliché," writes Penelope O'Sullivan, noting it is "a fast-growing, multi-stemmed shrub that spreads by suckers into a huge tangled mass."[27] "Oddly, or perhaps understandably, gardeners have a love/hate relationship with the Forsythia. For two weeks every year it is the darling wherever it grows. Then it is rather boring for 50 weeks," writes Green Deane.[28] Cultivation: Full sun, well-drained soil, pruning. Cold temperatures and late freezes cause flower bud damage. Ecological Threat: Naturalized throughout the Midwest; *SHOWY FORSYTHIA* (*F.* × *intermedia*). Ecological Threat: Naturalized in the Midwest; *WEEPING FORSYTHIA* (*F. suspensa*). Ecological Threat: Naturalized in the Midwest; *GREENSTEM FORSYTHIA* (*F. viridissima*). Ecological Threat: Naturalized in the Midwest; Zones: 5–8.

Forsythia (*Forsythia*)

Clove currant
(*Ribes odoratum*)

Native Alternatives:

CURRANT. **Family:** Currant (Grossulariaceae). **Genus:** *Ribes* (includes currants and goose-berries). **Note:** Currants have no spines or thorny prickles; gooseberries have at least some. GOLDEN CURRANT, BUFFALO CURRANT, CLOVE CURRANT, MISSOURI CURRANT (*R. aureum* var. *villosum,* syn. *R. odoratum*). **Height/Spread:** 3–6 feet. **Ornamental Attributes:** A thornless shrub with conspicuous clusters of tubular, clove-scented, edible, golden-yellow, red-centered flowers that bloom for weeks from March to June. Lobed blue-green leaves turn yellow or red in late summer; edible black fruits. "Before I even noticed the screaming yellow flowers, I followed my nose."[29] "By mid-April the too-little appreciated clove currant of the Midwest, *Ribes odoratum,* is as showy as forsythia but with the scent of a thousand pinks," wrote Wilson and Bell, experts in fragrant plants.[30] **Cultivation:** Best in full sun, tolerates light shade. Adaptable plants grows in moist to moderately dry (in summer) soil. Two or more plants provide cross-pollination and better fruiting. Any suckers can be easily removed. **Zones:** 4–8; RED CURRANT (*R. triste*). **Height:** 3 feet. **Ornamental Attributes:** Profuse clusters of red, pink, purple spring flowers followed by clusters of hard, bright red berries. **Cultivation:** Full sun, moist to wet soil. **Note:** Endangered or threatened in parts of the east coast and the Midwest. Some states ban some *Ribes* species, so check state law before planting,[31] and avoid planting currants in locations where white pines are growing. **Confusion Note:** Red currant is not the cultivated European red currant (*R. rubrum*). **Food Note:** Golden and red currants are used in jams and jellies. **Currant/Gooseberry Nature Note:** The Midwest is home to many native species of currant and gooseberry. Nectar and pollen attract butterflies, ruby-throated hummingbirds (p. 91), hummingbird moths (p. 72), beneficial wasps, and other insects. The plants attract and have special value to native bees, including their most effective pollinators, long-tongued bees. Low-dwelling bird species use them for shelter and nest sites. Currants and gooseberries host 99 species of moths and butterflies, including green comma (p. 103) and gray comma butterflies and the orange-barred carpet moth. Birds eat and feed the caterpillars to their offspring. At least 16 species of birds[32] eagerly

Ruffed grouse (*Bonasa umbellus*)

Cedar Waxwing (*Bombycilla cedrorum*)

Bobwhite quail (*Colinus virginianus*)

seek the midsummer fruits, including cedar waxwings, which—having waited until late in the season to nest—feed their nestlings mostly insects at first, but soon add fruits. Brown thrasher (p. 219), American robin (p. 62), northern cardinal (p. 61), blue jay (p. 79), ruffed grouse, mourning dove, and bobwhite quail also eat the fruits, as do red fox, eastern chipmunk (p. 94), other small mammals, and people. **Zones:** 3–8.

More Yellow-Flowering Native Alternatives:

NATIVE HONEYSUCKLE ALTERNATIVES, p. 38; OZARK WITCH HAZEL, p. 75; ROUGHLEAF DOGWOOD, p. 49; SPICEBUSH (FORSYTHIA OF THE WILDS), p. 22.

More Native Alternatives:

CHOKEBERRY SPP., p. 13; FOTHERGILLA SPP., p. 27; SERVICEBERRY SPP., pp. 20, 77; VIBURNUM SPP., p. 69.

See Summer Shrubs for AMERICAN BLACK CURRANT, p. 138 (and GOOSEBERRIES and DEERBERRY, p. 138); BUTTERFLY SHRUB, p. 129; ST. JOHN'S WORT, p. 145.

See Fall Shrubs for LEATHERWOOD, p. 232; SILVER BUFFALOBERRY, p. 229.

See Spring Trees for AMERICAN PLUM and other native plums, p. 78; CAROLINA SILVERBELL, p. 80; CHOKECHERRY, p. 83; SASSAFRAS (SHRUB FORM), p. 99.

Nonnative:

FILBERT. See Spring Trees, p. 102.

Nonnative:

FRINGE TREE. See Spring Trees, p. 103.

Nonnative:

HONEYSUCKLE, ASIAN BUSH HONEYSUCKLES. **Family:** Honeysuckle (Caprifoliaceae). **Genus:** *Lonicera.* **Origin:** Asia; ***AMUR HONEYSUCKLE*** (*L. maackii*); ***DWARF HONEYSUCKLE, EUROPEAN FLY HONEYSUCKLE*** (*L. xylosteum*); ***FLY HONEYSUCKLE*** (*L.* × *xylosteoides, tatarica* × *xylosteum*); ***HONEYSUCKLE*** (*L.* × *minutiflora*); ***HONEYSUCKLE*** (*L.* × *notha*); ***MANCHURIAN HONEYSUCKLE*** (*L. ruprechtiana*); ***MORROW'S HONEYSUCKLE*** (*L. morrowii*); ***SHOWY FLY HONEYSUCKLE, BELL'S HONEYSUCKLE*** (*L.* × *bella, morrowii* × *tatarica*) (hybrid of *L. tatarica* and *L. morrowii*); ***STANDISH'S HONEYSUCKLE*** (*L. standishii*); ***SWEET BREATH OF SPRING, WINTER HONEYSUCKLE, FRAGRANT HONEYSUCKLE*** (*L. fragrantissima*); ***TATARIAN HONEYSUCKLE*** (*L. tatarica*), and its well-known cultivar: ***'ARNOLD'S RED'*** (*L. tatarica* 'Arnold's Red'). **Height/Spread:** 5–12 feet. **Ornamental Attributes:** White, pink, or yellow flowers in spring; red, yellow, or orange berries in fall; weedy branches; suffer from honeysuckle witches broom aphids, causing unattractive branching. **Cultivation:** Full sun, medium soil. Shade out and inhibit native plant germination; difficult to eradicate. **Zones:** 3–7. **Differentiation Note:** Nonnative honeysuckle twigs have hollow stems; natives have solid stems. **Honeysuckle Ecological Threat:** Invasive in midwestern, eastern, and southern states. Birds experience higher nest predation due to branch structure when nesting in nonnative species, such as buckthorn, multiflora rose, and honeysuckle, than in comparable native shrubs, an adverse environmental consequence that—in addition to these plants' invasiveness—outweighs their ornamental or privacy benefits.[33] **Note:** Some nurseries still sell honeysuckles for ornamental purposes and some states still offer them for conservation programs. **Cultivar Note:** Cultivars of nonnative invasive species are also invasive. Invasive honeysuckles and their cultivars should be removed as soon as possible.[34]

Amur honeysuckle (*Lonicera maackii*)

Native Honeysuckle Alternatives:

Northern bush honeysuckle
(*Diervilla lonicera*)

NORTHERN BUSH HONEYSUCKLE, LOW BUSH HONEYSUCKLE, DWARF BUSH HONEYSUCKLE. **Family:** Honeysuckle (Caprifoliaceae). **Genus:** *Diervilla* (*D. lonicera*). **Height:** 3–4 feet. **Ornamental Attributes:** Fragrant, showy, tube-like bright yellow to orange or red flowers in June to August. Exfoliating bark—orange inner bark, bright yellow, orange or red fall leaves. **Cultivation:** Sun to shade, dry/moist well-drained soil. Drought tolerant. **Note:** Rare in parts of the Midwest. **Zones:** 3–6; AMERICAN FLY HONEYSUCKLE. **Family:** Honeysuckle (Caprifoliaceae). **Genus:** *Lonicera* (*L. canadensis*). **Height/Spread:** 3–7 feet. **Ornamental Attributes:** Fragrant yellow, red-tinged flowers in early April to May are harbingers of spring. Elongated red-orange berries in mid- to late summer. **Cultivation:** Easy to grow; full sun to part shade; variety of soil types. **Note:** Extirpated in part of the Midwest; MOUNTAIN FLY HONEYSUCKLE (*L. villosa*). **Height/Spread:** 2–3 feet. **Ornamental Attributes:** Fragrant white-yellow/chartreuse flowers in May, edible dark blue fruit in June to July mistaken for blueberries. Thick, blue-green leaves. **Cultivation:** Sun/part shade/shade, medium-moist soil. **Fly Honeysuckle Note:** Extirpated or presumed extirpated in parts of the Midwest. **Zones:** 3–8; TWINBERRY HONEYSUCKLE, BLACK TWINBERRY (*L. involucrata*). **Height/Spread:** 4–10 feet. **Ornamental Attributes:** Attention-grabbing, axillary pairs of fragrant, yellow tubular flowers from June to July. Showy red-bract-cupped "twin" black berries. Shiny green leaves turn yellow in fall. **Cultivation:** Sun best, prefers moist soil; succeeds in any fertile soil. **Note:** Threatened or endangered in parts of the Midwest. **Nature Note:** Native honeysuckles (*Lonicera*) host 37 species of butterflies and moths, including spring azure (p. 95), fawn and Kalm's sphinx moths, and snowberry clearwing moth. Birds and their nestlings eat the caterpillars. Pollinators, including ruby-

American fly honeysuckle
(*Lonicera canadensis*)

Twinberry honeysuckle
(*Lonicera involucrata*)

throated hummingbirds (p. 91), visit the flowers for nectar; the plants have special value to bumblebees and other native bees. American robin (p. 62), northern cardinal (p. 61), wood thrush (p. 175), wild turkey (p. 244), and small mammals seek the fruits. Native honeysuckles provide nesting cover for birds and tolerate black walnut tree toxicity. **Zones:** 4–10.

More Native Alternatives:

BLUEBERRY SPP., p. 27; CHOKEBERRY SPP., p. 13; CURRANT SPP., p. 35; DOG-WOOD SPP., p. 48; ELDERBERRY SPP., p. 29; FOTHERGILLA SPP., p. 27; NINE-BARK, p. 44; SERVICEBERRY SPP., pp. 20, 77; SPICEBUSH, p. 22; VIBURNUM SPP., p. 69.

See Summer Shrubs for CURRANT SPP., p. 35; DEERBERRY, p. 138; HYDRANGEA SPP., p. 143; ST. JOHN'S WORT, p. 145.

See Spring Trees for SNOWBELL, p. 116.

Note: For a good alternative to invasive nonnative honeysuckles, choose any native midwestern shrub.

Nonnative:

HYDRANGEA. See Summer Shrubs, p. 142.

Jetbead (*Rhodotypos scandens*)

Nonnative:

JETBEAD, BLACK JETBEAD. **Family:** Rose (Rosaceae). **Genus:** *Rhodotypos* (*R. scandens*). **Origin:** China, Korea, Japan. **Height:** 3–6 feet. **Spread:** 4–9 feet. **Ornamental Attributes:** White flowers in May to June, black fruits. No fall color. **Cultivation:** Full sun to part shade, medium soil. **Ecological Threat:** Invasive in midwestern states. **Zones:** 4–8.

Native Alternatives:

BLACK CHOKEBERRY, p. 13; BLACK HUCKLEBERRY, p. 28; CURRANT SPP., p. 35; FOTHERGILLA SPP., p. 27; NINEBARK, p. 44; SERVICEBERRY SPP., pp. 20, 77; TWINBERRY HONEYSUCKLE, p. 38; VIBURNUM SPP., p. 69.
See Summer Shrubs for AMERICAN BLACK CURRANT, p. 138; HYDRANGEA SPP., p. 143; NEW JERSEY TEA, p. 134.
See Fall Shrubs for AMERICAN BARBERRY, p. 233; AMERICAN BEAUTYBERRY, p. 235.
See Spring Trees for FRINGE TREE, p. 105.

Japanese kerria, Japanese rose
(*Kerria japonica*)

Nonnative:

***KERRIA, JAPANESE KERRIA, JAPA-
NESE ROSE.*** **Family:** Rose (Rosaceae). **Genus:** *Kerria* (*K. japonica*). **Origin:** Japan.
Height/Spread: 5–10 feet. **Ornamental Attributes:** Yellow flowers in April to May. Green,
weedy stems die back and sucker; requires
pruning. **Cultivation:** Sun; part shade prevents fading flowers; medium soil. **Ecological
Threat:** Invasive in some midwestern states.
Zones: 5–9.

Native Alternatives:

AMERICAN BLADDERNUT. **Family:**
Bladdernut (Staphyleaceae). **Genus:** *Staphylea* (*S. trifolia*). **Height:** 8–12 feet. **Spread:**
6–10 feet, may grow taller; shrub or small tree.
Ornamental Attributes: Bladdernut "is a
consummate Midwestern plant. . . . It has
beautiful chains of creamy flowers in early
spring, unusual, persistent pods and yellow
fall color. Its twigs are deep green and especially attractive in the winter months," note
Weeks and Weeks.[35] Unusual three-chambered
bladder-like seedpods resemble Chinese lanterns and persist into the winter months.
Greenish bark is textured with white cracks.
Cultivation: Native to moist, deep woods, the
plant prefers shade, moist well-drained sandy
or silty loams. Insect and disease resistant.
Suckering forms thickets. Good for shady
woodlands. Tolerates black walnut tree toxicity. **Nature Note:** Provides wildlife with protective cover and northern cardinal (p. 61),
gray catbird (p. 79), and wood thrush (p. 175)
with nesting sites. Hosts 2 species of butterflies and moths. Birds eat the caterpillars and
feed them to nestlings. **Zones:** 3–9.

More Native Alternatives:

AMERICAN FLY HONEYSUCKLE, p. 38;
CHOKEBERRY SPP., p. 13; GOLDEN
CURRANT, p. 35; NINEBARK, p. 44;
RHODODENDRON, AZALEA SPP., p.
56; ROSE SPP., p. 60; SPICEBUSH, p. 22;
VIBURNUM SPP., p. 69.

American bladdernut (*Staphylea trifolia*)

See Summer Shrubs for AMERICAN BLACK CURRANT, GOOSEBERRIES, DEERBERRY, p. 138; BUTTERFLY SHRUB, p. 129; HYDRANGEA SPP., p. 143.

See Fall Shrubs for AMERICAN BARBERRY, p. 233; LEATHERWOOD, p. 232; SILVER BUFFALOBERRY, p. 229; SUMAC SPP., p. 242.

See Spring Trees for SNOWBELL, p. 116.

Nonnative:

LILAC, COMMON LILAC. **Family:** Olive (Oleaceae). **Genus:** *Syringa* (*S. vulgaris*). **Origin:** Europe. **Height/Spread:** 8–10 feet. **Ornamental Attributes:** Clusters of often fragrant white, purple, or lavender flowers in April to May. **Cultivation:** Full sun, medium soil; pruning. "Lilacs are not a particularly attractive plant except in the spring when they are blooming," writes Melissa Howard.[36] Leggy, no fall color. **Ecological Threat:** Naturalized and potentially invasive in midwestern states; *JAPANESE LILAC* (*S. villosa*). **Origin:** China. **Height/Spread:** 12–15 feet. **Ornamental Attributes:** Briefly blooming flowers in May to June; *MEYER LILAC, DWARF KOREAN LILAC* (*S. meyeri*). **Origin:** China, Japan. **Height:** 4–8 feet. **Spread:** 6–12 feet. **Ornamental Attributes:** Flowers in May; *PERSIAN LILAC* (*S. × persica*); *LITTLELEAF LILAC* (*S. pubescens* subsp. *microphylla*). **Zones:** 3–7.

Lilac (*Syringa vulgaris*)

American wisteria
(*Wisteria frutescens*)

Native Alternatives:

AMERICAN WISTERIA. **Family:** Pea (Fabaceae). **Genus:** *Wisteria* (*W. frutescens*). **Height:** 15–30 feet. **Spread:** 4–8 feet. **Ornamental Attributes:** Woody vine; can be trained as a shrub. Large, showy clusters of lilac or purple flowers bloom on new wood in waves for two to four weeks in April and May and "evoke the same romantic feeling as the Asian types."[37] **Cultivation:** Full sun, part sun, moist to medium neutral to slightly acid sandy, clay, or loam well-drained soils. Tolerates black walnut tree toxicity. Well behaved; provide the trunk with good support. **Nature Note:** Attracts hummingbirds (p. 91) and butterflies; hosts 19 species of butterflies and moths, including longtailed skippers, silver-spotted skippers, and the marine blue butterfly. **Note:** Rare or threatened in parts of the Midwest. **Zones:** (4) 5–9. **Confusion Note:** Native wisteria is neither *CHINESE WISTERIA* (*W. sinensis*) nor *JAPANESE WISTERIA*

(*W. floribunda*); both invasive plants from Asia are "moderately well behaved" in cool climates "especially if you have a staff of gardeners to pull them off the window screens and telephone wires," observes William Cullina.[38]

Marine blue butterfly
(*Leptotes marina*)

Ninebark shrub (*Physocarpus opulifolius*)
Also see p. 268

NINEBARK, ATLANTIC NINEBARK. **Family:** Rose (Rosaceae). **Genus:** *Physocarpus* (*P. opulifolius*). **Height/Spread:** 5–10 feet. **Ornamental Attributes:** Long-lasting, showy white flowers with purple stamens in May to June; long-lasting papery bladder-like red fruit; leaves turn brilliant red, orange, or yellow in fall; exfoliating bark provides winter interest. "Domed clusters of creamy-white flowers smother the even, rounded crowns of ninebark in late spring and early summer," writes C. Colston Burrell.[39] **Cultivation:** Tough, adaptable to almost all conditions, easy to grow. Full sun to light shade. Dry to moist soil. Tolerates black walnut tree toxicity. **Nature Note:** Preferred site for many shrub-nesting songbirds. Used for cover, but not food, by deer and rabbits. Nectar and pollen support bees, butterflies, wasps, and the small flies sought by nesting birds. Birds eat the fruits. Ninebark hosts the specialist ninebark calligraphy beetle and 41 species of butterflies and moths, including the dark spotted palthis moth, whose disguise is to look like a leaf. **Cultivar/Nativar Note:** Although the naturally green-leaved species hosts the specialist ninebark calligraphy beetle,[40] the resulting damage is

Ninebark flowers
(*Physocarpus opulifolius*)

so minimal, experts describe the species as "largely left alone by animal pests."[41] Ninebark cultivars/nativars selected for dark (i.e., purple) foliage all year round instead of the normal green have changed leaf chemistry that makes the leaves indigestible to the ninebark's specialist beetle.[42] Its absence deprives birds of natural food for themselves and their nestlings. Dark-leaved cultivars like 'Mondo' Diablo are marketed as "pest-resistant"[43] and having "improved disease resistance," but complaints include fuzzy white coatings, mold, or powdery mildew infecting and killing whole branches.[44] **Zones:** 3–8.

Giant swallowtail butterfly (*Papilio cresphontes*)

WAFER ASH, HOPTREE. **Family:** Citrus (Rutaceae). **Genus:** *Ptelea* (*P. trifoliata*). **Height/Spread:** 10–20 feet. Multistemmed shrub or small tree. **Ornamental Attributes:** Pretty clusters of fragrant small greenish-white flowers in April; dark green trifoliate leaves turn yellow in fall; showy flat, wafer-like winged fruits provide winter interest, as does the slender crooked trunk with interwoven, ascending branches. Good as a specimen or screen. **Cultivation:** Sun, light shade; moist, humus-rich, well-drained soil. Hardy and easy-care. Wafer ash does not belong to the ash family, so isn't subject to their destruction by emerald ash borers. Its fruits resemble elm seeds, but it is not an elm, so not subject to Dutch elm disease. **Nature Note:** Wafer ash hosts 6 species of butterflies and moths. Along with pricklyash (Summer Shrubs, p. 124), wafer ash hosts the giant swallowtail butterfly. The moths it hosts include the brown-bordered ermine. The two-marked treehopper, whose frothy white egg masses are visible in winter, also relies on the wafer ash. Pollinators include small bees, wasps, flies, and ants that feed primarily on nectar. Songbirds use it for nesting. **Note:** One of Christopher Starbuck's selections for uncommon trees for specimen planting. **Zones:** 3–8.

More Native Alternatives:

AMERICAN BLADDERNUT, p. 41; AMERICAN SMOKETREE, p. 65; BLUEBERRY SPP., p. 27; CHOKEBERRY SPP., p. 13; DOGWOOD SPP., p. 48; ELDERBERRY SPP., p. 29; FOTHERGILLA SPP., p. 27; GOLDEN CURRANT, p. 35; OZARK WITCH HAZEL, p. 75, RHODODENDRON, AZALEA SPP., p. 56; SCENTLESS MOCK ORANGE, p. 46; SPICEBUSH, p. 22.

See Summer Shrubs for BUTTONBUSH, p. 131; HYDRANGEA SPP., p. 143; NEW JERSEY TEA (WILD LILAC), p. 134.

See Spring Trees for AMERICAN PLUM and other native plums, p. 78; CAROLINA SILVERBELL, p. 80; CHOKECHERRY, p. 83; FRINGE TREE, p. 105; SASSAFRAS (SHRUB FORM), p. 99; SERVICEBERRY SPP., p. 20; YELLOWWOOD, p. 96.

Nonnative:

MAGNOLIA. See Spring Trees, p. 109.

Nonnative:

MOCKORANGE, SWEET MOCKORANGE.
Family: Hydrangea (Hydrangeaceae). **Genus:** *Philadelphus* (*P. coronarius*). **Origin:** Europe. **Height/Spread:** 8–10 feet. **Ornamental Attributes:** White flowers in late spring to early summer, sometimes fragrant. Lanky plants with nondescript foliage. "To avoid disappointment it is well for the fragrant-minded to realize that many *Philadelphus* have no perfume, 'scentless, or souless . . . beautiful and dumb' in Mrs. [Louise Beebe] Wilder's words," wrote Wilson and Bell.[45] No fall color. **Cultivation:** Full sun to light shade, medium soil. **Ecological Threat:** Naturalized in midwestern states. **Zones:** 5–8.

Sweet mockorange (*Philadelphus coronarius*)

Native Alternative:

SCENTLESS MOCK ORANGE, APPALACHIAN MOCK-ORANGE. **Family:** Hydrangea (Hydrangeaceae). **Genus:** *Philadelphus* (*P. inodorus, P. grandiflorus*). **Height:** 6–12 feet. **Ornamental Attributes:** Fragrant, sweet citrus blossom–scented showy clusters of large bright white flowers decorate this erroneously named shrub in May to June. Its arching branches and exfoliating orange bark provide winter interest. **Cultivation:** Sun, or at least part sun, and moist soils best. Drought tolerant. **Note:** Threatened in parts of the Midwest.

Nature Note: Special value to native bees; hosts 4 species of butterflies and moths. **Zones:** 5–8.

Scentless mock orange
(*Philadelphus inodorus*)

More Native Alternatives:

AMERICAN BLADDERNUT, p. 41; CHOKEBERRY SPP., p. 13; FOTHERGILLIA, p. 27; GOLDEN CURRANT, p. 35; NINEBARK, p. 44; OZARK WITCH HAZEL, p. 75; SPICEBUSH, p. 22; WAFER ASH, p. 45.

See Spring Trees for CHOKECHERRY, p. 83; FRINGE TREE, p. 105; SASSAFRAS (SHRUB FORM), p. 99; SERVICEBERRY SPP., p. 20; SNOWBELL, p. 116.

Oriental photinia
(*Photinia villosa*)

Nonnative:

ORIENTAL PHOTINIA. **Family:** Rose. **Genus:** *Photinia* (*P. villosa*). **Origin:** Japan, Korea, China. **Height/Spread:** 10–15 feet. **Ornamental Attributes:** White flowers in May to June, red fall fruit. **Cultivation:** Sun or part sun; prolific seed producer, creates thickets. **Zones:** 4–8.

Native Alternatives:

NINEBARK, p. 44; RED CHOKEBERRY, p. 13; SCENTLESS MOCK ORANGE, p. 46; SERVICEBERRY SPP., p. 20; SPICEBUSH, p. 22.

See Spring Trees for AMERICAN PLUM and other native plums, p. 78; SERVICE-BERRY SPP., p. 77.

Nonnative:

PRIVET, PRIVET HEDGE. **Family:** Olive (Oleaceae). **Genus:** *Ligustrum.* **Note:** Several privet species occur and they are very hard to distinguish. **Cultivar Note:** Ornamentally, privet cultivars (ex: variegated) often revert to their original green; *AMUR PRIVET* (*L. obtusifolium* subsp. *suave,* syn. *L. amurense*). **Origin:** China. **Height:** 12–15 feet. **Spread:** 8–10 feet. **Ornamental Attributes:** A not particularly attractive shrub used for hedges, whose insignificant white flowers are often pruned to oblivion; black berry-like fruits; some find its fragrance objectionable; produces suckers. "In the Midwest, this species is as common as grass," writes Michael Dirr, recalling city blocks "where virtually every house had a hedge in front and in back and shared one on either side with the neighbor."[46] **Cultivation:** Full sun to part

European privet (*Ligustrum vulgare*)

shade, most soil types, regular pruning. **Zones:** 3–7; ***BORDER PRIVET, REGAL PRIVET, BLUNT-LEAVED PRIVET*** (*L. obtusifolium*). **Origin:** Japan, Korea, China. **Ornamental Attributes:** Resembles Amur privet. **Zones:** 3–7; ***CALIFORNIA PRIVET*** (*L. ovalifolium*). **Origin:** Japan. **Zones:** 7–10; ***CHINESE PRIVET*** (*L. sinense*). **Zones:** 6–9; ***EUROPEAN PRIVET, COMMON PRIVET*** (*L. vulgare*). **Origin:** Europe/Africa. **Zones:** 4–7; ***JAPANESE PRIVET*** (*L. japonica*). **Origin:** Japan. **Zones:** 7–10; **Privet Ecological Threat:** Amur, border, European, and Japanese privet are invasive in parts of the Midwest. In Indiana, California privet is ranked a "caution" invasive species. Privets are prolific producers of seed, and birds spread them far from the original plantings. All privet species are a major threat to all natural landscapes.[47] Neither the species nor their cultivars should be planted. Contrary to nursery representations, cultivars of invasive nonnative plants that are sold as not invasive and "safe to natural areas" do produce viable seeds and the seedlings—like their parents—naturalize or are invasive.[48]

Native Alternatives:

DOGWOOD. Family: Dogwood (Cornaceae). **Genus:** *Cornus.* **Cultivation Note:** Can grow dogwoods as shrubs, hedges, trees, clumps, or thickets. Dogwoods commonly grow as understory shrubs or trees in naturally moist, fertile soils high in organic matter, and never in poorly drained locations or hot dry areas; however, they are adaptable to several types of soils. Their primary demands are good soil drainage and protection from drought, including deep

Gray dogwood (*Cornus racemosa*)
Also see p. 268

watering during summer droughts. They do best when planted in association with larger trees that provide light or moderate shade, though some species do best in sun; ALTER-NATELEAF DOGWOOD, PAGODA DOGWOOD (*C. alternifolia*). **Height:** 15–25 feet. **Spread:** 20–30 feet. **Ornamental Attributes:** Fragrant, yellow- or creamy-white flowers in May to early June. Green fruits turn pink or red, then blue-black held in red pedicels in June or July, often with all the colors present at the same time. Fall leaves are deep reddish-purple. Tiers of horizontal branches tapering toward the top explain the common name, pagoda dogwood. This is "a highly prized ornamental tree," writes C. Colston Burrell.[49] "The shrub has year-round appeal. Everything about it is pretty and there is something unique for every season," write Weeks and Weeks.[50] **Cultivation:** For tree size, needs full or partial sun in moist soil. Remains a shrub in shade. To restrain golden canker disease, needs open sunny location, plenty of space, mulch over root system but away from the trunks, prune out affected branches, and, importantly, water deeply during summer droughts. Tolerates black walnut tree toxicity. **Zones:** 3–7; GRAY DOGWOOD, SWAMP DOGWOOD, RED-PANICLED DOGWOOD (*C. racemosa*). **Height:** Often 4–5 feet; sometimes attains 16 feet. **Spread:** 10–15 feet. **Ornamental Attributes:** Clusters of creamy-white flowers in late spring. White fruits held on bright red panicles that ripen July through October attract migrating and overwintering songbirds due to their high fat content. Leaves turn purple in fall. Red stems create red hazes. **Cultivation:** Tolerates alkaline soil. Fairly drought resistant. This tough shrub annoys prairie restorers, but it is a superb addition to other landscapes. **Zones:** 4–8; REDOSIER DOGWOOD, see Winter Shrubs, p. 310; ROUGHLEAF DOGWOOD, DRUMMOND'S

Roughleaf dogwood (*Cornus drummondii*)

DOGWOOD (*C. drummondii, C. asperifolia*). **Height:** To 16 feet. **Spread:** 10–15 feet. **Ornamental Attributes:** Large showy clusters of creamy-yellow flowers in April to June; red twigs; white fall fruits on orange-red pedicels accompany the deep red or purplish fall leaves. Once prairie fires restrained these woody plants in the prairie belt, "but because prairie fires are increasingly rare, roughleaf dogwoods can rise above their shrubby nature to become attractive small trees," write Sternberg and Wilson.[51] **Cultivation:** Full sun to shade; dry to moist soil; adapts to most conditions. **Zones:** 4–9; SILKY DOGWOOD, BLUE-FRUITED DOGWOOD (*C. amomum* subsp. *obliqua*). **Height/Spread:** 6–10 feet. **Ornamental Attributes:** Four-season interest includes showy, fragrant clusters of white flowers in May to June, gorgeously colored blue fruits displayed on bright red pedicels in August and September, reddish-purple fall leaves, and red twigs and stems resembling redosier dogwood that stand out in winter. Good in shrub borders, massing and naturalizing. **Cultivation:** Sun, but tolerates some shade and wet soil, where it forms thickets. Tolerates air pollution and black walnut tree toxicity. **Note:** Endangered in part of the Midwest. **Zones:** 4–8; SWAMP DOGWOOD, STIFF DOGWOOD (*C. foemina*). **Height:** 12 feet. **Ornamental Attributes:** Fragrant flowers. It is one of the blue-fruited species of its genus. **Cultivation:** Full or partial sun, wet to moist conditions containing significant organic matter. **Zones:** 5–9; ROUNDLEAF DOGWOOD (*C. rugosa*). **Height:** 3–10 feet. **Ornamental Attributes:** Conspicuous white or blue fruits mid-

Andrena spp.

August to late September. **Cultivation:** Shade, part shade. Dry soils and well-drained sandy loam soils. **Note:** Rare in part of the Midwest. **Zones:** 3–5. **Dogwood Nature Note:** Dogwood hosts 118 species of Lepidoptera (butterflies/moths), including the spring azure (p. 95) and summer azure (p. 128), giant silkmoths, polyphemus moth (p. 211), dogwood thyativid, and unicorn caterpillar moth. Birds eat the caterpillars and feed them to their offspring. The rare oligolectic bee, *Andrena fragilis*, prefers flowers in the genus *Cornus*. Dogwoods can be used as part of conservation biological control. Butterflies, wasps, flies, hummingbirds (p. 91), and other beneficial pollinators visit dogwood flowers; warblers and other nesting birds seek the small insects to feed their nestlings; dogwoods have special value to native bees. The specialist dogwood calligraphy beetle eats dogwood foliage; birds eat the beetles. The summer and fall fruits' (drupes) higher-than-average fat and calorie content causes them to be preferred foods for mammals and huge numbers of songbirds. High-fat berries are an important food source for wintering and migratory birds, which primarily use fat to fuel their migration. A study found fall migrating frugivorous (fruit-eating) birds have a preference for native dogwood fruits.[52] More than 98 bird species eat dogwood fruits, including American robin (p. 62), gray catbird (p. 79), yellow-shafted flicker, scarlet tanager, cedar waxwing (p. 36), eastern bluebird (p. 61), northern cardinal (p. 61), northern flicker (p. 99), downy woodpecker, long-tailed chat, eastern kingbird (p. 55), purple finch (p. 145), crested flycatcher, rose-breasted grosbeak (p. 200), evening grosbeak (p. 162), northern mockingbird (p. 256), brown thrasher (p. 219), wood thrush (p. 175), American crow (p. 244), Baltimore oriole (p. 167), vireos, yellow-bellied sapsucker (p. 79), tree swallow (p. 55), greater prairie chicken, bobwhite quail (p. 36), ruffed grouse (p. 36), red-bellied woodpecker (p. 55), red-headed woodpecker (p. 212), pileated woodpecker, wood duck (p. 162), wild turkey (p. 244), tufted titmouse (p. 169), song sparrow (p. 307), and chipping sparrow. Birds and other wildlife use dogwoods for shelter and nesting. Turtles in wetland areas eat the fallen leaves, fruit, and seeds. Mammals eating the fruit and foliage include black bear, beaver, cottontail rabbit, raccoon, squirrels, chipmunk, deer, and moose. The shrubs, especially when massed, provide excellent nesting habitat for songbirds. "These trees and shrubs are some of our most valuable plants for wildlife," write Sternberg and Wilson.[53] Also see Winter Shrubs for RE-DOSIER DOGWOOD, p. 310.

Also see Spring Trees for FLOWERING DOGWOOD, p. 94.

Chipping sparrow (*Spizella passerina*)

More Native Alternatives:

AMERICAN CRANBERRYBUSH, BLACKHAW & OTHER NATIVE VIBURNUMS, p. 69; CHOKEBERRY SPP., p. 13; CURRANT SPP., p. 35; ELDERBERRY SPP., p. 29; FOTHERGILLA SPP., p. 27; NINEBARK, p. 44; PUSSY WILLOW, p. 53; SCENTLESS MOCK ORANGE, p. 46; SERVICEBERRY SPP., p. 20; SPICEBUSH, p. 22; WAFER ASH, p. 45.

See Summer Shrubs for HYDRANGEA SPP., p. 143.

See Fall Shrubs for BAYBERRY, p. 232; POSSUMHAW, p. 237; SUMAC SPP., p. 242.

See Winter Shrubs for AMERICAN HOLLY, p. 313; REDOSIER DOGWOOD, p. 310.

See Spring Trees for AMERICAN HAZELNUT, p. 102; FRINGE TREE, p. 105; SERVICEBERRY SPP., p. 77.

See Fall Trees for OSAGE ORANGE, p. 259.

See Winter Trees for AMERICAN ARBORVITAE, p. 319; AMERICAN YEW, p. 314; RED CEDAR, p. 323.

Note: For a good alternative to privet, choose any native midwestern shrub.

Nonnative:

PUSSY WILLOW, GOAT WILLOW. **Family:** Willow (*Salicaceae*). **Genus:** *Salix* (*S. caprea*). **Origin:** Eurasia. **Height:** 12–20 feet. **Spread:** 6–9 feet. **Ornamental Attributes:** Small tree/shrub, catkins in March to April. **Cultivation:** Full sun best. Wet to moist soil; disease problems, naturalizes. **Ecological Threat:** Invasive in the eastern United States, parts of the Midwest, and Canada. **Zones:** 5–8; *LARGE GRAY WILLOW* (*S. cinerea*). **Origin:** Europe. **Ecological Threat:** Invasive in midwestern states. **Zones:** 4–8; *LAUREL WILLOW* (*S. pentandra*). **Origin:** Europe. **Ornamental Attributes:** Large shrub/small tree. **Ecological Threat:** Invasive in midwestern states.

For more willows, see Spring Trees, p. 117.

Pussy willow, goat willow
(*Salix caprea*)

Pussy willow (*Salix discolor*)

Native Alternatives:

PUSSY WILLOW. Family: Willow (Salicaceae). **Genus:** *Salix* (*S. discolor*). **Height:** 6–20 feet. **Spread:** 4–12 feet. Small tree/shrub. **Ornamental Attributes:** All willow species have alternate, usually narrow leaves and catkins, male and female on separate trees. Pussy willow's catkins appear each year in March to April; the pretty, velvety, silvery-gray male catkins fancifully resemble kittens climbing a twig. Female buds and flowers also conspicuously bloom on bare stems before leaves appear. **Cultivation:** Easy to grow and propagate. Full sun best, wet to moist soil, tolerates drier soil. **Zones:** 4–8; **MEADOW WILLOW** (*S. petriolaris*). **Height/Spread:** 10 feet. **Ornamental Attributes:** Low-growing clumped shrub with slender, upraised stems. **Cultivation:** Full sun, well-drained soil, tolerates many soil types. **Zones:** 3–8; **MISSOURI RIVER WILLOW** (*S. eriocephala*). **Height:** To 20 feet. **Ornamental Attributes:** Narrow shrub or small tree with multiple trunks, dark-gray scaly bark, thick lance-shaped leaves, and densely silky catkins. **Cultivation:** Sun, moist, wet, sandy soil. **Zones:** 5–9; **PRAIRIE WILLOW** (*S. humilis* var. *humilis;* var. *tristis*). **Height/Spread:** 2–12 feet. **Ornamental Attributes:** Gray-green to blue-green "extremely pretty foliage;"[54] yellow, green, or purple catkins emerge before the leaves in March to May; wandlike yellow-brown to red stems attractive in winter. **Cultivation:** Sun, dry to wet soil; tolerates salt and many soil types. Reproduces by reseeding. **Zones:** 3–7; **SANDBAR WILLOW** (*S. interior*). **Height:** 6–7, sometimes 20 feet. Small tree or thicket. **Zones:** 2–7; **SILKY WILLOW** (*S. sericea*). **Height:** 6–12 feet. **Ornamental Attributes:** Nonsuckering willow that "remains always a shrub."[55] Pussy-willow-like catkins; silvery leaves turn yellow in fall. **Cultivation:** Sun to light shade, moist to wet well-drained soil. **Note:** Endangered in Arkansas. **Zones:** 4–8. **Willow Ornamental Note:** "Of inestimable value to the opening season are the willows, for very early they put on their spring dress of silver sheen and thrust out buds of green, or combinations of colour almost too subtle to be accurately described," wrote Alice Lounsberry in 1901.[56] **Willow Cultivation Note:** Native willows tolerate black walnut tree toxicity. **Willow Nature Note:** "Willows do not spread their pollen via the wind. Instead, they rely on insects for pollination, despite having less than gaudy flowers. What they lack in visual cues, they clearly make up for in olfactory ones, producing large amounts of strongly scented nectar. Pollinators find willows to be superior food sources. Bees and flies are readily drawn to pussy willows in full bloom. One of the advantages of flowering early in spring is that there is very little competition for pollinators. The willows gain the full attention of the many bees and flies that also awaken early in the spring and are desperate for food," writes Johnny Caryopsis.[57] A few oligolectic or specialist bees, such as several Andrenid bees, use willow pollen almost exclusively. Pollination ecologists recognize willows as having special value to native and honeybees, meaning they attract them in large numbers. Willows host insects like wood-boring beetles; hungry woodpeckers eat the larvae during the winter. Native willows host 455 species of Lepidoptera (butterflies and moths), productivity exceeded only by oak (*Quercus*) and plum/cherry (*Prunus*). "If you have appropriate habitat, by all means use them liberally, for they support several of our showiest butterflies," writes Douglas Tallamy. If you want beautiful

Luna moth (*Actias luna*)

Acadian hairstreak butterfly
(*Satyrium acadica*)

butterflies and moths, plant the species they eat as larvae. If you want mourning cloaks, viceroys, or io moths, plant "any of our many native willows—and you will have them."[58] Willows also host green comma (p. 103), white admiral, red-spotted purple (p. 18), eastern tiger swallowtail (p. 18), mourning cloak (p. 62), luna moth, cecropia moth

Viceroy butterfly (*Limenitis archippus*)

(p. 18), and sphinx moths (p. 108). Also hosted by native willows are Compton tortoiseshell, northern finned prominent, and several hairstreak species such as Acadian hairstreak and striped hairstreak (p. 18). The viceroy butterfly, which resembles the monarch butterfly (p. 124), "is always found close to stands of willow and poplar, which are its larval host plants," writes David K. Parshall.[59] Snapping turtles and wood turtles eat fallen willow leaves. When planted along water, willows provide habitat for fish and other aquatic organisms. Nesting birds, including yellow warbler (p. 89), white-throated sparrow (p. 108), black-capped chicka-

dee (p. 322), golden and ruby-crowned kinglets (p. 233), American redstart (p. 89), and ruby-throated hummingbird (p. 91), dine on and feed their babies caterpillars and the small insects attracted to the willows' sugar-rich nectar. Northern harrier, yellow warbler

Common redpoll (*Acanthis flammea*)

Pine siskin (*Carduelis pinus*)

(*Left*) Tree swallow (*Tachycineta bicolor*)

(*Right*) **Sparrow hawk aka American kestrel** (*Falco sparverius*)

(*Below*) **Red-winged blackbird** (*Agelaius phoeniceus*)

(p. 89), American goldfinch (p. 145), gray catbird (p. 79), and willow flycatcher often construct their nests in willow thickets. Birds including ruffed grouse (p. 36) and ducks such as northern pintail, mallard, and wood duck (p. 162) eat willow seeds, buds, and/or catkins as emergency spring food, as do red-breasted nuthatch (p. 322), black-capped chickadee (p. 322), dark-eyed junco (p. 322), common redpoll (p. 54), fox sparrow (p. 322), pine siskin (p. 54), tree swallow, woodpeckers (pp. 55, 212), and hawks. Birds like the gray catbird (p. 79), rusty grackle, yellow warbler (p. 89), red-winged blackbird, warbling vireo, eastern kingbird, and herons nest in willows. Downy and red-bellied woodpeckers, prothonotary warblers, and tree swallows nest in shoreline willow snags. The yellow-bellied sapsucker (p. 79) drills into black willows for sap.

See Spring Trees for more native **WILLOWS**, p. 118.

More Native Alternatives:

OZARK WITCH HAZEL, p. 75.

See Fall Shrubs for SILVERBERRY, p. 229.

See Winter Shrubs for DWARF CHINKAPIN OAK, p. 311.

See Spring Trees for AMERICAN HAZELNUT, p. 102.

See Winter Trees for ALDER SPP., p. 316.

Red-bellied woodpecker (*Melanerpes carolinus*)

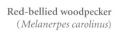

Eastern kingbird (*Tyrannus tyrannus*)

Korean rhododendron
(*Rhododendron mucronulatum*)

Nonnative:

RHODODENDRON, AZALEA. **Family:** Heath (Ericaceae). **Genus:** *Rhododendron*. **Origin:** Japan, China, Korea, Europe; *KOREAN RHODODENDRON* (*R. mucronulatum*). **Height/Spread:** 4–8 feet. **Ornamental Attributes:** Reddish-purple flowers in mid-spring. **Zones:** 5–7; *JAPANESE AZALEA* (*R. japonicum*). **Zones:** 5–8; *KOREAN AZALEA* (*R. yedoense*). **Zones:** 4–9; *YELLOW AZALEA* (*R. luteum*). **Zones:** 6–9; *HONEYSUCKLE AZALEA* (*R. ponticum*). **Zones:** 6–9; *TREE RHODODENDRON* (*R. arboreum*). **Origin:** Himalayas. **Ornamental Attributes:** Red flowers. **Cultivation:** Part to full shade. Some need sun. Moist, well-drained, acidic soil, fertilization, soil acidification, mulching, pruning, sheltered location, burlap screen, refraining from digging around shallow roots. In the United Kingdom, tree rhododendron is replacing the native woodland understory. **Genus Note:** Susceptibility to sun scorch, insect and disease pests, and leaf and flower frost damage applies to deciduous and evergreen rhododendrons/azaleas, including the species, hybrids, and cultivars. **Poison Note:** *Rhododendron* parts, including nectar, are poisonous, as is their honey, noted Aristotle and other observers from ancient days. **Ecological Threat:** Nectar produced by some species kills some species of bees.

Native Alternatives:

RHODODENDRON, AZALEA. **Family:** Heath (Ericaceae). **Genus:** *Rhododendron*. **Genus Note:** The *Rhododendron* genus includes rhododendrons and azaleas. Generally, rhododendrons are evergreen, while azaleas are deciduous. **Cultivation:** Rhododendrons perform best in partially shaded sites. Azaleas flower best with a few sunny hours. Both need the well-drained, organic-rich, acidic soil of their origins. To ensure a chosen plant suits the desired location, check with the purveyor. After planting, mulch to retain soil moisture. **Species and Range Note:** Like all plants, native azaleas generally grow best in the climates in which they

Flame azalea (*Rhododendron calendulaceum*)

naturally evolved. Species native to the northeast include rhodora. Species native to the Midwest include early azalea (roseshell azaela), rosebay rhododendron, Pinxterbloom azalea (pink azaela), and flame azalea.[60] According to Douglas Tallamy, the very showy azaleas that evolved in and around the Great Smoky Mountains in Tennessee and southwestern Virginia are an example of "cases where a plant can be moved outside its native range and still perform some or even most of its evolutionary roles within its new ecosystem. . . . This can happen because traits such as leaf chemistry, shape, and toughness can be so similar among congeners that adaptations enabling an insect to grow and reproduce on one member of the genus predispose that insect to using other members of the genus," he notes. "They can remain a functioning part of the ecosystem to which they are moved because insects adapted to local azalea species such as the Pinxterbloom azalea . . . should have no trouble using the southern species as a resource."[61] CATAWBA RHODODENDRON (*R. catawbiense*). **Height/Spread:** 6–15 feet. **Ornamental Attributes:** Evergreen shrub; clusters of large, rose or purple-lilac, funnel-shaped flowers late in spring. Hardy and easy to grow. "These evergreens [Rosebay and Catawba rhododendrons] are among the most spectacular of all flowering plants, native or exotic," write Sternberg and Wilson.[62] Natural hybrids between *R. catawbiense* and *R. maximum* occur in the wild where their ranges overlap. **Zones:** 4–7; EARLY AZALEA, ROSE-SHELL AZALEA (*R. prinophyllum;* syn. *R. roseum*). **Height/Spread:** 4–8 feet. **Ornamental Attributes:** Large, clove-scented, showy, pink flowers in April to May. Bright green leaves are woolly beneath and turn bronze in fall. Dense and rounded in full sun. **Zones:** 3–8; FLAME AZALEA (*R. calendulaceum*). **Height/Spread:** 4–8 feet. **Ornamental Attributes:** Spectacular large showy clusters of orange/apricot, yellow/gold, or brilliant scarlet long-lasting (even in sun) flowers for two weeks from mid-May to mid-June. Fall leaves are yellow-red to bronze. "This is certainly the most gay and brilliant shrub yet known," wrote eighteenth-century naturalist William Bartram.[63] **Note:** Endangered in Ohio. **Zones:** 4–8; MOUNTAIN AZALEA, PIEDMONT AZALEA (*R. canescens*). **Height/Spread:** 4–5 feet. **Ornamental Attributes:** Fragrant pink or occasionally white flowers in April. "This small shrub is perfect for gardeners with bitterly cold winters," writes Patricia A. Taylor. "Its rose purple flowers reliably burst forth every spring, almost seeming to defy snows and frosts."[64] **Note:** Endangered in Kentucky. **Zones:** 5–9; PINK AZALEA, PINXTERBLOOM AZALEA (*R. periclymenoides*, syn. *R. nudiflorum*). **Height:** 4–7 feet. **Ornamental Attributes:** Light to dark pink fragrant flowers in April to May, yellow fall foliage. **Note:** Threatened in Ohio. **Zones:** 4–8; PINK-SHELL AZALEA (*R. vaseyi*). **Height:** 10–15 feet. **Spread:** 3–10 feet. **Ornamental Attributes:** Eye-popping white to delicate pink flowers in late April, striking red fall foliage. **Note:** Very shade tolerant. Endemic to North Carolina. Endangered by development of its mountain habitats and over-collecting by horticulturalists. **Zones:** 5–7; RHODORA (*R. canadense*). **Height/Spread:** 2–4 feet. **Ornamental Attributes:** Bright purple blooms in early spring. Cold hardy species native to Canada south to Pennsylvania. **Zones:** 3–6; ROSEBAY RHODO-DENDRON, AMERICAN RHODODENDRON, GREAT LAUREL, WHITE LAUREL (*R. maximum*). **Height/Spread:** 4–15 feet. **Ornamental Attributes:** Showy, large white, pink, or purple flowers bloom June and July when few shade plants are flowering. "This old-fashioned favorite should be a staple in deep shade gardens."[65] Waxy, dark blue-green, leathery leaves on very cold-hardy plant that becomes a massive rounded shrub. **Note:** Threatened in Ohio. **Zones:** 3–7; SMOOTH AZALEA, SWEET AZALEA (*R. arborescens*). **Height/Spread:** 4–8 feet. **Ornamental Attributes:** Exceptionally hardy plant with clusters of very fragrant white or rose-tinged flowers perfuming a wide area in late spring to summer. Glossy orange-red fall leaves. Usually remains bush-like but can become tree-like with age. Readily crosses with other deciduous azaleas, so many plants labeled as true species are in fact natural hybrids. Native from New York to Alabama. **Zones:** 4–7; SWAMP AZALEA (*R. viscosum*). **Height:** 5 feet. **Spread:** 12 feet. **Ornamental Attributes:** Its very fragrant white to pink-flushed flowers bloom May to June; fall color is flame red to orange-maroon. **Cultivation:** Full sun, damp soil. A wetland shrub; does well in poorly drained areas. **Note:** Grows from Maine to Florida, and westward to Texas. **Zones:** 3–8; MOUNTAIN LAUREL. **Family:** Heath (Ericaceae). **Genus:** *Kalmia* (*K. latifolia*). **Height/Spread:** 5–15 feet. Large shrub, small tree. **Ornamental Attributes:** White or light pink flowers in May to July, contorted stems, twisted trunk. Writing about the Midwest, Weeks and Weeks note that "this is one of the most spectacular native shrubs."[66] Can use as a hedge. **Nature Note:** The native species have special value to native bees, including bumblebees (p. 61) and solitary native bees. The Cornell azalea bee is always found near azaleas; azalea pollen is its favorite food. Tiny insects and ruby-throated hum-

mingbirds (p. 91) visiting for nectar pollinate the flowers. Nesting birds, including hummingbirds, seek the tiny insects to eat and feed to their baby birds. Foliage provides wildlife and birds with shelter and nesting places. Native rhododendrons and azaleas host 51 species of butterflies and moths, including the gray comma butterfly, azalea sphinx, and the slender clearwing moth, which lays her eggs only on heath family plants. **Zones:** 5–9.

For more heath family plants see BEARBERRY, p. 156; BLUEBERRY, p. 27; CRANBERRY, p. 28; DEERBERRY, p. 138; HUCKLEBERRY, p. 28; SOURWOOD TREE, p. 186.

Orchard mason bee (*Osmia lignaria*)

Mountain laurel
(*Kalmia latifolia*)

Another Native Alternative:

RED BUCKEYE, p. 33.

Nonnative:

ROSE. **Family:** Rose (Rosaceae). **Genus:** *Rosa*. **Origin:** Europe, Asia. **Ornamental Attributes:** Pink flowers. Erect, climbing, or trailing woody species, varieties, and cultivars, often with suckers and sharp prickles, produce sometimes fragrant flowers in a variety of shapes and colors. "Distinguishing different species of roses (whether native or exotic) can be difficult," notes John Hilty.[67] **Cultivation:** Sun, well-drained soil. High maintenance: mounding, protection from freeze-thaw cycles, spraying, fertilizing, watering, pruning. Pesticides to fight black spot and other diseases also kill butterflies, bees, and other beneficial insects. Cultivars sold as disease "resistant" are resistant to some, but not all diseases. All cultivated roses (shrub

Nearly Wild rose (*Rosa* x 'Nearly Wild')

type, hybrid tea, floribunda, grandiflora, and miniature roses), including landscape roses in the popular Drift, Oso Easy, Flower Carpet, and Knock Out series, are considered susceptible to the highly contagious Rose Rosette Disease (RRD), which can destroy entire beds of roses. The increased use in residential and commercial landscapes of mass plantings of cultivated shrub roses is causing RRD to widely expand. In contrast, many native wild rose species have been reported as resistant to RRD.[68] *CABBAGE ROSE, PROVENCE ROSE* (*R. centifolia*). **Zones:** 5–8; *COMMON BRIAR, DOG ROSE* (*R. canina*). **Zones:** 6–9; *DAMASK ROSE* (*R.* × *damascena* [*gallica* × *moschata*]). **Zones:** 4–9; *FRENCH ROSE* (*R. gallica*). **Zones:** 4–8; *JAPANESE ROSE, RUGOSE ROSE* (*R. rugosa*). **Zones:** 4–8; *MEMORIAL ROSE* (*R. wichuraiana*). **Zones:** 3–8; *MULITIFLORA ROSE, JAPANESE ROSE* (*R. multiflora*). **Zones:** 3–8; *REDLEAF ROSE* (*R. ferruginea,* syn. *R. rubrifolia*). **Zones:** 2–8; *SCOTCH ROSE* (*R spinosissima*). **Zones:** 4–8; *SWEETBRIAR ROSE* (*R. rubiginosa*). **Zones:** 4–9. **Ecological Threat:** These nonnative roses are naturalized or invasive in midwestern states. Nonnative roses sometimes hybridize with native roses, raising the possibility of altering the gene pool of the native species.

Native Alternatives:

PRAIRIE ROSE, SUNSHINE ROSE, PRAIRIE WILD ROSE, ARKANSAS ROSE. **Family:** Rose (Rosaceae). **Genus:** *Rosa* (*R. arkansana* and *R. arkansana suffulta*). **Height:** 1–4 feet. **Ornamental Attributes:** Fragrant crimson to pink or sometimes bicolored yellow-centered flowers with golden stamens June to August. "An almost ever-present feature of native prai-

ries."[69] **Cultivation:** Full to part sun, dry or medium soil. Drought tolerant. Prairie icon John Weaver measured a taproot that descended more than 21 feet.[70] **Historical Note:** In 1820, Dr. Edwin James of the Long Expedition recorded "a large flowering rose ... diffusing a most grateful fragrance." **Note:** Extirpated in Ohio. **Zones:** 4–7; **CLIMBING ROSE, CLIMBING PRAIRIE ROSE, ILLINOIS ROSE, MICHIGAN ROSE, PRAIRIE ROSE** (*R. setigera*). **Height:** 6–15 feet. **Ornamental Attributes:** Fragrant deep pink flowers bloom for a month in May to July creating a wonderful multihued effect as they gradually fade to near white. Fall colors are a combination of bronze-purple, orange, and yellow. A thornless rose, with occasional prickles, it is perfect for a location where it can ramble or climb. **Cultivation:** Sun, part shade; dry to medium soil. Resists drought. A hardy rose, unlike most introduced climbing roses. **Zones:** 4–8.

Prairie rose (*Rosa arkansana*)
Also see pp. 269, 339

More Native Roses:

PASTURE ROSE, CAROLINA ROSE, LOW ROSE (*R. carolina*). **Height/Spread:** 2–3 feet. **Ornamental Attributes:** Fragrant pink flowers, red, orange, or purple fall foliage. **Zones:** 4–9; **PRICKLY ROSE** (*R. acicularis*). **Height/Spread:** 4 feet. **Ornamental Attributes:** Pink, sometimes white flowers. **Note:** Endangered in Illinois and Iowa. **Zones:** Hardy to Zone 3; **SMOOTH ROSE, EARLY WILD ROSE, MEADOW ROSE** (*R. blanda*). **Height/Spread:** 2–5 feet. **Ornamental Attributes:** Pink flowers in late May to June; thornless or nearly thornless stems. **Note:** Threatened in Ohio. **Zones:** 2–6; **SWAMP ROSE** (*R. palustris*). **Height/ Spread:** 5–8 feet. **Cultivation:** Moist to wet soil. **Zones:** 4–9; **VIRGINIA ROSE** (*R. virginiana*). **Height/Spread:** 3–6 feet. **Ornamental Attributes:** Yellow, purple, or pink flowers "open a few at a time and can scent a room if brought indoors."[71] Yellow to red fall color; reddish canes. **Zones:** 3–7; **WOODS' ROSE** (*R. woodsii* var. *woodsii*). **Height/Spread:** 5 feet. **Ornamental Attributes:** Pink flowers, spectacular yellow, red, and orange fall color. **Zones:** Hardy to Zone 4. **Native American Rose Note:** The beautiful rose hips (fruit) produced by all native roses provided emergency food in drought and winter. **Native Rose Note:** Our naturally beautiful, fragrant native roses are naturally resistant to the foliar or leaf diseases that plague most horticultural roses, including Rose Rosette Disease (RRD). The virtually maintenance-free natives need neither pesticides nor fertilizers. **Native Rose Fragrance Note:** "Every year we rediscover them, amazed that these simple flowers contain so much scent," wrote Wilson and Bell.[72] **Rose Nature Note:** Roses provide pollinators with a lot of pollen, but not much nectar. Wild roses have special value to bumble bees, their most important pollinators, but green metallic and other bees, flies, and various beetles visit the flowers. Wild rose shrubs provide native bees with nesting materials and structure. An oligolectic bee, *Synhalonia rosae,* is a specialist pollinator of *Rosa* spp. At least 38 species of birds rely on rose hips for emergency winter food, including northern cardinal, eastern bluebird, wood thrush (p. 175), brown

Bumblebee (*Bombus* spp.)

Northern cardinal (*Cardinalis cardinalis*)

Eastern bluebird (*Sialia sialis*)

Mourning cloak butterfly
(*Nymphalis antiopa*)

American robin (*Turdus migratorius*)

thrasher (p. 219), rose-breasted grosbeak (p. 200), cedar waxwing (p. 36), purple finch (p. 145), bobwhite quail (p. 36), and American robin. Birds easily swallow the small native rose hips. Chipmunks (p. 94), other small mammals, gray catbird (p. 79), and other birds use roses for cover and nesting sites. Native roses host 139 species of moths and butterflies, including mourning cloak butterflies.

More Rose Family Native Alternatives:

PURPLEFLOWERING RASPBERRY. **Genus:** *Rubus* (*R. odoratus* var. *odoratus*). **Height:** 3–6 feet. **Spread:** 6–12 feet. **Ornamental Attributes:** Ornamental raspberry; eye-catching, showy, long-blooming, fragrant, rose-purple, rose-like flowers in June to August; large maple-shaped leaves; thornless, arching stems; creates striking colonies; mid- to late summer fuzzy red raspberries; pale yellow fall color; exfoliating bark. **Cultivation:** Sun/light shade, well-drained soil. Low maintenance. Tolerates black walnut tree toxicity. **Note:** Threatened or endangered in parts of the Midwest. **Zones:** 3–8; THIMBLEBERRY (*R. parviflorus* var. *parviflorus*). **Height:** 1.5–5 feet. **Ornamental Attributes:** A flowering raspberry with clusters of large white (sometimes pink-tinged) flowers in May to June; red raspberries. **Zones:** 3–9.

Rubus Nature Note: See Summer Shrubs for BRAMBLE, p. 139.

Purpleflowering raspberry
(*Rubus odoratus* var.
odoratus)

Scotch broom
(*Cytisus scoparius*)

Nonnative:

SCOTCH BROOM, EUROPEAN BROOM, ENGLISH BROOM. **Family:** Pea (Fabaceae). **Genus:** *Cytisus* (*C. scoparius*). **Origin:** Europe, North Africa. **Height:** 3–12 feet. **Ornamental Attributes:** Yellow flowers March to June. **Cultivation:** Sun. Spreads by prodigious production of long-lived seeds. **Environmental Threat:** Invasive in parts of the Midwest and Canada. Designated a noxious weed by some states. **Zones:** 6–10.

Native Alternatives:

CHOKEBERRY SPP., p. 13; FOTHERGILLA SPP., p. 27; GOLDEN CURRANT, p. 35; NATIVE HONEYSUCKLE ALTERNATIVES, p. 38; NINEBARK, p. 44; SPICEBUSH (FORSYTHIA OF THE WILDS), p. 22.
　　See Summer Shrubs for BUTTERFLY SHRUB, p. 129; PRICKLYASH, p. 124.
　　See Fall Shrubs for LEATHERWOOD, p. 232; SILVERBERRY, p. 229.

Siberian peashrub
(*Caragana
arborescens*)

Nonnative:

SIBERIAN PEASHRUB. Family: Pea (Fabaceae). **Genus:** *Caragana* (*C. arborescens*). **Origin:** Siberia. **Height:** 10–15 feet. **Spread:** 8–12 feet. **Ornamental Attributes:** Thorny plant with yellow pea-like flowers in late May and alternate, compound leaves. "No beauty by most standards."[73] **Cultivation:** Full sun, most soils, pruning. Naturalizes by flinging seeds several feet away. **Ecological Threat:** Invasive in the Midwest. **Zones:** 2–7.

Native Alternatives:

CHOKEBERRY SPP., p. 13; FOTHERGILLA, p. 27; GOLDEN CURRANT, p. 35; NATIVE HONEYSUCKLE ALTERNATIVES, p. 38; NINEBARK, p. 44; OZARK WITCH HAZEL, p. 75; SERVICEBERRY SPP., p. 20; SPICEBUSH (FORSYTHIA OF THE WILDS), p. 22; VIBURNUM SPP., p. 69.

See Summer Shrubs for AMERICAN BLACK CURRANT, p. 138; PRICKLYASH, p. 124; ST. JOHN'S WORT, p. 145.

See Fall Shrubs for LEATHERWOOD, p. 232; SILVER BUFFALOBERRY, p. 229.

See Spring Trees for AMERICAN PLUM and other native plums, p. 78; CAROLINA SILVERBELL, p. 80; CHOKECHERRY, p. 83; SASSAFRAS (SHRUB FORM), p. 99; SERVICEBERRY SPP., p. 77.

Smoketree
(*Cotinus coggygria*)

Nonnative:

SMOKETREE, EUROPEAN SMOKETREE. **Family:** Sumac (Anacardiaceae). **Genus:** *Cotinus* (*C. coggygria*). **Origin:** Europe, China. **Height/Spread:** 10–15 feet. **Ornamental Attributes:** Yellow flowers, pedicels with pink-purplish hairs give smoke-like appearance; highly unreliable fall color. **Cultivation:** Full sun, well-drained soil. Pruning prevents flowering. "Its cultivars are very common in the landscape trade. Some of them maintain a raucous purple leaf color throughout the growing season."[74] The purple-leafed cultivars are susceptible to mildew.[75] Dioecious: male plant needed for females to produce fruit. **Ecological Threat:** Naturalized in parts of the Midwest. **Zones:** 5–8.

Native Alternatives:

AMERICAN SMOKETREE, SMOKETREE, SMOKE BUSH. **Family:** Sumac (Anacardiaceae). **Genus:** *Cotinus* (*C. obovatus*). **Height/Spread:** 10–30 feet. Large shrub or small tree. **Ornamental Attributes:** 6–10-inch clusters of red or purple flowers with pink-purplish hairs form ethereal clouds of pink and purple in spring, providing a smoke-like appearance. Silky pink spring leaves turn blue-green then flaming orange, red, yellow, or reddish purple in fall.

American smoketree (*Cotinus obovatus*)

Gnarled limbs and dark flaking bark provide winter interest. "This small tree has so much to offer us, it is a mystery to me why it is virtually unknown in gardens," writes William Cullina.[76] "Enough cannot be said about the fall color—it must be seen to be believed," write Gilman and Watson.[77] **Cultivation:** Full sun best. Wide range of soils; prefers well-drained, alkaline, rocky, and somewhat infertile loams; does well in somewhat acidic soil. Tolerates long droughts, urban conditions. Disease resistant. Rich soil and too much water create a weak plant. "Basically this tree can be planted and forgotten. Once established, it thrives on neglect."[78] Needs a male to enable females to produce flowers and fruits. Despite its rarity, the American smoketree is tough and easy to grow, writes Billy Bruce Winkles.[79] **Nature Note:** Visited by bees and butterflies, but few other insects; usually avoided by deer. Finches eat the female tree's small seeds. Though native to parts of the southern Midwest, it is designated a "tree for 2050" by the Chicago Botanic Garden. **Zones:** 4–8.

More Native Alternatives:

See Spring Trees for CAROLINA SILVERBELL, p. 80; CHOKECHERRY, p. 83.

Bridalwreath
spirea (*Spiraea
prunifolia*)

Nonnative:

SPIREA, BRIDALWREATH SPIREA. **Family:** Rose (Rosaceae). **Genus:** *Spiraea* (*S. prunifolia*). **Origin:** Japan, China, Korea. **Height:** 4–9 feet. **Spread:** 6–8 feet. **Ornamental Attributes:** White flowers in spring. **Cultivation:** Sun. Well-drained, preferably acid soil. **Zones:** 4–8; *SPIRAEA VANHOUTTEI, VAN HOUTTE SPIREA* (*Spiraea* × *vanhouttei*). **Origin:** China. **Height:** 10 feet. **Spread:** 20 feet. **Ornamental Attributes:** White spring flowers. **Ecological Threat:** Naturalized in much of the Midwest. **Zones:** 3–9.

See Summer Shrubs for *BUMALD SPIREA,* p. 126; *JAPANESE SPIREA,* p. 126.

Native Alternatives:

CHOKEBERRY SPP., p. 13; NINEBARK, p. 44; SCENTLESS MOCK ORANGE, p. 46; SERVICEBERRY SPP., p. 20; WAFER ASH, p. 45.

See Spring Trees for AMERICAN PLUM and other native plums, p. 78; AMERICAN SNOWBELL, p. 116; FRINGE TREE, p. 105.

European cranberry bush
(*Viburnum opulus*)

Nonnative:

VIBURNUM. Family: Elderberry (Adoxaceae). **Genus:** *Viburnum. EUROPEAN CRAN-BERRY BUSH, EUROPEAN HIGHBUSH CRANBERRY, COMMON SNOWBALL VIBURNUM, CRANBERRY VIBURNUM, GUELDER ROSE* (*V. opulus; V. opulus* subsp. *opulus,* syn. *V. opulus* var. *opulus*). **Origin:** Eurasia. **Height/Spread:** 8–15 feet. **Ornamental Attributes:** Large flat-topped clusters of white flowers in May. Its red fruit remind some people of cranberries; unreliable reddish-purple fall color. **Identification Note:** Viburnums are difficult to distinguish from each other. The glands of the leaf petioles of the European's are cup-shaped while the glands of the American's [see native alternatives] are columnar in shape and the fruit is "considerably more palatable."[80] **Cultivation:** Full sun best; moist to medium soil; naturalizes; susceptible to disfiguring aphids. **Ecological Threat:** Invasive in midwestern states. It interbreeds with the native highbush cranberry, creating hybrids that alter the gene pool of the native species. **Cultivar Note:** The invasive European cranberry bush has many hybrids and cultivars; they are also invasive.[81] **Zones:** 3–8; *BUDDLEJALEAF VIBURNUM* (*V. buddleifolium*). **Height:** 8–10 feet. **Ecological Threat:** Naturalized in Ohio. **Zones:** 6–9; *JAPANESE SNOWBALL VIBURNUM, DOUBLEFILE VIBURNUM* (*V. plicatum*). **Origin:** China, Japan. **Height/Spread:** 13 feet. Looks like the native mapleleaf and possumhaw viburnums. **Ecological Threat:** Naturalized in midwestern states. **Zone:** 5; *KO-REAN SPICE VIBURNUM* (*V. carlesii*). **Origin:** Korea, Japan. **Height/Spread:** 4–6 feet. **Ornamental Attributes:** Fragrant semisnowball-like flowers in April to May. Unspectacular fall color. **Ecological Threat:** Naturalized in Ohio. **Zones:** 5–7; *LANTANAPHYLLUM VI-BURNUM* (*Viburnum* × *rhytidophylloides*): Has its own hybrids and cultivars. **Ecological Threat:** Invasive in Ohio. **Zones:** 5–8; *LEATHERLEAF ARROWWOOD* (*V. rhytidophyl-lum*). **Origin:** China. **Height/Spread:** 6–10 feet. **Cultivation:** Best in protected location. **Ecological Threat:** Naturalized in midwestern states. **Zones:** 5–8; *SIEBOLD'S ARROWWOOD* (*V. sieboldii*). **Ecological Threat:** Naturalized in midwestern states. **Zones:** 4–8; *WAYFARING TREE* (*V. lantana*). **Origin:** Europe, Asia. **Height/Spread:** 10–5 feet. **Ecological Threat:** Natu-ralized in midwestern states. **Zones:** 4–8.

Native Alternatives:

American cranberrybush flowers
(*Viburnum opulus* var. *americanum*)

VIBURNUM. **Family:** Elderberry (Adoxaceae). **Genus:** *Viburnum*. **Viburnum Ornamental Attributes:** "Viburnums are treasured for their long season of interest: spring flowers, summer berries and colorful fall foliage."[82] The native species have dramatic branching structures, are adaptable, easily grown, and easily pruned to create dense hedges, and are "well-known for their splendid fall color, most of which are some shade of red."[83] For reliable heavy fruiting, plant at least 2 plants of the same species near each other. **AMERICAN CRANBERRYBUSH, HIGHBUSH CRANBERRY** (*V. opulus* var. *americanum; V. trilobum*). **Height/Spread:** 8–12 feet. **Ornamental Attributes:** Large showy white sterile flowers surround tiny white fertile flowers; maple-shaped leaves turn scarlet in fall; red fruit ripens in September and persists through

American cranberrybush (*Viburnum opulus* var. *americanum*)

Also see p. 262

Arrowwood viburnum (*Viburnum dentatum* var. *dentatum*)
Also see p. 263

February. **Cultivation:** Sun, part shade; dry, medium, moist, or wet soil; disease and pest resistant. Neither spreads nor creates thickets; easily pruned to create a dense hedge. **Note:** Endangered or threatened in parts of the Midwest. **Zones:** 2–7; ARROWWOOD VIBURNUM, SOUTHERN ARROWWOOD (*V. dentatum* var. *dentatum*). **Height/Spread:** 6–10 feet. Occasionally grows 20–25 feet as a small tree. **Ornamental Attributes:** White lace cap flowers, clusters of late August- to November-ripening blue-black fruit whose easy-to-eat small size and high fat content make them a preferred migrating and songbird food; brilliant red fall color. **Cultivation:** Sun best for flowers, takes part shade, most soils. Tolerant of black walnut tree toxicity. **Note:** Endangered, threatened, or rare in parts of the Midwest. **Zones:** 2–7; BLACKHAW (*V. prunifolium*). **Height:** 12–15 feet. **Spread:** 8–12 feet. Large shrub or small tree with horizontal branching. "Blackhaw is probably the most common viburnum in the Midwest."[84] **Ornamental Attributes:** Clusters of white flowers. "Rather a constant and pretty bloomer from April until June . . . the bluish-black drupes are covered with a bloom, and are agreeably sweet and good to eat. In the autumn the foliage turns to orange and purple"[85] (see p. 265). "This is another beautiful native that has aesthetic value year-round."[86] "Exceptionally ornamental but also easy care."[87] Recommended by Christopher Starbuck as an uncommon tree for specimen planting. **Cultivation:** Full sun best for flowers; takes deep shade. Moist to

Downy Arrowwood (*Viburnum rafinesqueanum*)

dry; tolerates wet soil, takes poor soil; drought resistant and tolerant of black walnut tree toxicity. **Historical Note:** In 1739, Peter Collinson thanked John Bartram for sending him a blackhaw. In 1771, Thomas Jefferson planted a blackhaw at Monticello. **Zones:** 3–9; DOWNY ARROWWOOD (*V. rafinesqueanum*). **Height/Spread:** 4–6 feet. **Ornamental Attributes:** White flowers in May to June. Bright red to burgundy fall color. "From the reddish-tinted new leaves in the spring, to the beautiful fall color that can begin in August while the black fruits are present, this is a species worthy of recognition," write Weeks and Weeks.[88] **Cultivation:** Full sun to shade, well-drained soil, tolerates drought. **Note:** Threatened in Kentucky. **Zones:** 2–7; MAPLELEAF VIBURNUM (*V. acerifolium*). **Height:** 4–6 feet. **Spread:** 3–4 feet. **Ornamental Attributes:** Pink buds become flat white flowers in May. Spring leaves have a reddish blush. In fall, the maple leaf–shaped green leaves turn pink to dark burgundy, contrasting with the shiny black fruit. "Mapleleaf viburnum is one of our more common viburnums that is underrated as an ornamental," write Weeks and Weeks.[89] **Cultivation:** Shade or half-day sun; an understory shrub of well-drained to dry soils. Tolerates black walnut tree toxicity. **Zones:** 4–8; NANNYBERRY (*V. lentago*). **Height:** 15–20 feet. **Spread:** 10–15 feet. Understory shrub or small tree of moist woods. **Ornamental Attributes:** Dense clusters of showy white flowers in May; drooping clusters of large black fruits in fall persist into winter; orange pedicels;

Possumhaw (*Viburnum nudum* var. *nudum*)

known for its exceptional maroon fall color. **Cultivation:** Full sun to part shade, medium soil. **Zones:** 2–7; **POSSUMHAW, POSSUMHAW VIBURNUM** (*V. nudum* var. *nudum*). **Confusion Note:** Possumhaw is also the common name for **POSSUMHAW HOLLY** (*Ilex decidua*); see Fall Shrubs, p. 237. **Height/Spread:** 5–12 feet. **Ornamental Attributes:** Showy white flowers. Fruits turn multiple colors before becoming showy blue or blue-black. Smooth, lustrous, lightly leathery foliage consistently turns purple and red. **Cultivation:** Prefers more sun than shade, moderately fertile, well-drained moist soil. **Note:** Endangered in Kentucky. **Zones:** 5–9; **RUSTY BLACKHAW, SOUTH-ERN BLACKHAW, BLUE HAW** (*V. rufidulum*). **Height:** 15–25 feet. **Ornamental Attributes:** Dark, rusty-colored buds, very large white flower clusters, brilliant red fall color, dark blocky bark. "Simply gorgeous any time of the year."[90] Tolerates black walnut tree toxicity. **Zones:** 5–8; **SQUASHBERRY, MOOSEWOOD VIBURNUM, LOWBUSH CRAN-BERRY** (*V. edule*). **Height:** 2–7 feet.

Hummingbird clearwing moth (*Hemaris thysbe*)

Rose hooktip moth (*Oreta rosea*)

Ornamental Attributes: A northern shrub with showy flowers; yellow fruit turns red or orange in late fall and makes good jam. Note: Threatened or endangered in parts of the Midwest. Zones: 3–5; WITHEROD (*V. nudum* var. *cassinoides*). Height: 5–8 feet. Ornamental Attributes: Domed clusters of creamy-white flowers in June; colors of serially ripening fruits range from pink, yellow, red, and powdery blue to black. Long-lasting fall color ranges from orange to purple; exfoliating bark. Cultivation: Full sun to part shade; wet, acidic soil; also found in drier sites. Note: Endangered in parts of the Midwest. Zones: 3–9. Viburnum Nature Note: Native viburnum flowers attract pollinators such as the red-spotted purple (p. 18) and other butterflies, Peck's skipper (p. 135) and other skipper butterflies, hummingbird moths (p. 72), bees, dance flies, wasps, ants, and beetles; have special value to native bees and can be used as part of conservation biological control. Viburnums host 104 Lepidoptera species (butterflies/moths), including Baltimore checkerspot, Henry's elfin (p. 93), spring azure (p. 95), and sphinx moths, hummingbird clearwing moth (p. 72), and the rose hooktip moth, a New World viburnum specialist. Baltimore butterfly caterpillars sometimes move off their host plants (false foxglove species) to feed on viburnum leaves. Butterfly and moth caterpillars are important food for birds and their offspring. Native viburnum species fruits attract at least 35 bird species, including many warblers, flycatchers, vireos, eastern bluebird (p. 61), wood thrush (p. 175), American robin (p. 62), northern mockingbird (p. 256), gray catbird (p. 79), cedar waxwing (p. 36), northern cardinal (p. 61), blue jay (p. 79), common redpoll (p. 54), and grosbeaks (pp. 162, 200). Fruit with high fat and carbohydrate content is crucial to birds battling cold temperatures where insects are not available and to migratory birds, which need sustenance for their long flights. At the top of the bird berry menu is northern bayberry (see Fall Shrubs, p. 232), with slightly over 50 percent fat; arrowwood viburnum (*V. dentatum*) is second, with 41.3 percent fat content. (The vine Virginia creeper (*Parthenocissus quinquefolia*) has 23.6 percent fat content.)[91] Mapleleaf viburnum berries' high sugar content makes them winter persistent and thus a very important food source for a wide variety of birds in the winter.[92] Small mammals and Bell's vireo and other birds seek the shrubs for cover and nesting.

More Native Alternatives:

AMERICAN SMOKE TREE, p. 65; CHOKEBERRY SPP., p. 13; DOGWOOD SPP., p. 48; ELDERBERRY SPP., p. 29; OZARK WITCH HAZEL, p. 75; SPICEBUSH, p. 22.
     See Summer Shrubs for HYDRANGEA SPP., p. 143.
     See Spring Trees for CAROLINA SILVERBELL, p. 80; CHOKECHERRY, p. 83; SERVICEBERRY SPP., p. 77.

Nonnative:

WEIGELA, CRIMSON WEIGELA. **Family:** Honeysuckle (Caprifoliaceae). **Genus:** *Weigela* (*W. floribunda*). **Origin:** China, Korea. **Height/Spread:** 6–10 feet. **Ornamental Attributes:** Red flowers in April to June; no fall color; ***OLD-FASHIONED WEIGELA*** (*W. florida*). **Ornamental Attributes:** Pink flowers in April to June; no fall color. **Cultivation:** Full to part sun, fertile well-drained soil. **Zones:** 4–8.

Native Alternatives:

CHOKEBERRY SPP., p. 13; DOGWOOD SPP., p. 48; NINEBARK, p. 44; SCENTLESS MOCK ORANGE, p. 46; SERVICEBERRY SPP., p. 20; SWEETSHRUB, p. 19; VIBURNUM SPP., p. 69.

See Summer Shrubs for HYDRANGEA SPP., p. 143.

See Spring Trees for AMERICAN PLUM and other native plums, p. 78; CHOKECHERRY, p. 83.

Weigela (*Weigela floribunda*)

Nonnative:

WILLOW. See ***PUSSY WILLOW,*** p. 52.

Nonnative:

WINTER HAZEL, FRAGRANT WINTERHAZEL. **Family:** Witch hazel (Hamamelidaceae). **Genus:** *Corylopsis* (*C. glabrescens*). **Origin:** Japan, Korea, China. **Height/Spread:** To 15 feet. **Ornamental Attributes:** Fragrant, pale yellow flowers in early spring. Bloom time depends heavily on the weather. **Cultivation:** Light shade, rich well-drained soil; water in dry weather. **Zones:** 5–8; ***CHINESE WITCH HAZEL*** (*Hamamelis mollis*). Flowers unlikely to be fragrant. **Zones:** 5–8; ***JAPANESE WITCH HAZEL*** (*H. japonica*). **Zones:** 5–8.

Winter hazel (*Corylopsis glabrescens*)

Native Alternatives:

OZARK WITCH HAZEL, VERNAL WITCH HAZEL. **Family:** Witch hazel (Hamamelidaceae). **Genus:** *Hamamelis* (*H. vernalis*). **Height:** 6–10 feet. Shrub or small tree. **Spread:** 8–15 feet. **Ornamental Attributes:** Extremely fragrant clusters of fringe-like flowers in January to April; yellow petals, red inner calyces. Bloom time depends heavily on the weather. "True spring is still a couple of months away, yet follow the scent and find an enchanting small tree in full bloom."[93] The flowers roll up on cold days to avoid freeze damage. Woody capsules release seeds in fall. Golden-yellow fall leaves. Picturesque winter branching structure. **Cultivation:** Full sun best for flowering; takes shade. Tolerant of black walnut tree toxicity. **Nature Note:** "Even more surprising is that, despite the wintery time of year, small native bees, moths and flies venture out on these occasional warm days to forage, and thus pollinate, witch hazel flowers,"[94] writes Cindy Gilberg. Hosts 63 species of butterflies and moths. American robin (p. 62), northern cardinal (p. 61), tufted titmouse (p. 169), dark-eyed junco (p. 322), and many other birds eat the seeds. **Zones:** 4–8.

Ozark witch hazel (*Hamamelis vernalis*)

More Native Alternatives:

FOTHERGILLA SPP., p. 27; SPICEBUSH, p. 22.
See Fall Shrubs for AMERICAN WITCH HAZEL, p. 244.
See Spring Trees for AMERICAN HAZELNUT, p. 102; AMERICAN PLUM and other native plums, p. 78; CAROLINA SILVERBELL, p. 80; CHERRY SPP., p. 82.

Nonnative:

WISTERIA, CHINESE WISTERIA, JAPANESE WISTERIA. See Confusion Note, p. 43.

Native Alternative:

AMERICAN WISTERIA, p. 43

Spring Trees

Nonnative:

ALDER. See Winter Trees, p. 316.

Nonnative:

AMUR MAACKIA. See *MAACKIA,* p. 109.

Nonnative:

AMUR MAPLE. See Fall Trees, p. 251.

Nonnative:

AUTUMN OLIVE; RUSSIAN OLIVE. See Fall Shrubs, p. 229.

Nonnative:

BIRCH. See Winter Trees, p. 320.

Nonnative:

BRADFORD PEAR, CALLERY PEAR. **Family:** Rose (Rosaceae). **Genus:** *Pyrus.* **Species:** *P. calleryana.* **Cultivar:** *P. calleryana* 'Bradford'. **Origin:** China. **Height:** 30–50 feet. **Spread:** 20–35 feet. **Ornamental Attributes:** White flowers in April to May with an odor many find unpleasant. Bees and butterflies ignore the flowers. Among the last trees to turn color in fall, leaves can turn yellow or red, ending up deep maroon. Some trees remain green until it is about to snow. Birds, such as the introduced European starling disperse its tiny inedible fruits. "'Bradford' . . . is as common as mud in landscapes across the United States," observes Michael Dirr, noting it "suffers from a fatal genetic flaw that causes it to self-destruct, literally falling apart with time—the many branches will cause

Bradford pear (*Pyrus calleryana* 'Bradford')

the tree to split in half after 10 to 15 years."[95] **Cultivation:** Sun, most soils. Shallow roots erupt out of lawns, lift sidewalks and patios, penetrate pipes. Shoots, suckers, and often long sharp thorns appear on grafted and non-grafted trees. Now affected by a new rust disease introduced from Europe.[96] **Callery Pear Cultivars:** Many communities have launched programs to stop planting the short-lived, invasive Callery pear cultivars that once were considered appealing landscape trees. There are over twenty genetically differing Callery pear cultivars, including such well-known selections as 'Bradford', 'Aristocrat', 'Glen's Form', 'Autumn Blaze', 'Chanticleer', and 'Cleveland Select' that are now identified as "problem plant pests."[97] Once considered self-incompatible, unable to self-pollinate or produce fertile fruit, the cultivars now sexually reproduce, interbreed, create hybrid fruits, and reacquire characteristics such as thorniness that had been purposely bred out. "Bradford pear is worse than kudzu, and the ill-conceived progeny of Bradford pear will be cursing our environment for decades or possibly centuries yet to come," writes Durant Ashmore.[98] The Morton Arboretum designates Callery pear "Not recommended." **Ecological Threat:** Invasive in midwestern states. **Zones:** 5–9.

Native Alternatives:

SERVICEBERRY, JUNEBERRY, SHADBUSH. Family: Rose (Rosaceae). **Genus:** *Amelanchier.* **Genus Note:** There are several wild species whose differences are not very great.
Ornamental Attributes: Showy, fragrant white five-petaled flowers bloom April to May, at the same time as the invasive Bradford pear, followed by edible showy purple fruits in June to July and fall leaves that turn brilliant shades of orange, red, and yellow at the same time as the invasive burning bush leaves (p. 239) turn pink or red. Graceful shapes and silver-gray bark provide winter beauty. Easy-to-grow deciduous trees with year-round interest. In 1900, the sight of blooming serviceberries inspired Alice Lounsberry to write, "It is then that the knowing ones sigh as with relief and feel grateful that the spring is indeed on its way. The winter has passed."[99] **Cultivation:** Sun for best fruit and color; takes part shade. Tolerates wide range of soils. No real disease or insect problems. Develops a deep, spreading root system, unlike a shallow-rooted 'Bradford' pear which will come up through lawns and lift sidewalks; **ALLEGHENY SERVICEBERRY, SMOOTH SERVICEBERRY** (*A. laevis*). **Height/Spread:** 25–40 feet. **Ornamental Attributes:** Bronzed purple spring foliage, large white flowers, particularly delicious fruits, orange-red fall color. "The tree *Amelanchier* of choice for gardens," writes William Cullina.[100] **Cultivation:** Prefers moist well-drained soil; **APPLE SERVICEBERRY** (*A. × grandiflora*). A naturally occurring hybrid of *A. arborea* and *A. laevis;* **COMMON SERVICEBERRY, DOWNY SERVICEBERRY, COMMON JUNEBERRY, SHADBLOW SERVICEBERRY** (*A. arborea* var. *arborea*). Sometimes sold as

Common serviceberry flowers
(*Amelanchier arborea* var. *arborea*)
Also see pp. 20, 271

American plum
(*Prunus americana*)

Canadian Serviceberry (*A. canadensis*). **Height/Spread:** 20–30 feet. The most tree-like and tallest of the native serviceberries. **Cultivation:** Prefers moist conditions; INLAND SHAD-BLOW, PACIFIC SERVICEBERRY (*A. interior*). **Height:** 15–20 feet. **Spread:** 10–15 feet. Despite its name, this serviceberry is native to the Midwest. **Nature Note:** See SERVICE-BERRY in Spring Shrubs, p. 20. **Cultivar/Nativar Note:** "We've been very disappointed to see that [*A. canadensis* 'Glenform'] produces very few berries. And of course, berries is what we bought this plant for! What a loss for birds!" writes Janet Allen.[101] Also sold as Rainbow Pillar Serviceberry, Plant Finder writes, "While it is considered to be somewhat self-pollinating, it tends to set heavier quantities of fruit with a different variety of the same species growing nearby."[102] **Tree Grafting Note:** Nursery trees are usually grafted, trained to a single trunk, and throw up root-suckers.[103] To purchase true or straight serviceberry species, patronize native plant nurseries. **Zones for All Species:** 4–9. For more native serviceberry species, see SER-VICEBERRY in Spring Shrubs, p. 20.

   PLUM. **Family:** Rose (Rosaceae). **Genus:** *Prunus.* **Plum Ornamental Attributes:** "No matter what the species, they all provide quite a show in early spring," state Weeks, Weeks, and Parker.[104] With their interesting shapes and bark, colorful fruits, and fall colors, all native plums provide summer, fall, and winter interest. **Cultivation:** Sun and more than one plant are best for flowers and fruit; well-drained soil; AMERICAN PLUM, WILD RED PLUM, WILD YELLOW PLUM (*P. americana*). **Height/Spread:** 15–25 feet. **Ornamental Attributes:** Pure white or pale pink flowers. "Plum flowers, especially on this species, rival those of any of our popular exotic flowering trees. . . . they bloom early, at the same time as the exotic orna-mental pears (*Pyrus calleryana*), and are every bit as attractive" and "reach their peak as the redbuds begin to bloom," creating a "spectacular" combination.[105] The delicious orange-red fruit ripens midsummer to fall and has a typical plum-like bloom; the fall leaves are orange-red or orange-yellow. The short, crooked trunk, scaly black bark, and spreading, sometimes thorny branches add winter interest. Grow as a small tree, a large shrub or a thicket. **Native American Note:** "Wild plum fruit was extensively consumed by the Indians of the prairies," writes Kelly Kindscher.[106] **Cultivation:** Tolerant of black walnut tree toxicity. **Zones:** 3–8;

Gray catbird (*Dumetella carolinensis*)

Blue jay (*Cyanocitta cristata*)

Yellow-bellied sapsucker
(*Sphyrapicus varius*)

CANADIAN PLUM (*P. nigra*). **Height/Spread:** 20–30 feet. **Ornamental Attributes:** "When this tree of the plum family is in bloom or hung with its translucent, radiant fruit it seems to elicit continual praise."[107] Small thorns provide winter interest. **Note:** Endangered or presumed extirpated in parts of the Midwest. **Zones:** 3–8; CHICKASAW PLUM (*P. angustifolia* var. *angustifolia*). **Height/Spread:** 12 feet, can attain 30 feet. **Zones:** 5–9; MEXICAN PLUM, BIGTREE PLUM (*P. mexicana*). **Height/Spread:** 15–30 feet. **Ornamental Attributes:** Edible purple plums. Does not sucker or create thickets or colonies. **Note:** Presumed extirpated in part of the Midwest. **Zones:** 6–8; HORTULAN PLUM, HOG PLUM (*P. hortulana*). Another midwestern native small non-suckering plum tree. **Zones:** 5–9. **Plum Native American Note:** Cultivated native plum orchards before Europeans arrived. **Note:** Native and heirloom plant sellers sometimes carry native plums. **Plum Nature Note:** The shrubby branches "provide an impenetrable fortress for a little animal to hide from hawks and cats,"[108] and offer nesting cover for many songbirds, particularly those preferring edges or thickets, including gray catbird, American robin (p. 62), and blue jay. Woodpeckers nibble at the largish fruits. (Birds prefer small fruits, like native roses and cherries, which they swallow whole.) Red and gray fox enjoy native plums. For more nature information, see Springs Shrubs for SAND CHERRY (p. 17).

Carolina silverbell (*Halesia carolina*)

CAROLINA SILVERBELL, SNOWDROP TREE. **Family:** Storax (Styracaceae). **Genus:** *Halesia* (*H. carolina*, syn. *H. tetraptera*). **Height:** 20–40 feet. **Spread:** 20–35 feet. **Ornamental Attributes:** Large shrub/small understory tree of southern midwestern regions where its abundant, showy mid- to late spring flowers resemble clusters of snow-white or pink-flushed silver bells. "Few trees can match the beauty of the silverbells."[109] Redbud blooms about the same time and the two provide a stunning contrast. Fall brings yellow leaves and showy four-winged brown fruits that persist during winter. It has exfoliating bark; its branches are low to the ground; when pruned, it makes a good street tree. "This is yet another case of a beautiful, unappreciated native plant,"[110] writes Patricia A. Taylor. One of Christopher Starbuck's selections for uncommon trees for specimen planting. **Cultivation:** Part shade; takes sun. Well-drained, mulched soil, preferably acidic. No serious insect pests or diseases. Tolerant of black walnut tree toxicity. **Note:** Endangered or presumed extirpated in parts of the Midwest. **Nature Note:** The flowers attract bees and ruby-throated hummingbirds (p. 91) and the tree hosts 7 species of butterflies and moths. "If you plant silverbell, oaks, birches, willows or black cherry in your yard, you may attract the spectacular prometha moth."[111] Squirrels use the trees for dens and eat the seeds; birds use the trees for nesting. **Zones:** 4–8.

More Native Alternatives:

CATALPA, p. 86; CHERRY SPP., p. 82; CRAB APPLE SPP., p. 89; CUCUMBERTREE, p. 111; FLOWERING DOGWOOD, p. 94; FRINGE TREE, p. 105; GREEN HAWTHORN, WASHINGTON HAWTHORN, and other native HAWTHORN SPP., p. 106; PAWPAW, p. 113; REDBUD, p. 92; SASSAFRAS, p. 99; SNOWBELL, p. 116; YELLOW BUCKEYE, p. 98; YELLOWWOOD, p. 96.

See Summer Trees for AMERICAN HORNBEAM, p. 182; AMERICAN LINDEN, p. 190; BLACKGUM, p. 218; HOP HORNBEAM, p. 183; OHIO BUCKEYE, p. 184; RED MAPLE, p. 197; SOURWOOD, p. 186.

See Fall Trees for AMERICAN MOUNTAIN ASH, p. 255; MOUNTAIN MAPLE, p. 252.

See Spring Shrubs for ALTERNATELEAF DOGWOOD & OTHER NATIVE DOGWOODS, p. 49; AMERICAN BLADDERNUT, p. 41; AMERICAN SMOKETREE, p. 65; RED BUCKEYE, p. 33; VIBURNUM SPP. (BLACKHAW, NANNYBERRY, RUSTY BLACKHAW VIBURNUMS), p. 69.

See Summer Shrubs for FRANKLIN TREE, p. 147.

Nonnative:

CALLERY PEAR. See *BRADFORD PEAR,* p. 76.

Nonnative:

CHERRY, PLUM. **Family:** Rosaceae. **Genus:** *Prunus.* **Cherry, Plum Disease and Cultivation Note:** "Unfortunately, countless insects and diseases contribute to the decline of many of these plants. In general, *Prunus* species prefer moist, well-drained, acid to near neutral soils," writes Michael A. Dirr.[112] Sun, regular pruning, and avoiding crowding are also needed. Early blooming creates susceptibility to frost damage. The period of full bloom for some introduced cherry blossoms is very limited, "usually less than a week."[113] Due to weather, blooming for introduced ornamental cherries is often limited to two or three days. Few have fall color. Despite their beauty, nonnative cherries and plums and their numerous cultivars have relatively short life spans, compared to other ornamental species. "On average, ornamental cherry trees live between 15 and 20 years."[114] **Cultivar Note:** Suckers from damaged roots of purple-leaved grafted cultivars will be green, not purple; *AMUR CHERRY, AMUR CHOKECHERRY, MANCHURIAN CHOKECHERRY* (*Padus maackii,* syn. *Prunus maackii*). **Origin:** Korea, Manchuria. **Height:** 20–30 feet. **Ornamental Attributes:** Exfoliating bark, fragrant white flowers in April to May, small black cherries. Maintaining tree form requires pruning. **Zone:** 2; *MYROBALAN PLUM, CHERRY PLUM* (*P. cerasifera, P. cerasifera* var. *pissardii*). **Origin:** Eurasia. **Height/Spread:** 15–30 feet. **Ornamental Attributes:** White or pinkish flowers in April. Purple foliage. The leaves will turn green if grown in the shade. Has a bad habit of cross-branching. May spread or naturalize by self-seeding. Sometimes used as a rootstock. Purple-leaf plums, including the many cultivars, are fast growing but disease susceptible and short lived, declining at 10–15 years. **Cultivar Note:** Suckers from

Japanese flowering cherry (*Prunus serrulata*)

green-leaved rootstock are green-leaved, not purple. **Ecological Threat:** Naturalized in mid-western states. **Zones:** 4–8; *EUROPEAN BIRD CHERRY* (*Padus avium* var. *avium*, syn. *Prunus padus*). **Origin:** Europe, Asia. **Height/Spread:** 20–40 feet. **Ornamental Attributes:** White flowers. **Ecological Threat:** Naturalized in midwestern states. **Zones:** 3–6; *JAPANESE FLOWERING CHERRY, ORIENTAL CHERRY* (*P. serrulata*). **Origin:** China, Japan, Korea. **Height/Spread:** 50–75 feet. **Ornamental Attributes:** White to pink flowers. Its cultivars often suffer from viruses, live 10–15 years, and are not hardy in Zone 5. **Zones:** 5–8; *MAHALEB CHERRY* (*Cerasus mahaleb*, syn. *Prunus mahaleb*). **Origin:** Europe, Asia. **Ornamental Attributes:** White flowers, black fruits. Invasive in the Chicago area. **Zones:** 5–8; *NANKING CHERRY.* See p. 17; *SARGENT CHERRY* (*Cerasus sachalinensis*, syn. *Prunus sargentii*). **Origin:** Japan, Korea, Russia. **Height/Spread:** 25–75 feet. **Ornamental Attributes:** Pink flowers. **Life Span:** Sometimes up to 20 years. **Zones:** 4–8; *SWEET CHERRY, MAZARD CHERRY* (*Cerasus avium*, syn. *Prunus avium*). **Origin:** Europe, Northern Africa. **Height/Spread:** 15–30 feet. **Ornamental Attributes:** White flowers. **Life Span:** Up to 25 years. **Zones:** 3–8; *WINTER-FLOWERING CHERRY, FLOWERING CHERRY* (*P. subhirtella*). **Origin:** Japan, Korea, Russia. **Height/Spread:** 20–45 feet. **Ornamental Attributes:** Nonfragrant pale pink to white flowers. **Ecological Threat:** Naturalized in Ohio. **Zones:** 4–7; **Cultivar:** *WEEPING FLOWERING CHERRY* (*P. subhirtella* 'Pendula'). **Height/Spread:** 20–30 feet. **Zones:** 5–8.

More Nonnatives:

PEACH (*Amygdalus persica*, syn. *Prunus persica* var. *persica*). **Ecological Threat:** Naturalized in midwestern states. **Zones:** 5–8.

See Spring Shrubs for *CHERRY, PLUM, ALMOND,* p. 16.

Native Alternatives:

CHERRY. **Family:** Rose (Rosaceae). **Genus:** *Prunus.* "Unfortunately, most nurseries sell only exotic varieties of *Prunus,* though none are more hardy or more beautiful than our natives,"[115] write Weeks, Weeks, and Parker. **Cultivation:** Sun. Prefer moist, well-drained acid to near neutral soils but tolerate a variety of soils. The twigs of all three of the cherry species in our area—black cherry, chokecherry, and pin cherry—have a diagnostic, almond smell when crushed and a bitter taste when chewed, so, if you touch a twig, you can easily determine whether or not it is from a cherry. Chokecherry is by far the shrubbiest of the cherries, but can

become a small tree; pin cherry is a small tree; and black cherry grows to be a large one.[116] BLACK CHERRY, WILD BLACK CHERRY, RUM CHERRY (*P. serotina* var. *serotina*). **Height/Spread:** 50–80 feet. **Ornamental Attributes:** Fragrant, showy, white flowers in long, slender, pendulous clusters or racemes appear with the foliage in late April to May. Drooping clusters of small red cherries ripen to purple-black in late summer. Yellow fall color. Crushed foliage and bark have cherry-like odor. "To the round black fruit there is a pleasant vinous flavour and often housewives prepare with it a good although rather insidious drink," wrote Alice Lounsberry

Black cherry leaves and flowers
(*Prunus serotina* var. *serotina*)

Black cherry (*Prunus serotina* var. *serotina*)

in 1901.[117] **Cultivation:** Easy to grow. Takes part sun; dry to medium-moist soil; propagates by seeds, not by suckers. Tolerant of black walnut tree toxicity. **Life Span:** 100–250 years. **Black Cherry Nature Note:** Like all native cherries, black cherry provides wildlife with extraordinary benefits. "If you want to enjoy tiger swallowtails (*Papilio glaucus*) [p. 18], plant tulip trees, sweetbay magnolia, or black cherry trees," writes Douglas Tallamy. "Black cherries will also provide food for red-spotted purples" and "over 400 other moths and butterfly species."[118] The tree is the favorite host plant for giant silk moths such as the Columbia silkmoth. Wild black cherry's "value to wildlife is exceptional," notes John Hilty.[119] **Zones:** 3–9; **CHOKE-CHERRY, AMERICAN WILD RED CHERRY, COMMON CHOKECHERRY. Family:** Rose (Rosaceae). **Genus:** *Prunus* (*P. virginiana* var. *virginiana*). **Confusion Note:** The names chokecherry and chokeberry (p. 13) are easily confused. **Height/Spread:** 8–10 feet. Sometimes grows taller. **Ornamental Attributes:** A dazzling display of showy, fragrant white flowers in late April to early May. Spectacular red-orange early fall color. "However lovely the flowers, chokecherry is even more beautiful in the autumn, when its shining fruits turn from green to red and then proceed to develop their final, rich purple color," writes Virginia Barlow.[120] **Life Span:** A woody plant that does well in almost every location, it reportedly lives 40 years. **Native American Note:** "Chokecherries were an ancient food of the Prairie Indians," writes Kelly Kindscher.[121] **Nature Note:** Chokecherries mature in late August with reliable and prodigious pendant clusters of sugary fruits that are irresistible to birds, especially those preparing for migration and seeking fruits rich in carbohydrates. The trees also provide important cover habitat. **Zones:** 2–8; **PIN CHERRY, BIRD CHERRY, RED CHERRY** (*P. pensylvanica* var. *pensylvanica*) **Height/Spread:** 15–50 feet. **Ornamental Attributes:** A non-suckering small tree with umbels (flower stalks arising from a common point) of showy, fragrant white flowers,

Pin cherry
(*Prunus pensylvanica*
var. *pensylvanica*)

bright red horizontal branches, aromatic reddish- to yellow-orange bark, clusters of bright red edible fruit, lustrous green, sometimes blue-tinted leaves that turn bright red or orange in fall. "This is an old-fashioned garden tree, and one of the choicest, producing in May a great abundance of its tiny white flowers," noted an 1893 book on hardy ornamental flowering shrubs and trees.[122] **Cultivation:** Needs full sun. Sometimes called fire cherry because it helps reforest areas after forest fires. Tolerant of black walnut tree toxicity and air pollution. **Note:** Rare in parts of the Midwest. **Zones:** 3–7. **Cherry Nature Note:** See Spring Shrubs for SAND CHERRY (p. 17).

More Native Alternatives:

AMERICAN PLUM and other native plums, p. 78; CAROLINA SILVERBELL, p. 80; CRAB APPLE SPP., p. 89; CUCUMBERTREE, p. 111; FLOWERING DOGWOOD, p. 94; FRINGE TREE, p. 105; PAWPAW, p. 113; REDBUD, p. 92; SERVICEBERRY SPP., p. 77; SNOWBELL, p. 116; YELLOWWOOD, p. 96.
See Winter Trees for BIRCH SPP., p. 320.

See Spring Shrubs for ALTERNATELEAF DOGWOOD & OTHER NATIVE DOG-WOODS, p. 48; AMERICAN BLADDERNUT, p. 41; AMERICAN SMOKETREE, p. 65; RED BUCKEYE, p. 33; VIBURNUM SPP. (BLACKHAW, NANNYBERRY, RUSTY BLACKHAW VIBURNUMS), p. 69; WAFER ASH, p. 45.

For EXFOLIATING BARK, see YELLOW BUCKEYE, p. 98.

Nonnative:

CHINESE CATALPA, JAPANESE CATALPA, ORIENTAL CATALPA, YELLOW CA-TALPA. **Family:** Trumpet creeper (Bignoniaceae). **Genus:** *Catalpa* (*C. ovata*). **Origin:** China. **Height/Spread:** To 30 feet. **Ornamental Attributes:** Looks like native catalpas; its May–June flowers are attractive, but not as showy as *C. bignonioides* (southern catalpa) and *C. speciosa* (northern catalpa). Heart-shaped leaves tend to depreciate as the growing season progresses. Long slender brown fall seedpods. **Cultivation:** Full to part sun, medium to wet soil; naturalizes. **Ecological Threat:** Naturalized in midwestern states. Chinese catalpa trees crossbreed with native catalpa trees and degrade the the native catalpas. **Zones:** 4–8.

Chinese catalpa
(*Catalpa ovata*)

Northern catalpa tree flowers (*Catalpa speciosa*)

Native Alternatives:

CATALPA, NORTHERN CATALPA, CIGAR TREE, INDIAN BEAN. **Family:** Trumpet creeper (Bignoniaceae). **Genus:** *Catalpa* (*C. speciosa*). **Height:** 40–70 feet. **Spread:** 20–40 feet. **Ornamental Attributes:** Clusters of orchid-like white flowers with ruffled edges in May to July "appear in upright panicles like those of a horse chestnut—white, speckled with purple and yellow."[123] In spring to early summer, the tree is a huge intensely fragrant bouquet. "Many of our choicest exotics are not more exquisite."[124] In fall, the bright green heart-shaped leaves turn yellow. As the tree ages, its branching structure becomes more dramatic. The heavy branches along with its persistent cigar-like seedpods create a dramatic winter silhouette. Writing in 1900, before attitudes about smoking had changed, Alice Lounsberry noted, "When they have become dried and brown, little country boys are credited with finding them good to smoke . . . however . . . they burn the throat most horribly."[125] **Note:** In the summer, catalpas of any size can be mistaken for the Asian invader, the empress tree, as both have big heart-shaped leaves. **Cultivation:** Easy to grow. Full to part sun; prefers moist deep soil; tolerates wet, dry, and alkaline soils and hot, dry environments, drought, and air pollution. **Life Span:** 100 years. **Zones:** 4–8; SOUTHERN CATALPA (*C. bignonioides*). **Height/Spread:** 25–40 feet. **Ornamental Attributes:** Blooms later with slightly smaller flowers. **Cultivation:** Not as hardy as northern catalpa. **Zones:** 5–9. **Catalpa Nature Note:** Catalpas host 8 species of butterflies and moths, including the catalpa sphinx moth. Pollinators—including

Northern catalpa tree(*Catalpa speciosa*)
Also see pp. 280, 345

ruby-throated hummingbirds (p. 91)—love the flowers, which are cross-pollinated by bumblebees (p. 61), the large carpenter bee, and various nocturnal moths. Honeybees (p. 19), skippers, ants, and flies visit for nectar. The leaves' extrafloral nectaries secrete nectar in greater amounts than normal when the leaves are damaged, attracting predacious insects like ants, ladybird beetles, and parasitoid wasps that protect the tree from leaf-eating insects. Older trees develop cavities used as dens by tree squirrels, screech owls, and other cavity-nesting birds. American robins (p. 62) and other birds build nests in the branches. **Interesting Theory:** "How come the northern catalpa is built to withstand the −30°F temperatures in Montreal, if its original range was only in the southern Mississippi Valley?" asks Sue Sweeney. Maybe it was here before the Ice Age and is reclaiming its original territory, she speculates.[126]

More Native Alternatives:

More trees with heart-shaped leaves: REDBUD, p. 92.

See Summer Trees for AMERICAN LINDEN, p. 190; COTTONWOOD, p. 166. Also see AMERICAN BEECH, p. 168; TULIP TREE, p. 179.

Sargent crab apple (*Malus sargentii*)

Nonnative:

CRAB APPLE. Family: Rose (Rosaceae). Genus: *Malus.* Genus Note: These exotics are ubiquitous for their flowers in April or May. Most nonnative crab apples do not have outstanding fall color and many are scentless. In the Midwest, crab apple species and their cultivars often do poorly due to diseases like apple scab, frogeye leaf spot, fire blight, cedar-apple rust, powdery mildew, cankers, and root rot. They can also have structural problems, such as basal suckering from rootstock and water sprouts on branches. They can be intolerant of poor drainage, and susceptible to pests like Japanese beetles. Some cultivars create litter due to either large or nonpersistent fruit. Some are alternate bearing (flower/fruit heavily every other year).[127] "The bigger, badder crabs look fried in July. By August each year, I want to wield an axe and relieve these trees of their ugly, half-dead lives," writes Penelope O'Sullivan, who urges, "Buyers beware! These seemingly perfect ornamental trees are related to finicky roses and are susceptible to some of their pests and diseases plus some problems of their own."[128] Cultivation: Sun, medium, well-drained soil; *EUROPEAN CRAB APPLE* (*M. sylvestris*). Origin: Europe. Height: 40 feet. Ornamental Attributes: White flowers, red fruits. Zones: 4–8; *JAPANESE FLOWERING CRAB APPLE* (*M. floribunda*). Origin: Japan. Height/Spread: 15–25 feet. Ornamental Attributes: Pink flowers turn white. Ecological Threat: Naturalized in midwestern states; invasive in Illinois. Zones: 4–8; *O-ZUMI CRAB APPLE* (*M. × zumi*). Pink buds, white flowers, red fruits. Ecological Threat: Naturalized in Ohio and Virginia. Zones: 4–8; *PARADISE APPLE* (*M. pumila* Mill., syn. *M. communis, M. domestica, M. sylvestris, Pyrus malus*). Origin: Europe. Height/Spread: 10–30 feet. Ornamental Attributes: Pink, white flowers. Ecological Threat: Naturalized across much of the United States. Zones: 4–8; *PLUM-LEAVED CRAB APPLE* (*M. prunifolia*). Origin: Japan; *SIBERIAN CRAB APPLE, MANCHURIAN CRAB APPLE* (*M. baccata*). Origin: Asia. Height/Spread: 15–25 feet. Ornamental Attributes: White flowers. Ecological Threat: Naturalized in midwestern states; invasive in Illinois. Zones: 2–8; *TORINGO CRAB APPLE* (*M. sieboldii*, syn. *M. toringo*). Origin: Japan. Ecological Threat: Naturalized in midwestern states. Zones: 4–8.

Native Alternatives:

CRAB APPLE. Family: Rose (Rosaceae). Genus: *Malus.* Genus Note: "American crabapples differ from European and Asiatic species in that flowers do not open until mid-May when the leaves are developed. . . . If fruit sets, it is green, bitter, yet pleasantly aromatic."[129] "I have yet to know if anything can surpass [the American crab apple] in wealth of bloom," wrote Eloise Butler, born in 1851. Nesting birds were part of Butler's spring plan. On June 1, 1902, she wrote in her diary, "Raining hard, but I went into the woods. I wanted to see how the nests were coming on. The redstart's nest was fully completed. . . . The yellow warbler's nest had four eggs in it."[130] AMERICAN CRAB APPLE, SWEET CRAB APPLE, SWEET-SCENTED

American redstart (*Setophaga ruticilla*)

Yellow warbler (*Setophaga petechia*)

Prairie crab apple (*Malus ioensis* var. *ioensis*)

CRAB APPLE, WILD CRAB APPLE (*M. coronaria*). **Height:** 20–30 feet. **Spread:** 10–30 feet. **Ornamental Attributes:** Extravagant spring floral displays in May to June as breathtaking clusters of very fragrant rosy pink buds unfurl to reveal profusions of delicate white flowers. Bright red fall foliage. Fragrant green fruits that become tinged with red and yellow "clings to the branches . . . long after the leaves have fallen," wrote Harriet L. Keeler in 1900.[131] "When seen as a small tree in cultivation hardly one more beautiful can be imagined," wrote Alice Lounsberry in 1900.[132] **Cultivation:** Full to part sun; adapts to most soils; thrives on neglect; PRAIRIE CRAB APPLE, WILD CRAB APPLE, IOWA CRAB APPLE, WILD SWEET CRAB APPLE, AMERICAN CRABAPPLE. (*M. ioensis* var. *ioensis*). **Height:** 20–35 feet. **Spread:** 10–30 feet. **Ornamental Attributes:** Pink to white buds. Lavish display of clusters of large rose-colored single or double fragrant flowers every May to June that fade to white, sometimes tinged with rose. Extraordinarily shiny chartreuse-colored fruits have firm, white flesh. In fall, leaves turn deep crimson color. Flaking bark that is silvery-gray, creating winter interest. **Cultivation:** Full to part sun, moist to moderately dry soil, uncrowded environment. Resistant to cedar apple rust. For a breathtaking spring display, permit the trees to form thickets. If a single stem is desired, pull rooted suckers and replant or give away. "The value of Prairie Crab Apple to various kinds of wildlife is quite high," writes John Hilty.[133] Well represented in the nursery trade; SOUTHERN CRAB APPLE, NARROW-LEAVED CRAB APPLE (*M. angustifolia* var. *angustifolia*). **Height:** 25–30 feet. **Ornamental Attributes:** Its profuse pink flowers have an incomparably fragrant scent. Emerging leaves are red. When "its exquisite rosy and fragrant blossoms come into full bloom" it is "still so early in the season

Io moth (*Automeris io*)

Andrenid bees (Andrenidae)

Ruby-throated hummingbird
(*Archilochus colubris*)

that the purplish grey colouring of its twigs forms for them a misty background and only such other wide-awake shrubs as the thorn [hawthorn], the shad-bush [serviceberry] and the spice-bush are laden with flowers."[134] Colorful scaly bark adds winter interest. **Cultivation:** Part sun, moist well-drained soil. **Note:** Threatened or endangered in parts of the Midwest, including Illinois; Special Concern in Kentucky. **Nature Note:** Crab apple nectar and pollen have special value for, and attract pollinators like, honeybees (p. 19), bumblebees (p. 61), digger bees and other long-tongued bees, small short-tongued bees, and the black, red, or metallic blue ground-nesting miner bees (andrenids) that emerge in early spring. The fragrant flowers attract adult butterflies and ruby-throated hummingbirds. Native crab apples serve as host plants for 308 species of moths and butterflies, including the white-lined sphinx moth (p. 108), Io moth, cecropia moth (p. 18), viceroy (p. 54), red-spotted purple (p. 18), tiger swallowtail butterfly (p. 18), and gray and striped hairstreaks (p. 18). Beetles and weevils with "apple" in their names are, not surprisingly, attracted to all crab apples, and provide birds with insect food. Mammals like foxes, meadow voles, and squirrels eat crab apple fruits, as do more than 29 species of birds, including American robin (p. 62), red-bellied woodpecker (p. 55), yellow-bellied sapsucker (p. 79), blue jay (p. 79), gray catbird (p. 79), northern cardinal (p. 61), Baltimore oriole (p. 167), eastern bluebird (p. 61), tufted titmouse (p. 169), purple finch (p. 145), northern mockingbird (p. 256), northern flicker (p. 99), and white-throated sparrow (p. 108). Songbirds peck at the larger fruits, but don't carry them around. The dense and sometimes thorny branches provide nesting habitat and cover for the birds like yellow-breasted chat, song sparrow (p. 307), and orchard oriole. **Nativar/Cultivar Note:** Fruitless nativars, such as *Malas ioensis* 'Prairie Rose' deprive birds and animals of food and people of ornamental beauty. **Zones for All Native Crab Apples:** 4–8.

Eastern redbud (*Cercis canadensis* var. *canadensis*)
Also see pp. 297, 355

Another Native Alternative:

REDBUD, EASTERN REDBUD. **Family:** Pea (Fabaceae). **Genus:** *Cercis* (*C. canadensis* var. *canadensis*). **Height/Spread:** 20–30 feet. **Ornamental Attributes:** Shockingly beautiful long-lasting magenta flowers in April and May, followed by pretty heart-shaped leaves tinted purple in spring and bright yellow in fall. Arching limbs and clinging seedpods add winter interest. "This little tree . . . is handsome at all seasons of the year, but it is truly a sight in the early days of spring when it is radiant with its exquisitely bright and cheery blossoms," wrote Alice Lounsberry.[135] "Its arching branches are covered with rose-pink blossoms in early spring, as colorful as those of any flowering Oriental tree," write Sternberg and Wilson.[136] "No garden should be without at least a few," writes William Cullina.[137] For a continuous spring parade of showy native blooming trees, supplement redbud with earlier white-flowering serviceberries (p. 77) and wild plums (p. 78), overlapping flowering dogwood (p. 94) and Carolina silverbell (p. 80), and the slightly later pink-flowering prairie crab apple (p. 90). **Cultivation:** Full to part sun, adapts to a variety of well-drained soils. Tolerant of black walnut toxicity. **Nature Note:** Has special value to native bees, its primary pollinators, which visit for nectar and pollen. Redbud, Kentucky coffee tree, honeylocust, black locust, and wisteria are legumes that fix nitrogen, naturally enriching the soil. Redbud hosts 19 species of butterflies and moths, including the grape redbud leaf-folder moth and Henry's elfin. Where redbud is the caterpillar host, its flowers are the main nectar supply for the adult butterflies. The seeds are eaten by northern cardinal (p. 61), rose-breasted grosbeak (p. 200), and bobwhite quail (p. 36). **Life Span:** 50 years. **Cultivar/ Nativar Note:** Variegated and purple-leaved cultivars have changed chemistry that reduces beneficial insect populations that birds depend on to feed their offspring.[138] **Zones:** 4–8.

More Native Alternatives:

CAROLINA SILVERBELL, p. 80; CHERRY SPP., p. 17; FLOWERING DOGWOOD, p. 94; HAWTHORN SPP., p. 106; PLUM SPP., p. 78; SERVICEBERRY SPP., p. 77; SNOW-BELL, p. 116.

See Spring Shrubs for ALTERNATE-LEAF DOGWOOD and other native dogwoods, p. 49; AMERICAN SMOKETREE, p. 65; RED BUCKEYE, p. 33; VIBURNUM SPP. (BLACKHAW, NANNYBERRY, RUSTY BLACKHAW VIBURNUMS), p. 69; WAFER ASH, p. 45.

Henry's elfin butterfly (*Callophrys henrici*)

Nonnative:

DOGWOOD, KOUSA DOGWOOD, JAPANESE DOGWOOD. **Family:** Dogwood (Cornaceae). **Genus:** *Cornus* (*C. kousa*). **Origin:** Japan, Korea, China. **Height/Spread:** 15–30 feet. **Ornamental Attributes:** White flowers in May to June, may have reddish-yellow fall foliage; interesting bark. Unlike our native dogwoods, like flowering dogwood, Kousa dogwood's red summer fruits are too large for midwestern birds to swallow whole. **Cultivation:** Full sun, well-drained soil; drought intolerant; needs mulching; naturalizes. **Ecological Threat:** "We have planted Kousa dogwood, a species from China that supports no insect herbivores, instead of our native flowering dogwood (*Cornus florida*) that supports 117 species of moths and butterflies alone";[139] *ASIATIC DOG-WOOD, JAPANESE CORNEL DOGWOOD* (*C. officinalis*). **Origin:** Japan, Korea, China. **Height/Spread:** 15–25 feet. **Ornamental Attributes:** Yellow flowers in March to April. **Zones:** 5–8.

Dogwood (*Cornus kousa*)

Flowering dogwood tree
(*Cornus florida*)

Native Alternative:

FLOWERING DOGWOOD. Family: Dogwood (Cornaceae). **Genus:** *Cornus* (*C. florida*). **Height/ Spread:** 15–25 feet. **Ornamental Attributes:** This tree has all-season interest. Spring brings beautiful, long-lasting flowers in April to May with large showy white, sometimes pink, bracts surrounding a button of tiny bright green fertile flowers. Bright red, long-lasting fall fruits highlight the fall foliage and persist into winter. Horizontally layered, pagoda-like, violet-tinted branches and interesting bark texture create winter interest. "Matchless beauty when in bloom," writes William Cullina. "The tree that elevates the clan to the horticultural aristocracy, *C. florida*, comes as close to perfection as nature is willing to tread."[140] "The long blooming period overlaps with redbud. The two species are often found together and provide a spring flowering spectacle that, once seen, is never forgotten," write Sternberg and Wilson, adding, "If the flowers were not so impressive, this tree would be more famous for its radiant red fall color."[141] This showy native tree received an admiring review back in 1690 in Ray's *Historia Plantarum*. **Cultivation:** Light shade; moist well-drained soil, benefits from mulching. Its own calcium-rich leaf litter makes excellent mulch. Tolerant of black walnut tree toxicity. The native species is more winter hardy than the nonnative hybrids and cultivars. **Nature Note:** From eastern bluebird (p. 61) to wild turkey (p. 244), its small, calcium- and fat-rich, shiny red fruits are sought by 93 bird species, including migrating warblers though fall and early winter, as well as by squirrels, chipmunks, and foxes. Wildlife uses the tree for shelter and habitat. Flowering dogwood hosts 117 species of butterflies and moths, including "the diminutive spring azure, . . . one of the first butterflies to become active as the days warm

Eastern chipmunk
(*Tamias striatus*)

Flowering dogwood flowers (*Cornus florida*)

Spring azure butterfly (*Celastrina ladon*)

in the spring. [The spring azure] may become a resident of your yard if you plant flowering dogwood . . . or any of our native *Viburnum* species. They won't appear if you insist on kousa dogwood . . . from Asia. Azures will have nothing to do with that alien," writes Douglas Tallamy.[142] Flowering dogwood is the state tree of Missouri. **Life Span:** 125 years. **Zones:** 5–9.

More Native Alternatives:

CAROLINA SILVERBELL, p. 80; CHERRY SPP., p. 17; CRAB APPLE SPP., p. 89; RED-BUD, p. 92; SASSAFRAS, p. 99; SERVICE-BERRY SPP., p. 77; YELLOWWOOD, p. 96.

See Spring Shrubs for ALTERNATELEAF (PAGODA) DOGWOOD, p. 49; AMERICAN BLADDERNUT, p. 41; AMERICAN SMOKETREE, p. 65; DOGWOOD, p. 48, for dogwood species that can be grown as trees; RED BUCKEYE, p. 33; WAFER ASH, p. 45.

Empress tree
(*Paulownia tomentosa*)

Nonnative:

EMPRESS TREE, PRINCESSTREE, ROYAL PAULOWNIA. **Family:** Paulownia (Paulowniaceae). **Genus:** *Paulownia* (*P. tomentosa*). **Origin:** China. **Height/Spread:** 30–40 feet. **Ornamental Attributes:** Lavender flowers in April become dry brown capsules, each holding several thousand tiny winged seeds. A single tree is capable of producing 20 million seeds. Heart-shaped green leaves. Lacks winter interest. **Cultivation:** Sun, many habitats, naturalizes from seed and root sprouts. **Ecological Threat:** Widely invasive in the Midwest. The Morton Arboretum lists this extremely aggressive tree as "Not recommended" for planting. **Zones:** 5–8.

Native Alternatives:

YELLOWWOOD, KENTUCKY YELLOWWOOD. **Family:** Pea (Fabaceae). **Genus:** *Cladrastis* (*C. kentukea*, syn. *C. lutea*). **Height:** 30–50 feet. **Spread:** 40–55 feet. **Ornamental Attributes:** "To say that this tree is spectacular in flower may be an understatement! Large clusters of fragrant, white flowers reminiscent of wisteria hang gracefully from the ends of branches. Fall color is a bright yellow, and its smooth gray bark is attractive year-round. . . . yellowwood is a perfect ornamental for just about any area where a medium-sized spreading tree is desired," wrote Weeks, Weeks, and Parker in 2010.[143] More than a century earlier, Alice Lounsberry wrote, "There is something mystical about the great bunches of this tree's flowers when they unfold. It is, moreover, always beautiful."[144] **Cultivation:** Full sun to shade, well-drained soil, tolerates urban conditions. This slow-growing tree flowers at about 8–10 years old, producing profuse blooms every 2 or 3 years. **Nature Note:** Used by songbirds for food and nesting; attracts bees. Not known to host moths or butterflies. **Zones:** 3–8.

Yellowwood flowers (*Cladrastis kentukea*)

Yellowwood (*Cladrastis kentukea*)
Also see pp. 301, 354

Yellow buckeye
(*Aesculus flava*)

YELLOW BUCKEYE, SWEET BUCKEYE. **Family:** Soapberry (Sapindaceae). **Genus:** *Aesculus* (*A. flava; A. octandra*). **Height:** 50–70 feet. **Ornamental Attributes:** Panicles of yellow or creamy-white flowers suffused with red in April to June. Palmately compound, deciduous leaves turn yellow, orange or red in fall; split smooth-husks reveal two shiny brown seeds. Stout, picturesque branches sweep the ground. Exfoliating bark adds to winter interest. "In the early spring when it is covered with its yellow flowers it seems to have suddenly become quite frivolous."[145] **Cultivation:** Young trees do well in shade; adults flourish in full to part sun. Likes rich, moist, well-drained soil; disease resistant. It is the largest of the buckeyes, least susceptible to leaf scorch, and best adapted to urban situations. Tolerates black walnut toxity. **Buckeye Nature Note:** Hosts 32 species of butterflies and moths and some leafhoppers. Important food source for nectar- and pollen-seeking bumblebees (p. 61), other long-tongued bees, butterflies, and ruby-throated hummingbirds (p. 91), pollinators of the showy flowers. Squirrels are the only known animals to consume toxic buckeye seeds. Provides wildlife with shelter and nesting sites. **Zones:** 4–8.

Leafhopper (*Cicadellidae* spp.)

Other Native Buckeyes:

See Summer Trees for OHIO BUCKEYE, p. 184.
   See Spring Shrubs for RED BUCKEYE, p. 33.
   See Summer Shrubs for BOTTLEBRUSH BUCKEYE, p. 130.
   SASSAFRAS. **Family:** Laurel (Lauraceae). **Genus:** *Sassafras* (*S. albidum*). **Height:** 30–60 feet. **Spread:** 25–40 feet. **Shrub Form Height:** 20–30 feet. **Shrub Form Spread:** 15–25 feet. **Ornamental Attributes:** Clusters of profuse fragrant yellow or chartreuse female flowers bloom over two weeks during March to May. "The fruit is a beautiful, dark blue, shining berry set on a bright red, club-shaped, fleshy stem," wrote Harriet L. Keeler in 1900.[146] In fall, the mitten-, ghost-, or football-shaped leaves turn wildly brilliant shades of yellow, orange, red, to almost pink. Deeply furrowed bark adds winter interest. Like its relative, spicebush, all parts of sassafras are strongly aromatic. In 1900, Alice Lounsberry wrote, "It is always pleasant to come upon the sassafras. . . . In the spring especially its drooping clusters of flowers attract us."[147] In 2006, C. Colston Burrell wrote, "The sweet scent of fresh sassafras is merely a memory for most of us. This lovely and familiar tree is often ignored in favor of trendier ornamentals, but few can rival sassafras for season-long interest."[148] **Cultivation:** Full to part sun; adaptable to almost every site, except very wet. Fast growing, long lived. "Sassafras is highly underrated as an ornamental. It is reportedly difficult to transplant. . . . This myth is due to the fact that people try to dig suckers that have inadequate root systems," state Weeks, Weeks, and Parker.[149] Tolerates black walnut tree toxicity. **Life Span:** 100–500 years. **Nature Note:** Nectar- and pollen-seeking pollinators include small native bees, dance flies and other flies, wasps, and beetles that birds seek to feed their nestlings. It hosts 38 species of Lepidoptera (butterflies/moth), including tiger swallowtail butterflies (p. 18), the Promethea silkmoth and other moths, and is one of the preferred host plants for the spicebush swallowtail (p. 22). Its fat-rich fruits, much appreciated by migrating and overwintering birds, feed at least 23 species of birds,[150] including wood thrush (p. 175), northern flicker, gray catbird (p. 79), wild turkey (p. 244), flycatchers, eastern bluebird (p. 61), red-headed woodpecker (p. 212), red-bellied woodpecker (p. 55), American robin (p. 62), vireos, and warblers. **Zones:** 4–9.

Northern flicker
(*Colaptes auratus*)

Hooded warbler (*Setophaga citrina*)

Black locust leaves and flowers (*Robinia pseudoacacia*)

BLACK LOCUST. **Family:** Pea (Fabaceae). **Genus:** *Robinia* (*R. pseudoacacia*). **Height:** 30–50 feet. **Ornamental Attributes:** Its spectacular white, pea-like flowers in April to May belong in depictions of Eden in primitive art. Pinnately compound blue-green leaves, thorns. "The flowers exhale one of the most exquisite of flower scents and when the air is moist and still, the perfume spreads over a great area."[151] Large trees can be "burly and contorted, singularly picturesque," and "among the most photogenic of trees."[152] **Cultivation:** Sun, easily established. Trees tend to sucker vigorously from the roots and dominate open habitats. To have a single tree, remove any suckers. Most soils; fixes nitrogen. Because of its soil-improving properties, black locust has often been used as a nurse crop and underplanted among other trees; it is tolerant of black walnut tree toxicity. **Range Note:** Black locust has a disjunct or separate native range, the extent of which is not accurately known, which includes parts of the Midwest.[153] **Ecological Threat:** "Although it has a reputation for suckering, we only wish that certain superb specimens we know of, did!," wrote Wilson and Bell.[154] "Many say the black locust is an invader in the Northeast, but geologists have found that black locust was here before the Ice Age. So, the black locust is only reclaiming its original territory," writes Sue Sweeney.[155] "Black locusts have invasive traits that enable them to spread aggressively. While these trees have demonstrated invasive traits, there is insufficient supporting research to declare them so pervasive that they cannot be recommended for any planting sites. Review of risks should be undertaken before selecting these trees for planting sites," states the Morton

Clockwise, from upper left: Clouded sulphur butterfly (*Colias philodice*); Orange sulphur butterfly (*Colias eurytheme*); Locust underwing moth (*Euparthenos nubilis*); Silver-spotted skipper (*Epargyreus clarus*)

Arboretum, which finds black locust "Not recommended." Several midwestern states find black locust invasive. **Nativar/Cultivar Note:** Black locust nativars have the same invasive traits. **Life Span:** 60–100 years. **Nature Note:** Favorite of bumblebees (p. 61), other bees and insect pollinators, and ruby-throated hummingbirds (p. 91). Hosts 72 species of Lepidoptera (butterflies/moths), including the clouded sulphur, orange sulphur, silver-spotted skipper, and the locust underwing moth. **Zones:** 3–8.

More Native Alternatives:

CAROLINA SILVERBELL, p. 80; CATALPA SPP., p. 86; CHERRY SPP., p. 17; FLOWERING DOGWOOD, p. 94; MAGNOLIA SPP., p. 110; PAWPAW, p. 113; REDBUD, p. 92; SERVICEBERRY SPP., p. 77.
   See Summer Trees for AMERICAN BEECH, p. 168; AMERICAN LINDEN, p. 190; HONEY LOCUST, p. 163; SHAGBARK HICKORY, p. 222.
   See Fall Trees for PERSIMMON, p. 256.
   See Spring Shrubs for RED BUCKEYE, p. 33; SPICEBUSH, p. 22.

Nonnative:

FILBERT, COMMON FILBERT, HAZEL, EUROPEAN FILBERT. **Family:** Birch (Betula). **Genus:** *Corylus* (*C. avellana*). **Origin:** Europe. **Height:** 19 feet. **Spread:** 9 feet. **Ornamental Attributes:** Early spring flowers, nuts. **Cultivation:** Sun/shade, most soils. **Zones:** 4–8.
See Winter Shrubs for *HARRY LAUDER'S WALKING STICK,* p. 311.

Native Alternatives:

AMERICAN HAZELNUT. **Family:** Birch (Betulaceae). **Genus:** *Corylus.* AMERICAN HAZELNUT, AMERICAN FILBERT (*C. americana*). **Height:** 6–12 feet. **Spread:** 4–6 feet. **Ornamental Attributes:** The greatest bloom appears in spring, with seed and fruit production on this monoecious plant occurring in fall when clusters of male flowers or catkins (staminate) appear. Regarding the male flowers opening the following spring, Alice Lounsberry wrote, "This indeed is the shrub known to almost every country urchin and which when its catkins begin to loosen and its golden pollen to fall proclaims loudly the coming of the springtime."[156] In fall, female flowers (pistillate) occupy a scaly bud with protruding bright red pollen receiving stigma and styles. The fruit, a light brown, acorn-like nut enclosed

American hazelnut (*Corylus americana* var. *indehiscens*)
Also see p. 274

by two husk-like bracts, matures in September and October. Fall color varies from bright yellow to deep wine-red to various shades of oranges and yellows, providing a kaleidoscope of colors. "Free food is there for the taking, if you can beat the wildlife to it," write Weeks and Weeks.[157] **Cultivation:** Easily grown, sun, sun for about half a day, part shade. Soil can be well-drained, soggy or marshy for long periods, or have poor drainage. Tolerates drought and black walnut toxicity. Size is easy to control. Best to plant 2 or 3 plants for pollination. A colony-forming shrub, it is good for naturalizing and providing cover. **Native American Note:** "Hazelnuts have been found in archaeological remains along the eastern border of the Prairie Bioregion, such as the Middle Woodland sites in Illinois," writes Kelly Kindscher;[158] BEAKED

HAZELNUT (*C. cornuta* var. *cornuta*). **Height:** 10 feet. Its nuts are held by "beak-like" husks. **Note:** Presumed extirpated in Ohio. **Zones:** 4–9; **Nature Note:** Hazelnut hosts 131 Lepidoptera species, including Juvenal's duskywing skipper, mourning cloak (p. 62), red-

Juvenal's duskywing skipper
(*Erynnis juvenalis*)

Green comma butterfly (*Polygonia faunus*)

spotted purple (p. 18), viceroy (p. 54), Compton tortoiseshell (p. 322), green comma, polyphemus moth (p. 211), and saddled prominent butterfly. Birds eat the caterpillars and feed them to their nestlings. Hazelnuts attract pollinating insects that in turn attract birds seeking food for themselves and their babies. The nuts are heavily used by wild turkey (p. 244), red-headed woodpecker (p. 212), red-bellied woodpecker (p. 55), American goldfinch (p. 145), warblers, blue jay (p. 79), ruffed grouse (p. 36), chipmunks (p. 94), squirrels, and deer mice. The shrubs' dense branching structure and large leaves provide excellent cover and nesting for wildlife and songbirds. **Zones:** 4–9.

Nonnative:

FRINGE TREE, CHINESE FRINGE TREE. **Family:** Olive (Oleaceae). **Genus:** *Chionanthus* (*C. retusus*). **Origin:** China, Korea, Japan. **Height/Spread:** 10–25 feet. **Ornamental Attributes:** Fragrant, showy white flowers in May to June that are smaller than the native species; female trees produce blue fruit. **Cultivation:** Full sun to part shade, well-drained soil. **Name Note:** Named after its beautiful North American cousin by sixteenth-century botanist Carl Linnaeus. **Zones:** 5–8.

Chinese fringe tree
(*Chionanthus retusus*)

Fringe tree flowers
(*Chionanthus virginicus*)

Fringe tree
(*Chionanthus virginicus*)
Also see p. 283

Native Alternative:

FRINGE TREE, WHITE FRINGE TREE. Family: Olive (*Oleaceae*). **Genus:** *Chionanthus* (*C. virginicus*). **Height/Spread:** 10–25 feet. **Ornamental Attributes:** Fringes of beautiful fragrant white flowers at a very young age. Magnolia-like leaves turn yellow in fall. A multiple-trunked shrub or small tree, it smooth gray branches, thick twiggy form, and beautiful shapes provide winter interest. "The fragrant late-spring blossoms signal the closure of spring and the onset of summer. The flowers are cloud-like, pure white and brilliant when viewed *en masse* against the expanding green foliage . . . looks especially stunning almost ethereal, at peak bloom at night," write Sternberg and Wilson.[159] "We have planted it to take full advantage of its two weeks of exquisite scent," noted the fragrant plant expert, Helen Van Pelt Wilson.[160] The dioecious trees have male and female flowers on separate plants; occasional trees have both kinds of flowers. Female trees' grape-like clusters of dark blue fruit are attractive to birds. To ensure fruit, plant 3 or more. Selected by Christopher Starbuck as an uncommon tree for specimen planting. **Cultivation:** Low maintenance. Full sun, part shade, prefers moist, deep, well-drained, acidic soils; adapts to most soils. Tolerates black walnut toxicity. **Note:** Threatened in Ohio. **Nature Note:** Host plant for 8 species of butterflies and moths, including the rustic sphinx moth. Flowers attract butterflies and bees, and birds seeking insects to feed their young. The fruits attract small mammals and birds, including wild turkeys (p. 244). **Zones:** 3–9.

More Native Alternatives:

AMERICAN HAZELNUT, p. 102; CAROLINA SILVERBELL, p. 80; SNOWBELL, p. 116.

See Spring Shrubs for AMERICAN BLADDERNUT, p. 41; WAFER ASH, p. 45.

Nonnative:

HAWTHORN. **Family:** Rose (Rosaceae). **Genus:** *Crataegus.* **Note:** As a group, hawthorns are difficult to identify. Highly susceptible to a large number of insect and disease problems. Nonnative hawthorns can hybridize with native hawthorn species, leading to alteration of the gene pool of the native species. Some nonnative hawthorns don't do well in the Midwest;[161] *ENGLISH HAWTHORN, COMMON HAWTHORN, SMOOTH HAWTHORN* (*C. laevigata* sometimes incorrectly called *C. oxyacantha*). **Origin:** Europe. **Height/Spread:** 15–20 feet. **Ornamental Attributes:** White or pink flowers in April to May emit a musky scent that some find unpleasant. It has red fall fruits and sharp thorns. No fall color. **Cultivation:** Full sun, medium soil; creates dense shade, naturalizes. Particularly

English hawthorn (*Crataegus laevigata*)

susceptible to leaf blight; don't plant near junipers. It has numerous cultivars with thorns, including 'Punicea', 'Crimson Cloud', 'Superba', and 'Paul's Scarlet', which is defoliated by August. **Ecological Threat:** Naturalized in midwestern states. **Zones:** 5–8; *ONESEED HAWTHORN, SINGLESEED HAWTHORN, COMMON HAWTHORN* (*C. monogyna*). **Origin:** Europe. 6–30 feet. White or pinkish flowers; the strong thorns that appear along each branch are modified branches; red berries. Resembles other ornamental hawthorns. **Ecological Threat:** Naturalized in much of the country. **Zones:** 5–8.

Native Alternatives:

HAWTHORN. **Family:** Rose (Rosaceae). **Genus:** *Crataegus*. **Height/Spread:** Generally 20–25 feet. **Hawthorn Ornamental Attributes:** Like the native crab apples, native hawthorns have beautiful spring flowers, long-lasting striking fruits, colorful leaves that brighten fall and interesting shapes, dense, intricate branch patterns, bark, and thorns that provide winter interest. "All our thorns are attractive in habit, foliage, flower and fruit and are worthy of cultivation," wrote Harriet Keeler in 1900.[162] "Many are the allusions to the hawthorns of England in poetry and prose," wrote Eloise Butler in 1911. "It is pertinent to ask why writers neglect to extol the American species. For our hawthorn trees or shrubs are of extreme beauty, when covered with their snowy fleece of bloom, or when glowing with the sweet tasting, stony bright red 'thorn apples.'"[163] **Cultivation:** Full sun best; plants tolerate light shade, a wide range of well-drained soils, some drought, and many urban pollutants. "Hawthorns will survive conditions that thwart most other flowering trees," conclude Sternberg and Wilson.[164] Hawthorns readily hybridize, complicating identification; some species seem like large shrubs; COCKSPUR THORN, COCKSPUR HAWTHORN (*C. crus-galli*). **Height/**

Spread: 25–35 feet. Clusters of white flowers, showy dark red fruit, orange, scarlet, purple-red fall color. Wide-spreading, horizontal, thorny branches, thick, leathery, shiny dark green leaves; dramatic long sharp thorns. Four-season interest. Provides many smaller birds with excellent cover and nesting sites and small fruit that many birds eat in winter and spring, especially cedar waxwing (p. 36), fox sparrow (p. 322), and ruffed grouse (p. 36); THORNLESS COCKSPUR HAWTHORN (*C. crus-gall* var. *inermis*). A naturally occurring variety, it has all of the features of the species except it is thornless; COPENHAGEN HAWTHORN, SCARLET HAWTHORN, ONTARIO HAWTHORN (*C. intricata*). Sometimes a large multistemmed shrub; DOWNY HAWTHORN, RED HAW (*C. mollis*). **Height/Spread:** 20–30 feet. **Ornamental Attributes:** Early, profuse, white, musk-scented, rose-like flowers; large persistent scarlet fruit; fuzzy or downy leaves drop in late summer after turning yellow to bronze; silvery scaly bark provides winter interest. "This is the handsomest

Downy hawthorn (*Crataegus mollis*)

Washington hawthorn (*Crataegus phaenopyrum*)
Also see pp. 299, 354

of the American Hawthorns and bears the only haws that by any stretch of the imagination could be considered edible," wrote Harriet Keeler.[165] "Tough little flowering tree" with "a dense crown of spreading, thorny branches. . . . The white flowers of red haw are bourne in baseball-sized clusters," write Sternberg and Wilson.[166] Spreads by seed; GREEN HAW-THORN (*C. viridis*). **Height/Spread:** 30–40 feet. **Ornamental Attributes:** Showy white flowers in May, orange-red fall color. Often thornless. "One of the best of the native hawthorns for gardens, with fruits that rival many crabapples in winter effect, scarlet-orange fall color, exfoliating bark, and good disease resistance," writes William Cullina.[167] Reportedly doesn't suffer from cedar-hawthorn rust. Bird-friendly fruits make it preferable to its popular nativar, the larger-fruited 'Winter King'; WASHINGTON HAWTHORN (*C. phaenopyrum*). **Height:** 25 feet. "The Washington thorn . . . is an amazingly beautiful tree, especially when seen under a blue October sky, with its scarlet foliage a background for a tremendous abundance of large, shiny red corymbs of fruit." Its "spectacular" fruit "lasts into winter . . . heavy fruiting looks like a second blooming";[168] BIGFRUIT HAWTHORN (*C. macrosperma*); DOTTED HAWTHORN (*C. punctata*); DOUGLAS HAWTHORN, BLACK HAWTHORN (*C. douglasii*); FIREBERRY HAWTHORN (*C. chrysocarpa*); FORT SHERIDAN HAW-THORN (*C. apiomorpha*); MARGARETT'S HAWTHORN (*C. margarettae*); PEAR HAWTHORN (*C. calpodendron*); WAXY-FRUITED HAWTHORN, FROSTED HAW (*C. pruinosa*). **Anachronistic Note:** Long ago, huge "ground sloths and mastodons" ate haw-thorn berries, but "the thorns are too long and insufficiently dense" and too high on the tree to provide a defense against deer, today's herbivores, "so perhaps hawthorn thorns can be regarded as anachronistic," writes Connie Barlow.[169] **Nature Note:** Native hawthorns have special value to bees, which, along with small beneficial flies, are their primary pollinators.

Wasps, beetles, and butterflies also visit the flowers. Hawthorns host 159 Lepidoptera (butterfly/moth) species, including the striped hairstreak butterfly (p. 18), sphinx moths, hummingbird clearwing (p. 72), the hawthorn underwing, and dagger moths. Several species of leafhoppers (p. 98) prefer hawthorns as host plants. The caterpillars and leafhoppers serve as food for nesting birds. In winter and early spring, hawthorns' fall berries are sought by more than 39 bird species—including American robin (p. 62), wood thrush (p. 175), cedar waxwing (p. 36), northern cardinal (p. 61), eastern kingbird (p. 55), rose-breasted grosbeak (p. 200), purple finch (p. 145), ruffed grouse (p. 36), and such native sparrows as fox sparrow (p. 322) and white-throated sparrow, along with upland game birds, foxes, squirrels, and other mammals. Sternberg and Wilson rank hawthorns "among the most useful of all woody plants for wildlife habitat."[170] Their dense structure and thorns provide protective cover, roosting sites, and safe nesting habitat, especially when the plants are permitted to become living fences and thickets, for mammals and for birds like yellow-breasted chat, brown thrasher (p. 219), northern cardinal (p. 61), and loggerhead shrike (p. 259). The shrike also uses the thorns to impale

White-lined sphinx moth (*Hyles lineata*)

its prey. Native hawthorns are drought and black walnut tree toxicity tolerant. "Overall, the ecological value of hawthorns to wildlife is high," writes John Hilty.[171] **Hawthorn Zones:** 4–8.

White-throated sparrow
(*Zonotrichia albicollis*)

More Native Alternatives:

CRAB APPLE, p. 89.
    See Spring Shrubs for RED BUCKEYE, p. 33; VIBURNUM SPP., p. 69.
    See Fall Shrubs for SILVER BUFFALOBERRY, p. 229.

Nonnative:

HORSE CHESTNUT. See Summer Trees, p. 184.

Nonnative:

LINDEN. See Summer Trees, p. 190.

Amur maackia
(*Maackia amurensis*)

Nonnative:

MAACKIA, AMUR MAACKIA. **Family:** Pea (Fabaceae). **Genus:** *Maackia* (*M. amurensis*). **Origin:** China. **Height/Spread:** 20–30 feet. **Ornamental Attributes:** Late spring spike-like clusters of fragrant, dull white, pea-like flowers. No fall color. Similar in appearance to the slightly larger yellowwood, but yellowwood has more attractive flowers and excellent fall color. **Cultivation:** Full sun to part shade, most soils. **Zones:** 3–7.

Native Alternatives:

FRINGE TREE, p. 105; YELLOW BUCKEYE, p. 98; YELLOWWOOD, p. 96.

Nonnative:

MAGNOLIA. **Family:** Magnolia (Magnoliaceae). **Genus:** *Magnolia.* **Asian Bloom Time Note:** "Asian magnolias . . . grow naturally in areas without late-season frost and safely open their large lustrous flowers in early spring before their leaves emerge. Not so here; more often than not a gorgeous Asian magnolia blossom . . . becomes a soggy brown mess, and a reminder that frosts and cold weather are still not the norms," writes Patricia A. Taylor.[172] **Pollination Note:** Pollinated by beetles. **Fall Color Note:** Most magnolias lack good fall color; *KOBUS MAGNOLIA* (*M. kobus*). **Origin:** Japan. **Height:** 25–30 feet. **Spread:** 15–20 feet. **Ornamental Attributes:** Takes 25 years to produce its white flowers in March to April. **Cultivation:** Full sun to part shade; well-drained but not dry soil. Intolerant of urban pollutants;

Magnolia tree (*Magnolia × soulangeana*)

naturalizes. **Zones:** 5–8; *LILY-FLOWERED MAGNOLIA, JAPANESE MAGNOLIA, TU-LIP MAGNOLIA, MULAN MAGNOLIA* (*M. liliiflora*). **Origin:** China. **Height/Spread:** 10–15 feet. **Ornamental Attributes:** Large shrub/tree. The brief bloom of pink or reddish-purple flowers in April creates piles of browning petals. Full sun, most soils. **Zones:** 5–8; *SAU-CER MAGNOLIA* (*Yulania × soulangeana*, syn. *M. × soulangeana*). Hybrid. **Origin:** China. **Height/Spread:** 20–25 feet. **Ornamental Attributes:** Pinkish-white blooms in early spring. **Cultivation:** Sun, part shade, well-drained soil. Prune to prevent multiple stems. Performs poorly in urban environments; flowers often suffer early frost damage. **Zones:** 4–9; *STAR MAGNOLIA* (*M. stellata*). **Origin:** Japan. **Height/Spread:** 10–20 feet. **Ornamental Attri-butes:** Star-shaped white flowers in March to April can suffer spring frost damage. **Cultiva-tion:** Full sun, rich acidic soil. **Zones:** 4–8.

Native Alternatives:

MAGNOLIA. Family: Magnolia (Magnoliaceae). **Genus:** *Magnolia.* **American Bloom Time Note:** "American magnolias, on the other hand, do not bloom until after the leaves have emerged. The leaves and the later blooming time ensure that the flowers will not be damaged by frost, and thus that your garden will be filled with delicious summer scents and will remain neat, tidy, and low maintenance," writes Patricia A. Taylor.[173] **Cultivation Note:** Sun to light shade, moist well-drained soil, easy to grow. Watering around tree base keeps soil moist, en-suring tree thrives during periods of drought. **BIGLEAF MAGNOLIA** (*M. macrophylla*).

Cucumbertree
(*Magnolia acuminata*)

Height: To 40 feet. Fragrant, large (up to 16 inches), creamy-white spring flowers with purple-tinted petal bases. Huge (up to 3 feet long), tropical-looking leaves with fuzzy, silver-gray undersides create beautiful, two-toned effects with passing breezes and turn yellow in fall. "The only way to describe this tree is magnificent," notes Taylor, adding it "provides year-round interest and only needs well-drained soil."[174] **Note:** Endangered in Arkansas and Ohio. **Zones:** 5–8; CUCUMBERTREE, CUCUMBER MAGNOLIA (*M. acuminata*). **Height:** 40–75 feet. **Spread:** 20–35 feet. **Ornamental Attributes:** Tropical-looking shade tree. Fragrant yellow, tulip-like flowers in April to May followed by green, warty, cucumber-like fruits (seed-cones) for which tree is named. In fall, the fruits turn red and the foliage turns yellow, providing a colorful contrast. "It is a magificent tree for lawn planting, and thrives with but little attention," wrote Helen Keeler.[175] One of Christopher Starbuck's selections for uncommon trees for specimen planting. **Cultivation:** Sun–part sun, adequate moisture. Pest and problem free, the hardiest of all magnolias. Tolerant of black walnut tree toxicity. **Note:** Endangered in Indiana. It is Canada's only native magnolia, but threatened with extirpation. **Life Span:** 80–250 years. **Zones:** 3–8; SWEETBAY MAGNOLIA (*M. virginiana*). **Height/Spread:** 10–30 feet. **Ornamental Attributes:** Creamy-white, showy, solitary, very fragrant, month-long blooms resemble southern magnolias. The lush, enlongated, oval leathery leaves shimmer in a breeze due to silvery leaf undersides; in fall they turn russet to yellow. The fruit is red.

Umbrella-tree
(*Magnolia tripetala*)

Cultivation: Sun best for flowers; takes part shade; easily grown in evenly moist, humus-rich acidic soil, tolerates wet, boggy soils, flooding, salt, heavy clay and moderate air pollution. Can be a tree or shrub. **Zones:** 5–10; in Zone 5, it appreciates a protected location; SWAMP MAGNOLIA (*M. virginiana* var. *australis*). A taller, more fragrant natural variation; UMBRELLA-TREE, UMBRELLA MAGNOLIA (*M. tripetala*). **Height/Spread:** 15–30 feet. **Ornamental Attributes:** Large creamy-white flowers, attractive red fruits, yellow fall color, smooth gray bark. **Cultivation:** Sun. Moist soil; appreciates a protected site. The flowers do not have a pleasant fragrance, "but they keep it to themselves," remarked a fragrant plant expert.[176] **Note:** Endangered in parts of the Midwest. **Zones:** 5–8. **Magnolia Nature Note:** Host 21 species of butterflies and moths. Nesting birds seek the caterpillars and the pollinating insects that visit the flowers. The trees provide homes and shelter for wildlife. The fruits and seeds provide food for small mammals and birds such as eastern towhee (p. 235), red-eyed vireo, American redstart (p. 89), American robin (p. 62), wild turkey (p. 244), northern flicker (p. 99), pileated woodpecker, great crested flycatcher, blue jay (p. 79), ruffed grouse (p. 36), and—when they fall to the ground—other ground-feeding birds. A seed's brightly colored fleshy exterior covering is high in fat and provides migrating birds with a good source of energy as they fly south. Magnolias, tuliptrees (p. 179), and black cherry trees (p. 82) host the eastern tiger

Red-eyed vireo (*Vireo olivaceus*)

swallowtail butterfly (p. 18). Magnolias also host the spicebush swallowtail and nocturnal sweetbay silk moth. **Historical Note:** Fossilized remains indicate that magnolias are among the earliest known flowering plants dating back about 130 million years, before bees appeared, relying on beetles for pollination. The flowers retain some of their primitive and exotic features.

Pawpaw flower (*Asimina triloba*)

PAWPAW, CUSTARD APPLE, DOG BANANA. Family: Custard-apple (Annonaceae). **Genus:** *Asimina* (*A. triloba*). **Height/Spread:** 15–20 feet. **Ornamental Attributes:** Flowers in April to May are maroon or purple. Fruit is large and green. In fall, the green leaves become spectacularly golden. One of Christopher Starbuck's selections for uncommon trees for specimen planting. **Cultivation:** Easy to grow. Full sun to light shade. Moist well-drained soil; tolerates wet soil. Cross-pollination from an unrelated pawpaw tree required for fruiting. "Pawpaw tends to grow in clonal groups, or patches."[177] Good for erosion control. **Food Note:** The unique fruit is sometimes used for custard-type desserts. **Anachronistic Note:** Like magnolias and sweetshrub, pawpaw is a survivor from "that distant time when insect pollination first developed," writes William Cullina.[178] "If pawpaw, persimmon, or osage orange are in the neighborhood, you should be able to make out the ghosts of their extinct partners," writes Connie Barlow. The fruits are too large for songbirds to eat but are sought by raccoon, opossum, fox, skunk, squirrel, wild turkey, and woodland box turtle. "Even the smallest pawpaw specimens are too big for foxes and raccoons to take into their mouths whole."[179] **Nature**

Zebra swallowtail butterfly
(*Eurytides marcellus*)

Pawpaw sphinx moth (*Dolba hyloeus*)

Note: Hosts 12 species of Lepidoptera (butterflies/moths); sole host for zebra swallowtail butterfly and pawpaw sphinx moth. Flower color and scent attract various pollinating beetles and flies that birds use to feed their offspring. Tolerant of black walnut toxicity, resistant to white-tailed deer and most herbivores, which object to its odor and toxicity. **Zones:** 5–9.

More Native Alternatives:

CAROLINA SILVERBELL, p. 80; CRAB APPLE SPP., p. 89; DOWNY HAWTHORN, WASHINGTON HAWTHORN, OTHER HAW-THORNS, p. 106; FLOWERING DOGWOOD, p. 94; FRINGE TREE, p. 105; PLUM SPP., p. 78; REDBUD, p. 92; SERVICEBERRY SPP., p. 77; YELLOWWOOD, p. 96.

See Spring Shrubs for ALTER-NATELEAF DOGWOOD, OTHER NATIVE DOGWOODS, p. 49; AMERICAN SMOKETREE, p. 65; BLACKHAW & OTHER VIBUR-NUM SPP., p. 69; WAFER ASH, p. 45.

Pawpaw tree (*Asimina triloba*)

Nonnative:

OAK. See Summer Trees, p. 201.

Nonnative:

PLUM. See *CHERRY, PLUM,* p. 81. Also see Spring Shrubs for *CHERRY, PLUM, ALMOND,* p. 16.

Nonnative:

REDBUD, CHINESE REDBUD. **Family:** Pea (Fabaceae). **Genus:** *Cercis* (*C. chinensis*). **Origin:** China, **Height:** 8–15 feet. **Spread:** 6–12 feet. **Ornamental Attributes:** Showy rose-colored flowers in March to April. Yellow fall color. **Cultivation:** Full to part sun, medium soil. **Zones:** 6–9.

Native Alternatives:

REDBUD, p. 92.
See Spring Shrubs for RED BUCKEYE, p. 33.

Chinese redbud (*Cercis chinensis*)

Japanese snowbell
(*Styrax japonicus*)

Nonnative:

SNOWBELL. Family: Storax (Styracaceae). **Genus:** *Styrax.* **Origin:** China, Japan, Korea. **Height/Spread:** 20–30 feet. **Ornamental Attributes:** Showy white flowers in May to June. **Cultivation:** Full to part sun, medium soil; *JAPANESE SNOWBELL* (*S. japonicus*). Naturalizes; *FRAGRANT SNOWBELL* (*S. obassis*). **Zones:** 5–8.

Native Alternatives:

SNOWBELL. Family: Storax (Styracaceae). **Genus:** *Styrax.* **Height/Spread:** 10–25 feet. Shrub/small tree. **Ornamental Attributes:** Dainty, fragrant white and yellow bell-shaped flowers in April to July create a white cloud and remind some of honeysuckle. Bright green, glossy foliage turns yellow in fall. Smooth gray bark. "Snowbells are among the most ornamental and least appreciated of our flowering shrubs." Their "heady aroma lofts out on the slightest breeze," writes William Cullina.[180] **Cultivation:** Part sun, light shade; wet, moist, and medium soils. Preference for acidic soils but does well in limestone soils. Propagation is by

American snowbell (*Styrax americanus*)

self-seeding; AMERICAN SNOWBELL (*S. americanus*). **Note:** Threatened in Illinois, presumed extirpated in Ohio. **Zones:** 5–9; BIGLEAF SNOWBELL (*S. grandifolius*). Native to southern portions of the Midwest. **Note:** Endangered in Illinois and Indiana. Presumed extirpated in Ohio. **Zones:** (6) 7–9. **Snowbell Nature Note:** Attracts butterflies; bees are the major pollinators. Birds and other animals eat the fruit. A claim that snowbell hosts the promethea moth is disputed.

More Native Alternatives:

CAROLINA SILVERBELL, p. 80.
    See Summer Trees for SOURWOOD, p. 186.
    See Spring Shrubs for AMERICAN BLADDERNUT, p. 41; WAFER ASH, p. 45.

Nonnative:

WILLOW. **Family:** Willow (Salicaceae). **Genus:** *Salix.* **Willow Problems:** Subject to pests and diseases. Nonnative willows, due to weak and easily broken branches, are considered "dirty trees"; *WEEPING WILLOW, BABYLON WEEPING WILLOW* (*S. babylonica*; *S.* × *sepulcralis* [*alba* × *babylonica*]). **Origin:** China. **Height/Spread:** 30–50 feet. **Zones:** 4–9; *WISCONSIN WEEPING WILLOW* (*S.* ×*pendulina*, syn. *S.* × *blanda.* [*babylonica* × *fragilis*]). **Origin:** Europe. **Height/Spread:** 20–40 feet. **Zones:** 5–9. **Cultivation:** The Babylon weeping willow and Wisconsin weeping willow are very similar. Both do best in full to part sun, medium to wet soil; messy trees with aggressive roots that may clog underground pipes and

Weeping willow
(*Salix babylonica*)

drainage systems; brittle limbs. **Ecological Threat:** Naturalized in midwestern states; ***CORK-SCREW WILLOW, CURLY WILLOW.*** See Winter Shrubs, p. 311; ***CRACK WILLOW*** (*S.* × *fragilis*). **Origin:** Eurasia. **Height/Spread:** 40 feet. "This large willow is such a common feature in the upper Midwestern landscape that most people assume it is native," writes Sally S. Weeks.[181] "It is naturalized across North America, thanks in part to its popularity with immigrating Europeans who used its wood and twigs in basketwork," write Weeks, Weeks, and Parker.[182] **Ecological Threat:** Naturalized in parts of the Midwest. **Zones:** 4–7; ***GOLDEN WILLOW*** (*S. alba* var. *vitellina*). Dies back during drought. **Zones:** 2–8; ***LARGE GRAY WILLOW*** (*S. cinerea*), see p. 118; ***LAUREL WILLOW, BAY WILLOW*** (*S. pentandra*), see p. 118; ***OSIER WILLOW*** (*S. viminalis*); ***PURPLEOSIER WILLOW*** (*S. purpurea*). **Origin:** Europe. **Ecological Threat:** Naturalized in midwestern states; ***WHITE WILLOW, EUROPEAN WILLOW*** (*S. alba*). **Origin:** Europe, Asia. **Height:** 50–80 feet. Upright tree. There are weeping forms. Leaves are green above, nearly white below; can turn yellow in fall. **Cultivation:** Full to part sun, medium to wet soil; naturalizes. **Ecological Threat:** Naturalized in midwestern states. **Medicinal Note:** Because so many nonnative willows have been planted for medicinal purposes, many have become naturalized.

For more willows, see Spring Shrubs for ***PUSSY WILLOW,*** p. 52.

Native Alternatives:

WILLOW. **Family:** Willow (Salicaceae). **Genus:** *Salix.* **Genus Note:** Native willows are considered clean trees and shrubs. **BLACK WILLOW** (*S. nigra*). **Height:** 30–60 feet. **Spread:** 30–40 feet. **Ornamental Attributes:** In March and April, its bright yellow-green twigs bear long catkins composed of many small yellow-green flowers creating a soft chartreuse haze that develop into orange capsules full of seeds by summer. The male and female flowers are on separate trees. Silky hairs on seeds help the seeds blow in the wind. The bark is deeply furrowed. Black willow is a shade tree that also looks good massed. "Rather than a graceful weeping form, this native willow has a billowing, soft shape that is passed over for exotic relatives," writes C. Colston Burrell.[183] **Cultivation:** Full to light sun, wet to moist upland sites; adapts to wide range of soils. **Life Span:** 70–85 years. **Zones:** 2–9; **PEACH-LEAVED WILLOW** (*S. amygdaloides*). **Height:** 70 feet. **Historical Note:** "Willows were very adept at claiming ground at the edges of glaciers, and underwent explosive evolution after the most recent ice ages."[184] **Zones:** 5–9. **Nature Note:** See Spring Shrubs for PUSSY WILLOW, p. 53.

More Native Alternatives:

AMERICAN HAZELNUT, p. 102.
See Summer Trees for COTTONWOOD, p. 166; SWAMP WHITE OAK, p. 207; WILLOW OAK, p. 209.
See Winter Trees for ALDER SPP., p. 316.
See Spring Shrubs for PRAIRIE WILLOW, p. 53; PUSSY WILLOW, p. 53.

Black willow (*Salix nigra*)

2

SUMMER

A FTER THE COOL of spring gives way to summer's sunshine and heat, we start appreciating the shade and soothing green color that characterize native shrubs and trees. This chapter presents midwestern native shrubs, trees, and vines that produce shade, flowers, or fruit during the summer.

Native Americans negotiated the summer forests of birch, elm, maple, cedar, and hickory, traversing a vast network of trails. Using live bur, post, and white oak saplings, they bent and fastened the upper ends to the ground, creating distinctively shaped trail markers, some of which still survive.[1] While there was a lull in activities before buffalo hunting time in fall, tribes gathered rose hips. Their subsistence activities, obtaining bark to build wigwams and canoes, gathering medicinal plants and berries from shrubs, planting corn, and fishing and hunting, interconnected with religion and the social order.[2]

The bounty produced by native trees, shrubs, and vines also played a vital role in the lives of Euro-American explorers and settlers. In 1672, exploring what would soon be called the Illinois Country, Canadian mapmaker Louis Jolliet and French-born Jesuit missionary Jacques Marquette documented herds of buffalo roaming prairies lined with groves of elm, oak, plum, and apple trees laced with the vines of the wild grape.[3]

Spring is the pinnacle for flowering shrubs and trees, but summer has a goodly share. Virginia sweetspire's fragrant white flowers in early to midsummer attract as many butterflies as the butterfly bush introduced from China. A butterfly and hummingbird magnet, this beautiful shrub is a guilt-free choice because—a native—it is not invasive like introductions from Asia, such as butterfly bush and Japanese meadowsweet. Native summer-blooming butterfly-, bee-, and hummingbird-attracting shrubs include, among others, New Jersey tea, buttonbush, clethra (sweetpepperbush), steeplebush, white meadowsweet, and butterfly shrub. Native summer-flowering butterfly-, bee-, and hummingbird-attracting small trees include Stewartia, Franklin, and sourwood trees. Many of the summer-blooming woody species display gorgeous fall color. Native ornamental shrubs and trees offer much all-season beauty and attract insect and bird pollinators. Why choose introduced species?

A typical late-1800s midwestern woodland held "timber tall, and of the best sort, such as oak hickerie [sic] and locust; and for game, both for plenty and variety, perhaps exceeded by no part of the world," wrote Major Robert Rogers in his 1883 journal. Landscapes of wild [crab] apple, "white, black and yellow oak, black and white walnut, 'cypress,' chestnut, and locust," and areas where "chestnut and oak predominated" gave him "a good opinion of the soil."[4]

Our streets can be lined and our yards and parks landscaped with midwestern trees "of the best sort." Oaks are a keystone species, provide wonderful shade, and deserve special acknowledgment. Acorns provide birds and mammals with food at critical times. Hosting 534 species of butterflies and moths, no other plant genus supports more species of Lepidoptera than oak. The caterpillar stage of butterflies and moths is vital food for birds and their offspring. Universally, each oak tree, in terms of the hundreds of species it hosts, feeds, and supports, "is like a little rain forest."[5] "Restoring large stands of oaks to suburbia would go a long way toward shoring up the future of our nation's biodiversity," writes Douglas Tallamy.[6] "I have to admit being a tad overwhelmed by this amazing genus," writes William Cullina. "Oaks are generally slow growing, but planting an oak is in a sense like sowing the seeds of your own immortality by helping something to take root that will likely live for 200 years or more. In fact, there are few broad-leaved trees that will reliably grow to a venerable age like an oak. A maple may wither, a pine may break, and a poplar may be just a distant memory when the huge limbs of a mighty oak still stand triumphantly to link earth and sky."[7]

Planting oaks can be as easy as leaving acorns out for gray squirrels, furry acrobats that cover the acorns with earth, literally planting them. People can plant acorns too. In Riverside, Illinois, volunteers collect native acorns, buckeyes, and walnut and hickory seeds and plant them on the shores of the Des Plaines River. "If you're responsible for adding even just one tree to the landscape, you're leaving an important legacy," says Tom Sisulak, the originator of the 1,000 Tree Planting Project. "Some of the trees we plant through this project will be here in Riverside 100 or 200 years from now," he tells the volunteers.[8]

To improve our natural environment we must become aware of the diminishment of our butterfly, bee, and bird populations and connect our awareness with the loss of our native flora. Gardening and landscaping with midwestern native shrubs, trees, and herbaceous species, which also possess intrinsic beauty, then seems obvious. When planting a new shrub or tree or replacing an existing cultivar or introduced species, we suggest choosing from among the following summer-flowering, summer-fruiting, and shade-producing native shrubs and trees.

Summer Shrubs

Nonnative:

ANGELICA TREE, JAPANESE ANGEL-ICA TREE. Family: Ginseng (Araliaceae). **Genus:** *Aralia* (*A. elata*). **Origin:** China, Japan, Korea. **Height:** 12–15 feet. Can grow taller. **Spread:** 6–10 feet. **Ornamental Attributes:** Looks like the native Devil's walking stick. Large suckering spiny shrub/tree. Large compound leaves; clumps of small, white flowers in August, purplish fruit. **Cultivation:** Full sun best; moist well-drained soil. Rapid grower, produces suckers that form dense spiny thickets. **Ecological Threat:** Naturalized in midwestern states. **Zones:** 4–8.

Angelica tree (*Aralia elata*)

Native Alternatives:

DEVIL'S WALKING STICK, ANGELICA TREE, ARALIA. Family: Ginseng (Araliaceae). **Genus:** *Aralia* (*A. spinosa*). **Height:** 10–20 feet. **Spread:** 6–10 feet. **Ornamental Attributes:** This angelica tree look-alike has large panicles of small creamy-white flowers in late summer followed by purple clusters of fruits resembling American elderberries. The very large compound leaves turn bronze-red touched with yellow in fall. This prickly, exotic, tropical-looking native is included by Christopher Starbuck on his list of uncommon trees for specimen plantings. "The stunningly beautiful species makes a formidable barrier," writes C. Colston Burrell.[9] **Cultivation:** Low maintenance; full sun best, takes part sun; moist, humus-rich, neutral or acidic well-drained soil. Pull or transplant suckers; in drier areas restrain thickets by mowing.

Devil's walking stick (*Aralia spinosa*)

Monarch butterfly (*Danaus plexippus*)

Monarch butterfly caterpillar (*Danaus plexippus*)

Deer resistant, tolerates black walnut tree toxicity. **Anachronistic Note:** The plant's sharp, spiny stems are far above the height of deer, today's woodland browser. "Is the plant still defending against mastodons?" asks Connie Barlow.[10] **Life Span:** 55 years. **Nature Note:** Bees and butterflies, including eastern tiger swallowtail (p. 18), monarch, and hairstreaks eagerly visit for nectar and cross-pollinate the huge clusters of flowers. Fruit-eating birds, chipmunks, and other mammals relish the abundant berries. **Zones:** 4–9.

PRICKLYASH, COMMON PRICKLYASH, TOOTHACHE TREE. **Family:** Citrus, Rue (Rutaceae). **Genus:** *Zanthoxylum* (*Z. americanum*). **Height:** To 15 feet. **Spread:** 5–8 feet. **Ornamental Attributes:** The delicate yellow flowers covering the thorny twigs make the plant easy to spot in early spring. The females bear clusters of small, dark red fruits in late summer.

The jet-black seeds smell strongly like citrus. In fall, the leaves turn yellow. All parts of plant are fragrant. **Cultivation:** Full sun to part shade, well-drained soil; it often forms dense spiny thickets. Tolerates black walnut tree toxicity. **Nature Note:** Beneficial pollinators, including butterflies, native bees, and flies, visit for nectar and pollen. The plant hosts 6 species of butter-

Pricklyash (*Zanthoxylum americanum*)

Bee fly (*Bombyliidae*)

flies and moths, including spicebush swallow-tail butterflies (p. 22), skipper species, and along with wafer ash, the giant swallowtail butterfly (p. 45). Birds and mammals use it for shelter; the red-eyed vireo (p. 112) and eastern chipmunk (p. 94) eat the seeds. **Emerald Ash Borer Note:** This problem affects only true ash (*Fraxinus*) species, but not mountain ash, pricklyash, or wafer ash. **Zones:** 3–7.

ADAM'S NEEDLE. **Family:** Century-plant family (Asparagaceae). **Subfamily:** Agavaceae. **Genus:** *Yucca* (*Y. filamentosa*). **Height:** 3 feet. **Ornamental Attributes:** More typical of western deserts and grasslands, this yucca's native habitat includes midwestern dry, sandy, open woods, hills and prairies. A shrub with stiff sword-like foliage, it produces 3–4-foot spikes of showy white flowers in summer. **Cultivation:** Sun to light shade, well-drained soil. Tolerant of black walnut tree toxicity. **Nature Note:** Fragrance attracts hummingbirds, butterflies and night-flying moths and bats. **Zones:** 4–9.

Flower fly (*Syrphidae*)

Other Native Alternatives:

BOTTLEBRUSH BUCKEYE, p. 130.

See Spring Shrubs for ELDERBERRY SPP., p. 29.

See Fall Shrubs for SILVER BUFFALO-BERRY, p. 229.

See Spring Trees for HAWTHORN SPP., p. 106.

See Summer Trees for ALLEGHENY CHINKAPIN, p. 171.

Nonnative:

BEAUTYBERRY. See Fall Shrubs, p. 234.

Nonnative:

BUCKTHORN. See Summer Shrubs (Hedges), p. 140.

Adam's needle (*Yucca filamentosa*)

Japanese spirea (*Spiraea japonica* **var.** *fortunei*)

Nonnative:

BUMALD SPIREA. **Family:** Rose (Rosaceae). **Genus:** *Spiraea* (*Spiraea* × *bumalda*). **Origin:** Asia. **Ornamental Attributes:** White-pink flowers from early to late summer. **Zones:** 4–8; *JAPANESE SPIREA, JAPANESE MEADOWSWEET, FORTUNE MEADOWSWEET* (*S. japonica* var. *fortunei*). **Origin:** Japan, China. **Height/Spread:** 4–6 feet. **Ornamental Attributes:** Pink flowers from June to July; looks weedy; branches die back and need frequent pruning. **Cultivation:** Full sun; well-drained soil. Self-sows freely, needs deadheading to prevent seedlings. **Ecological Threat:** Invasive and naturalized in midwestern states. It creates dense colonies in natural areas, displacing existing native flowers and shrubs. Single plants produce hundreds of small seeds that last in the soil for many years, making restoration of native vegetation especially difficult. The shrub and its various cultivars (some have yellow foliage) entice gardeners seeking cheap ornamentals. **Zones:** 3–8.

Native Alternatives:

VIRGINIA SWEETSPIRE, VIRGINIA WILLOW. **Family:** Sweetspire (Iteaceae). **Genus:** *Itea* (*I. virginica*). **Height/Spread:** 2–5 feet. **Ornamental Attributes:** Very fragrant, white bottlebrush-like flowers open in early to midsummer at a time when few other shrubs are blooming and bloom for several weeks. Fall color from early October to early December is crimson-burgundy in full sun and a mixture of green, yellow, orange, and scarlet in partial sun to full shade. **Cultivation:** Full sun best; takes partial shade. "Though inhabiting partially shaded, wet places in nature, this plant seems equally happy in garden soils that are sunny and dry," writes Patricia Taylor.[11] "It has made its way into the horticultural trade because of its ability to thrive in upland sites and for its gorgeous flowers," writes Sally S. Weeks.[12] Most at-

Virginia sweetspire
(*Itea virginica*)

tractive when massed, it can be used as a hedge. **Note:** Extirpated or endangered in parts of the Midwest. **Nature Note:** Attracts at least as many butterflies as the invasive Chinese but-

terfly bush. Attracts pollinating insects that provide birds with food for their nestlings. Colonies of this shrub provide nesting habitat and cover for birds and other wildlife. **Zones:** 5–9.

STEEPLEBUSH, PINK SPIREA, HARD-HACK. **Family:** Rose (Rosaceae). **Genus:** *Spiraea* (*S. tomentosa*). **Height/Spread:** 2–5 feet. **Ornamental Attributes: Showy** spires of bright pink flowers bloom from July to September; gold or auburn fall foliage; exfoliating reddish-brown bark. "A spectacular native shrub," write Weeks and Weeks.[13] **Cultivation:** Full sun best; rich, moist, medium, wet soil. Woody stems often die to the ground during winter. **Nature Note:** Though steeplebush produces abundant pollen but little nectar, the nectar it produces attracts many butterflies, including the monarch butterfly (p. 124) and the endangered Karner blue butterfly (p. 128). The shrub hosts 89 species of butterflies, including the spring azure (p. 95) and summer azure (p. 128) butterflies, and moths, including the scallop shell, sharp-lined yellow, spirea leaf-tier, Columbia silkmoth, and northern apple sphinx moth. The

Steeplebush (*Spiraea tomentosa*)

Karner blue butterfly (*Lycaeides melissa samuelis*)

Summer azure butterfly (*Celastrina neglecta*)

bees, flies, and beetles that are its primary pollinators are fed to baby birds by their parents. Native field sparrows (p. 307), indigo buntings, common yellow-throats (p. 330), red-winged blackbirds (p. 55), American goldfinches (p. 145), yellow warblers (p. 89), and willow flycatchers seek it for nesting. **Zones:** 4–8; WHITE MEADOWSWEET, WHITE SPIREA (*S. alba* var. *alba*; *S. alba* var. *latifolia*). **Height/Spread:** 3–4 feet. **Ornamental Attributes:** Dense fluffy clusters/spikes of white or pale pink flowers from June to September produce nectar and pollen. Fall color is golden yellow. Seed capsules persist into winter. The flowers bloom "over an extended period of several weeks, so the show seems to go on and on," observe Weeks and Weeks.[14] **Cultivation:** Sun best; tolerates many soil conditions. Can grow in standing water. Tolerant of drought and heat. Produces flowers even if cut to ground in March. **Note:** Endangered in Kentucky and Tennessee. **Nature Note:** See STEEPLEBUSH, above. **Zones:** 3–7.

Other Native Alternatives:

CLETHRA SPP., p. 132; HYDRANGEA SPP., p. 143; NEW JERSEY TEA, p. 134; and NATIVE ALTERNATIVES TO *BUTTERFLY BUSH,* p. 129.

See Spring Shrubs for Native Honeysuckle Alternatives: AMERICAN FLY HONEYSUCKLE, p. 38; MOUNTAIN FLY HONEYSUCKLE, p. 38; TWINBERRY HONEYSUCKLE, p. 38; for Native Rhododendron Alternatives: FLAME

White meadowsweet (*Spiraea alba* var. *alba*)

AZALEA, p. 57; MOUNTAIN LAUREL, p. 58; ROSEBAY RHODODENDRON, p. 58; SWAMP AZALEA, p. 58; SWAMP ROSE, p. 61.

Also see Spring Shrubs for SNOWBELL, p. 116; SWEETSHRUB, p. 19.

See Spring Trees for FRINGE TREE, p. 105; CAROLINA SILVERBELL, p. 80.

Nonnative:

BUTTERFLY BUSH, ORANGE-EYE BUTTERFLYBUSH. Family: Figwort (Scrophulariaceae). **Genus:** *Buddleja* (*B. davidii*). **Origin:** China, Japan. **Height:** 5–15 feet. **Spread:** 6–8 feet. **Ornamental Attributes:** Ornamental only when sprays of colorful flowers are present in midsummer. **Cultivation:** Full sun; well-drained soil; mulch. Dies to the ground in winter. "Butterfly bush used to be one of my favorite summer-blooming shrubs until it started seeding itself into different garden beds," writes Penelope O'Sullivan. "I've seen *B. davidii* growing in gutters, railways, and cracks in the stonework of ancient cathedrals. In my own garden . . . Buddleia became a weed growing where I never planted it. Three years ago I removed butterfly bushes from my mixed border, but I still find seedlings in my big perennial bed."[15] **Note:** Rather than deadheading every bloom and the millions of seeds it holds, eliminate the problem by choosing beautiful native butterfly-attracting species. **Butterfly Reproduction Note:** "Not one species of butterfly in North America can use buddleias as larval host plants," writes entomologist Douglas Tallamy.[16] Widespread landscaping use of butterfly bush helped it naturalize, become invasive, and crowd out the native butterfly-attracting shrubs that serve as "host plants" on which butterflies lay their eggs. **Ecological Threat:** Naturalized and invasive in midwestern states. "In fact, *Buddleja davidii* has life history traits that make it invasive in most environments," writes Tallamy.[17] **Buddleja Cultivar/Hybrid Invasiveness Note:** *Buddleja* breeders claim cultivars and hybrids produce less than 2 percent of the seeds of traditional butterfly bushes, characterizing them as "in effect, sterile" and selling them as "noninvasive varieties," or "safe" alternatives to invasive relatives. Following independent studies, researchers find that marketing less fecund cultivars as "safe" is premature at this time.[18] If you want a pretty butterfly-attracting plant that benefits the environment, plant a native alternative. **Zones:** 5–10.

Native Alternatives:

BUTTERFLY SHRUB, SHRUBBY CINQUEFOIL, SHRUBBY POTENTILLA. Family: Rose (Rosaceae). **Genus:** *Potentilla*, *Dasiphora*, or *Pentaphylloides* (*D.* or *P. fruticosa*). **Height:** 2–4 feet. **Spread:** 8–20 feet. **Ornamental Attributes:** Masses of bright yellow flowers bloom for 2 or 3 months, from summer through fall; in fall the gray-green leaves turn yellow-brown; reddish-brown exfoliating bark. A circumpolar species

Butterfly bush (*Buddleja davidii*)

Butterfly shrub
(*Potentilla fruticosa*)

native to northern parts, this long-lived and maintenance-free plant flourishes in the Midwest. Use as focal point, groundcover, in borders, mass plantings, and foundation plantings. **Cultivation:** Easily grown in full sun, moderately fertile, medium moisture, well-drained soils; tolerates part shade and poor soils. A dioecious shrub, it has separate male and female plants. **Note:** Threatened in Iowa. **Nature Note:** Long-term bloom enables long-term butterfly viewing, including butterflies drawn to yellow flowers like the Gorgone checkerspot. *Potentilla* spp., including shrubby cinquefoil, are the sole hosts for the

Gorgone checkerspot butterfly
(*Chlosyne gorgone*)

Clayton's copper butterfly, found wherever the plants grow. Special value to native bees. Supports conservation biological control. Deer mostly ignore it. **Zones:** 2–7.

　　BOTTLEBRUSH BUCKEYE. **Family:** Soapberry (Sapindaceae). **Genus:** *Aesculus* (*A. parviflora*). **Height/Spread:** 8–12 feet. **Ornamental Attributes:** Early to midsummer blooms of spectacular feathery spires of fragrant white flowers with conspicuous red anthers; palmate green leaves turn glorious gold or yellow in fall. A dramatic shrub noted for being one of the best summer-flowering ones in shade. "A sublime shrub," writes William Cullina.[19] Its elegant curving branch structure graces the winter garden. "This shrub is suitable for even the most difficult growing situation—under the dreaded Norway maple," writes Catherine Siddall, and also for small gardens as "it grows so slowly that it is not likely to exceed its allotted space."[20] Native to the southeastern United States, but hardy in northern areas, especially when grown in the Midwest. **Cultivation:** Low maintenance. Sun, part shade best for flowers; best in moist well-drained soil; absorbs toxic pollutants like herbicides. **Nature Note:** Hosts 32 species of butterflies and moths. Attracts ruby-throated hummingbirds (p. 91), bees, and butterflies, including eastern tiger swallowtail (p. 18). Virtually pest- and disease-free. **Zones:** 4–8.

Bottlebrush buckeye (*Aesculus parviflora*)
Also see p. 266

BUTTONBUSH, HONEY-BUSH, HONEYBALLS. **Family:** Madder (Rubiaceae). **Genus:** *Cephalanthus* (*C. occidentalis*). **Height:** 5–12 feet. **Spread:** 4–8 feet. **Ornamental Attributes:** Tiny, tubular, fragrant, nectar-rich white flowers reminiscent of pincushions appear in dense, spherical, long-stalked flower heads and bloom from June to August followed by showy red ball-like fruit clusters that persist into winter. In fall, the glossy leaves turn partially red. "The striking flower balls of *Cephalanthus occidentalis*, buttonbush, are wonderful nectar sources for butterflies in midsummer," writes Douglas Tallamy, who includes the plant among his "favorites for the butterfly garden."[21] "I'm aware of no better shrub for attracting various pollinators . . . as well as occasional hummingbirds," writes Alonso Abugattas, who lists buttonbush as one of the "Top 13 Native Shrubs/Small Trees" as wildlife plants for homeowners.[22] **Cultivation:** Easily grown; full sun best. Succeeds in upland sites and is "the best native shrub for a wet, poorly drained site."[23] Perfect for a rain garden. **Confusion Note:** Do not confuse native buttonbush with **CHINESE BUTTONBUSH** (*Adina rubella*). **Nature Note:** Large showy butterflies cover

Buttonbush (*Cephalanthus occidentalis*)

the flowers of this favorite nectar source, including monarch (p. 124), eastern tiger swallowtail (p. 18), painted lady, silver-spotted skipper (p. 101), fritillaries, and important pollinators like the small insects needed throughout the season by nesting birds. The shrub hosts 19 species of Lepidoptera (butterflies/moths), including beauties such as the titan and the rare hydrangea sphinx moths and the promethean moth. A honey plant, it has special value to bees. Attracts more than 24 bird species to its nutlets, including eastern kingbird (p. 55), American robin (p. 62), and eastern towhee (p. 235). Songbirds use it for nesting; frogs use it for cover. **Zones:** 5–9.

Painted lady butterfly (*Vanessa cardui*)

CLETHRA, SWEETPEPPERBUSH, SUMMERSWEET, COASTAL SWEET-PEPPERBUSH. **Family:** Clethra (Clethraceae). **Genus:** *Clethra* (*C. alnifolia*). **Height:** 3–8 feet; sometimes taller. **Spread:** 4–6 feet. **Ornamental Attributes:** Very fragrant white or pink flower spikes resembling butterfly bush bloom for 4–6 weeks in July and August. Fall leaves are golden or yellow. The shrub masses well in conspicuous areas where its attractive foliage, fragrant summer bloom, good fall color, and tidy winter appearance can be showcased and its slender, upright habit makes it ideal for planting in narrow spaces. "Summersweet is something that no gardener whould be without. Its carefree disposition, fragrant blooms—which appear during the midsummer lull when not much else is in bloom—and glossy deep green leaves are as at home in a formal garden as they are naturalized in a swamp," writes William Cullina.[24] "Summersweet has intensely scented, creamy-white summer flowers adored by butterflies," writes C. Colston Burrell.[25] **Cultiva-**

Clethra (sweetpepperbush) (*Clethra alnifolia*)

tion: Sun to some shade; very adaptable; likes moist to wet soil; if dry, needs watering; tolerates salt and many soil conditions. Easily grown, trouble-free. Remove root suckers unless naturalized look is desired. Blooms on new wood, so if pruning needed, do so in late winter. **Nature Note:** Hosts 10 species of butterflies and moths. Attracts ruby-throated hummingbird (p. 91) and many adult butterflies, including swallowtails; has special value to bees. American robin (p. 62), American goldfinch (p. 145), warblers, and many other birds and mammals eat the fruit (brown capsules) that persist through the winter. **Zones:** 3–9.

FALSE INDIGO BUSH, INDIGO BUSH. **Family:** Pea (Fabaceae). **Genus:** *Amorpha* (*A. fruticosa*). **Height:** 3–10 feet. **Ornamental Attributes:** Large open shrub with conspicuous masses of large, unusual, fragrant, purple to blue-violet upright flowers studded with bright orange/yellow stamens from June to August; fragrant, pinnate, gray, downy leaves turn yellow in fall. Persistent pods in winter. **Cultivation:** Full sun; wet to moist soil; poor, dry sites.

False indigo bush
(*Amorpha fruticosa*)

Drought and salt tolerant. Nitrogen fixing. **Note:** "It is likely that populations of this shrub have been declining because of habitat destruction."[26] **Nature Note:** Hosts many moths, butterflies, and skippers, including marine blue (p. 43), clouded sulphur (p. 101), orange sulphur (p. 101), and southern dogface. Has special value to its primary pollinators, nectar- and pollen-seeking small to medium-sized bees. The *Andrena quintiles* bee is a specialist pollinator (*oligolege*) of all *Amorpha* species. Deer resistant. **Zones:** 4–9; LEADPLANT, PRAIRIE SHOESTRINGS, DEVIL'S SHOESTRINGS, BUFFALO BELLOWS (*A. canescens*). **Height:** 2–4 feet. **Spread:** 4–5 feet. **Ornamental Attributes:** A small, nitrogen-fixing prairie shrub with flowers May to August when few other shrubs are blooming. "In early summer, the purple and orange flower spikes on this plant gleam among its silvery gray foliage and make a powerful presence in dry, sunny gardens. Because of its shortness and neat appearance, this shrub is often planted in perennial borders, where it looks particularly smashing when paired with orange butterfly weeds (*Asclepias tuberosa*) and lavender wild petunias (*Ruellia humilis*). In such a setting it is easy to see why leadplant has been called one of the most ornamental of the prairie natives," writes Patricia A. Taylor, calling it "a star attraction."[27] Its seeds persist into the winter. **Cultivation:** Best in full sun; dry well-drained soil. Can form a dense thicket. **Name Note:** Blooms when rutting buffalo bellow. Its long, stringy, tough roots (shoestrings) caused plowing difficulties for early settlers. **Nature Note:** Attracts adult monarch butterflies (p. 124)

Southern dogface butterfly (*Zerene cesonia*)

Leadplant (*Amorpha canescens*)

and other butterflies throughout the season. Hosts Lepidoptera including the southern dog-face (p. 133), marine blue (p. 43), gray hairstreak, silver spotted skipper (p. 101), leadplant flower moth, and black-spotted prominent. Has special value to native bees. Attracts insects like grasshoppers, beetles, and leafhoppers (p. 98) that provide insectivorous birds, bird nestlings, and mammals with important food. The bee *Andrena quintiles* is a leadplant oligolege. American goldfinch (p. 145), native sparrows, tufted titmouse (p. 169), and dark-eyed junco (p. 322) eat the seeds. **Zones:** 2–9.

NEW JERSEY TEA, WILD LILAC. **Family:** Buckthorn (Rhamnaceae). **Genus:** *Ceanothus* (*C. americanus*). **Height/Spread:** 3 feet. **Ornamental Attributes:** Low-growing, compact, dense, rounded shrub. Billowing cylindrical clusters of tiny, fragrant, white flowers bloom several weeks in late spring and summer. Clusters of small black fruit in July and August. Gray-green oval leaves turn yellow in fall; bright yellow twigs stand out in winter. Fills in difficult hot, dry, sunny locations; looks good massed. **Cultivation:** Full sun best. Well-drained dry to medium soil; intolerant of wet soil. Deep-rooted prairie/savanna plant tolerates drought and heat. Tolerates black walnut tree toxicity. **Note:** One of William Cullina's top 10 native shrubs for butterfly gardens. **Nature Note:** Hosts 45 species of butterflies and moths, including the red-fronted emerald moth, spring azure butterfly (p. 95), summer azure (p. 128), dreamy duskywing, mottled duskywing, northern broken dash, Peck's skipper, and hoary edge. Nectar and the tiny insects the nectar attracts bring in pollinators like bees, beneficial parasitic wasps, hoverflies, and 13 species of butterflies, including the monarch (p. 124). Ruby-throated hummingbirds (p. 91) eat and feed the small insects to their nestlings. Songbirds use the shrubs for nesting and, along with bobwhite quail (p. 36) and wild turkey (p. 244), eat the fruits. Special value to native bees; supports conservation biological control. **Zones:** 4–8.

New Jersey tea (*Ceanothus americanus*)

Peck's skipper (*Polites peckius*)

Northern broken dash butterfly
(*Wallengrenia egeremet*)

Hoary edge butterfly (*Achalarus lyciades*)

More Native Alternatives:

CRIMSONEYED ROSEMALLOW & OTHER MALLOWS, p. 145; HYDRANGEA SPP., p. 143; STEEPLEBUSH, p. 127; VIRGINIA SWEETSPIRE, p. 126; WHITE MEADOW-SWEET, p. 128.

See Spring Shrubs for FOTHERGILLA SPP., p. 27; HONEYSUCKLE SPP., p. 38; MAPLELEAF VIBURNUM, p. 71; NINEBARK, p. 44; SPICEBUSH, p. 22; SWEET-SHRUB, p. 19.

For native herbaceous butterfly and moth host plants, see Native Herbaceous Species (Perennials) in Descending Order of Lepidoptera Productivity in Selected Bibliography and Resources at p. 395.

Nonnative:

CHASTE TREE, LILAC CHASTE TREE. **Family:** Mint (Lamiaceae). **Genus:** *Vitex* (*V. agnus-castus* var. *agnus-castus*). **Origin:** Mediterranean, Asia. **Height/Spread:** 15–20 feet. Large shrub/small tree. **Ornamental Attributes:** Panicles of bluish summer flowers. Cultivars have white or pink flowers. **Cultivation:** Full sun, partial shade. Moist to dry well-drained soil, sheltered location. May die to the ground in winter. **Zones:** 6–9.

Chaste tree (*Vitex agnus-castus* var. *agnus-castus*)

Native Alternatives:

BOTTLEBRUSH BUCKEYE, p. 130; BUTTERFLY SHRUB, p. 129; BUTTONBUSH, p. 131; CLETHRA, p. 132; CRIMSONEYED ROSEMALLOW and other mallows, p. 146; FALSE INDIGO BUSH, p. 132; HYDRANGEA SPP., p. 143; NEW JERSEY TEA, p. 134; STEEPLEBUSH, p. 127; VIRGINIA SWEETSPIRE, p. 126; WHITE MEADOWSWEET, p. 128.

See Spring Shrubs for FOTHERGILLA, p. 27; HONEYSUCKLE SPP., p. 38; MAPLE-LEAF VIBURNUM, p. 71; NINEBARK, p. 44; SWEETSHRUB, p. 19.

Nonnative:

CURRANT. Family: Currant (Grossulariaceae). **Genus:** *Ribes. ALPINE CURRANT* (*R. alpinum*). **Origin:** Europe. **Height/Spread:** 3–6 feet. **Ornamental Attributes:** Insignificant flowers in April. Scarlet berries on female plants in June/July masked by foliage. Dull yellow fall color. Ornamental appeal limited to green foliage. Often used as a hedge. **Cultivation:** Full sun to full shade, well-drained soil. Dioecious (separate male and female plants). Most commercially sold plants are cultivars (male clones) billed as resistant to rust diseases that may afflict females.[28] **Ecological Threat:** Naturalized in Michigan. **Zones:** 2–7; *EUROPEAN BLACK CURRANT* (*R. nigrum*). **Origin:** Europe, Asia. **Height/Spread:** 5–6 feet. **Ornamental Attributes:** Insignificant spring flowers. Small edible black berries. **Cultivation:** Half day sun; moist well-drained soil. Extremely susceptible to white pine blister rust. **Ecological Threat:** Naturalized in midwestern states. **Zones:** 4–7; *EUROPEAN GOOSEBERRY* (*R. uva-crispa*). Severe mildew susceptibility. **Zones:** 4–7; *CULTIVATED CURRANT, EUROPEAN RED CURRANT* (*R. rubrum*). Invasive in parts of the Midwest. **Zones:** 3–7. **Genus Legal Note:** Check with county extension offices regarding laws on planting these species.

Alpine currant (*Ribes alpinum*)

American black currant
(*Ribes americanum*)

Native Alternatives:

CURRANT. **Family:** Currant (Grossulariaceae). **Genus:** *Ribes* (includes currants and goose-berries). **Note:** Currants have no spines or thorny prickles; gooseberries have at least some. AMERICAN BLACK CURRANT, WILD BLACK CURRANT, EASTERN BLACK CURRANT. (*R. americanum*). **Height:** 2–6 feet. **Ornamental Attributes:** Prolific production of clusters of showy, green-tinted, bell-like yellow flowers in late April to May. Drooping clusters of sweet edible (high in vitamins and antioxidants) purple-black fruits in July. In fall sun, aromatic maple-shaped leaves glistening with golden glands turn crimson, yellow, gold, and deep purple; pink twigs. "When in flower, the black currant can rival exotic horticultural currants in beauty," write Weeks and Weeks.[29] **Cultivation:** Easy to grow. Sun best for flowers, berries; takes light shade; moist to moderately dry soils. Does not sucker; can form thickets desirable for habitat. Drought tolerant. **Nature Note:** Visitors include bumblebees sucking nectar and sweat bees collecting pollen. Unlike its European counterpart, USDA considers American black currant low risk for serving as a white pine blister rust host,[30] and it is recommended by the Morton Arboretum for its suitability and desirability in the Midwest; MISSOURI GOOSE-BERRY, WILD GOOSEBERRY (*R. missouriense*). **Height:** To 5 feet. **Ornamental Attributes:** Greenish-white, trumpet-shaped flowers in April to May that "are

Missouri gooseberry (*Ribes missouriense*)

very beautiful, elongated and graceful in appearance," write Weeks and Weeks.[31] Edible smooth-surfaced, transluscent summer purple berries. Round-lobed leaves change from yellow-orange to red then purple in the fall. **Cultivation:** Gooseberries are self fertile. This adaptable shrub takes more sun than most gooseberries; medium, rich, dry, poor soils. **Note:** Threatened in Ohio; AMERICAN GOOSEBERRY (*R. hirtellum*); PRICKLY GOOSE-BERRY (*R. cynosbati*). Undeterred by each juicy berry's daunting prickles, birds find them delicious. **Currant/Gooseberry Nature Note:** See CURRANT in Spring Shrubs, p. 35. **Zones:** 3–8.

DEERBERRY. **Family:** Heath (Ericaceae). **Genus:** *Vaccinium* (*V. stamineum*). **Height:** 6–16 feet. **Ornamental Attributes:** Blueberry-like nodding, greenish-white, pink-tinged, bell-shaped flowers in spring and summer. Greenish to blue-black or purple edible summer berries with whitish bloom. Foliage turns a variety of colors through the seasons. Birds and mammals eat berries. **Vaccinium Species Nature Note:** Host 294 species of butterflies and moths. By including heath family plants in addition to "rosids," a group that includes trees and shrubs like oaks, willows, beeches, maples, and elms, we help increase Lepidoptera (butterfly/moth) diversity because these plants host different insects. The slender clearwing only lays her eggs on deerberry and other plants in the heath family such as RHODODEN-DRON, AZALEA, p. 56; BLUEBERRY, p. 27; CRANBERRY, p. 28; LEATHERWOOD, p. 232; SOURWOOD, p. 186. **Zones:** 5–9.

BRAMBLE. **Family:** Rose (Rosaceae). **Genus:** *Rubus.* **Native species include:** AMERI-CAN RED RASPBERRY (*R. idaeus*); GRAYLEAF RED RASPBERRY (*R. idaeus* ssp. *strigosus*); BLACK RASPBERRY (*R. occidentalis*); COMMON BLACKBERRY, WILD BLACKBERRY (*R. allegheniensis*); DEWBERRY, NORTHERN DEWBERRY (*R. flagellaris*). **Ornamental Attributes:** Colorful berries. Orange, red, or purple fall color. Blackberry has showy white flowers in spring. **Nature Note:** Raspberries and blackberries have very high value for songbirds, game birds, and large and small mammals. More than 149 species of birds eat wild blackberry; at least 63 species of birds eat raspberries.[32] Blackberries can become aggressive and difficult to eliminate. *Rubus* plants provide shelter, cover, and nesting sites. The fruits are eaten by wood thrush (p. 175), brown thrasher (p. 219), eastern towhee (p. 235), northern cardinal (p. 61), evening grosbeak (p. 162), rose-breasted grosbeak (p. 200), eastern kingbird (p. 55), gray catbird (p. 79), scarlet tanager, Baltimore oriole (p. 167), white-crowned and white-throated sparrows (p. 108). *Rubus* hosts 163 species of butterflies and moths, including the yellow-banded sphinx moth and Henry's elfin (p. 93). The flowers attract nectar-seeking butterflies, ruby-throated hummingbirds (p. 91); have special value to native bees. Raccoons, fox squirrels, and chipmunks (p. 94) occasionally eat the fruits; rabbits and deer browse on foliage and stems. **Zones:** blackberry: 5–9; dewberry: 3–8; raspberry: 3–8.

More Native Alternatives:

NEW JERSEY TEA, p. 134.

See Spring Shrubs for more shrubs with colorful (sometimes edible) summer fruits: CHOKEBERRY SPP., p. 13; CURRANT SPP., p. 35; DOGWOOD SPP., p. 48; ELDER-BERRY SPP., p. 29; HIGHBUSH BLUEBERRY, p. 27; PURPLEFLOWERING RASP-BERRY, p. 62; ROSE SPP., p. 60; SERVICEBERRY SPP., p. 20; SPICEBUSH, p. 22; THIMBLEBERRY, p. 62.

See Fall Shrubs for AMERICAN BARBERRY, p. 233.

Nonnative:

Hedges:

BUCKTHORN. Family: Buckthorn (Rhamnaceae). **Genuses:** *Frangula* and *Rhamnus.* Origin: Eurasia; *GLOSSY BUCKTHORN, EUROPEAN BUCKTHORN, ALDER BUCKTHORN, FERNLEAF BUCKTHORN, TALLHEDGE BUCKTHORN* (*F. alnus, R. frangula*). "This weedy species' cultivar, 'Columnaris', has been widely planted for hedges in the upper Midwest."[33] **Cultivars include:** 'Ron Williams' and 'Asplenifolia'; *BUCKTHORN* (*R. arguta*). Exotic weed in Illinois; *CHINESE BUCKTHORN* (*R. utilis*). Invasive in Illinois; *COMMON BUCKTHORN, DAHURIAN BUCKTHORN* (*R. davurica*). Invasive in Illinois; *EUROPEAN BUCKTHORN, COMMON BUCKTHORN* (*R. cathartica*). **Height:** To 15 feet; *JAPANESE BUCKTHORN* (*R. japonica*). Invasive in Illinois. **Buckthorn Ornamental Attributes:** Neither attractive spring flowers nor fall color; messy berries. Used as specimens and hedges. Have thorny lower branches. Leaf out early and drop leaves late. **Cultivation:** These weedy species are not particular about where they grow. Buckthorn berries have a high diuretic content and act as laxatives upon birds, ensuring their wide and efficient spread of the invasive seeds. **Buckthorn Ecological Threat:** Invasive or naturalized throughout the Midwest; they shade out entire native plant communities and destroy dependent wildlife. Buckthorns are **allelopathic: they** produce chemical compounds inhibiting the growth of other vegetation. Branch structure causes nesting birds to experience higher nest predation than in comparable native shrubs. This adverse environmental consequence (in addition to their invasiveness) outweighs ornamental or privacy benefits.[34] The Morton Arboretum designates common buckthorn "Not recommended."[35] **Cultivar Note:** Independent studies demonstrate that cultivars of invasive nonnative buckthorns remain invasive and are not "safe."[36] Fortunately, many bird-attracting berry-producing native alternatives exist. **Zones:** 3–9.

Common buckthorn
(*Frangula cathartica*)

Other Popular Nonnative Shrub Hedge Choices:

ROSE OF SHARON, p. 146.
See Spring Shrubs for *FORSYTHIA,* p. 34; *HONEYSUCKLE SPP. (BUSH HONEY-SUCKLE, AMUR HONEYSUCKLE),* p. 37; *LILAC,* p. 42; *PRIVET SPP.,* p. 47.
See Fall Shrubs for *BARBERRY SPP.,* p. 231; *BURNING BUSH,* p. 239; *COTONEAS-TER SPP.,* p. 246.
See Winter Shrubs for *BOXWOOD SPP.,* p. 308.

Native Alternatives:

CAROLINA BUCKTHORN, CAROLINA FALSE BUCKTHORN, INDIAN CHERRY.
Family: Buckthorn (Rhamnaceae). **Genus:** *Frangula* (*F. caroliniana*). **Height:** 12–25 feet. Can become tree-like. **Spread:** 10–15 feet. **Ornamental Attributes:** Insignificant yellow spring flowers, yellow to orange fall color lasts into the winter. Airy and tiered in light shade, somewhat like flowering dogwoods; a good specimen. "Glossy, deep green oval, quilted leaves accented by red berries that ripen to black make this underutilized shrub a perfect substitute for tall hedge buckthorn. The two are so similar that they are often confused," writes C. Colston Burrell.[37] **Cultivation:** Best with 3–4 hours of sun; well-drained soil. Native to southern regions of the Midwest. **Zones:** 5–9; LANCELEAF BUCKTHORN. **Genus:** *Rhamnus* (*R. lanceolata* subsp. *glabrata*; *R. lanceolata* subsp. *lanceolata*). **Height:** 4–12 feet. Can be used as a part of conservation biological control. **Zones:** Hardy to Zone 4; ALDERLEAF BUCKTHORN, AMERICAN ALDER BUCKTHORN (*R. alnifolia*). **Height:** 3 feet. **Cultivation:** Part shade, shade; moist, wet soil. **Note:** Native to northern Midwest. Endangered in Illinois. **Nature Note:** Native buckthorns host 11 species of butterflies and moths, including the American snout butterfly. Native buckthorns are excellent cover for birds and small mammals and provide birds with safe nesting sites; the fruits attract and support many birds and other wildlife. A native buckthorn is "safe to plant without fear of it becoming another biological pest," write Sternberg and Wilson.[38] **Zones:** Hardy to Zone 2.

Carolina buckthorn (*Frangula caroliniana*)

American snout butterfly
(*Libytheana carinenta*)

More Hedge and Buckthorn Native Alternatives:

AMERICAN BLACK CURRANT, p. 138; CLETHRA, p. 132; DEVIL'S WALKING STICK, p. 123; HYDRANGEA SPP., p. 143; MALLOW SPP., p. 146; NEW JERSEY TEA, p. 134; PRICKLYASH, p. 124; ST. JOHN'S WORT, p. 145; VIRGINIA SWEETSPIRE, p. 126.

See Spring Shrubs for AMERICAN CRANBERRYBUSH and other native VIBURNUMS, p. 69; AMERICAN SMOKETREE, p. 65; CHOKEBERRY SPP., p. 13; DOGWOOD SPP., including SILKY DOGWOOD, p. 50; ELDERBERRY SPP., p. 29; FOTHERGILLA SPP., p. 27; GOLDEN CURRANT, p. 35; MOUNTAIN LAUREL, p. 58; NINEBARK, p. 44; ROSE SPP., p. 60; SERVICEBERRY SPP., p. 20; SPICEBUSH, p. 22.

See Fall Shrubs for AMERICAN BARBERRY, p. 233; BAYBERRY, p. 232; POSSUMHAW HOLLY, p. 237; SUMAC SPP., p. 242.

See Winter Shrubs for AMERICAN YEW, p. 314; DWARF CHINKAPIN OAK, p. 311; INKBERRY, p. 308; REDOSIER DOGWOOD, p. 310.

See Spring Trees for AMERICAN HAZELNUT, p. 102; CHERRY SPP., p. 82; FRINGE TREE, p. 105; HAWTHORN SPP., p. 106; REDBUD, p. 92; SERVICEBERRY SPP., p. 77.

See Fall Trees for OSAGE ORANGE, p. 259.

See Winter Trees for ALDER SPP., p. 316; AMERICAN ARBORVITAE, p. 319; EASTERN WHITE PINE, p. 328; HEMLOCK, p. 325; RED CEDAR, p. 323; VIRGINIA PINE, p. 329.

Note: Instead of nonnative buckthorn, plant any native shrub or tree.

Nonnative:

HYDRANGEA. **Family:** Hydrangea (Hydrangeaceae). **Genus:** *Hydrangea; FRENCH HYDRANGEA, BIGLEAF HYDRANGEA* (*H. macrophylla*). **Origin:** China, Japan. **Height/Spread:** 3–4 feet. **Ornamental Attributes:** Big heavy balls of sterile flowers that hold neither pollen nor nectar. **Lacecaps:** discs of fertile flowers ringed by showy, sterile flowers. There are numerous cultivars, subspecies, and varieties in various shapes and colors. **Cultivation:** Part sun/part shade; moist well-drained soil. **Zones:** 6–9; *PANICLED HYDRANGEA, TREE HYDRANGEA* (*H. paniculata*). **Origin:** Japan. **Height/Spread:** 10–15 feet. **Ornamental Attributes:** Writing in 1905 about flowering shrubs in England, G. Clarke Nuttall described this "Oriental Hydrangea" as "too massive and a shade too pretentious for some tastes."[39] Messy suckering habit; tidy folks prefer to train them as small trees. Small inner flowers surrounded by white outer sterile flowers turn purplish-pink. To avoid problems, use the look-alike native wild hydrangea (see below). **Cultivation:** Full sun. Well-drained, constantly moist soil. **Zones:** 4–7. Cultivars include *PEE-GEE HYDRANGEA, SNOWBALL BUSH* (*H. paniculata* 'Grandiflora'). **Zones:** 6–9.

Hydrangea arborescens 'Annabelle'

Native Alternatives:

HYDRANGEA. Family: Hydrangea (Hydrangeaceae). **Genus:** *Hydrangea.* **Note:** "For far too long, native hydrangeas have taken a garden back seat to the ubiquitous blue hydrangeas from Asia. The [natives] are superb, good-looking, trouble-free plants that you will most certainly want to incorporate in your landscape once you have read their descriptions," writes Patricia A. Taylor;[40] **ASHY HYDRANGEA, AMERICAN HYDRANGEA** (*H. cinerea*). **Height/ Spread:** 3–5 feet. **Ornamental Attributes:** From May to early summer, its showy white infertile flowers surround tiny fertile flowers, creating large fragrant clusters of "lacecap" flowers. The infertile flowers persist into fall; the flower-like seed heads persist through winter. **Name Note:** Refers to the gray undersides of the leaves. **Cultivation:** Full to part sun, tolerates deep shade; well-drained soil. **Zones:** 4–9; **WILD HYDRANGEA, SMOOTH HYDRANGEA** (*H. arborescens*). **Height/Spread:** 3–6 feet. **Ornamental Attributes:** Fragrant, large, showy sterile flowers surround tiny fertile flowers, creating a "lacecap" effect that persists from June to September. Persistent capsules of seeds add winter interest to the landscape. "This undemanding shrub is covered with white flowers during the height of summer heat."[41] **Cultivation:** Low maintenance; thrives in areas sunny for about half the day. Tolerates full sun with consistent moisture. Best in moist well-drained soil. Does well in soggy or marshy soil; tolerates poor drainage. Foliage tends to decline in dry conditions. Intolerant of drought, tolerant of black walnut tree toxicity. May die to the ground in harsh winters. Blooms on new wood. Naturally found in high-quality natural areas. "Even if your garden is shady and you live where winters are cold, you can still grow this hydrangea with good results," writes Penelope O'Sullivan, noting its "long-lasting floral interest . . .

Ashy hydrangea (*Hydrangea cinerea*)
Also see p. 336

when little else is blooming" and how they "light up shady borders, woodland gardens, and perennial gardens, blending in discreetly when not in bloom."[42] **Zones:** 4–9. **Cultivar/Nativar Note:** The sterile flowers adorning native hydrangea flowers advertise the fertile flowers and attract pollinators. Nativars with no fertile flowers attract no pollinators, so the sterile flowers have no role. The nativar Annabelle hydrangea (*H. arborescens* 'Annabelle'), which "barely resembles our native,"[43] produces clusters of sterile green flowers that turn briefly white and are larger than the straight or true species. "'Annabelle' borders playfully on the absurd, with heads that enlarge to the size of basketballs. . . . Of course this enormous weight on top of rather thin stems means the plants have a tendency to bend over after a heavy rain," writes William Cullina.[44] Many cultivars of wild hydrangea have only sterile flowers, "which don't provide any nectar or pollen to flower-visiting insects. From an ecological perspective, this makes them less desirable," writes John Hilty.[45] For beauty, butterflies and

Oakleaf hydrangea
(*Hydrangea quercifolia*)
Also see pp. 269, 336

birds choose the true native species; OAKLEAF HYDRANGEA (*H. quercifolia*). **Height/Spread:** 6–8 feet. **Ornamental Attributes:** Long cones of flowers remain white for weeks in summer before darkening to pink-rose, crimson, or purple. Oak-leaf-like leaves turn shades of red in fall. Exfoliating bark. In 1776, naturalist William Bartram described it as "a very singular and beautiful shrub."[46] The shrub is a good alternative to nonnative burning bush. **Cultivation:** Sun, light shade, moist to moderately dry soil. **Zones:** 5–9. **Native Hydrangea Nature Note:** Butterflies, native bees, beneficial wasps, dance flies, tumbling flower beetles, and long-horned beetles visit native hydrangeas for nectar and pollen and pollinate the fertile flowers. Nesting birds collect many of these insects to feed their babies. Native hydrangeas host 5 species of moths and butterflies, including hydrangea sphinx and hydrangea leaf-tier moths. Songbirds use the shrubs for cover and nesting, and feed their offspring the caterpillars.

Tumbling flower beetle (*Tomoxia* spp.)

More Native Alternatives:

BUTTONBUSH, p. 131; NEW JERSEY TEA, p. 134.

See Spring Shrubs for CHOKEBERRY SPP., p. 13; FOTHERGILLA SPP., p. 27; HONEYSUCKLE SPP., p. 38; NINEBARK, p. 44; RHODODENDRON, AZALEA SPP., p. 56; SCENTLESS MOCK ORANGE, p. 46; SWEETSHRUB, p. 19.

See Spring Trees for FRINGE TREE, p. 105; SNOWBELL, p. 116.

See Summer Trees for STEWARTIA, p. 215.

Nonnative:

PURPLELEAF CHERRY. See Spring Shrubs, p. 215.

Nonnative:

ROSE. See Spring Shrubs, p. 59.

Native Alternatives:

ST. JOHN'S WORT, SHRUBBY ST. JOHN'S WORT. Family: St. John's wort (Hypericaceae). **Genus:** *Hypericum* (*H. prolificum*). **Height/Spread:** 2–5 feet. **Ornamental Attributes:** Small shrub with showy yellow flowers that bloom during July and August. Conspicuous seed capsules, exfoliating bark, and colorful late fall foliage. "From a landscape perspective, St. John's wort puts on a show of exploding yellow fireworks (its flowers) when nearly all the other native shrubs have finished flowering. Their extended flowering period of a month or longer adds to their appeal," write Weeks and Weeks.[47] **Cultivation:** Sun, part sun. Moist to dry, well-drained soils. Adaptable, easily grown. Tolerates black walnut tree toxicity. **Zones:** 3–8; **KALM'S ST. JOHN'S WORT** (*H. kalmianum*). **Height/Spread:** 2–3 feet. **Ornamental Attributes:** Neat, mounded shrub with bright yellow flowers for about six weeks in June to July; teardrop-shaped fruit turns dark red and persists winter to spring. **Cultivation:** Sun; prefers moist sites; tolerates some dryness, alkaline soil, and salt. **Note:** Threatened in Ohio, endangered in Illinois. **Zones:** 4–7; **ST. ANDREW'S CROSS** (*H. hypericoides*). **Height:** 6 inches to 3 feet. Slowly spreads low to the ground. **Zone:** 5–9. **Hypericum Nature Note:** Adult butterflies visiting for nectar face disappointment because *Hypericum* species offer only pollen, but in abundance. This is fine with bumblebees, which collect the pollen for their larvae, along with large numbers of small bees and beneficial flies, simultaneously cross-pollinating the flowers. Mammalian herbivores avoid the toxic foliage. Host 20 species of butterflies and moths, including the gray hairstreak butterfly. Goldfinch, purple finch, field sparrow (p. 307), fox sparrow (p. 322), chipping sparrow (p. 51), song sparrow (p. 307), dark-eyed junco (p. 322), and other native sparrows and finches love the seeds and use the plant for cover. **St. John's Wort Confusion Note:** Do not confuse native species with the nonnative invasive common St. Johnswort (*Hypericum perforatum*) sold as an antidepressant.

Shrubby St. John's wort
(*Hypericum prolificum*)
Also see p. 339

Purple finch (*Haemorhous purpureus*)

American goldfinch (*Spinus tristis*)

Rose of Sharon (*Hibiscus syriacus*)

More Native Alternatives:

See Spring Shrubs for ROSE SPP., p. 60; PUR-
PLEFLOWERING RASPBERRY, p. 62.
See Fall Shrubs for SILVERBERRY, p. 229.

Nonnative:

*ROSE OF SHARON, ALTHAEA, HARDY
HIBISCUS.* **Family:** Mallow (Malvaceae). **Genus:** *Hibisicus* (*H. syriacus*). **Origin:** India, China.
Height: 8–12 feet. **Spread:** 6–10 feet. **Ornamental
Attributes:** Unpleasant-smelling pink, white, or
blue flowers in late summer. Anxious homeowners fear its death annually because it doesn't leaf
out until about June. When it does come to life,
its buds and full blooms can inexplicably fall off.
Cultivation: Full to part sun, medium soil. Top-
heaviness and legginess can require tying or
pruning. Particularly attractive to Japanese beetles.
The shrub self-sows aggressively and becomes invasive in average garden soils and natural environments. When the unattractive seeds "ripen and
disperse, they can be annoying, creating seedlings
everywhere; self-sowing cultivars do not come
true."[48] **Ecological Threat:** Naturalized in midwestern states. **Zones:** 5–9.

Native Alternatives:

MALLOW, CRIMSONEYED ROSEMALLOW, ROSE MALLOW, HARDY HIBIS-
CUS. **Family:** Mallow (Malvaceae). **Genus:** *Hibiscus* (*H. moscheutos*). **Height/Spread:** 3–5
feet. **Ornamental Attributes:** Large, often dinner-plate-size, red, pink, or white long-blooming flowers with brilliant red eyes and yellow stamens bloom from July to September. This
subshrub has large, heart-shaped, gray-green leaves. "Crimson-eyed rose mallow looks similar to the non-native Rose of Sharon, making it a great native alternative," writes Emily

Crimsoneyed rose mallow
(*Hibiscis moscheutos*)

DeBolt.[49] **Cultivation:** Sun; wet, moist,
and medium soils. Clumps start growing
late in the season. Good seasonal hedge
or specimen. **Zones:** 4–9; HALBERD-
LEAVED MALLOW (*H. laevis*). **Height:**
4–6 feet. **Spread:** 2–3 feet. **Ornamental
Attributes:** Large pink flowers in August
to September. **Cultivation:** Full sun, wet
soil. **Zones:** 4–9; ROSEMALLOW (*H.
lasiocarpos*). **Height:** 3–7 feet. **Spread:** 2–3
feet. **Ornamental Attributes:** Large white
or pink flowers in July to October. **Cultivation:** Full sun, medium to wet soil.
Zones: 5–9. **Mallow Nature Note:** Native
hibiscus flowers attract ruby-throated

Mallow hedge (*Hibiscus*)

hummingbirds (p. 91), bees, and butterflies; the plants host butterflies, including gray hair-streak, cloudless sulphur, marine blue (p. 43), and coppers. Bobwhite quail (p. 36), blue-winged teals, pintails, and wood ducks (p. 162) eat the seeds. The plants provide nesting sites for red-winged blackbirds (p. 55).

FRANKLIN TREE, FRANKLINIA. **Family:** Tea (Theaceae). **Genus:** *Franklinia* (*F. alatamaha*). **Height:** 10–20 feet. **Spread:** 6–15 feet. **Ornamental Attributes:** Large, showy, fragrant, white camellia-like flowers bloom late July to September. Glossy dark green leaves turn red to orange and purple in fall. "This beautiful plant dispels the notion that August gardens are tired, worn-out affairs," writes Patricia A. Taylor.[50] Franklin tree is a good alternative to the nonnative Bradford pear and burning bush. Included by Christopher Starbuck on his list of uncommon trees suited for specimen planting. **Cultivation:** Sun to shade; well-drained, preferably acid soil. **Historical Note:** "History buffs and plant collectors love this small flowering tree or shrub which botanist John Bartram found in southeastern Georgia in 1765 and named for his buddy Benjamin Franklin," writes Penelope O'Sullivan."[51] Extinct in the wild since 1803. "Some of the best specimens of this species occur north of its native range."[52] **Zones:** 5–8.

More Native Alternatives:

CLETHRA, p. 132.

See Spring Shrubs for AMERICAN FLY HONEYSUCKLE & NORTHERN BUSH HONEYSUCKLE, p. 38; ELDERBERRY SPP., p. 29; NINEBARK, p. 44; SPICEBUSH, p. 22.

See Fall Shrubs for AMERICAN BEAUTYBERRY, p. 235.

See Summer Trees for STEWARTIA, p. 215.

Note: For an alternative to the invasive, introduced rose of Sharon, choose any native midwestern shrub.

Symplocos spp.

Nonnative:

SAPPHIRE-BERRY. **Family:** Sweetleaf (Symplocaceae). **Genus:** *Symplocos* (*S. paniculata*). **Origin:** Asia. **Height/Spread:** 15 feet; can be a small tree. **Ornamental Attributes:** White flowers in spring; blue berries in late summer to early fall. **Cultivation:** Full sun to part shade, well-drained soil. Self-sows, creating seedlings that need removal. **Ecological Threat:** Naturalized in midwestern states. **Zones:** 4–8.

Native Alternatives:

See Spring Shrubs for BLUEBERRY. SPP., p. 27; BLUE-FRUITED DOGWOOD, p. 50; FRINGE TREE, p. 105; MOUNTAIN FLY HONEYSUCKLE, p. 38; ROUNDLEAF DOGWOOD, p. 50; SILKY DOGWOOD, p. 50, SWAMP DOGWOOD, p. 50.
See Fall Shrubs for AMERICAN BEAUTYBERRY, p. 235.

Nonnative:

SEVEN-SON FLOWER. **Family:** Honeysuckle (Caprifoliaceae). **Genus:** *Heptacodium* (*H. miconioides*). **Origin:** China. **Height:** 15–20 feet. **Spread:** 8–10 feet. **Ornamental Attributes:** White flowers in late summer to early fall. Small, purplish-red fruits. Can train as single-trunk tree. **Cultivation:** Full sun, medium to moist well-drained soil. Like ginkgo, believed to be extinct in the wild in China. **Zones:** 5–9.

Seven-son flower
(*Heptacodium miconioides*)

Native Alternatives:

CAROLINA BUCKTHORN, p. 141; FRANKLIN TREE, p. 147.
See Fall Trees for AMERICAN MOUNTAIN ASH, p. 255; MOUNTAIN MAPLE, p. 252; and native alternatives to *AMUR MAPLE,* p. 251.

Nonnative:

SHRUBBY LESPEDEZA, BUSH CLOVER. **Family:** Pea (Fabaceae, Leguminosae). **Genus:** *Lespedeza* (*L. bicolor*). **Origin:** China, Japan. **Height/Spread:** 5–10 feet. **Ornamental Attributes:** Rose-purple flowers in August to September. **Cultivation:** Full sun, part shade, dry to medium soil. **Ecological Threat:** Invasive in midwestern states. **Zones:** 4–8.

Native Alternatives:

ASHY HYDRANGEA, p. 143; BUTTONBUSH, p. 131; CLETHRA, p. 132; FALSE INDIGO BUSH, p. 132; FRANKLIN TREE, p. 147; LEADPLANT, p. 133; NEW JERSEY TEA, p. 134; OAKLEAF HYDRANGEA, p. 144; ST. JOHN'S WORT, p. 145; VIRGINIA SWEETSPIRE, p. 126; WHITE MEADOWSWEET, p. 128.

Nonnative:

TAMARISK, SALT CEDAR. **Family:** Tamarix (Tamaricaceae). **Genus:** *Tamarix* (*T. chinensis, T. gallica, T. parviflora, T. ramosissima*). **Origin:** Eurasia. **Height/Spread:** 10–15 feet. **Ornamental Attributes:** Thicket-producing shrubs, small trees; fine-textured, willow-like foliage with feathery pink or white flowers in June to August. **Cultivation:** Full sun, medium to dry

soil; in gardens grows best in consistently moist soil; naturalizes. **Ecological Threat:** Fire-adapted species with long taproots that intercept deep water tables and interfere with natural aquatic systems. Once considered a "western state" problem,[53] several species are now widely naturalized. Small flower tamarisk (*T. parviflora*) is naturalized in some midwestern states and invasive in Indiana. **Zones:** 3–8.

Native Alternatives:

BOTTLEBRUSH BUCKEYE, p. 130; BUTTONBUSH, p. 131; CLETHRA, p. 132; FALSE INDIGO BUSH, p. 132; STEEPLEBUSH, p. 127; VIRGINIA SWEETSPIRE, p. 126; WHITE MEADOWSWEET, p. 128.

See Spring Shrubs for PEACH-LEAVED WILLOW, p. 118; OZARK WITCH HAZEL, p. 75; PRAIRIE WILLOW, p. 53; PUSSY WILLOW, p. 53; SILKY WILLOW, p. 53.

See Spring Trees for FRINGE TREE, p. 105.

Nonnative:

WILLOW—See *PUSSY WILLOW* in Spring Shrubs, p. 52.

Wineberry (*Rubus phoenicolasius*)

Nonnative:

WINEBERRY, JAPANESE WINEBERRY, WINE RASPBERRY. Family: Rose (Rosaceae). **Genus:** *Rubus* (*R. phoenicolasius*). **Origin:** Japan, Korea, China. **Height:** Grows to 9 feet. **Ornamental Attributes:** Spiny stems/canes, bright red fruit in June to July. **Cultivation:** Sun, dappled shade; moist conditions. Forms large, dense, impenetrable thickets. **Ecological Threat:** Invasive in midwestern states. **Zones:** 6–8; **HIMALAYAN BLACKBERRY** (*R. ulmifolius*, syn. *R. discolor*; *R. bifrons*, syn. *R. armeniacus*). **Origin:** Asia. **Ecological Threat:** Naturalized in midwestern states. **Zones:** 6–9.

Native Alternatives:

AMERICAN BLACK CURRANT, p. 138; BRAMBLE, p. 139; GOOSEBERRY, p. 138; DEVIL'S WALKING STICK, p. 123; PRICKLYASH, p. 124.

See Spring Shrubs for ELDERBERRY SPP., p. 29; DOGWOOD SPP., p. 48: GOLDEN CURRANT, p. 35; HIGHBUSH BLUEBERRY, p. 27; HUCKLEBERRY, p. 28; NATIVE HONEYSUCKLE ALTERNATIVES, p. 38; PURPLEFLOWERING RASPBERRY, p. 62; THIMBLEBERRY, p. 62; VIBURNUM SPP., p. 69.

See Winter Shrubs for REDOSIER DOGWOOD, p. 310.

Nonnative:

Vines, Groundcovers:

WINTERCREEPER, CLIMBING EUONYMUS, PARA-SITIC IVY. **Family:** Bittersweet (Celastraceae). **Genus:** *Euonymus* (*E. fortunei*). **Origin:** China, Korea, Japan. **Height:** 3–70 feet. **Ornamental Attributes:** Sold as groundcover; becomes a shrub, thicket, or vine that can climb 70 feet. Woody, dense, dark green broadleaf evergreen. **Cultivation:** Full sun to dense shade, most soils; spreads by seed, runners, and parasitic suckers; by inserting their roots into trees, they eventually kill them. **Authors' Note:** A native hawthorn tree in our yard suffered this fate. Requires pruning; is high-maintenance and difficult to eradicate. **Ecological Threat:** Invasive in midwestern states. Appears many miles from the nearest planting because birds eat its fruits and disperse them. "Its ability to gradually invade woodlands is rather shocking. It has been overly planted as an ornamental. . . . Even though it is a menace to our natural environment, it is available in practically every nursery, greenhouse and garden shop in the Midwest," write Weeks and Weeks.[54] "Instead of winter creeper, try native ground cover, shrubs, and vines," writes Penelope O'Sullivan.[55] **Cultivar Note:** "There are at least 50 cultivars,"[56] including *'EMERALD'N GOLD'* and *'GAIETY'.* Cultivars of wintercreeper are also invasive.[57] **Zones:** 4–9.

More Nonnative Vine and Groundcover Species:

ENGLISH IVY. **Family:** Ginseng (Araliaceae). **Genus:** *Hedera* (*H. helix*). **Origin:** Europe. **Height/Spread:** 50–100 feet. **Ornamental Attributes:** Groundcover or climbing vine. **Cultivation:** Sun, shade, range of soils. Birds disperse seeds; roots where stems touch the ground. **Ecological Threat:** Invasive in natural areas in 18 states, including the Midwest. Aggressively smothers, shades out, and kills native ground vegetation and trees, which it clings to by aerial rootlets. **Zones:** 4–9.

Wintercreeper (*Euonymus fortunei*)

    PORCELAINBERRY VINE, AMUR PEPPERVINE. **Family:** Grape (Vitaceae). **Genus:** *Ampelopsis* (*A. brevipedunculata*). **Origin:** China, Korea, Japan. **Height:** Can grow 15 feet in a single growing season, eventually reaching 25 feet. **Ornamental Attributes:** Woody, perennial vine has beautifully colored fruits that look like the native HEARTLEAF PEPPER-VINE (p. 153). **Note:** Invasive in midwestern states. Covers and shades out native shrubs and young trees. **Cultivar Note:** Widely sold along with its invasive cultivars, including *A. brevipedunculata* 'Elegans'. **Zones:** 5–8.

    FIVE LEAF AKEBIA, CHOCOLATE VINE. **Family:** Lardizabalaceae. **Genus:** *Akebia* (*A. quinata*). **Origin:** Asia. **Height/Spread:** 20–40 feet. **Ornamental Attributes:** Vine with brown-purple flowers. **Cultivation:** Sun, part shade, medium soil. **Ecological Threat:** Invasive in midwestern states; outlawed in Chicago. **Zones:** 4–8.

Climbing hydrangea
(*Hydrangea anomala*
subsp. *petiolaris*)

Native Alternatives:

CLIMBING HYDRANGEA, DECUMARIA, WOODVAMP. **Family:** Hydrangea (Hydrangeaceae). **Genus:** *Decumaria* (*D. barbara*). **Height:** To 30 feet. **Ornamental Attributes:** Fragrant, ethereal, pale white flowers in late spring, early summer. Glossy, dark green foliage turns yellow in fall. **Cultivation:** Sun, light shade; moist, rich, well-drained soil; tolerates seasonal flooding, intolerant of drought. Blooms on new wood and only when climbing. A southeastern native, it takes cold. **Zones:** (5) 6–9. **Confusion Note:** Do not confuse the native with the lookalike nonnative *CLIMBING HYDRANGEA* (*H. anomala* subsp. *petiolaris*).

GRAPE. **Family:** Grape (Vitaceae). **Genus:** *Vitas;* RIVERBANK GRAPE (*V. riparia*). **Height:** 35 feet or more. **Ornamental Attributes:** Attractive vine with beautiful fruit. **Cultivation:** Full sun to light shade, moist to slightly dry soil. In small properties, needs control. Tolerates black walnut tree toxicity. Native *Vitas* species include SUMMER GRAPE (*V. aestivalis*); FOX GRAPE (*V. labrusca*); FROST GRAPE (*V. vulpina*); and GRAYBARK GRAPE, WINTER GRAPE (*V. cinerea*). **Zones:** 5–9.

More Grape Family Native Alternatives:

HEARTLEAF PEPPERVINE, RACCOON GRAPE, AMERICAN AMPELOPSIS, FALSE-GRAPE. **Genus:** *Ampelopsis* (*A. cordata*). **Ornamental Attributes:** Clusters of round fruits in September and October with colors transitioning from green to chartreuse to lavender to porcelain blue, often with all colors present on the same vine. **Cultivation:** Full sun,

Virginia creeper
(*Parthenocissus
quinquefolia*)

part shade; moist well-drained soil; adapts to poor and dry soils, heat, and drought. **Zones:** 4–9; VIRGINIA CREEPER, WOODVINE. **Genus:** *Parthenocissus* (*P. quinquefolia*). **Height:** Vine or groundcover. **Ornamental Attributes:** Pretty leaves; brilliant red or maroon fall color; red stalks hold showy indigo-blue berries that persist into winter. "Virginia creeper will enable the majestic Pandora sphinx [p. 155] to reproduce (by contrast, English ivy, the vine of choice in suburbia, hosts nothing)," writes Douglas Tallamy.[58] Northern cardinal (p. 61), wood thrush (p. 175), and many other birds rely on its high-fat fruit in the winter. **Cultivation:** Sun best for bright color. Good groundcover in shade. Moist, medium, or dry soil. Tolerates black walnut tree toxicity and a wide range of soil and environmental conditions. **Zones:** 3–9; WOODBINE, HIEDRA CREEPER, THICKET CREEPER (*P. vitacea*). **Ornamental Attributes:** Vine produces blue-black fruit. **Cultivation:** Sun, part shade; dry, moist, medium soil. **Zones:** 4–9. **Grape Family Nature Note:** Native grape family fruits provide valuable food and cover for many insects, birds, and small and large animals. Bumblebees, small bees, and flower flies primarily seeking pollen visit the flowers. Grape family species host 79 species of butterflies and moths, including Pandora sphinx (p. 155), white-lined sphinx or hawk moth (p. 108), eight-spotted forester, and Abbott's sphinx moth, which mimics a bumblebee by buzzing while feeding. Also hosted are the grape leaffolder moth, whose larvae hide in the folded leaves but become active when disturbed; silver-spotted skipper; and grape vine epimenis moth. The fruits are favorites of at least 52 species of birds, including eastern bluebird (p. 61), northern cardinal (p. 61), gray catbird (p. 79), American crow (p. 244), purple finch (p. 145), northern flicker (p. 99), common grackle, blue jay (p. 79), eastern kingbird (p. 55), Baltimore oriole (p. 167), American robin (p. 62), yellow-bellied sapsucker (p. 79), scarlet tanager, brown thrasher (p. 219), wood thrush (p. 175), tufted titmouse (p. 169), eastern towhee (p. 235), cedar waxwing (p. 36), pileated woodpecker, northern mockingbird (p. 256), red-bellied woodpecker (p. 55), red-headed woodpecker (p. 212), red- (p. 322) and white-breasted nuthatches (p. 30), warbling vireo, bobwhite quail (p. 36), and wild turkey (p. 244).

HONEYSUCKLE. **Family:** Honeysuckle (Caprifoliaceae). **Genus:** *Lonicera;* CORAL HONEYSUCKLE, TRUMPET HONEYSUCKLE (*L. sempervirens*). **Ornamental Attributes:** Well-behaved twining vine or groundcover supports multitudes of spring-to-fall showy tubular flowers, red outside, yellow inside, followed by red to black berries. Upper leaves are united. **Cultivation:** Sun, various soils. Prefers rich well-drained soil. Tolerates black walnut toxicity. **Zones:** 4–9; LIMBER HONEYSUCKLE, WILD HONEYSUCKLE, RED HONEYSUCKLE (*L. dioica*). **Height:** 13 feet. **Ornamental Attributes:** Vine with deep tubular red flowers followed by orange-red berries. **Note:** Endangered in Illinois; YELLOW HONEYSUCKLE (*L. flava*). **Height/Spread:** 4–10 feet. **Ornamental Attributes:** Small shrub or vine; showy, fragrant orange-yellow flowers in April to July; orange-red berries. **Cultivation:** Low maintenance, easily grown. Needs half day of sun, average well-drained soil. Does best with supportive structure. **Note:** Endangered, presumed extirpated, or imperiled in parts of the Midwest. **Confusion Note:** Do not confuse native honeysuckles with the nonnative invasive Japanese honeysuckle (*Lonicera japonica*) or the nonnative invasive hybrid vine or shrub, Lonicera × heckrottii 'Gold Flame' [× americana × sempervirens]. **Zones:** 5–8. **Native Honeysuckle Nature Note:** Host 37 species of Lepidoptera (butterflies/moths), including the spring azure (p. 95) and snowberry clearwing moth. Tubular flowers attract ruby-throated

hummingbirds (p. 91) and butterflies. Purple finch (p. 145), goldfinch (p. 145), hermit thrush, bobwhite quail (p. 36), and American robin (p. 62) eat the fruits. During migration, the Baltimore oriole (p. 167) eats the flowers to access the nectar. Used as vines, honeysuckles can climb a trellis, tree snag, or other support.

TRUMPET CREEPER, TRUMPET VINE. **Family:** Trumpet creeper (Bignoniaceae). **Genus:** *Campsis* (*C. radicans*). **Ornamental Attributes:** Vine produces clusters of large red trumpet-shaped flowers; pinnate leaves. **Cultivation:** Easily grown; full sun, most soils; aggressive; develops an impressive trunk. **Nature Note:** Attracts hummingbirds (p. 91), butterflies. Hosts 7 species of butterflies and moths, including silver-spotted skipper (p. 101), little grapevine epimenis, and Pandora sphinx moth. Woodpeckers (pp. 55, 212) and chipmunks (p. 94) eat the fruits. **Zones:** 4–9.

Trumpet vine (*Campsis radicans*)

Pandora sphinx moth (*Eumorpha pandorus*)

Dutchman's pipe
(*Aristolochia tomentosa*)

DUTCHMAN'S PIPE. **Family:** Birthwort (Aristolochiaceae). **Genus:** *Aristolochia* (*A. tomentosa*). **Ornamental Attributes:** Pretty leaves and flowers. **Cultivation:** Full sun or part shade; medium wet or moist soil; intolerant of dry soils. Provide a stout support to climb on. **Nature Note:** Host plant for the pipevine swallowtail butterfly. **Zones:** 5–8.

See Spring Shrubs for **AMERICAN WISTERIA**, p. 43.

Pipevine swallowtail butterfly
(*Battus philenor*)

Native Groundcover Alternatives:

BEARBERRY, KINNIKINNICK. **Family:** Heath (Ericaceae). **Genus:** *Arctostaphylos* (*A. uva-ursi*). **Height/Spread:** 2–6 inches. **Ornamental Attributes:** White to pink flowers. Large red berries persist into winter. Leaves turn bronze in fall. **Cultivation:** Sun best for flowers, tolerates shade. Well-drained acidic soil. **Nature Note:** The slender clearwing moth lays her eggs only on plants in the heath family. Birds eat the fruits. **Note:** Endangered in parts of the Midwest. **Zones:** 2–8.

Another Heath Family Plant:

BLACK HUCKLEBERRY. See Spring Shrubs, p. 28.

BUNCHBERRY DOGWOOD, CREEP-ING DOGWOOD. **Family:** Dogwood (Cornaceae). **Genus:** *Cornus (C. canadensis)*. **Height:** 3–6 inches. **Ornamental Attributes:** Perennial, woodland groundcover. Showy white to greenish dogwood flowers in spring. Wine-red berries. Red leaves in fall. **Cultivation:** Part sun to shade; moist, acid soil. Benefits from pine needle mulch. Spreads by underground stems. **Note:** Endangered in Illinois and Indiana, threatened in Iowa and Ohio. Spruce grouse, warbling vireo, and other birds eat the berries and help distribute the seeds. **Nature Note:** See DOGWOOD in Spring Shrubs, p. 48. **Zones:** 2–6.

RUNNING STRAWBERRY BUSH. **Family:** Bittersweet (Celastraceae). **Genus:** *Euonymus (E. obovatus)*. **Ornamental Attributes:** Flowers in spring decorate this prostrate shrub or groundcover. Dense green foliage turns brilliant shades of purple, maroon, or pink in fall. Showy orange or pink seedpods hold bright red seeds. **Cultivation:** Fast-growing. Part sun to part shade, dry to moist well-drained soil. **Nature Note:** See AMERICAN STRAWBERRY BUSH in Fall Shrubs, p. 241. **Zones:** 4–9.

Bearberry (*Arctostaphylos uva-ursi*)

SWEET-FERN. **Family:** Bayberry (Myricaceae). **Genus:** *Comptonia (C. peregrina)*. **Height:** 2–4 feet. **Spread:** 4–8 feet. **Ornamental Attributes:** Aromatic, fuzzy green fern-like plant forms colonies. **Cultivation:** Sun to part shade; prefers acidic sandy to gravelly soil, adapts to poor infertile soil. Aggressively colony forming. Resistant to drought, salt, and heat. **Note:** Endangered in parts of the Midwest. **Zones:** 2–5.

YELLOWROOT. **Family:** Buttercup (Ranunculaceae). **Genus:** *Xanthorhiza (X. simplicissima)*. **Height:** 2–3 feet. **Ornamental Attributes:** Spreading shrub, leaves turn purple; good groundcover. **Cultivation:** Shade, moist soil. **Zones:** 3–9.

More Native Alternatives:

NEW JERSEY TEA, p. 134; ST. ANDREW'S CROSS, p. 145.

See Spring Shrubs for AMERICAN WISTERIA, p. 43; CRANBERRY and MOUN-TAIN CRANBERRY, p. 28; CREEPING SAND CHERRY, p. 17; LOWBUSH BLUE-BERRY, p. 28; PRAIRIE ROSE and other native roses, p. 60; SERVICEBERRY SPP., p. 20.

See Fall Shrubs for FRAGRANT SUMAC, p. 242.

See Winter Shrubs for CREEPING JUNIPER, p. 306.

Nonnative:

AMUR CORK TREE. **Family:** Rue (Rutaceae). **Genus:** *Phellodendron* (*P. amurense*). **Origin:** China, Korea, Japan. **Height/Spread:** 30–45 feet. **Ornamental Attributes:** Boldly branched; fleeting yellow fall color; corky bark. **Cultivation:** Full sun, moist well-drained soil. Females produce abundant ill-smelling fruits. Male-only cultivars like 'His Majesty' and 'Macho' can cross-pollinate with female trees.[59] "Amur corktree has received plaudits for its urban tolerance, but my experiences indicate otherwise," writes Michael A. Dirr.[60] "Although some have recommended cork tree for use in landscaping and as a street tree in parts of the U.S., its ability to withstand urban pollution, root constriction, and frost is highly variable," writes Dani Simons, who notes: "The best way to control Amur corktree is not to plant it in the first place. An ounce of prevention is worth hundreds of hours of labor and thousands of dollars spent that are needed to remove it once established."[61] **Also:** *JAPANESE CORK TREE* (*P. japonicum*); *LAVALLE CORK TREE* (*P. lavallei*); *SAKHALIN CORK TREE* (*P. sachalinense*). **Ecological Threat:** Amur and Japanese cork trees are invasive in the Chicago area. Amur cork trees are invasive in midwestern states. The fruits have low nutritional value, to the detriment of native birds and small mammals.[62] **Zones:** 3–7.

Amur cork tree
(*Phellodendron amurense*)

Kentucky coffee tree leaves and seeds (*Gymnocladus dioicus*)

Native Alternatives:

KENTUCKY COFFEE TREE, COFFEETREE. **Family:** Pea (Fabaceae). **Genus:** *Gymnocladus* (*G. dioicus*). **Height:** 60–80 feet. **Spread:** 40–55 feet. **Ornamental Attributes:** Fragrant greenish-white flowers; showy pinnate leaves leaf out late in spring and turn yellow or brown in fall; dramatic waxy brown pods on female trees remain through winter and well into spring. Its shape, robust twigs, and beautiful bark give it a stark, bold, "very individual look."[63] **Anachronistic Note:** "If you share habitat in North America with. Kentucky coffeetree . . . you live among ecological anachronisms."[64] **Cultivation:** Best in full sun, well-drained, organically rich soil; tolerates dry, poor, alkaline soils, salt, and urban conditions. A dioecious tree. **Note:** A species of special concern in Wisconsin. **Nature Note:** The flowers are pollinated by bees, tiger swallowtail butterflies (p. 18), and ruby-throated hummingbirds (p. 91). Hosts 5 species of butterflies and moths, including—along with the honey locust tree—the bicolored and the bisected honey locust moths. Like all legumes, including redbud, honeylocust, and wisteria, the tree fixes nitrogen but at a lower rate. **Zones:** 3–8.

More Native Alternatives:

AMERICAN BEECH, p. 168; AMERICAN SYCAMORE, p. 214; BLACKGUM, p. 218; BLACK WALNUT, p. 220; HACKBERRY, p. 174; HONEY LOCUST, p. 163; MAPLE SPP., p. 197; OAK SPP., p. 202; OHIO BUCKEYE, p. 184; RED MULBERRY, p. 195; SWEETGUM, p. 216; TULIP TREE, p. 179.
See Fall Trees for AMERICAN MOUNTAIN ASH, p. 255.

Kentucky coffee tree (*Gymnocladus dioicus*)
Also see pp. 286, 346

Nonnative:

ASH. **Family:** Olive (Oleaceae). **Genus:** *Fraxinus.* **Genus Note:** These shade trees are subject to the ravages of the emerald ash borer; *FLOWERING ASH* (*F. ornus*). **Origin:** Europe, Asia. **Height/Spread:** 40–50 feet. **Ornamental Attributes:** White flowers in April to May. Winged seeds (samaras) may remain through the winter. **Cultivation:** Full sun, well-drained soil. **Zones:** 6–9; *CHINESE ASH* (*F. chinensis*). **Origin:** China, Japan, Korea. **Height/Spread:** 25–50 feet. **Ornamental Attributes:** White flowers in June. **Zones:** 6–9.

Native Alternatives:

ASH. **Family:** Olive (Oleaceae). **Genus:** *Fraxinus.* **Genus Note:** These shade trees are subject to the ravages of the invasive Asian emerald ash borer (EAB). The beetle is responsible for the loss of millions of ash trees with environmental and maintenance consequences that include increased stormwater runoff. Management strategies include cutting the trees down and replacing them with alternative native trees, quarantining forests, or preserving targeted trees with pesticide treatments. In some areas, ash trees are sold and continue to flourish.[65] "With the discovery of the Emerald Ash Borer in Illinois in 2006, we are no longer recommending ash species (*Fraxinus*)," warns the Morton Arboretum.[66] **Ash Tree Ornamental Attributes:** Pinnate leaves, fall panicles of winged seeds (samaras) that persist through winter; many have yellow or purple flowers in spring. **Cultivation:** Prefer sun, moist well-drained soil; WHITE ASH (*F. americana*). **Height:** 60–80 feet. **Ornamental Attributes:** Showy yellow and purple fall color. **Cultivation:** Sun to light shade, moist soil. **Life Span:** 260–300 years. **Zones:** 3–9; BLACK ASH (*F. nigra*). **Height/Spread:** 40–60 feet. **Cultivation:** Shade-intolerant northern species; prefers moist to wet soils. **Zones:** 4–8; BLUE ASH (*F. quadrangulata*). **Height/Spread:** 50–75 feet. **Cultivation:** Sun to light shade, moist to moderately dry soil. **EAB Note:** Resistance enables survival of 60–70 percent of trees in infested areas.[67] **Zones:** 4–7; GREEN ASH (*F. pennsylvanica*). **Cultivation:** Sun to light shade, moist to dry soil. **Zones:** 3–9. **Ash Tree Nature Note:** Ash trees host 149 species of butterflies and moth, such as the tiger

Flowering ash (*Fraxinus ornus*)

White ash leaves (*Fraxinus americana*)

White ash
(*Fraxinus americana*)
Also see p. 300

swallowtail butterfly (p. 18) and several species of sphinx moths including the great ash sphinx moth. The arrival of the EAB put these native insects at risk as well as nesting birds and other wildlife that rely on the insects for food. Wood duck, wild turkey (p. 244), northern cardinal (p. 61), evening grosbeak, purple finch (p. 145), squirrels, and woodland mice eat ash seeds. Older trees often have cavities that provide good nesting habitat for tree squirrels, woodpeckers, wood ducks, owls, and white-breasted nuthatches (p. 30). Larvae-eating downy, hairy, and red-bellied woodpeckers (p. 55) and the red-breasted nuthatch (p. 322) became EAB's leading predators, although there aren't enough bark-gleaning species to make any significant dent in the population.[68]

Great ash sphinx moth
(*Sphinx chersis*)

Evening grosbeak
(*Coccothraustes vespertinus*)

Wood duck (*Aix sponsa*)

Another Native Alternative:

HONEY LOCUST, THORNY LOCUST, SWEET LOCUST. Family: Pea (Fabaceae). **Genus:** *Gleditsia* (*G. triacanthos*). **Height/Spread:** 30–80 feet. **Ornamental Attributes:** Alternate, compound leaves create filtered shade, permitting plants and grass to grow underneath, and turn brilliant yellow in fall. Long, twisted pods (fruit) can persist into winter. Its beautiful bark resembles an oil painting applied with a palette knife, providing winter interest. "The arching form and fern-like foliage of honey locust would make it appear at home with the acacias of tropical Africa, to which it is related."[69] **Cultivation:** Sun, light shade; wide range of soils; tolerates pollution, drought, salt, and black walnut tree toxicity. **Anachronistic**

Honey locust leaves (*Gleditsia triacanthos*)

Honey locust tree (*Gleditsia triacanthos*) Also see pp. 285, 353

Note: "Growing on the branches just about the axils of the leaves . . . the long, sharply-pointed and richly-coloured thorns appear. But they are not more curious to look at than are the great pods which hang on the tree late in the season. . . . They produce an eccentric effect. . . . One is really inclined to wonder where they came from," wrote a prescient Alice Lounsberry in 1900.[70] Exactly 100 years later, Connie Barlow provided an answer. "The pod of the honey locust . . . along with the fruits of several other North American trees is anachronistic."[71] Its sweet fruits became adapted for animals that have gone extinct. "No animals with mouths big enough to take in a pod whole are now native to the home range of honey locust."[72] Squirrels and other small animals disperse today's honey locust seeds; THORNLESS HONEY LO-CUST (*G. triacanthos f. inermis*). This thornless variety occurs naturally in the wild. It is the only true native sold by most nurseries.[73] The thornless, fruitless cultivars/nativars that are sold are expected to produce little fruit, but occasionally do the opposite. **Nature Note:** The insignificant but fragrant flowers' abundant nectar attracts pollinating bees, flies, moths, butterflies, and silver-spotted skipper (p. 101) and other skipper butterflies. Honeylocust hosts 46 species of butterflies and moths, including bicolored honey locust moth and bisected honey locust moth. Squirrels eat the seeds. Shrikes (p. 259) use the thorns of honey locust and Osage orange (see Fall Trees, p. 259) to hold their prey. **Life Span:** 60–100 years. **Zones:** 3–9.

More Native Alternatives:

BLACKGUM, p. 218; BLACK WALNUT, p. 220; HACKBERRY, p. 174; KENTUCKY COFFEE TREE, p. 159; MAPLE SPP., p. 197; OAK SPP., p. 202.
    See Spring Trees for YELLOW BUCKEYE, p. 98; YELLOWWOOD, p. 96.
    See Fall Trees for AMERICAN MOUNTAIN ASH, p. 255.
    See Spring Shrubs for WAFER ASH, p. 45.

Nonnative:

ASPEN, EUROPEAN ASPEN. **Family:** Willow (Salicaceae). **Genus:** *Populus* (*P. tremula*). **Genus Note:** The willow family has two genera: *Populus* (aspen, cottonwood, poplar) and *Salix* (willow). The dioecious *Populus* has male and female flowers (catkins that hang in clusters) on separate plants. The male catkins bloom first and produce pollen. The females produce seeds attached to cotton-like fluff that are blown by the wind. Pollen from male trees elicits allergies. **Origin:** Europe. **Height:** 30–70 feet. **Spread:** 10–30 feet. **Ornamental Attributes:** Yellow fall foliage. **Cultivation:** Full sun, moist well-drained soil; disease susceptible. **Ecological Threat:** Naturalized in some midwestern states. **Zones:** 1–6; *BLACK POPLAR, LOMBARDY POPLAR* (*P. nigra, P. nigra* var. *italica; P. dilatata*). **Origin:** Asia, Europe. **Ornamental Attributes:** An American landscaper noted, in 1841, that "the Lombardy poplar is too well known among us to need any description."[74] Lombardy poplar "illustrates that there are fashions in trees just as in all else," writes Christina D. Wood in 1994, calling Lombardy poplar "a most dangerous tree."[75] This short-lived, disease-susceptible tree is used as a stop-

European aspen (*Populus tremula*)

gap measure for privacy screens and windbreaks. **Ecological Threat:** Naturalized in midwestern states. **Zones:** 3–9; *GRAY POPLAR* (*P. × canescens* [*alba × tremula*]). **Origin:** Europe. **Height:** 100 feet. **Ornamental Attributes:** Grows rapidly, leaves have woolly grayish undersides. **Ecological Threat:** A Michigan invasive with isolated distribution. Naturalized in midwestern states; *WHITE POPLAR, SILVER POPLAR* (*P. alba*). **Origin:** Asia, Europe. **Height:** 60–90 feet. **Spread:** 10 feet. **Ornamental Attributes:** Sometimes it is confused with the native silver maple. **Cultivation:** Very aggressive; water-hungry root suckers around the base of parent tree require regular cutting. Poor choice for a landscape tree. **Ecological Threat:** Brought here early in the Colonial era, it has invaded most of North America,[76] including midwestern states. **Zones:** 2–9.

Native Alternatives:

ASPEN. Family: Willow (Salicaceae). **Genus:** *Populus.* AMERICAN ASPEN, QUAKING ASPEN, TREMBLING ASPEN (*P. tremuloides*). **Height:** 20–50 feet. **Spread:** 10–30 feet. **Ornamental Attributes:** This shade and ornamental tree has small, nearly round, shiny leaves that quiver in the slightest breeze and turn a bright yellow in fall. Smooth, whitish-green or silvery-gray bark with diamond markings becomes furrowed at the trunk's base with age. Silvery catkins appear before leaves. **Cultivation:** Sun—at least four hours a day—to light shade, dry, moist, wet soil. Like most aspens, it is a pioneer species that reproduces rapidly from root suckers, forming dense stands. **Range Note:** North America's most widely distributed tree species. It grows in Alaska and Canada south to Mexico.[77] **Bird Note:** Ruffed grouse is especially dependent on this tree for food and nesting habitat. **Zones:** 2–7; BIGTOOTH ASPEN, LARGE-TOOTHED ASPEN (*P. grandidentata*). **Height:** 50–70 feet. **Spread:** 20–40 feet. **Ornamental Attributes:** Leaves tremble in the wind. When young, they are silvery. In fall they are bright yellow. The smooth bark develops thick picturesque patches. Best used as small groves of trees because of its root-sprouting characteristic. **Cultivation:** See American aspen, above. **Life Span:** 40 years, sometimes longer. **Zones:** 3–7; BALSAM POPLAR, BALM OF GILEAD (*P. balsamifera* subsp. *balsamifera*; syn. *P. candicans*). **Cultivation:** Sun, moist soil. Considered the wetland member of the

American aspen (*Populus tremuloides*)

Cottonwood leaves (*Populus deltoides*)

aspen group. **Ornamental Attributes:** Leaf undersides covered with amber resin giving the tree a distinctive look and wonderful fragrance. It is a pioneer species. **Life Span:** 100–150 years. **Note:** Endangered in Illinois and Ohio. Extirpated in Indiana. **Zones:** 1–6; **COTTONWOOD, EASTERN COTTONWOOD** (*P. deltoides*). **Height:** 50–80 feet. **Spread:** 35–60 feet. **Ornamental Attributes:** The imposing cottonwood's glossy, toothed, heart-shaped leaves move with the wind, performing like musical instruments, and turn yellow in fall. Its bark is dark gray and ridged; it has a vase-like shape. Male trees produce showy red male catkins in March to April. Female trees produce small seeds attached to the white cottony substance

Cottonwood tree (*Populus deltoides*)
Also see pp. 282, 345

for which the tree is named. Usually recommended for highway and park plantings, not for residential landscapes, but to my great delight huge, cotton-producing cottonwoods have occupied every yard where I've lived. Alice Lounsberry praised the cottonwood: "With its ashy grey stem and bright, fluttering leaves which turn in the autumn to a brilliant yellow, the tree appears among our silva an individual so striking and beautiful that it must call largely upon the admiration of all."[78] **Cultivation:** Easily grown. Sun, dry, medium, to very moist well-drained soil. Unlike aspens, cottonwood does not develop sprouts. Tolerate drought, air pollution. **Prairie Note:** By developing thick, corky, fire-resistant bark and growing on the edges of streams and rivers, cottonwood adapted itself to life on the prairie; to thirsty pioneers, its presence signaled life-giving water. Cottonwood can live more than 100 years. **Zones:** 2–9; SWAMP COTTONWOOD, RIVER COTTONWOOD, DOWNY POPLAR, BLACK POPLAR (*P. heterophylla*). Nearly eliminated from its original range by farming and development, this cottonwood tolerates wetter sites; it is used for nesting by waterbirds like green-backed herons. **Note:** Endangered in Michigan. **Hayfever Note:** Some people afflicted by hayfever attribute their suffering to the cotton produced by female aspen, cottonwood, and poplar trees, but the cotton is not allergenic. The cause is pollen produced by male trees. **Cottonless Note:** Attempts at creating cottonless cottonwoods are mostly ineffective. Canker fungi on cottonwoods is most severe on "cottonless hybrids of cottonwood." The short-lived hybrid trees typically accrue health issues after about 25 years of growth and quickly decline thereafter, a factor to be considered when landscaping.[79] **Nature Note:** Our native aspens, cottonwoods, and poplars host 367 species of butterflies and moths, including great ash sphinx moth (pp. 162), twin spotted sphinx moth, eastern tiger swallowtail butterfly (p. 18), red-spotted purple (p. 18), dreamy dusky wing skipper, and satin and virgin moths. The viceroy butterfly (p. 54), which resembles the monarch butterfly (p. 124), "is always found close to stands of willow and poplar, which are its larval host plants," writes David K. Parshall.[80] Along with black willow, American elm, aspen, canoe/paper birch, hackberry, and red mulberry, cottonwoods are host plants for the mourning cloak butterfly (p. 62). Because this butterfly roams and migrates, it can be found almost anywhere its host plants occur. The tiny insects the trees attract are sought by nesting birds and insectivorous birds. When food is scarce in spring, tree squirrels, purple finches, (p. 145), and other birds eat the buds and catkins. Woodpeckers (pp. 55, 212) nest in the trees' cavities. Second to American elm, cottonwood may be the nesting favorite of the Baltimore oriole.[81] Warbling vireo, northern parula, and yellow warbler (p. 89) also often nest in the branches. **Zones:** 4–9.

Baltimore oriole (*Icterus galbula*)

Northern parula warbler
(*Setophaga americana*)

Beech (**European beech**) (*Fagus sylvatica*)

More Native Alternatives:

SILVER MAPLE, p. 193.
　See Winter Trees for ALDER
SPP., p. 316; BIRCH SPP., p. 320.

Nonnative:

AUTUMN OLIVE; RUSSIAN OLIVE. For both, see Fall Shrubs, p. 229.

Nonnative:

BEECH, EUROPEAN BEECH, COMMON BEECH. **Family:** Beech (Fagaceae). **Genus:** *Fagus* (*F. sylvatica*; *Fagus sylvatica var. atropunicea*). **Origin:** Europe. **Height:** 50–60 feet. **Spread:** 35–50 feet. **Ornamental Attributes:** Looks like American beech. Low-branched tree with golden-bronze fall foliage and prickly husked beechnuts. "The European beech is planted in this country and was for a long time confused by early travelers with the American species. It may be known by its broader leaves . . . and . . . the abundance of fine hairs on their under surface," noted Alice Lounsberry.[82] **Cultivation:** Sun to part shade; moist, well-drained, acidic soil. Grass tends not to grow under tree. European beech trees generally have relatively shallow but expansive root systems that do not tolerate extended periods of drought; *COPPER BEECH* (*F. sylvatica* Purpurea group). One of European beech's many mutations. Many cultivars also exist. **Beech Ecological Threat:** Naturalized in a few midwestern states. **Zones:** 5–7.

Native Alternative:

AMERICAN BEECH. **Family:** Beech (Fagaceae). **Genus:** *Fagus* (*F. grandifolia*). **Height:** 50–80 feet. **Spread:** 40 feet. **Ornamental Attributes:** This large, graceful tree's unusual bark is sleek, smooth, and silvery or steel-blue gray. The flowers are small; the female's are yellow-green with red borders; the male's are yellow. The beechnuts (fruits) are triangular. The oval, serrated leaves change from green to brown, gold, yellow, and red and persist through winter, providing shelter to wildlife and ornamental interest to people.

American beech leaves (*Fagus grandifolia*)

Tufted titmouse (*Baeolophus bicolor*)

American beech (*Fagus grandifolia*)
Also see p. 342

Prickly husks split open, revealing two or three triangular, edible nuts. Harriet L. Keeler described this as a tree for all seasons. Beech is "charming in early spring, when the half-opened leaves clinging to the branches make a shimmering mist of soft green and pearly white. In midsummer, because of the lateral arrangement of the branches, the foliage lies in great shelving masses and as the leaves are short petioled they have little independent motion but sway with the branch. In autumn, the head becomes a glowing sphere of golden yellow touched with russet, and as the last leaf flutters to the ground it marks the close of a cycle of unequalled beauty."[83] "In a winter woodland, its gold-bronze foliage shines out among the leafless branches of other trees. . . . It is a tree to 'see' and enjoy for its color wherever it is found, alone or in groves," wrote Helen Van Pelt Wilson."[84] **Cultivation:** Sun, moist well-drained soil. Don't disturb its extensive root system with plantings. **Life Span:** 300–400 years. Tolerant of black walnut tree toxicity. **Nature Note:** Beech supports 127 Lepidoptera species, including early hairstreak. It hosts many of the same insects as oaks, which also belong to the beech family. Planting them together is good for wildlife. The high-protein, high-fat nuts, or "beech mast," are highly preferred by many birds and mammals and attract woodpeckers (pp. 55, 212), tufted titmouse, white-breasted nuthatch (p. 30), blue jay (p. 79), ruffed grouse (p. 36), wild turkey (p. 244), wood duck (p. 162), squirrels, chipmunks (p. 94), and bears. Purple finches (p. 145) eat beech buds, and yellow-bellied sapsuckers (p. 79) visit for the sap. Red-shouldered hawks, pileated woodpeckers, tufted titmouse, Acadian flycatcher, and wood thrush (p. 175) use the trees for nesting. Tree cavities provide dens for mammals like tree squirrels. **Zones:** 3–9.

Nonnative:

BIRCH. See Winter Trees, p. 320.
BUCKTHORN. See Summer Shrubs (Hedges), p. 140.

Chestnut (Chinese Chestnut)
(*Castanea mollissima*)

Nonnative:

CATALPA. See Spring Trees, p. 85.

Nonnative:

CHERRY. See Spring Trees, p. 81.

Nonnative:

CHESTNUT, CHINESE CHESTNUT. **Family:** Beech (Fagaceae). **Genus:** *Castanea* (*C. mollissima*). **Origin:** China, Korea. **Height/Spread:** 40–60 feet. **Ornamental Attributes:** White, yellow flowers in June. Though an ideal orchard tree to commercially replace the now nearly extinct American chestnut, it is "far from ideal as a shade tree or ornamental tree that couples as a nut tree. In addition, its flowers are extremely noxious and ill-smelling when it is in bloom in early summer."[85] Its fall color is yellow. **Cultivation:** Full sun; moist, well-drained, acidic soil. "Chinese chestnut is not immune to Chestnut blight, it is simply resistant. . . . In addition, this tree suffers from the ravages of twig canker (another disease affecting the bark) and several insects, including root weevils and gall wasps."[86] **Ecological Threat:** Naturalized in midwestern states. **Zones:** 4–8; *EUROPEAN CHESTNUT* (*C. sativa*); *JAPANESE CHESTNUT* (*C. crenata*).

Native Alternatives:

AMERICAN CHESTNUT. **Family:** Beech (Fagaceae). **Genus:** *Castanea* (*C. dentata*). **Height/Spread:** 50–75 feet. **Ornamental Attributes:** Ornamental white or yellow flowers in summer, edible chestnuts, yellow fall foliage. **Cultivation:** Young trees persist in shade and grow toward the sun through other trees. Best in moist, fertile, well-drained acidic soil but thrives in dry, rocky soil. Tolerant of black walnut toxicity. **Historical Note:** The king of the forest until a blight arrived in the northeastern United States in 1876 on Japanese chestnut trees. In 1901, when the fungus was still unknown, Alice Lounsberry wrote, "American chestnut is thoroughly well known and in nobility of outline stands almost as a rival of the white oak," and is "indeed one of the most majestic figures of the woodlands."[87] In 1904, the fungus was discovered on Asian chestnut trees in the Bronx. A result was the Plant Quarantine Act of 1912. However, like most pathogens, their "microscopic nature" rendered the act of Congress ineffective.[88] By 1950, gone were four billion American chestnut trees, more than 99.9 percent of the population. "Backcross breeding" is developing blight-resistant American chestnut trees. But altering the American "chestnut's genome—the code of life that has evolved over millenniums . . . could be a Trojan horse that may seduce the public into accepting other genetically engineered trees," writes Bernd Heinrich. "It is possible to bring back the American

American chestnut
(*Castanea dentata*)

chestnut to the forest where it belongs without genetic engineering."[89] **Note:** Kentucky and Michigan classify the tree as endangered. American chestnut is not extinct; hundreds of large chestnut trees survive outside its natural range. The tree still grows by root suckering within its natural range. American chestnuts can be obtained from native plant nurseries that sell trees grown from seeds harvested from existing stands. **Life Span:** 100–300 years. **Zones:** 4–9; **ALLEGHENY CHINKAPIN OR CHINQUAPIN; DWARF CHESTNUT** (*C. pumila* var. *pumila*). **Height:** To 30 feet. **Ornamental Attributes:** Single- or multi-trunked small tree or large, thicket-forming shrub; pale yellow flowers borne in spikes; glossy, dark green, toothed leaves turn yellowish or purple in fall; prickly, bur-like husked nuts. **Cultivation:** Sun to light shade, moist to dry well-drained soil. This tree was less affected by chestnut blight. **Historical Note:** Captain John Smith published the first record of this species in 1612.[90] In 1901, Alice Lounsberry wrote of country children selling bags of chinquapin nuts for a nickel.[91] **Note:** Threatened in Kentucky. **Chestnut Nature Note:** Wildlife from deer and bears to squirrels and blue jays (p. 79), wild turkeys (p. 244), woodpeckers, and other birds (including the now-extinct passenger pigeon) relied on the native chestnuts as a dependable and highly preferred source of food. The trees continue to support birds and mammals and host at least 127 Lepidoptera (butterflies/moths) species. **Zones:** 5–8.

More Native Alternatives:

AMERICAN BEECH, p. 168; OAK SPP., p. 202; OHIO BUCKEYE, p. 184; WALNUT SPP., p. 219; YELLOW BUCKEYE, p. 98.

See Spring Trees for AMERICAN HAZELNUT, p. 102; PAWPAW, p. 113; YELLOW-WOOD, p. 96.

See Fall Trees for PERSIMMON, p. 256.

See Spring Shrubs for RED BUCKEYE, p. 33.

Dawn redwood
(*Metasequoia
glyptostroboides*)

Nonnative:

DAWN REDWOOD. Family: Cypress (Cupressaceae). **Genus:** *Metasequoia* (*M. glyptostroboides*). **Origin:** China. **Height:** 70–100 feet. **Spread:** 15–25 feet. **Ornamental Attributes:** Non-blooming, deciduous coniferous tree closely resembles its close native relative, bald cypress. Feathery fern-like foliage drops quickly in the fall. **Cultivation:** Full sun, rich moist soil. **Zones:** 4–8.

Native Alternatives:

BALD CYPRESS. Family: Cypress (Cupressaceae). **Genus:** *Taxodium* (*T. distichum*). **Height:** 50–80 feet. **Spread:** 20–40 feet. **Ornamental Attributes:** Deciduous conifer with feathery sage-green foliage turns copper or burnt orange around Thanksgiving, when the needles fall, like the larches to the north. Exfoliating, reddish-brown to silver bark, showy cones. Beautiful in stands; out of place as specimen. **Cultivation:** Full sun, easily grown in a wide range of soils from standing water (in ponds supporting nesting herons) to medium and dry. Sends up large root projections, called "knees," around the base of the tree, which can be hidden in lawns with mulch or native ground cover. **Nature Note:** Hosts 16 species of butterflies and moths, including angle-winged emerald, baldcypress sphinx, and cypress emerald

Bald cypress needles (*Taxodium distichum*)

Bald cypress (*Taxodium distichum*)
Also see p. 277

moths. Wood duck (p. 162), gadwall, mallard, wild turkey (p. 244), and tree squirrels eat the seeds. Woodpeckers, herons, egrets, bald eagle, osprey, and yellow-throated warbler (p. 330) use the tree for nesting, and some eat the seeds. In swampy areas, barred owls use it for roosting. It is deer resistant. **Life Span:** 600–1,800 years. **Note:** Threatened in Indiana. **Zones:** 4–9.

Another Native Alternative:

AMERICAN LARCH, p. 189.

Nonnative:

ELM. **Family:** Elm (Ulmaceae). **Genus:** *Ulmus.* *CHINESE ELM* (*U. parvifolia*). **Origin:** China, Korea. **Height:** 40–50 feet. **Spread:** 25–40 feet. **Ornamental Attributes:** Green leaves may turn red in fall. **Cultivation:** Full sun, wide range of soil types. Fast grower, naturalizes. **Ecological Threat:** Listed on Iowa's General Invasive Plant List. Naturalized in midwestern states. **Zones:** 4–9; *ENGLISH ELM, COMMON ELM* (*U. procera*). **Origin:** Europe. Naturalized in midwestern states; *SIBERIAN ELM* (*U. pumila*). **Origin:** Asia. **Height/Spread:**

Chinese elm (*Ulmus parvifolia*)

40–70 feet. **Ornamental Attributes:** Green leaves, brittle branches, unattractive shape. Very susceptible to the elm leaf beetle, but "unscrupulous plant peddlers sometimes sell this tree as a Dutch Elm Disease resistant alternative to the majestic American Elm," writes Seth Harper. "Unfortunately, it lacks the impeccable vase-like form of its American cousin, leaving it with—let me do the math here—ah yes, precisely zero ornamental characteristics. . . . Let me leave you with a few comments from the renowned plantsman Michael Dirr: 'A poor ornamental tree that does not deserve to be planted anywhere! . . . One of, if not the, world's worst trees. . . . Native to eastern Siberia, northern China, Manchuria, Korea and, unfortunately, was not left there.' I think there's a lesson there for us all."[92] **Cultivation:** Full sun, dry to medium soil. **Ecological Threat:** Invasive in several midwestern states; Siberian elm is reported to be invasive in natural areas in 25 states, but some still promote it as a conservation tree. **Zones:** 4–9; *ZELKOVA, JAPANESE ZELKOVA.* **Family:** Elm (Ulmaceae). **Genus:** *Zelkova* (*Z. serrata*). **Origin:** Japan, China. **Height/Spread:** 50–80 feet. Its resistance to Dutch elm disease led to its use as a replacement for American elm. **Cultivation:** Sun. Moderately drought tolerant, may need supplemental watering. **Ecological Threat:** Invasive in Ohio. **Zones:** 5–8. **Disease Resistance Note:** "All species of elm are more or less susceptible to Dutch elm disease. Individual trees, especially in the Chinese and Siberian elm group, have some resistance but are not immune."[93] The solution is to plant a variety of beautiful native trees and avoid future disasters such as Dutch elm disease.

Native Alternatives:

HACKBERRY, AMERICAN HACKBERRY, COMMON HACKBERRY, NORTHERN HACKBERRY. **Family:** Hemp (Cannabaceae). **Genus:** *Celtis* (*C. occidentalis*). **Height:** 40–80 feet. **Ornamental Attributes:** Vase-shaped, elm-like shade tree. Purple berries; distinctive knobby, corky bark; yellow to yellow-brown fall color. **Cultivation:** Sun to shade. Wet to dry. Tolerates many soils, drought, salt, pollution, and other urban conditions. Sometimes develops bushy growths called witches' brooms. **Life Span:** 150–200 years. **Zones:** 2–9; SUGARBERRY, SOUTHERN HACKBERRY (*C. laevigata* var. *laevigata*). **Height/Spread:** 60–80 feet. It

Hackberry berries and leaves
(*Celtis occidentalis*)

Hackberry tree (*Celtis occidentalis*)
Also see p. 284

has been planted in the Midwest "with great success."[94] Its fruits are sugary sweet. **Zones:** 5–9. **Hackberry Nature Note:** Hackberries are among the best food, nesting, and shelter plants and have high value for wildlife. The high-fat, late-summer sweet, dark purple fruits' persistence through the winter provides emergency food for mammals and more than 48 species of migrating and overwintering birds, including woodpeckers (pp. 55, 212), American robin (p. 62), wood thrush, northern cardinal (p. 61), brown thrasher (p. 219), northern mockingbird (p. 256), northern flicker (p. 99), yellow-bellied sapsucker (p. 79), gray catbird (p. 79), wild turkey (p. 244), and cedar waxwing (p. 36). Hackberries host 43 species of moths and

Wood thrush (*Hylocichla mustelina*)

Hackberry emperor butterfly
(*Asterocampa celtis*)

Question mark butterfly (*Polygonia interrogationis*)

American elm leaves (*Ulmus americana*)

butterflies, including the hackberry emperor. In late fall, its caterpillars sew hackberry leaf nests to a tree and move in for their diapause or overwintering stage. In spring, they crawl out and eat fresh leaves. Hackberries also host tawny emperor, question mark, and American snout (p. 141) butterflies, and moths, including Io, thin-lined owlet, and ruddy dagger. Along with American elm, aspen, willows, red mulberry, and canoe birch, hackberries are a host plant for the mourning cloak butterfly (p. 62). A turtle, *Trachemys scripta*, eats the leaves when they fall into the water; **ELM: AMERICAN ELM. Genus:** *Ulmus* (*U. americana*). Native elms, like nonnative elms, are susceptible to Dutch elm disease. **Height:** 60–80 feet. **Spread:** 30–50 feet. **Ornamental Attributes:** Red-yellow flowers in early spring, vase-like shape, yellow fall color. **Cultivation:** Sun, well-drained soil. Tolerates black walnut tree toxicity. **Historical Note:** After 1930, the introduction of Dutch elm disease from Asian elms killed great numbers of American elms, depriving Americans of one of their iconic trees. **Cultivar Note:** "I question the logic of planting large numbers of these resistant cultivars, for as with all monocultures, some other problem will undoubtedly crop up to trouble them. Luckily, there is enough natural resistance in the natural populations that young, breeding-size elms are everywhere apparent and this suggests that in time they will outwit the disease on their own," writes William Cullina.[95] **Life Span:** 175–300 years. **Zones:** 3–9; **ROCK ELM, CORK ELM** (*U. thomasii*). **Height:** 40–60 feet. **Spread:** 20–40 feet. **Ornamental Attributes:** Yellow-purple flowers in early spring. Straight trunk, corky, furrowed bark, yellow fall color. **Cultivation:** Sun, well-drained soil. **Note:** Endangered in Illinois. **Zones:** 4–8; **SLIPPERY ELM, RED ELM** (*U. rubra*). **Height:** 40–60 feet. **Spread:** 30–50 feet. **Ornamental Attributes:** Vase-shaped and similar in appearance to the revered American elm. Red flowers in March to April, yellow fall color. **Cultivation:** Sun, part shade. Dry to moist soil. Tolerates black walnut tree toxicity. **Life Span:** 200–300 years. **Zones:** 3–9; **WINGED ELM, CORK ELM, WAHOO** (*U. alata*). **Height:** 30–40 feet. **Orna-**

American elm (*Ulmus americana*)
Also see pp. 274, 343

Eastern comma butterfly
(*Polygonia comma*)

mental Attributes: Yellow-red flowers in early spring; fast-growing attractive tree; branches have decorative corky ridges; yellow fall color. **Cultivation:** Sun, moist soil. **Native American Note:** Wahoo was the Creek Indian name. **Zones:** 5–9. **Elm Nature Note:** Elms attract birds and butterflies; the native trees host 215 Lepidoptera species (butterflies/moths), including mourning cloak (p. 62), question mark (p. 176), eastern comma, and comma angelwing butterflies, as well as moths like the Columbia silkmoth (p. 18). One of several elm specialists is the double-toothed prominent; its caterpillars look like, and eat only, elm leaves. Elms provide mammals and birds with cover, nesting sites, seeds, and in spring attract tiny insects that migrating and other nesting birds eagerly collect to feed their offspring. The Baltimore oriole (p. 167) seems to prefer American elms for nesting, but also likes cottonwood, willow, oak, and poplar.

More Native Alternatives:

AMERICAN HORNBEAM, p. 182; BLACKGUM, p. 218; COTTONWOOD, p. 166; HONEY LOCUST, p. 163; HOP HORNBEAM, p. 183; KENTUCKY COFFEE TREE, p. 159; MAPLE SPP., p. 197; OAK SPP., p. 202.

See Spring Trees for BLACK CHERRY, p. 82; YELLOWWOOD, p. 96.
See Winter Trees for EASTERN WHITE PINE, p. 328.

Nonnative:

GINKGO, MAIDENHAIR TREE. **Family:** Ginkgo (Ginkgoaceae). **Genus:** *Ginkgo* (*G. biloba*). **Origin:** China. **Height:** 60–100 feet. **Spread:** 40–60 feet. **Ornamental Attributes:** Leaves with an appealing shape turn yellow in fall. **Problems:** A deciduous conifer (a true gymnosperm), it often looks spindly, can become irregular with age, and branches can cross the trunk. Females produce orange, fleshy, long-lasting, ill-smelling seeds which, due to their butyric acid content, contain the same odorous chemical found in soured butter and cheese, body odor, and vomit. The seeds become slimy, stick to pedestrians' shoes, and present slipping hazards. Selecting a male is difficult as male and female trees appear identical until they start reproducing when 20 to 50 years old. For this reason, male clones have been developed, with propagation primarily by cuttings from male cultivars grafted onto seedling rootstock. Sometimes, a "certified male" cutting, such as 'Princeton Sentry', doesn't take, and when a plant sprouts below the graft, a tree is created whose gender will be unknown for decades.[96] **Cultivation:** Full to part sun, medium soil, creates numerous seedlings. Challenging ginkgo's reputation as a "trouble-free" tree, Frank S. Santamour notes it suffers "breakage of main trunks and premature tree death."[97] "Trees in urban areas can support many other species—birds, small mammals, insects. In fact, a highly diverse urban canopy can appear to many organisms as a forest," writes Tom Kimmerer. "Most resident birds spend time in trees where food is available. Since there

Ginkgo (*Ginkgo biloba*)

are no insects in ginkgo, birds tend to avoid them." Instead of endless planting of ginkgo, we urgently need to diversify our urban forests with diverse plantings of seedlings of many species. We need to prepare our cities for climate change, and greatly increase not just our urban forest canopy, but our urban forest diversity. "We have more than enough ginkgo trees now. Let's resolve to stop planting them."[98] **Anachronistic Note:** "Ginkgo disappeared from North America seven million years ago," note Darke and Tallamy. "Ginkgos are contributing little if anything to the local food webs compared to most contemporary indigenous plants." Whatever complex food webs ginkgo may have supported in the past, "did not survive its seven-million-year hiatus."[99] Parkways and landscapes planted with ginkgo create butterfly- and bird-free zones. For beautiful native North American trees that are relics of the past but continue to contribute to the ecosystem, see HONEY LOCUST, p. 163; KENTUCKY COFFEE TREE, p. 159; HAWTHORN, MAGNOLIA, and PAWPAW (all: see Spring Trees, pp. 106, 110, 113), and PERSIMMON and OSAGE ORANGE (both: see Fall Trees, pp. 256, 259). **Ginkgo Ecological Threat:** Naturalized in parts of the Midwest. **Zones:** 3–8.

Native Alternatives:

TULIP TREE, YELLOW POPLAR. Family: Magnolia (Magnoliaceae). **Genus:** *Liriodendron* (*L. tulipifera*). **Height:** 60–90 feet. **Spread:** 30–50 feet. **Ornamental Attributes:** The large, showy, tulip-shaped flowers—yellow-green on the outside, deep orange and yellow on the inside—open over an extended period in late spring and early summer but may go unnoticed on very tall trees until, like rose petals, intact, they fall to the ground, waiting to be collected. The large leaves also resemble tulips in profile. The cone-shaped fruit clusters are chartreuse. The bark is deeply fissured. The leaves turn golden yellow in fall. This majestic fast-growing tree is the tallest of eastern forests. "There is something to make one tremble in the gigantic proportions, the tall, column-like trunk and the strangely cut leaves of this tree when it is approached for the first time," wrote Alice Lounsberry. "It is a tree that at all times is readily recognized; but in the spring when it is covered with its tulip-like flowers it is truly a surprising sight."[100] **Cultivation:** Full sun, part shade; well-drained soil. Resistant to black walnut tree toxicity and to deer. **Native American Note:** Huge canoes were made from huge single logs. **Magnolia Family Note:** Like tulip tree, spring-blooming magnolia trees belong to the ancient Magnolia family. **Nature Note:**

Tulip tree leaves (*Liriodendron tulipifera*)

Flower nectar and pollen attract a variety of pollinators, such as flies, beetles, honeybees, bumblebees (p. 61), other long-tongued bees, as well as Baltimore orioles (p. 167) and ruby-throated hummingbirds (p. 91). Hosts 21 species of Lepidoptera (butterflies/moths), including, along with spicebush, sassafras, white ash, pawpaw, poplar, cherry, sweetbay magnolia, basswood, birch, cottonwood, mountain ash, and willow, the spicebush swallowtail butterfly (p. 22). Favorite host plant for the spectacular promethea silkmoth that also feeds on ash,

Tulip tree silkmoth (*Callosamia angulifera*)

Tulip tree (*Liriodendron tulipifera*)
Also see pp. 299, 349

azalea, bayberry, birch, button bush, cherry, plum, poplar, sassafras, spice bush, and sweetgum. Named for its host, the tulip tree silkmoth caterpillar spins a dark brown cocoon in a curled leaf and spends its winter on the ground. Another moth associated with the tulip tree is the tulip-tree beauty moth, our largest inchworm species. "If you want to enjoy tiger swallowtails (*Papilio glaucus*) plant tulip trees, sweetbay magnolia, or black cherry trees," writes Douglas Tallamy.[101] Northern cardinal (p. 61), American goldfinch (p. 145), Carolina chickadee, purple finch (p. 145), white-footed and woodland deer mice, and fox, gray, and red squirrels eat the seeds. Yellow-bellied sapsuckers (p. 79) access sap by drilling holes; later the holes are used by Baltimores orioles (p. 167) and ruby-throated hummingbirds (p. 91). **Note:** Tulip tree is the state tree of Indiana and Tennessee. **Life Span:** 250–450 years. **Zones:** 4–9.

More Native Alternatives:

AMERICAN BEECH, p. 168; BLACKGUM, p. 218; BLACK WALNUT, p. 220: HACK-BERRY, p. 174; HONEY LOCUST, p. 163; MAPLE SPP., p. 197; OAK SPP., p. 202.
    See Spring Trees for CATALPA SPP., p. 86.

Golden rain tree
(*Koelreuteria paniculata*)

Nonnative:

GOLDEN RAIN TREE. **Family:** Soapberry (Sapindaceae). **Genus:** *Koelreuteria* (*K. paniculata*). **Origin:** China, Korea. **Height/Spread:** 30–40 feet. **Ornamental Attributes:** Yellow flowers in summer, compound leaves, papery seed capsules. **Cultivation:** Full sun, dry to medium soil. Naturalizes; creates nuisance seedlings, twig and seed litter. **Ecological Threat:** Naturalized and invasive in midwestern states. "In hundreds of thousands of acres we have planted golden raintree from China instead of one of our beautiful oaks and lost the chance to grow 532 species of caterpillars, all of them nutritious bird food. My research has shown that alien ornamentals support 29 times less biodiversity than do native ornamentals," writes Douglas Tallamy.[102] **Zones:** 5–9.

Native Alternatives:

AMERICAN LINDEN, p. 190; HONEY LOCUST, p. 163; KENTUCKY COFFEE TREE, p. 159; OAK SPP., p. 202; SOURWOOD, p. 186; WHITE BASSWOOD, p. 191.

See Spring Trees for BIGLEAF MAGNOLIA, p. 110; BLACK CHERRY, p. 82; CATALPA SPP., p. 86; FRINGE TREE, p. 105; RED BUCKEYE, p. 33; YELLOW BUCKEYE, p. 98; YELLOWWOOD, p. 96.

See Fall Trees for AMERICAN MOUNTAIN ASH, p. 255.

See Spring Shrubs for SPICEBUSH, p. 22; WAFER ASH, p. 45.

See Summer Shrubs for FRANKLIN TREE, p. 147.

Hornbeam (European hornbeam)
(*Carpinus betulus*)

Nonnative:

HORNBEAM, EUROPEAN HORNBEAM, COMMON HORNBEAM, IRONWOOD. **Family:** Birch (Betulaceae). **Genus:** *Carpinus* (*C. betulus*). **Origin:** Europe. **Height:** 40–60 feet. **Spread:** 30–40 feet. **Ornamental Attributes:** Difficult to distinguish from the American species. "Some of the best gardeners in the world have confused the two species," writes Michael A. Dirr.[103] Has less desirable fall foliage and is somewhat larger. **Cultivation:** Full to part sun, well-drained soil. **Zones:** 4–8.

American hornbeam leaves (*Carpinus caroliniana*)

Native Alternatives:

AMERICAN HORNBEAM, IRONWOOD, BLUE BEECH, WATER BEECH, MUSCLEWOOD. **Family:** Birch (Betulaceae). **Genus:** *Carpinus* (*C. caroliniana*). **Height:** 20–35 feet. **Spread:** 20–35 feet. **Ornamental Attributes:** Spring's female flowers or catkins give way to attractive and distinctive clusters of papery nutlets. Shiny, bluish-green, serrated leaves turn scarlet-orange in the fall. The thin, smooth, blue-gray bark has sinewy, muscle-like ripples. This tough understory tree for shade or specimen planting can be grown single-stemmed or multistemmed. Christopher Starbuck designates American hornbeam as an uncommon tree for specimen planting. **Cultivation:** Easily grown, problem free. Part sun to moderate shade; moist, well-drained, preferably rich acidic soil. Tolerates wet conditions and moderate drought and dry soil. Salt intolerant. Tolerant of black walnut toxicity. Disease resistant. Benefits from shade during hot weather. **Life Span:** 100 years. **Nature Note:** Hosts 68 species of butterflies and moths, including luna moth (p. 54), eyed moth, cecropia moth (p. 18), polyphemus moth, striped hairstreak (p. 18), red-spotted

American hornbeam (*Carpinus caroliniana*)
Also see p. 275

purple (p. 18), marine blue (p. 43), and eastern tiger swallowtail butterfly (p. 18). The nutlets are particularly popular with northern cardinal (p. 61) and American goldfinch (p. 145). Also eaten by wood duck (p. 162), ruffed grouse (p. 36), bobwhite (p. 36), and yellow-rumped warbler, as well as gray and fox squirrels. Birds that nest in its branches include wood thrush (p. 175). Black-capped chickadees (p. 322) nest in small cavities of older trees. **Zones:** 2–9.

HOP HORNBEAM, IRON-WOOD, AMERICAN HOP HORNBEAM, EASTERN HOP HORNBEAM. **Family:** Hazelnut (Corylaceae). **Genus:** *Ostrya* (*O. virginiana*). **Height:** 30–50 feet. **Ornamental Attributes:** Graceful understory tree with twisted trunk, flaky bark, clusters of yellow-tinted fruit, and birch-like leaves that turn yellow in fall. Attractive

Yellow-rumped warbler (*Setophaga coronata*)

Horse chestnut
(*Aesculus hippocastanum*)

and persistent clusters of overlapping inflated hop-like fruits give the tree the appearance of being covered with flowers and make it easily identifiable. Like American hornbeam, this native is considered an unusual tree that is suitable for specimen planting. It was different in 1901, when Alice Lounsberry could say, "For its beauty, in fact, it is much planted."[104] **Cultivation:** Sun, part to full shade, dry or moist soil; insect and disease free. Slow growing. Creates no vegetative offsets; reproduces by reseeding. **Nature Note:** Host plant for 94 species of moths and butterflies, including the ironwood tubemaker moth. Bobwhite (p. 36), grouse, woodpeckers (pp. 55, 212), American robin (p. 62), gray catbird (p. 79), northern cardinal (p. 61), purple finch (p. 145), deer, rabbits, and squirrels eat the buds and seeds, and use it for shelter. **Zones:** 3–9.

Nonnative:

HORSE CHESTNUT, COMMON HORSE CHESTNUT, EUROPEAN HORSE CHESTNUT. **Family:** Soapberry (Sapindaceae). **Genus:** *Aesculus* (*A. hippocastanum*). **Origin:** Europe. **Height:** 50–75 feet. **Spread:** 50–60 feet. **Ornamental Attributes:** Showy white flowers in May. Spiny brown fruit in summer. Midsummer leaf scorch, with its brown, fall-like appearance, mars its beauty; it may be nearly defoliated by late summer. **Cultivation:** Sun to part shade. Moist, fertile soil; does poorly in dry soil. **Ecological Threat:** Naturalized in midwestern states. **Zones:** 3–7.

Native Alternatives:

OHIO BUCKEYE. **Family:** Soapberry (Sapindaceae). **Genus:** *Aesculus* (*A._glabra* var. *glabra*). **Height/Spread:** 20–40 feet. **Ornamental Attributes:** Yellow flowers turn red after pollination and look beautiful against the palmately compound leaves leafing out early each spring, an understory adaptation. Spiny brown seed-holding husks are ornamental from September to early October; leaves turn red, yellow, or orange in fall, making it a good alternative to Bradford pear. Prominent buds remain over the winter, elongating and turning a bright salmon color before bursting open in spring to reveal the leaves. **Cultivation:** Young trees prefer shady conditions. Adult trees thrive, and produce best flowers and colorful leaves, in areas that are sunny for about half a day. Soil can have poor drainage or be soggy or marshy for long periods. Tree prefers slightly acid moist deep soils, but with sufficient moisture can grow in calcareous soils. Unlike yellow buckeye, leaf scorch may render Ohio buckeye leafless by end of summer when planted in hot, dry conditions. Tolerates black walnut toxicity. Recommended for woodland areas, but not for parkways by Missouri Botanic Garden. **Note:** State tree of Ohio. **Nature Note:** See Spring Trees for YELLOW BUCKEYE, p. 98. See Spring Shrubs for RED BUCKEYE, p. 33. See Summer Shrubs for BOTTLEBRUSH BUCKEYE, p. 130. **Zones:** 3–7.

More Native Alternatives:

AMERICAN HORNBEAM, p. 182; BLACK-GUM, p. 218; BLACK WALNUT, p. 220; HOP HORNBEAM, p. 183; MAPLE SPP., p. 197; OAK SPP., p. 202; TULIP TREE, p. 179.

See Spring Trees for BLACK CHERRY, p. 82; CATALPA SPP., p. 86.

Nonnative:

JAPANESE ANGELICA TREE. See *ANGELICA TREE* in Summer Shrubs, p. 123.

Ohio buckeye flowers and leaves (*Aesculus glabra* var. *glabra*)

Ohio buckeye (*Aesculus glabra* var. *glabra*)

Japanese lilac tree (*Syringa reticulata*)

Nonnative:

JAPANESE LILAC TREE, JAPANESE TREE LILAC. **Family:** Olive (Oleaceae). **Genus:** *Syringa* (*S. reticulata*). **Origin:** China. **Height:** 20–30 feet. **Spread:** 15–20 feet. **Ornamental Attributes:** White flowers in early summer whose fragrance resembles privet, not lilac. Very large shrub usually trained as a small tree. Becoming a popular parkway tree. **Cultivation:** Full sun, medium soil. Fragile tree suffers from winds and storms. Once damaged, it takes a long time to recover. **Zones:** 3–7.

Sourwood (*Oxydendrum arboreum*)

Native Alternative:

SOURWOOD, SORREL TREE, LILY OF THE VALLEY TREE. Family: Heath (Ericaceae). **Genus:** *Oxydendrum* (*O. arboreum*). **Height:** 20–50 feet. **Spread:** 10–25 feet. **Ornamental Attributes:** Fragrant sprays of small bell-like white flowers in summer. Fall color is spectacular deep red and crimson. One of the first trees to turn color, it is a great alternative to the Bradford pear's very late (or tenacious green) fall color. Twigs can be distinctively reddish. Showy yellow fruit capsules, crooked stems, and silver-gray seed capsules provide winter interest. "Many are not in the habit of watching the trees as they come into bloom, and for them to find the sour-wood hung with its delicate sprays of flowers so suggestive of the lily-of-the-valley must indeed be a revelation," wrote Alice Lounsberry.[105]

Considered by Christopher Starbuck an uncommon tree for specimen planting. **Cultivation:** Sun is best for flowering and brilliant fall color; well-drained soil, preferably acidic. Deer avoid the sour-tasting leaves. This tree is problem free. **Nature Note:** Particularly important to bees because it provides food when little else is flowering. Hosts 14 species of butterflies and moths, including the azalea sphinx. A heath family plant, it helps increase Lepidoptera (butterfly/moth) diversity because these plants host different insects, like the slender clearwing who only lays her eggs on sourwood and other heath family plants. **Note:** Rare in Indiana. **Life Span:** 99 years. **Zones:** 5–9.

More Native Alternatives:

STEWARTIA, p. 215.

See Spring Trees for BIGLEAF MAGNOLIA, p. 110; BLACK CHERRY, p. 82; FLOWERING DOGWOOD, p. 94; FRINGE TREE, p. 105; YELLOWWOOD, p. 96.

See Fall Trees for MOUNTAIN MAPLE, p. 252.

See Spring Shrubs for AMERICAN BLADDERNUT, p. 41.

See Summer Shrubs for FRANKLIN TREE, p. 147.

Nonnative:

JAPANESE PAGODA TREE. **Family:** Pea (Fabaceae). **Genus:** *Sophora* (*S. japonica*, syn. *Styphnolobium japonicum*). **Origin:** China, Korea. **Height/Spread:** 50–75 feet. **Ornamental Attributes:** Somewhat showy white flowers in July to August. Bean-like brown pods last into winter. Pinnately compound leaves turn briefly yellow in fall. **Cultivation:** Full to part sun, medium soil. **Ecological Threat:** Naturalized in midwestern states. **Zones:** 4–8.

Native Alternatives:

AMERICAN HORNBEAM, p. 182; AMERICAN LINDEN, p. 190; HONEY LOCUST, p. 163; KENTUCKY COFFEE TREE, p. 159; OHIO BUCKEYE, p. 184; RED MAPLE, p. 197; SOURWOOD, p. 186.

See Spring Trees for BIGLEAF MAGNOLIA, p. 110; BLACK CHERRY, p. 82; CATALPA SPP., p. 86; YELLOW BUCKEYE, p. 98; YELLOWWOOD, p. 96.

See Fall Trees for MOUNTAIN MAPLE, p. 252.

See Summer Shrubs for FRANKLIN TREE, p. 147.

Japanese pagoda tree
(*Styphnolobium japonicum*)

Katsura tree
(*Cercidiphyllum*
japonicum)

Nonnative:

KATSURA TREE. **Family:** Katsura-tree (Cercidiphyllaceae). **Genus:** *Cercidiphyllum* (*C. japonicum*). **Origin:** China, Korea. **Height:** 40–60 feet. **Spread:** 25–60 feet. **Ornamental Attributes:** Reddish-purple heart-shaped leaves turn green in summer, yellow in fall. **Cultivation:** Full to part sun. Adapts to a variety of soils; needs watering during drought. Bark of young trees subject to sun scald and needs protection. **Ecological Threat:** Naturalized in midwestern states. **Zones:** 4–8.

Native Alternatives:

AMERICAN HORNBEAM, p. 182; HOP HORNBEAM, p. 183; MAPLE SPP., p. 197; OAK SPECIES, p. 202; SHAGBARK HICKORY, p. 222.
    See Spring Trees for CATALPA SPP., p. 86; REDBUD, p. 92.

Nonnative:

KOREAN EVODIA. Family: Rue (Rutaceae). Genus: *Tetradium* (*T. daniellii*). Origin: Korea. Height: 50 feet. Ornamental Attributes: Short-trunked tree; small fragrant white flowers with yellow anthers bloom in late spring or summer. Looks like both Amur cork tree and native yellowwood. Cultivation: Sun. Zones: 4–8.

Native Alternatives:

AMERICAN LINDEN, p. 190; SOURWOOD, p. 186.

See Spring Trees for YELLOWWOOD, p. 96.

Nonnative:

LARCH, EUROPEAN LARCH. Family: Pine (Pinaceae). Genus: *Larix* (*L. decidua*). Origin: Europe. Height: 60–100 feet. Spread: 20–30 feet. Ornamental Attributes: Soft green foliage turns golden yellow in fall. Cultivation: Full sun, rich moist soil. Ecological Threat: Naturalized in midwestern states. Zones: 4–7; *GOLDEN LARCH.* Family: Pine (Pinaceae). Genus: *Pseudolarix* (*P. amabilis*, syn. *P. kaempferi*). Origin: China. Height: 20–40 feet. Ornamental Attributes: Looks like American larch. Zones: 5–7.

Native Alternatives:

AMERICAN LARCH, EASTERN LARCH, TAMARACK. Family: Pine (Pinaceae). Genus: *Larix* (*L. laricina*). Height: 40–80 feet. Spread: 15–30 feet. Ornamental Attributes: Deciduous conifer with soft green foliage turning golden yellow in fall before falling. One of the northern-most trees, this hardy tree is a useful ornamental in very cold climates. Naturally often grows in pure stands, so looks best and presents the most dramatic fall color planted in groups or groves. Cultivation: Full sun, moist to wet acidic conditions; adapts to well-drained sites. Can underplant with acid-loving wildflowers and shrubs.

Korean evodia (*Tetradium daniellii*)

Intolerant of shade, heat, dry shallow soils, and polluted areas. Nearly immune to winter road salt. Note: Threatened in Illinois. Nature Note: Hosts 121 species of butterflies and moths, including Columbia silkmoth. Seeds are a favorite of crossbills (p. 317), pine siskins (p. 54), mice, voles, and shrews. Spruce grouse eat the buds. Birds use the tree as nesting sites. Tree has limited cover value because it sheds its needles in the winter. Zones: 1–6.

Another Native Alternative:

BALD CYPRESS, p. 172.

Nonnative:

LINDEN. **Family:** Mallow (Malvaceae; formerly Tiliaceae). **Genus:** *Tilia.* **Origin:** Europe, Asia. **Ornamental Attributes:** Heart-shaped leaves. Yellow- to white-tinged fragrant flowers in late June or early July, some poisonous to bees; fruits are nutlets. **Cultivation:** Sun, part shade; well-drained soil. All lindens are susceptible to a long list of pests, making maintenance difficult. Japanese beetle and aphid control becomes impossible when the trees grow to mature sizes; defoliation often results; *LITTLELEAF LINDEN* (*T. cordata*). **Height:** 40–60 feet. **Spread:** 35–50 feet. Looks like American linden or basswood with smaller leaves. **Midwest Problems:** Avoid planting littleleaf linden and its cultivar 'Greenspire' due to structural problems, basal suckering, girdling roots, deep planting decline, storm damage, trunk sunscald,

Littleleaf linden (*Tilia cordata*)

leaf scorch, road salt sensitivity, intolerance to poor drainage, and Japanese beetle and other pest susceptibility.[106] Its cultivars are less hardy. **Ecological Threat:** Naturalized in eastern states and parts of Canada. **Zones:** 4–7; *BIGLEAF LINDEN* (*T. platyphyllos*). Looks like American linden with the same size of leaves but smaller flowers. **Zones:** 5–7; *MONGOLIAN LINDEN* (*T. mongolica*). Leaves are not heart shaped. Difficult to grow. **Zones:** 5–7; *SILVER LINDEN* (*T. tomentosa*). **Zones:** 4–7; *CAUCASIAN LINDEN, CRIMEAN LINDEN* (*T.* × *euchlora*). **Zones:** 3–8. **Ecological Threat:** Nonnative lindens hybridize with native lindens growing in the wild, raising the possibility of altering the gene pool of the native species.

Native Alternatives:

LINDEN: AMERICAN LINDEN, AMERICAN BASSWOOD, BEE TREE. **Family:** Mallow (Malvaceae; formerly Tiliaceae). **Genus:** *Tilia* (*T. americana*). **Name Note:** "Basswood" usually refers to North American species. **Height:** 50–80 feet. **Spread:** 30–50 feet. **Ornamental Attributes:** Handsome shade and street tree with small fragrant yellow flowers in April to July, accompanied by conspicuous, showy, lime-colored, curving bracts. Heart-shaped foliage may turn chartreuse, yellow, gold, or golden brown in fall. Late summer seeds (nutlets). **Cultivation:** Best in sun. Prefers moist well-drained soil but adapts to seasonally dry, average soils. Has the ability to propagate itself through suckers, which develop from the root system. It is the northernmost *Tilia* species. **Life Span:** 100–140 years.

American linden
leaves and flowers
(*Tilia americana*)

Zones: 2–8; WHITE BASSWOOD, SILVER-LEAVED LINDEN, WHITE LINDEN, BEE TREE (*T. heterophylla, T. americana* var. *heterophylla*). **Ornamental Attributes:** Stately tree with white/silver leaf undersides. Botanists describe linden flowers as perfect, meaning they have both male and female reproductive parts. **Zones:** 3–8. **Linden Nature Note:** "Perhaps the linden is more famed among the bee community than any other tree of our silva," wrote Alice Lounsberry. "Most assiduously they seek its fragrant, cream-colored blossoms to gather nectar and then produce a honey which is highly regarded in Europe as well as in this country. Truly also it is a beautiful tree of high bred, refined expression."[107] Hollow linden trees found in the woods are often filled with honey. Lindens have special value for bumblebees, halictid bees including green metallic bees, and other native bees. Bees cross-pollinate the flowers and produce very high-quality honey. Native linden trees host 149 species of Lepidoptera (butterflies/moths), including eastern tiger swallowtail (p. 18), question mark (p. 176), red-spotted purple (p. 18), mourning cloak (p. 62), yellow-banded underwing, Linden prominent, basswood leafroller, and saturniid moths including the cecropia moth (p. 18). Other pollinators include various native flies (p. 125), moths, and butterflies such as red admiral,

American linden tree (*Tilia americana*)

Also see p. 275

Red admiral butterfly (*Vanessa atalanta*)

monarch (p. 124), silver-spotted skipper (p. 101), spring azure (p. 95), and question mark (p. 176). Native lindens can be used as a part of conservation biological control,[108] which means they attract predatory or parasitoid insects that naturally prey upon pest insects. By attracting many insects, including a variety of long-horned beetles, native basswoods provide an important and major food source to nesting birds whose babies require a huge insect supply. Birds, including bobwhite (p. 36), eat the seeds as do fox and gray squirrels, eastern chipmunk (p. 94), and white-footed and woodland deer mice. Cavities provide nesting habitat for cavity-nesting birds like wood ducks (p. 162) and woodpeckers (pp. 55, 212), and dens for squirrels and other mammals. **Japanese Beetle Control Note:** Lindens attract Japanese beetles. Hand picking is one way to control them, but this is impossible in tall trees. Forgo insecticides, soaps, oils, and sprays because they indiscriminately kill all insects, including bees and butterflies. Pheromone beetle traps (for both sexes) selectively attract *only* Japanese beetles. Claims that beetle traps should not be used because they attract beetles from far away are inconsistent with the authors' experience. A favorite Japanese beetle egg-laying site, home to their white grubs, is mowed lawn. "The irony of white grub infestations is that they usually attack lawns that are well maintained and irrigated. By nurturing a beautiful lawn and surrounding landscape we actually invite beetles and their destructive grubs."[109] Turning lawn into a garden or landscape of native shrubs, trees, and perennials is a safe and aesthetic method of solving the Japanese beetle problem and helping birds and butterflies.

More Native Alternatives:

BLACKGUM, p. 218; HACKBERRY, p. 174; HONEY LOCUST, p. 163; MAPLE SPP., p. 197; OAK SPP., p. 202; OHIO BUCKEYE, p. 184.

See Spring Trees for BIGLEAF MAGNOLIA, p. 110; CATALPA SPP., p. 86; REDBUD, p. 92; YELLOW BUCKEYE, p. 98; YELLOWWOOD, p. 96.

Nonnative:

MAPLE, SYCAMORE MAPLE, LARGE MAPLE. **Family:** Soapberry (Sapindaceae). **Genus:** *Acer* (*A. pseudoplatanus*). **Origin:** Eurasia. **Height/Spread:** 40–60 feet. **Ornamental Attributes:** Green leaves, no fall color. **Cultivation:** Part to full sun, medium soil, naturalizes. **Zones:** 4–7; *NORWAY MAPLE,* p. 196. Also see Fall Trees for *MAPLE SPP.,* p. 251.

Sycamore maple (*Acer pseudoplatanus*)

Native Alternatives:

SILVER MAPLE. **Family:** Soapberry (Sapindaceae). **Genus:** *Acer* (*A. saccharinum*). **Height:** 50–80 feet. **Spread:** 35–70 feet. **Ornamental Attributes:** Spectacular red flowers in March to April; beautiful silver-backed leaves turn golden in fall. Individual trees sometimes change their gender from year to year. **Cultivation:** Full to part sun, medium to wet soil. Grows naturally in bottomlands. Unlike most native maples, it is sensitive to black walnut toxicity. **Life Span:** 100–125 years. **Zones:** 2–10; BOXELDER, ASHLEAF MAPLE (*A. negundo* var. *negundo*). **Height/Spread:** 30–50 feet. **Ornamental Attributes:** Greenish-yellow flowers in March to April. Showy seed clusters persist into winter, yellow fall color. Sturdy trees with dramatic twisted growth habit, sometimes multiple trunks. In defense of box elder, Caitlin Reinartz describes their growth form as "pretty cool. Every tree is different, and their individuality gives them a bit of personality and interest." Also, "many different types of wildlife rely on those fruits and leaves that persist on the tree, especially late in the season when food supplies become scarce."[110] **Cultivation:** Easily grown in sun and many soil types. Tolerates periodic flooding, cold, dry weather, and black walnut toxicity. Survives where others would not. **Life Span:** 75–100 years. **Zones:** 2–10.

Silver Maple and Box Elder Nature Note: See MAPLE, p. 197.

Silver maple (*Acer saccharinum*)
Also see p. 288

More Native Alternatives:

AMERICAN SYCAMORE, p. 214.

See Native Alternatives to *NORWAY MAPLE,* p. 196.

See Spring Trees for CATALPA SPP., p. 86.

Boxelder (*Acer negundo*)

Mimosa (silk tree)
(*Albizia julibrissin*)

Nonnative:

MIMOSA, SILK TREE. **Family:** Bean (Fabaceae). **Genus:** *Albizia* (*A. julibrissin*). **Origin:** Asia. **Height:** To 40 feet. **Ornamental Attributes:** Fragrant fluffy pink flowers in May to August, pinnately compound leaves. Long brown seedpods. **Cultivation:** Sun, shade, moist soil. Short lived, prolific seeder; dies back in cold weather, becomes weedy, subject to infestations of mimosa webworm. **Ecological Threat:** Naturalized in parts of the Midwest. **Zones:** 6–9.

Native Alternatives:

HONEY LOCUST, p. 163; SOURWOOD, p. 186; SWEETGUM, p. 216.

See Spring Trees for BIGLEAF MAGNOLIA, p. 110; CATALPA SPP., p. 86; CRAB APPLE SPP., p. 89; FLOWERING DOGWOOD, p. 94; FRINGE TREE, p. 105; RED-BUD, p. 92; SERVICEBERRY SPP., p. 77; YELLOW BUCKEYE, p. 98; YELLOW-WOOD, p. 96.

See Fall Trees for AMERICAN MOUNTAIN ASH, p. 255.

See Spring Shrubs for RED BUCKEYE, p. 33.

Nonnative:

MULBERRY, WHITE MULBERRY, RUSSIAN MULBERRY, SILKWORM MULBERRY. **Family:** Mulberry (Moraceae). **Genus:** *Morus* (*M. alba*). **Origin:** China. **Historical Information:** In 1624, the Virginia legislature required every male resident to plant at least four white mulberries to promote a North American silk industry. **Height:** 50 feet. **Ornamental Attributes:** Large shrub/tree. Deeply lobed or heart-shaped leaves. Fruits are purple in the wild, white to pink in many cultivated varieties. **Cultivation:** Most sites. **Ecological**

Mulberry tree (*Morus alba*)

Red mulberry (*Morus rubra*)

Threat: Invasive in the Midwest. Hybridizes readily with the native mulberry, causing concern for the native's long-term genetic viability; transmits a root disease. **Zones:** 4–8; ***PAPER MULBERRY.*** **Genus:** *Broussonetia* (*B. papyrifera*). **Origin:** Japan. **Height:** 45 feet. **Ornamental Attributes:** Reddish-purple/orange summer fruits. Lobed or mitten-shaped leaves. **Ecological Threat:** Naturalized in Midwest. **Zones:** 7–11; ***BLACK MULBERRY*** (*Morus nigra*). **Origin:** Asia. **Ecological Threat:** Naturalized in Midwest. **Zones:** 5–9.

Native Alternative:

RED MULBERRY. **Family:** Mulberry (Moraceae). **Genus:** *Morus* (*M. rubra* var. *rubra*). **Height:** 35–50 feet. **Spread:** 35–40 feet. **Ornamental Attributes:** Attractive tree resembling white mulberry with reddish or dark purple fruits. **Cultivation:** Full sun best, well-drained soil. Males do not fruit. To have fruit and enjoy the many birds they attract, choose a female tree and plant it where dropping fruit won't be a problem. Tolerant of black walnut tree toxicity. **Nature Note:** At least 44 bird species eagerly eat its summer fruits,[111] including American robin (p. 62), gray catbird (p. 79), Baltimore oriole (p. 167), northern flicker (p. 99), eastern kingbird (p. 55), wood duck (p. 162), great crested flycatcher, cuckoos, and tanagers. Squirrels, raccoons, opossums, people, and creatures like the eastern box turtle eagerly seek the abundant and long-lasting fruits. Red mulberry hosts 9 species of butterflies and moths. Along with black willow, American elm, cottonwood, aspen, canoe/paper birch, and hackberry, red mulberry is a host plant for the mourning cloak butterfly (p. 62). **Note:** Threatened in Michigan. **Life Span:** 125 years. **Zones:** 4–8.

More Native Alternatives:

See Spring Trees for CATALPA SPP., p. 86; PAWPAW, p. 113; REDBUD, p. 92; SASSAFRAS, p. 99; SERVICEBERRY SPP., p. 77.

See Fall Trees for OSAGE ORANGE, p. 259; PERSIMMON, p. 256.

Norway maple leaves
(*Acer platanoides*)

Nonnative:

NORWAY MAPLE. **Family:** Soapberry (Sapindaceae). **Genus:** *Acer* (*A. platanoides*). **Origin:** Eurasia. **Height:** 40–50 feet. **Spread:** 30–50 feet. **Ornamental Attributes:** Yellow fall color. **Cultivation:** Sun to shade; tolerates many soil conditions, naturalizes. Shallow roots and dense shade prevent native flowers and shrubs from growing beneath it. "Wherever you are in the city of Chicago, statistically speaking, a well-swung dead cat will either hit the side of a

Norway maple (*Acer platanoides*)

Red maple (*Acer rubrum*)
Also see p. 351

Dunkin Donuts or the trunk of a Norway Maple," observes Seth Harper.[112] **Ecological Threat:** Invasive in several midwestern states. **Historical Note:** Introduced in Philadelphia in 1756 by John Bartram.[113] "It wasn't until the early 1900s that plant identification manuals began to include it with the notation 'occasionally escaped.'"[114] **Cultivar Note:** There are more than 100 Norway maple cultivars, including *A. platanoides* 'Crimson King'. Studies show that cultivars of invasive species are invasive.[115] Some invasive trees and shrubs have seeds that are spread by the wind and water, such as Norway maple, notes the Morton Arboretum, designating Norway maple "Not recommended."[116] **Zones:** 3–7.

Native Alternatives:

MAPLE. **Family:** Soapberry (Sapindaceae). **Genus:** *Acer.* **Note:** The Midwest has an abundance of beautiful native maples. To enjoy maple shade and magnificent fall beauty, and to protect the midwestern environment, eschew nonnative maples, hybrids, and "native" cultivars/nativars. **Seed Note:** The winged seeds, called samaras, spin as they descend to the ground; RED MAPLE (*A. rubrum*). Natural midwestern varieties include *A. rubrum* var. *rubrum*; var. *drummondii*; var. *trilobum.* **Height:** 40–60 feet. **Spread:** 30–50 feet. **Ornamental Attributes:** Red flowers,

Red maple leaves (*Acer rubrum*)

Sugar maple leaves (*Acer saccharum*)

petioles, samaras, twigs, and deep red fall color. **Cultivation:** Full sun to part shade, moist to average well-drained soil. "The red maple is one of our finest ornamentals, a tree for all seasons that develops into an attractive yard specimen in a great range of soils and climates."[117] It can adapt to a particular site due to its roots' unique abilities. **Nativar/Cultivar Fall Color Note:** Conditions beyond human control determine changing leaf color, such as shorter days of sunlight, temperature, and moisture. "Optimum fall foliage is dependent upon sunny days and crisp nights at the beginning of the autumn season." Red maple's leaves are sometimes yellow in fall. "Even relatively consistent cultivars such as 'Red Sunset' maple trees . . . are at the mercy of the weather."[118] **Life Span:** 130–300 years. **Zones:** 3–9; SUGAR MAPLE (*A. saccharum* var. *saccharum*).

Sugar maple (*Acer saccharum*)
Also see p. 289

Black maple leaves
(*Acer nigrum*)

Height: 40–80 feet. **Spread:** 30–60 feet. **Ornamental Attributes:** Pale yellow spring flowers. Beautiful orange, red, and yellow fall color. They do best in large lawns and parks and in groups. **Cultivation:** Full sun to shade, moist well-drained soil. Large trees can suffer from heat rot; prefer cooler climate. Depending on many factors, fall foliage color may vary from year to year and place to place. **Ecological Note:** The tree's shade tolerance enables it to germinate, persist as an understory plant, and shade out native herbaceous plants and slower growing basswood, cherry, walnut, hickory, and oak seedlings, depriving wildlife of important winter food. **Life Span:** 300–400 years. **Zones:** 3–8; **BLACK MAPLE** (*A. nigrum*). **Height/Spread:** 75–120 feet. **Ornamental Attributes:** Fall color ranges from bright yellow and orange to red-orange. Taller but similar in all characteristics to the sugar maple; sometimes treated as belonging to that species. **Zones:** 5–7; see also **BOXELDER**, p. 193; **SILVER MAPLE**, p. 193; **MOUNTAIN MAPLE** and **STRIPED MAPLE**, see Fall Trees, p. 252. **Hybrid/Male Selection Note:** Male-only trees and shrubs dominate modern landscapes, favored by landscapers because they are "litter-free" and

Black maple (*Acer nigrum*)

Rosy maple moth
(*Dryocampa rubicunda*)

Rose-breasted grosbeak (*Pheucticus ludovicianus*)

produce no seeds, seedpods, or fruit. "Several seedless maple varieties are available, either hybrids or male selections that do not produce seeds. Most notable are the *freemanii* cultivars."[119] However, male trees and shrubs do produce pollen, and increasing their plantings causes an increase in pollen.[120] A tip that experts provide to hayfever sufferers is "Avoid planting male (pollen-producing) plants."[121] Another negative result is that male plant–dominated landscapes deprive wildlife of seeds, buds, nuts, and fruits provided by female trees. Commonsense landscaping includes a good mix of naturally sexed native trees. **Nature Note:** Native maples (including boxelder) host 297 species of Lepidoptera, including eastern tiger swallowtail butterfly (p. 18), Io moth (p. 91), oval-based prominent, saddled prominent, retarded dagger moth, the rosy maple moth with variable colors that include pink, yellow, and white, luna moth (p. 54), and imperial moth (p. 329). Maple sap is sought by the yellow-bellied sapsucker (p. 79), honeybees, and adult butterflies, including mourning cloak (p. 62), commas (p. 103), and red admiral (p. 192). Insect-eating birds devour flies seeking sap. Ruffed grouse (p. 36), wild turkey (p. 244), rose-breasted grosbeak, purple finch (p. 145), American goldfinch (p. 145), native sparrows (p. 108), red-breasted nuthatch (p. 322), eastern chipmunk (p. 94), bears, foxes, meadow voles, white-footed mice, and gray, red, and flying squirrels eat the winged seeds and buds in spring and winter. Female maple flowers offer neither nectar nor pollen, but bees sometimes seek pollen from male flowers. Snapping turtles sometimes feed on fallen leaves. Some songbirds nest in the trees. Large blocks of mature upland and lowland oak-hickory-maple forests are breeding sites for the rare and endangered cerulean warbler. Old trees provide dens for squirrels, raccoons, opossums, and cavity-nesting birds like the black-capped chickadee (p. 322), northern flicker (p. 99), pileated woodpecker, wood duck (p. 162), and screech owl. Birds such as prairie warbler construct nests on the branches.

Prairie warbler (*Setophaga discolor*)

Note: A native maple is a better choice than any nonnative tree. "I don't recommend maples, though, unless a homeowner really wants one," states a landscaper, who finds one of the more than 50 species of oaks found in the United States and Canada a better choice for wildlife.[122] Although maple trees are beautiful, they don't provide as much food value to wildlife, and allowing them to dominate reduces plant and wildlife diversity.[123]

More Native Alternatives:

AMERICAN BEECH, p. 168; BLACKGUM, p. 218; BOXELDER, p. 193; HICKORY SPP., p. 221; OAK SPP.: BLACK OAK, PIN OAK, RED OAK, SCARLET OAK, and others, p. 202; SILVER MAPLE, p. 193; SOURWOOD, p. 186; and many other beautiful native trees. Also see Fall Trees for MOUNTAIN MAPLE, p. 252; STRIPED MAPLE, p. 252.

Nonnative:

OAK, ENGLISH OAK. **Family:** Beech (Fagaceae). **Genus:** *Quercus* (*Q. robur*). White Oak Group. **Origin:** Europe, Asia. **Height/Spread:** 40–70 feet. **Ornamental Attributes:** Dull brown-yellow fall color. **Cultivation:** Full sun, medium soil, prone to mildew. **Zones:** 5–8; *JAPANESE WHITE OAK, ORIENTAL WHITE OAK* (*Q. aliena*). **Origin:** Korea, Japan. **Ornamental Attributes:** Red fall leaves. **Zones:** 3–9; *MONGOLIAN OAK* (*Q. mongolica*).

Oak (English oak) (*Quercus robur*)

Oak (English oak) leaves
(*Quercus robur*)

Zones: 5–8; *SAWTOOTH OAK* (*Q. acutissima*). **Origin:** China, Korea, Japan. **Height/ Spread:** 40–60 feet. **Ornamental Attributes:** Has occasional yellow fall color. **Cultivation:** Full sun, medium soil, naturalizes. **Ecological Threat:** Classified as invasive in Wisconsin, a "caution" in Indiana. **Zones:** 5–9. **Nonnative Oak Problem Note:** Nonnative oaks are susceptible to two-lined chestnut borer attacks. All native North American oak species have some resistance.[124]

Native Alternatives:

OAK. Family: Beech (Fagaceae). **Genus:** *Quercus*. Native oaks are "quintessential wildlife plants," writes Douglas Tallamy.[125] **Note to the Future:** "If you have the space, you should . . . consider planting the larger oak species," writes Billy Bruce Winkles. "Every year in the United States thousands of large old oaks are cut down, but far fewer are planted. Many of the destroyed trees are at least a hundred years old, and it would take that long to grow similar-size replacements. In fact, some of the large oaks can live for five hundred years. If you want to leave a lasting legacy to the future, plant one (or several) now. No tree is more majestic, and it's hard to find a better wildlife plant."[126] "No other group of trees that I'm aware of provides more wildlife value than the genus *Quercus*," writes Alonso Abugattas, putting oaks first in his list of "Top 10 Trees" for homeowners to use to support wildlife.[127] Oaks are not regenerating in adequate numbers in many midwestern forests. By planting oaks in our backyards, gardens, schoolgrounds, parks, and other landscapes, we can help prevent these trees from becoming rare or disappearing. Long after maple trees are bare, the oaks remain full of fall color. **Oak Groups:** Red-Black and White. Native oaks are generally disease resistant, but some problems of oaks are restricted to, or are more severe in, one group versus the other, so it can be helpful to know your oak's group. Ultimately, acorns produced by trees in the white oak group tend to be consumed more regularly by wildlife than acorns from trees in the red oak group.[128] BUR OAK, BURR OAK (*Q. macrocarpa*). White Oak Group. **Midwestern Variety:** *Quercus macrocarpa* var. *macrocarpa*. Overlapping varieties include *Quercus macrocarpa* var. *depressa*. **Height/Spread:** 70–80 feet; in an open setting can reach 100 feet. **Ornamental**

Bur oak leaves and acorns (*Quercus macrocarpa*)
Also see p. 279

Bur oak (*Quercus macrocarpa*)
Also see p. 350

Attributes: Rugged-looking shade tree produces large fringed-capped acorns. Its beautiful summer foliage turns yellow, purple, golden brown, or dull orange in fall. Massive trunk and deeply furrowed bark. The bur oak is "the preeminent tree of the Midwest savannas" and "a most appreciated shade tree on the hot prairie. . . . Perhaps no other tree can match the rugged venerability of an old bur oak," write Sternberg and Wilson.[129] "Hardly a more beautiful tree can be imagined when in cultivation when enough room has been given it to follow its own bent of development," wrote Alice Lounsberry. "One then looks upon its great head and branches with almost a feeling of awe."[130] **Cultivation:** Full sun, takes numerous soil conditions; prefers heavier soils, including clay. **Urban Use Note:** Tolerant of city smoke, ozone, other air pollutants, and drought; resistant to salt, fire, wind, and ice damage. The region's most cold-hardy oak, bur oak is commonly planted as a shade tree in many urban areas, and is easy to find in nurseries. **Midwestern Prairie Note:** Before the destruction of the prairie, the tree's deep taproot and thick fire- and drought-resistant bark enabled it to coexist with prairie in the form of "beautiful parklike savannas that were neither prairie nor forest."[131] **Life Span:** 200–400 years. **Zones:** 3–8; BLACK OAK (*Q. velutina*). Red-Black Oak Group. **Height/Spread:** 60–85 feet. **Ornamental Attributes:** Leaves of different shapes may be found on an individual tree; in fall they turn red, orange, yellow, or brown. **Cultivation:** Full sun. Moist or dry well-drained soils; handles many soil types. Tolerates black walnut tree toxicity. Nearly as common in the Midwest as white oak and northern red oak. **Life Span:** 100–225 years. **Zones:** 4–8; BLACKJACK OAK (*Q. marilandica*). Red-Black Oak Group. **Height/Spread:** 20–40 feet. **Ornamental Attributes:** Thick, leathery, 3-lobed leaves turn red or brown in fall. Has a twisted trunk and thick, chunky bark that developed to resist fire. This striking small oak tree "is underappreciated" in the Midwest.[132] **Cultivation:** Full sun; acidic, dry to medium, well-drained soils. The leaves persist through winter, providing wildlife with shelter. **Life Span:** 125 years. **Zones:** 5–9; CHESTNUT OAK (*Q. montana, Q. prinus*). White Oak Group. **Height/Spread:** 60–70 feet. **Ornamental Attributes:** Chestnut-like foliage unfurls pink and becomes silvery before becoming dark green, then red or gold in fall. Bark is beautiful silvery-white. **Cultivation:** Full sun best; moist or dry well-drained soil, intolerant of poorly drained soil. Survival in unfavorable conditions, like steep, rocky hills, is due to well-developed taproot. **Life Span:** 300–400 years. **Note:** Threatened in Illinois. **Zones:** 4–8; CHINKAPIN OAK, CHINQUAPIN OAK, YELLOW CHESTNUT OAK (*Q. muehlenbergii*). White Oak Group. **Height:** 60–80 feet. "In the primeval forests," these trees "commonly grew 160 feet tall."[133] **Ornamental Attributes:** Relatively fast-growing beautiful shade and ornamental tree, its leaves are unlobed, serrated, chestnut tree–like, and its acorns are small and unusually sweet. Fall color is golden yellow. **Cultivation:** Full sun best when tree grows in soils that are dry or of average moisture. Thrives in rich, deep soils. Intolerant of flooding and acidic soil; salt resistant. Its liking for alkaline soils and drought resistance make it a good street tree. **Note:** Be sure not to purchase a mildew-susceptible hybrid. Also

Chinkapin oak leaves
(*Quercus muehlenbergii*)

Chinkapin oak
(*Quercus muehlenbergii*)
Also see p. 281

see Winter Shrubs for **DWARF CHINKAPIN OAK**, p. 311. **Life Span:** 400 years. **Zones:** 4–8; **HILL'S OAK, NORTHERN PIN OAK, JACK OAK** (*Q. ellipsoidalis*). Red-Black Oak Group. **Height/ Spread:** 40–50 feet. **Ornamental Attributes:** Reliable bright red fall color (see p. 291) and tolerance of poor conditions make these trees popular. Trees generally retain leaves through winter, so used as a screen; provides wildlife with cover. Good yard, park, and parkway tree. **Cultivation:** Sun; dry, sandy, and heavy clay soils. Relatively fast growing. **Zones:** 4–7; **PIN OAK** (*Q. palustris*). Red-Black Oak Group. **Height:** 50–70 feet. **Spread:** 40–60 feet. **Ornamental Attributes:** Broad pyramidal shape. A popular urban tree in the Midwest. Pendulous drooping lower limbs often touch the ground when grown in the open. Numerous small, pin-like branches line the trunk. Heavy crops of small acorns appeal to songbirds and woodpeckers. Red, yellow, orange fall foliage persists through winter, providing wildlife with cover. **Cultivation:** Sun; rich, moist, wet, acidic soil; flood tolerant, resistant to road salt and urban pollution. **Life Span:** 100–150 years. **Zones:** 4–8; **POST OAK** (*Q. stellata*). White Oak Group. **Height/Spread:** 35–50 feet. **Ornamental Attributes:** The leaves, often mistaken for white oak, turn excellent shades of yellow and brown in fall. **Cultivation:** Full sun, shade intolerant. Dry to moist, rocky or sandy acidic soils. Considered the ultimate drought-resistant tree, but also grows in soggy, flatwood soils. Slow-growing, small acorns appeal to songbirds and woodpeckers. **Life Span:** 250–450 years. **Zones:** 5–9; **RED OAK, NORTHERN RED OAK** (*Q. rubra* var. *ambigua, Q. rubra* var. *rubra*). Red-Black Oak Group. **Height:** 60–70 feet. **Spread:** 50 feet. The Midwest's most northerly red oak. Along with white oak, it is one of the region's two most common oaks. **Ornamental Attributes:** Fall color

Red oak leaves (*Quercus rubra* var. *rubra*)

is an outstanding red, hence the name *rubrum*. Distinctive gray-striped bark. "Under the right conditions, the quality of the red color of the leaves is not far inferior to that on *Acer rubrum* [red maple], the standard by which all other specimens are judged. Their fall foliage comes later than that on the maples. For the impatient, this may seem a bad thing. But it's a boon to those who desire to see the season for autumn color extended for as long as possible," writes David Beaulieu.[134] **Cultivation:** Sun; tolerates light shade; can grow under existing trees. Best in moist, well-drained loamy acidic soils; tolerates clay soil, intolerant of wet soil and flooding. Tolerant of air pollution, salt, and black walnut tree toxicity. **Life Span:** 200–400 years. **Zones:** 3–8; SCARLET OAK (*Q. coccinea*). Red-Black Oak Group. **Height:** 50–80 feet. **Spread:** 40–50 feet. **Ornamental Attributes:** "'Spectacular fall color,' 'brilliant scarlet leaves,' and 'a standout for fall color' are some popular descriptions for this tree.'"[135] "All minor characteristics of the scarlet oak seem to be immersed in the brilliant bright red of its autumn foliage, the most exquisite tint displayed by any

Red oak
(*Quercus rubra*)
Also see p. 292

one of the family," wrote Alice Lounsberry.[136] (See p. 293.) **Cultivation:** Full sun, dry to medium soil; considered a dry-site species. Tolerates black walnut tree toxicity. Grows rapidly. **Life Span:** 80–180 years. **Zones:** 4–9; SHINGLE OAK (*Q. imbricaria*). Red-Black Oak Group. **Height:** 40–60 feet. **Ornamental Attributes:** Leathery, banana-shaped leaves with neither lobes nor teeth turn red, golden yellow, or brown in fall and persist through winter, providing animals with shelter. May be used as a screen instead of evergreens, or as a shade tree for lawns, parks, or parkways. **Cultivation:** Sun; shade intolerant. Can grow in gravel, dry sand, heavy clay. Low maintenance. Tolerates black walnut tree toxicity. A pioneer species; like eastern red cedar and honey locust, it is one of the first to colonize a disturbed area. **Zones:** 4–8; SHUMARD OAK, SWAMP RED OAK (*Q. shumardii* var. *schneckii*, Q. *shumardii* var. *shumardii*, Q. *shumardii* var. *stenocarpa*). Red-Black Oak Group. **Height:** 60–80 feet. **Ornamental Attributes:** Looks like northern red oak. Fast-growing tree; fluted base, large acorns, red fall leaves. **Cultivation:** Sun. Average, dry to medium, acidic, well-drained soils. Tolerates a wide range of soil conditions, including wet and moist soils. Easily grown shade tree for lawn or parkway. **Life Span:** 200 years. **Zones:** 5–8; SWAMP WHITE OAK, BICOLOR OAK (*Q. bicolor*). White Oak Group. **Height/Spread:** 50–70 feet. **Ornamental Attributes:** Striking shade tree has lustrous, lobed leaves with a two-tone appearance (bicolor), dark green on top and a silvery-white underside. On sunny days when the wind ruffles the leaves, the brightly shining undersides help identify the tree. **Young trees have** peeling or plate-like bark. Fall

Swamp white oak
(*Quercus bicolor*)
Also see p. 296

Swamp white oak leaves
(*Quercus bicolor*)

color is intense orange-gold to yellow (see p. 296). **Confusion Note:** Bur oak acorn caps are fringed, unlike those of swamp white oak. **Cultivation:** Sun. Prefers lowlands and mildly acidic soil. Does poorly in high dry sites. Resistant to disease, drought, salt, poorly drained urban soils, heat, and black walnut tree toxicity. Grows quickly. **Note:** Special concern species in Minnesota. **Life Span:** More than 300 years. **Zones:** 4–8; WHITE OAK (*Q. alba*). White Oak Group. **Height:** 60–100 feet, sometimes 150 feet. **Spread:** 50–70 feet. **Ornamental Attributes:** Can be a massive spreading tree. "In spring the young leaves are exquisite in their delicate silvery pink, covered with soft down as with a blanket." In summer, it is "the most stately and beautiful of our oaks." In fall, it is "also beautiful; its rich purplish red glows in the forest

and gives a splendor to November days long after the maples and sumachs have shed their leaves," wrote Harriet L. Keeler.[137] It is the only oak of the white oak group with russet red fall color. "The white oak . . . so-called for its pale trunk, and one of our truly magnificent trees, has large leaves that turn russet in late fall and gradually turn to a browner tone until February," wrote Helen Pelt Wilson.[138] **Cultivation:** Sun best, well-drained acidic sites. Grows in sand and clay but never in very wet soils. Tolerates drought and black walnut tree toxicity. **Life Span:** 300–600 years. **Note:** State tree of Illinois. **Zones:** 3–9.

White oak leaves (*Quercus alba*)

Oaks Native to the Southern Midwest:

CHERRYBARK OAK (*Q. pagoda*). Red-Black Oak Group. **Height/Spread:** 75 feet. Can reach 120 feet. **Ornamental Attributes:** Fast-growing, spectacular shade tree; black cherry tree–like bark. Produces small acorns in alternate years. **Cultivation:** Sun, dry to moist soil. Best in rich, loamy soils, intolerant of compacted soil. Does well further north but remains smaller. **Zones:** 6–9; OVERCUP OAK (*Q. lyrata*). White Oak Group. **Height:** 35–65 feet. **Ornamental Attributes:** Leaves resembling white oak turn yellow, orange, and red in fall. Acorn almost completely covered by cap. **Cultivation:** Sun to part shade. Flood tolerant; thought of as the bur oak of wet, low areas and floodplains. Native to southern Illinois and Indiana; found growing in northern parts of the states. Not widely available, but is likely to become an important landscape tree, states the Lady Bird Johnson Wildflower Center.[139] **Life Span:** 300–400 years. **Zones:** 5–8; SOUTHERN RED OAK, SPANISH OAK (*Q. falcata*). Red-Black Oak Group. **Height:** 80 feet. **Cultivation:** Full sun, shade intolerant. Clay, sand, loam, acidic, occasionally wet, well-drained soils. Tolerates drought. **Note:** Threatened in Ohio. **Life Span:** 200–275 years. **Zones:** 5/6–8; SWAMP CHESTNUT OAK, COW OAK, BASKET OAK (*Q. michauxii*). White Oak Group. **Height:** 80 feet. Native to low, well-drained bottomlands and floodplains and moist uplands. **Ornamental Attributes:** Bright red fall color. **Cultivation:** Sun; shade intolerant. **Life Span:** 100–200 years. **Zones:** 5–8; WATER OAK (*Q. nigra*). Red-Black Oak Group. **Height/Spread:** 50–80 feet. **Ornamental Attributes:** Full sun to partial shade. Tolerates clay, sand, loam, acidic, and alkaline soils, extended flooding, and drought. Can grow on moist, well-drained uplands. Fast growing. **Life Span:** 175 years. **Zones:** 6–9; WILLOW OAK, PEACH LEAVED OAK (*Q. phellos*). Red-Black Oak Group. **Height:** 75 feet. **Spread:** 50 feet. **Ornamental Attributes:** Small, willow-like leaves provide fine shade and are often retained into winter, providing wildlife with shelter. It is said to have been President Thomas Jefferson's favorite tree. **Cultivation:** Sun; shade intolerant. Medium to wet soil; tolerates compacted soil and urban environments. "Willow oak is extensively used as an

White oak (*Quercus alba*)

ornamental in the South, but handles Midwestern winters fairly well."[140] Grows quickly. **Life Span:** Up to 300 years. **Note:** Threatened in Illinois. **Zones:** 5–9. **Native American Oak Note:** Native Americans roasted or ground the acorns into nutritious food after removing the bitter tannic acid by placing a bag of acorns in a clean, flowing stream for a few days until brown-colored water around the acorns was no longer visible.[141] **Oak Nature Note:** "When oaks burst into life in spring populations of oak-leaf-eating caterpillars boom: this offers a food bonanza for caterpillar-munching birds looking to raise a family," observe researchers.[142] To find "caterpillars unlike any you have seen before," Douglas Tallamy suggests "careful inspection" of oak leaf undersides.[143] "The value of oaks for supporting both vertebrate and invertebrate wildlife cannot be overstated," he writes. "Since the demise of the American chestnut, oaks have joined hickories, walnuts, and the American beech in supplying the bulk of nut forage so necessary for maintaining populations of vertebrate wildlife. What we have underappreciated in the past, however, is the diversity of insect herbivores that oaks add to forest ecosystems. From this perspective, oaks are the quintessential wildlife plants: no other plant genus supports more species of Lepidoptera; thus providing more types of bird food, than the mighty oak."[144] Oak trees host an astounding 534 species of Lepidoptera (butterflies/moths), the greatest number of any known North American plant. Oaks enable chickadees (p. 322), whose nestlings eat mostly caterpillars, to successfully reproduce. Insects, particularly caterpillars, contain fat and more protein than beef, and 96 percent of North American land birds feed them to their young.[145] When nonnative trees, such as ginkgo, dominate street plantings, fewer birds can nest successfully. When oaks are plentiful, so are caterpillars, enabling butterflies and birds to successfully coexist. The great number of butterflies hosted by oaks makes it accurate to call them butterfly trees. The sleepy duskywing lays her eggs on bur oak. Juvenal's

Sleepy duskywing skipper (*Erynnis brizo*)

Horace's duskywing butterfly (*Erynnis horatius*)

Banded hairstreak butterfly (*Satyrium calanus*)

Edwards' hairstreak butterfly (*Satyrium edwardsii*)

Oak hairstreak butterfly
(*Satyrium favonius*)

White M hairstreak butterfly
(*Parrhasius m-album*)

duskywing (p. 102), Horace's duskywing (p. 210), and several species of hairstreak butterflies, including the banded hairstreak (p. 210) and northern hairstreak, lay their eggs on many oaks, including black oak, blackjack oak, bur oak, northern red oak, post oak, scrub oak, water oak, white oak, and willow oak. Edwards' hairstreak (p. 210) lays her eggs on many oaks, including bur oak, scrub oak, and black oak. "The easiest way to find a colony of the Edwards' hairstreak is to look for large ant mounds in association with small oak trees," writes David K. Parshall. "The ants receive sweet nectar from the larvae and in turn provide protection for the larvae and adult butterflies."[146] The striped hairstreak (p. 18), red-banded hairstreak, and oak hairstreak lay their eggs on most oak trees. The red-spotted purple (p. 18) and white M hairstreak lay their eggs on all oak trees, as well as on cherry, aspen, poplar, and hawthorn. "If you plant silverbell, oaks, birches, willows or black cherry in your yard, you may attract the spectacular prometha moth," writes Douglas Tallamy. "Oaks will provide food for the polyphemus moth . . . and the bizarrely attractive larvae of moths in the family Limacodidae."[147] Oaks host the imperial moth (p. 329) and moths with names ranging from Acorn Moth to Slowpoke and Girl Friend Underwing.[148] Oaks support leafhoppers, walking sticks, katydids, long-horned beetles, leaf beetles, treehoppers, and other small insects that nesting birds need to feed their offspring. Butterflies such as red admiral (p. 192), mourning cloak (p. 62), and painted lady (p. 132) sip sap from holes drilled by yellow-bellied sapsucker woodpeckers (p. 79) in plum and bur oak trees, a woodland butterfly adaptation to shady areas with few nectar-producing flowers.[149] Harmless wasps lay eggs on oaks that produce harmless galls that contain larvae eaten by woodpeckers, chickadees, raccoons, and opossums. Snout beetles (acorn weevils) lay eggs inside acorns, providing wildlife with extra protein. Acorns become most abundant on

Polyphemus moth (*Antheraea polyphemus*)

Green leaf katydid
(*Microcentrum rhombifolium*)

Red-headed woodpecker (*Melanerpes erythrocephalus*)

the ground in autumn and winter, when availability and nutritional quality of many other plant food resources are lowest. Another reason acorns are critically important is that they supply energy in fall, a time of year when animals need extra food to prepare for winter's harsh weather. Oaks also provide many types of animals with shelter and homes in strong branches and hollow places in trunks. Animals also shelter in and inhabit the trees after they fall. More than 60 species of birds frequent live and dead oaks for shelter and nesting sites, including the cavity-nesting eastern flycatcher. Birds feeding on acorns include ruffed grouse (p. 36), bobwhite quail (p. 36), greater prairie chicken, brown thrasher (p. 219), mallard and wood ducks (p. 162), northern parula, blue-gray gnatcatcher, yellow-throated vireo, summer tanager, red-tailed and Swainson's hawks, black-capped chickadee (p. 322), Carolina chickadee, screech owl, eastern bluebird (p. 61), and wild turkeys (p. 244) that rely on strong gizzards to grind them up; red- and white-breasted nuthatches (pp. 322, 30) and blue jays (p. 79) crack acorns open with their strong beaks and eat the nuts. Acorns are important food for the red-headed woodpecker, American crow (p. 244), and tufted titmouse (p. 169). Oaks provide food and shelter for more than 100 species of vertebrate animals,[150] including squirrels (fox, gray, red, flying), voles, rabbits, opossums, raccoons, chipmunks (p. 94), and larger mammals such as bear and white-tailed deer, which dig through the snow to locate the acorns. The blue jay is credited with planting the acorns, chestnuts, and beechnuts that developed into the North American forests that grew in the newly ice-free areas that followed the melting of the Wisconsin Glacier about 10,000 years ago. To this day, the birds accurately select the nuts not infested with weevils, transport several at a time as far as five miles, and systematically bury them individually to eat them over the winter, thereby planting them in new areas.[151] Chipmunks store acorns for winter, as do gray squirrels, covering them with earth and literally planting them. Creating some individual trees (or even creating an oak forest) is as easy as leaving acorns out for the squirrels, which sometimes forget where they have hidden some of them. Masting, an evolutionary strategy, enables many oaks to produce bumper crops approximately every two to seven years. Because more acorns are often produced than wildlife can eat, some remain to turn into new trees. Hummingbirds (p. 91) use the fuzz on the undersides of the first oak leaves to build nests. **Natural Oak Hybrids:** Because they are wind pollinated, under certain conditions, especially near their habitat margins, oaks—like many other trees—can create natural hybrids.

More Native Alternatives:

AMERICAN BEECH, p. 168; AMERICAN HORNBEAM, p. 182; BLACK WALNUT, p. 220; HICKORY SPP., p. 221; HOP HORNBEAM, p. 183.

Plane tree
(*Platanus* × *hispanica*)

Nonnative:

PLANE TREE, LONDON PLANE TREE, HYBRID PLANE. **Family:** Plane-tree (Platanaceae). **Genus:** *Platanus (P.* × *hispanica).* **Origin:** Despite its name, it is not native to England. It is not native anywhere, as it is a hybrid of Oriental plane tree from southeastern Europe to Asia Minor and American sycamore, trees from opposite sides of the globe. **Height:** 75–100 feet. **Spread:** 60–75 feet. **Ornamental Attributes:** This tree is very difficult to distinguish from the American sycamore. It has yellow and red flowers in April, brown fruit balls in fall. Exfoliating brown bark reveals creamy-white inner bark. **Cultivation:** Full sun, medium to wet soil. The *Platanus* genus is highly susceptible to anthracnose, leaf, shoot, or twig blight. Cultivars, often male, are susceptible to a variety of diseases. Male tree pollen causes hayfever. **Zones:** 4–8.

American sycamore leaves (*Platanus occidentalis*)

American sycamore tree (*Platanus occidentalis*)
Also see pp. 276, 352

Native Alternative:

AMERICAN SYCAMORE, EASTERN SYCAMORE, AMERICAN PLANETREE, OCCIDENTAL PLANE, BUTTONWOOD. **Family:** Plane-tree (Platanaceae). **Genus:** *Platanus* (*P. occidentalis*). **Note:** This genus has survived for 100 million years, since the late Cretaceous Period. **Height/Spread:** 75–100 feet. **Ornamental Attributes:** In April, it produces red and yellow flowers; its fall leaves are yellow. Dark bark with showy splashes of creamy white— snowy white bark adorns upper branches of some sycamores; single "button ball" fruits add winter interest. **Cultivation:** Full to part full sun, many soils, preferably deep and moist. Tolerant of black walnut tree toxicity. **Nature Note:** Purple finch (p. 145), American goldfinch (p. 145), black-capped (p. 322) and Carolina chickadees, and dark-eyed junco (p. 322) eat the seeds in winter; some birds dine on the leafhoppers (p. 98) the tree hosts. The cerulean warbler, a once-abundant migratory bird, preferred nesting in old sycamore trees. Habitat destruction helped endanger sycamores and cerulean warblers. "Some of them live on for centuries," but owners of huge old trees can cut them down. "Stewardship connotes responsibility to the future," observe Sternberg and Wilson.[152] Owls, chimney swifts, red-bellied and red-headed woodpeckers (pp. 55, 212), and wood ducks (p. 162) use older or dead tree cavities for nesting. Pairs of great crested flycatchers use live trees to create nests adorned with a piece of snakeskin. Squirrels, raccoons, and bats use them for dens. In pioneer days, people lived in huge, hollow trees. Today, black bears have reclaimed these living quarters. The tree hosts 45 species of butterflies and moths, including the white-marked sycamore tussock moth, whose caterpillars provide chickadee and other bird babies with needed food. **Zones:** 4–9.

Nonnative:

POPLAR. See *ASPEN*, p. 164.

Nonnative:

PURPLELEAF CHERRY. See Spring Shrubs, p. 17.

Nonnative:

SEVEN-SON FLOWER. See Summer Shrubs, p. 148.

Nonnative:

STEWARTIA, JAPANESE STEWARTIA. **Family:** Tea (Theaceae). **Genus:** *Stewartia* (*S. pseudocamellia*). **Origin:** Japan. **Height:** 12–40 feet. **Spread:** 8–25 feet. **Ornamental Attributes:** Small tree, multistemmed shrub. Camellia-like white flowers in early summer. **Cultivation:** Sun to part shade; well-drained soil. Needs winter protection. **Zones:** 5–8.

Stewartia (Japanese stewartia)
(*Stewartia pseudocamellia*)

Native Alternative:

STEWARTIA, MOUNTAIN CAMELLIA, MOUNTAIN STUARTIA, ANGEL-FRUITED STUARTIA. **Family:** Tea (Theaceae). **Genus:** *Stewartia* (*S. ovata*). **Height/Spread:** 10–20 feet. **Ornamental Attributes:** Large shrub/small tree. When few other trees are blooming in May to July, the native stewartia produces showy, large, frilly white camellia flowers with orange-scarlet fall color and zigzag branching. "It seems strange that a shrub so bold and striking and fairly enchanting as the mountain Stuartia should be so little known by the country people through its range," wrote Alice Lounsberry in 1901, noting, "It is also rarely seen in cultivation, although it is hardy, as far northward as New England."[153] **Cultivation:** Early morning sun; appreciates afternoon shade in heat of the day. Well-drained soil. Native to southeastern United States, it is well adapted to cold winters. "This uncommon tree deserves a prominent position in the landscape," writes the Missouri Botanical Garden.[154] **Nature Note:** Hosts 1 species of Lepidoptera. Its fragrance attracts butterflies, bees, and other pollinators. **Zones:** 5–9.

Stewartia (*Stewartia ovata*)

Another Native Alternative:

See Summer Shrubs for FRANKLIN TREE, p. 147.

Nonnative:

SWEETGUM, ORIENTAL SWEETGUM. **Family:** Altingia (Altingiaceae). **Genus:** *Liquidambar* (*L. orientalis*). **Origin:** Asia. **Height:** 15–25 feet. **Spread:** 20–30 feet. **Ornamental Attributes:** Produces gumballs. Fall foliage is sometimes colorful. **Cultivation:** Sun, medium soil. **Zones:** 6–9.

Sweetgum (Oriental sweetgum) (*Liquidambar orientalis*)

Native Alternatives:

SWEETGUM. **Family:** Altingia (Altingiaceae). **Genus:** *Liquidambar* (*L. styraciflua*). **Height:** 60–80 feet. **Spread:** 40–60 feet. **Ornamental Attributes:** Star-shaped leaves often go through shades of yellow and orange before culminating in hues of brilliant red, crimson, burgundy, and purple. Distinctive spiky brown seed balls (gumballs) persist through winter. The sap can be made into chewing gum. All parts of the tree are fragrant. **Cultivation:** Sun; moist, acidic soil; tolerates poor drainage; a rapidly growing low-maintenance tree. **Nature Note:** Seeds provide food for birds, chipmunks (p. 94), and squirrels. Hummingbirds (p. 91) visit the flowers for nectar. Hosts 35 species of butterflies and moths. If you wish to enable reproduction by the beautiful luna moth (p. 54), "sweetgum . . . is your best bet," notes Douglas Tallamy.[155] **Life Span:** 200–300 years. **Zones:** 4–9.

Sweetgum leaves and
fruits (*Liquidambar
styraciflua*)

Sweetgum (*Liquidambar
styraciflua*)
Also see pp. 298, 348

Blackgum (*Nyssa sylvatica*)

BLACKGUM, BLACK TUPELO, SOUR-
GUM. **Family:** Dogwood (Cornaceae). **Genus:**
Nyssa (*N. sylvatica*). **Height:** 30–50 feet. **Spread:**
20–30 feet. **Ornamental Attributes:** Small
greenish-white flowers in May to June are followed by small blue-black berries. "The dark
green glossy summer foliage takes center stage in
fall when the leaves turn bright scarlet," notes the
Morton Arboretum.[156] Gray scaly bark, horizontal, pagoda-like limbs provide winter interest.
Cultivation: Full sun best for fall color. Does well
in light shade. Best in rich, fertile, well-drained
moist soil, adapts to seasonal flooding and dry
uplands. To set fruit, female trees need a male
pollinator. Tolerant of black walnut tree toxicity.
This tree is uncommon only because its taproot
once made transplanting difficult; today, there
should be more plantings of this beautiful tree.
Life Span: 250–600 years; WATER TUPELO,
SWAMP TUPELO, WATER GUM (*N. aquat-
ica*). Found in swamps and bottomlands in pure
stands or in combination with bald cypress, water oaks, and swamp cottonwoods. *Nyssa* **Nature
Note:** Flowers are an excellent nectar source for
bees. Beekeepers prize them to create delicious
tupelo honey. Trees host 26 species of Lepidoptera (butterflies/moths), including the false underwing, tupelo leaf miner, and azalea sphinx.
The high-fat dark blue fruits produced by the
female trees attract more than 30 species of song

Blackgum leaves and
fruit (*Nyssa sylvatica*)

and game birds, including American robin, wood thrush (p. 175), northern flicker (p. 99), wild turkey (p. 244), and brown thrasher, and are an important food source for many mammals. Older trees often develop cavities that provide dens for various small mammals and nesting habitat for birds. **Zones:** 3–9.

More Native Alternatives:

SOURWOOD, p. 186; STEWARTIA, p. 215.
See Fall Trees for MOUNTAIN MAPLE, p. 252; STRIPED MAPLE, p. 252.

Nonnative:

TULIP TREE, CHINESE TULIP TREE. **Family:** Magnolia (Magnoliaceae). **Genus:** *Liriodendron* (*L. chinense*). **Origin:** Asia. **Height:** 50–70 feet. **Spread:** 30–40 feet. **Ornamental Attributes:** Very similar to the native tulip tree (*L. tulipifera*) but less cold hardy; also smaller, less colorful flowers. **Zones:** 6–9.

Brown thrasher (*Toxostoma rufum*)

Native Alternative:

TULIP TREE, p. 179.

Nonnative:

WALNUT, ENGLISH WALNUT. **Family:** Walnut/Hickory (Juglandaceae). **Chemical Reaction Note:** The walnut family produces a chemical that can inhibit the growth of nearby plants. **Genus:** *Juglans* (*J. regia*). **Origin:** Middle East. **Height/Spread:** 40–60 feet. **Ornamental Attributes:** Shade tree with edible nuts. **Cultivation:** Full sun, moist rich soil, naturalizes. **Ecological Threat:** Naturalized in Michigan. It is the source of a fungus that is harming our native butternuts. **Zones:** 3–7.

Walnut (English walnut) (*Juglans regia*)

Black walnut nuts and leaves (*Juglans nigra*)

Native Alternatives:

BLACK WALNUT. Family: Walnut/Hickory (Juglandaceae). **Genus:** *Juglans* (*J. nigra*). **Height/Spread:** 50–75 feet. **Ornamental Attributes:** Dramatic-looking shade tree. Sweet, protein-rich, fragrant, green ornamental-looking edible nuts. Chocolate-brown, furrowed, diamond-patterned bark. Yellow fall foliage. "There are few trees indeed that hold a more assured place in the plant world than the black walnuts. In personality they are attractive with foliage that is noticeable from the odd-pinnate growth of its leaflets; their nuts are abundant in a richly flavoured, oily meat," wrote Alice Lounsberry."[157] **Cultivation:** Full sun; moist, rich soil. The tree produces a chemical, juglone, that is toxic to some other plants, so when landscaping, choose an appropriate site. **Chemical Reaction Note:** "The greatest quantities of juglone are found in the area immediately under the walnut tree," writes Lynn M. Steiner.[158] "The most sensitive plants however are alien ornamentals, because they have no evolutionary experience with juglone," writes Douglas Tallamy. "Most natives that evolved within the range of walnuts are unfazed by their allelochemicals."[159] Black walnuts can receive undeserved blame for failures due to underwatering plants and other cultivation mistakes. **Life Span:** 150–250 years. **Zones:** 3–9;

BUTTERNUT, WHITE WALNUT (*J. cinerea*). **Height:** To 60 feet. **Spread:** To 50 feet. **Ornamental Attributes:** Resembles black walnut. **Cultivation:** Similar to black walnut. Butternut is now threatened everywhere by an Asian canker disease. **Native American Note:** The sweet nuts were planted, collected, and boiled to extract oil, which was used like butter. **Zones:** 3–7. **Nature Note:** Black walnut and butternut host 129 species of butterflies and moths. Both are "excellent wildlife trees because their foliage hosts well over 100 species of Lepidoptera 'bird food' and because they produce large nuts that sustain squirrels and other rodents through the long winter months," writes Douglas Tallamy.[160] Squirrels can forget where they hid some nuts, which makes planting a black walnut tree as easy as putting out some black walnuts. Raccoons, bears, chipmunks, wild turkeys (p. 244), woodpeckers (pp. 55, 212), and American crows (p. 244) also eat the nuts. The tree's large limbs serve as roosts for wild turkeys and eastern screech owls; its cavities shelter woodpeckers, swallows (p. 55), wrens (p. 28), red- and white-breasted

Black walnut tree (*Juglans nigra*)

nuthatches (pp. 322, 30), and owls. Black walnut and butternut host "the larva of the walnut sphinx moth, a moth unusual because of the squeaking sound it makes."[161] They are the sole hosts of the gray-edged bomolocha and the Angus' datana, specialists whose caterpillars can eat only these species. They are the preferred hosts of the beautiful luna moth (p. 54) and the immense regal moth, also called royal walnut moth, which can fill the palm of a hand. This moth lays its eggs on walnut, hickory, sweetgum, ash, and sumac trees and "is parent to the awe-inspiring larva of the hickory horned devil. Once seen, neither can be forgotten," write Sternberg and Wilson.[162] The young caterpillars rest on the tops of leaves and resemble bird droppings, while older caterpillars appear menacing because they are very large and brightly colored with red "horns" near the head. Caterpillars pupate in a burrow in the soil.[163] Only one generation is produced every year regardless of region. Sadly, "as with many of our larger moths, light pollution has all but eliminated royal walnut moths from developed areas," writes Douglas Tallamy, noting, "Royal walnut moths have already disappeared entirely from New England. (A plea: switch off unnecessary lights when you retire at night!)."[164] This plea also applies to fireflies, which cannot survive loss of habitat, poisonous pesticides and fertilizers, suburban sprawl, and light pollution;[165] HICKORY. **Genus:** *Carya.* **Hickory Note:** "Like many oaks, hickories are large trees that in full sun can spread as wide as they are tall. They thus make excellent specimen trees and their large compound leaves throw nice shade," writes Douglas Tallamy. "Hickories are noted for their production of tough nuts that are important sources of winter forage for several mammals, but they also have excellent fall color of brilliant yellows and golds. If I were a homeowner with the opportunity to convert a section of my property from lawn to trees, I would rely heavily on hickories, oak and beeches for my canopy species."[166] Hickories are good home landscape trees because their large taproots do not lift up sidewalks but do ensure trees won't blow over easily in wind storms. Taproot-shaped containers enable the propagation and sale of these stately shade and ornamental trees; BITTERNUT HICKORY, SWAMP HICKORY (*C. cordiformis*). **Height:** 40–60 feet. **Spread:** 30–40 feet. **Ornamental Attributes:** Highly conspicuous yellow buds in winter. Smooth bark. Its open shade enables underplanted species to thrive. **Cultivation:** Fast-growing tree that thrives in areas that are sunny for about half the day. Soil can be medium to moist, soggy or marshy for long periods, or have poor drainage. **Nature Note:** Its bitter nuts are not a preferred wildlife food, but they do get eaten. **Food Use:** Smoke from burning hickory logs imparts distinctive flavor to bacon and smoked ham. **Life Span:** 175–200 years; BLACK HICKORY (*C. texana*). **Height:** To 80 feet.

Hickory (*Carya*)

Ornamental Attributes: Short, crooked branches, narrow crown. Sweet, edible, brown nuts covered with yellow scales. Zones: 4–9; KINGNUT, SHELLBARK HICKORY (*C. laciniosa*). Height: 75–90 feet. Ornamental Attributes: Bark peels away in plates, similar to shagbark hickory, with which it hybridizes producing *C.x dunbarii*. "A Shellbark just about to put forth its leaves presents a unique and striking appearance, as if covered with brilliant flowers," wrote Harriet L. Keeler in 1900, referring to the "astonishing" large "gorgeous red or salmon yellow" inner buds.[167] Orange young branches. King-size tree produces king-size, great-tasting nuts eaten by a wide range of wildlife. Cultivation: Sun, part sun, fertile moist soil. Slow growing. Zones: (4)5–9; MOCKERNUT HICKORY (*C. tomentosa*). Height: 50–75 feet. Ornamental Attributes: Leaves, husks, and buds have pleasant resinous fragrance. Big husk holds small, sweet nut. Cultivation: Part sun. Dry, well-drained soil. Life Span: 200–300 years. Zones: 4–9; PIGNUT HICKORY (*C. glabra*, syn. *C. porcina*). Height: 50–70 feet. Spread: 45–60 feet. Ornamental Attributes: Pignut hickory "is a beautiful tree and certainly worthy of a pleasanter name than that of Pignut. But the early settlers of this country judged trees by the standard of use rather than beauty; and as the fruit of this tree did not compare favorably with that of the Shellbark, both tree and fruit were given over to the pigs without question," wrote Harriet L. Keeler.[168] Tall, evenly branched; tightly woven bark. Cultivation: Sun, well-drained dry or moist acidic soil. Life Span: 200–300 years. Zones: 4–9; RED HICKORY, FALSE SHAGBARK HICKORY (*C. ovalis*). Height: 50–75 feet. Spread: 40–50 feet. Ornamental Attributes: Bark is slightly shaggy, has good golden-yellow fall color. Cultivation: Part sun, dry/well-drained soil. Nature Note: The edible nuts are attractive to wildlife; SHAGBARK HICKORY (*C. ovata*). Height: 70–90 feet. Spread: 50–70 feet. Ornamental Attributes: It is a distinct surprise to come upon its large, beautiful, bright red, flower-like buds in the spring. It has large compound leaves that turn an unbelievably beautiful golden yellow in fall. Its distinctively shaggy bark, developed over time, makes it the most widely recognized hickory. Its seed husks are thick and green. Cultivation: Full to part sun, medium-dry well-drained soil best; tree is very adaptable and problem free. Life Span: 250–300 years. Zones: 4–9; PECAN, HARDY PECAN (*C. illinoinensis*). Height: 70–100 feet. Ornamental Attributes: Tall, massive shade tree with upright branching and delicious nuts. Cultivation: Full

Shagbark hickory leaves
(*Carya ovata*)

sun, well-drained moist soil; two trees for best pollination. Native Carya species are tolerant of black walnut toxicity. **Range Note:** Iowa and Indiana south to Texas and Mexico. Sparse nut production in the northern part of growing range. **Native American Note:** In 1532, Spaniard Cabeza de Vaca observed pecans furnishing "the sole subsistence of [western Indians] for two months of the year."[169] **Life Span:** 300 years. **Zones:** 5–9; **Hickory Nature Note:** These trees host 235 Lepidoptera (moth/butterfly) species, including Io moth (p. 91), hag moth, polyphemus moth (p. 211), pale tussock moth, hickory tussock moth, American dagger moth, luna moth (p. 54), several species of skipper and hairstreak butterflies including the gray hairstreak, hickory hairstreak, and banded hairstreak butterflies (p. 210), and the regal or royal walnut moth. (See Walnut Nature Note, p. 220.) Hickory nuts contain protein, calcium, and phosphorus and are high in crude fat, making them an important food for a variety of mammals such as bears, foxes, rabbits, woodland mice, squirrels, American crow (p. 244), mallard and wood ducks (p. 162), wild turkeys (p. 244), and bobwhite quail (p. 36) and a highly nutritious and tasty food for people. Birds including flycatchers use hickories for cover and nesting. The shagbark hickory's peeling bark is a favored roosting site for little brown bats and a nesting spot for brown creepers, a small streaked, migrating bird that creeps up tree trunks in spring, searching for insects and spiders. "If you are lucky enough to have a shagbark hickory on your property, leave it there, it is far better than any artificial bat box, bird house or bird feeder," writes Sue Pike.[170]

Shagbark hickory (*Carya ovata*)
Also see p. 294

Nonnative:

WILLOW. See Spring Trees, p. 117.

3

FALL

Midwesterners enjoy watching the leaves of trees and shrubs change in fall from soothing green to vivid shades of orange, red, purple, brown, or yellow. In preparation for winter, Illinois Indian women gathered the inner bark of many plants, fruits, berries, acorns, and hickory, hazel, and beechnuts.[1] The men hunted bison by setting fire to the grass "everywhere around these animals," killing those seeking to escape with bows and arrows.[2]

Visiting Illinois in 1846, Eliza W. Farnham wrote, "Autumn in the prairie land is scarcely excelled for the richness of its charms by any other season. A few flowers linger in the borders of the woodlands. . . . The squirrel searches timidly about amongst the fallen leaves, making provisions for winter."[3] In 1993, Sara Stein wrote, "This fall commotion—these scurryings of squirrels and twitterings of birds among flights of painted leaves and twirling maple wings—takes me by surprise after the drowsy quietude of summer."[4]

Midwesterners love the idea of choosing shade-producing and ornamental woody plants that help our region's wildlife survive, including its butterflies and birds. To achieve this, we must reevaluate the trees and shrubs we choose for fall color. Take burning bush, for example. This shrub was introduced from China about 1860. Though it is only attractive once a year, its red or pinkish autumn hues made it an obligatory plant for midwesterners. With innumerable burning bushes intentionally installed throughout the region, no wonder burning bushes and their cultivars became invasive in the Midwest. In 1875, Japanese barberry was introduced. Despite having sharp thorns, its red fall leaves made it very popular and led to a huge number of cultivars. It took about a hundred years, but Japanese barberry started taking over in the 1970s and, along with its cultivars, is invasive in the Midwest. In the 1960s, the nursery industry promoted 'Bradford' pear tree, a Chinese Callery pear cultivar, for its white spring flowers and red fall foliage. Before long, this popular ornamental became an invasive species in the Midwest. The USDA Forest Service featured Callery pear/'Bradford' pear in 2005 as a "Weed of the Week."[5]

It is not as if burning bush, Japanese barberry, and 'Bradford' pear are the only red-leaved fall shrubs and trees. The Midwest is home to a great many equally and even more beautiful fall red-leaved native shrubs and trees. In northern Europe, except for four species that turn red, tree leaves turn yellow and orange. In all the rest of Europe, the leaves of only 24 tree species turn red. "Here on this side of the pond there are at least 89 species that have red leaves in the fall, such as sugar maple, mountain ash, sumac, scarlet oak, dogwood, sweetgum, and sourwood, just to name a few," writes Matt Estep.[6] Asymmetry in red fall color inspires scientific theories and enables midwesterners to celebrate our region's abundance of red fall woody color. One result of choosing native fall red-leaved woody host plants is future generations of moths and butterflies. With so many native shrubs and trees whose leaves turn wonderfully red in fall, surely enough exist to satisfy any midwestern lover of red fall color.

The ubiquitous, invasive, nonnative burning bush, Japanese barberry, and 'Bradford' pear relentlessly degrade America's natural environment, but their sales produce lots of money. Revenues from burning bush annually exceed $38 million nationwide.[7] When burning bush's invasiveness belatedly caught the attention of the nursery industry, did this deter its sales? Was the nursery industry inspired to prioritize offering native North American trees and shrubs with red leaves in fall? Well-funded universities, arboretums, and the USDA spend energy, time, and money seeking "safe" seedless, sterile, noninvasive versions.[8] The nursery industry hopes for a burning bush breakthrough they see as "a big win for everyone," because "we get to keep selling a popular plant, the public gets to keep using it in their landscapes, and the environment is safe from invasives."[9]

Is it realistic to create "sterile" plants to keep the environment safe from invasive species? "History shows that this theory hasn't worked well for other ornamental invasives," writes Ellen Sousa in *Developing Sterile Invasives . . . Why Bother?* Cultivars marked "sterile" of the invasive purple loosestrife and the invasive 'Bradford' pear eventually produced pollen and seed and now they "happily cross-pollinate with the wild species."[10] Studies show "sterile" burning bush and Japanese barberry cultivars are not "safe" for the environment because the cultivars remain invasive.[11] As said in *Jurassic Park,* "Nature will find a way."

If sterile cultivars of nonnative species could be created, would this be good for the environment? No, because a sterile nonnative barberry remains a nonnative barberry. Plants that are good for the environment are the natives upon which butterflies and moths lay their eggs, producing caterpillars which birds feed their nestlings. Comparing the production of butterfly, moth, and sawfly caterpillars of two groups of woody species, common natives and common nonnatives, Douglas Tallamy found the native species supported "a whopping 35 times more caterpillar biomass than the aliens."[12] Sterilizing nonnative invasive plants cannot transform them into host plants for butterflies and moths.

It took thousands of years for local insects to overcome the chemical defenses of the local plants they rely on for reproduction. "Because native insects did not evolve with nonnative plants, most lack the ability to overcome the plants' chemical defenses and cannot eat them."[13] Caterpillars, the larval stage of butterflies and moths and a particularly important food for breeding birds, tend to be among the most specialized insect groups of all. "According to Tallamy, more than 90 percent of butterfly and moth larvae eat only particular plants or groups of plants. Evolving the ability to feed on a radically new host would take an insect species tens of thousands of years, he says."[14] Most popular nonnative shrubs and trees, whether sterile or fertile, host few or no midwestern butterflies. How can one think that yards and communities planted with sterile nonnative shrubs and trees will be beautiful when their presence leads to an absence of butterflies and the birds that eat and feed caterpillars and other insects to their nestlings?

Midwesterners who love fall color and birds have the choice of many native fruit-, nut-, and seed-bearing trees and shrubs whose leaves turn beautiful colors in fall and that also provide us with opportunities to observe migrating birds. Fueled by high-fat berries and fruits, most migrants generally stop to feed and rest about every 165 miles. "Consequently, these migrants depend on the availability of these feeding and resting sites," writes backyard wildlife expert Terry W. Johnson. Native plants "have co-evolved with the songbirds that migrate through [our region]. As such, they often bear fruit when the migrants are passing through." Unfortunately, "a dramatic loss in suitable stopover areas used by the birds on their spring and fall migrations [plays] a significant role in their alarming population losses. Believe it or not our yards can help in conserving these migratory songbirds by providing high-quality stopover areas."[15] A wide array of native woody plants provides natural, renewable food sources for birds and animals, as well as butterfly reproduction sites. When we choose native species for our premises, it is convenient to observe these amazing and beautiful long-distance travelers visiting shrubs and trees we planted that produce nutritious spring and fall food.

Fall cleanup poses hazards for wildlife. Removing leaf litter, a life-giving resource for hibernating butterflies, moths, and fireflies, makes it difficult for insectivorous birds to survive the resource-scarce winter. Without fallen leaves there is nothing for the squirrel to search timidly to make provisions for winter. Leaf litter removal deprives shrubs and trees (often installed at considerable cost) of the natural and cost-free mulch needed to properly grow. Cleanup alternatives include sparing host plants, decreasing lawn size, increasing tree and shrub borders and raking leaf litter under them, and creating compost and wood piles. Thoughtful and restrained seasonal cleanups that help butterflies, fireflies, and birds can incorporate natural elements without sacrificing attractiveness.

It is hard to believe, but dead trees can provide habitat for wildlife. When standing, dead and dying trees, called "snags" or "wildlife trees," are important for wildlife in both natural and landscaped settings. Over thousands of years, midwestern wildlife evolved in unmanaged forests where snags and cavities were a natural part of their environment. Sap oozing from winter-damaged trees, and holes drilled into willow, beech, and poplar trees by woodpeckers such as the yellow-bellied sapsucker, provide food to many butterflies, including many that overwinter in tree crevices and loose bark.[16] (See the introduction to Spring.) Nuthatches, woodpeckers, black-capped chickadees, and chimney swifts continue to use snags for nesting, shelter, and a source of food. The importance and benefits derived from insectivorous birds as biological control agents for unwanted insect pests are receiving more attention.[17]

If you do not have snags on your property, consider creating one.[18] All trees of all sizes, alive or dead, are potential snags that will likely be used by wildlife. Unfortunately, many wildlife trees are cut down without much thought to their wildlife value or the potential management options that can safely prolong the existence of the tree. To locate an expert tree service to create a wildlife tree, check with the International Society of Arboriculture for certified arborists specializing in wildlife tree creation and maintenance. Alternatively, obtain a dead tree salvaged from a seller of firewood, a developer clearing land, or a construction or logging site. Again, professional help and special equipment may be needed, as well as the landowner's permission.[19] The National Museum of Natural History turned a declining pine tree into an ornamental and ecologically productive snag. "Through creative thinking the Smithsonian Gardens' staff discovered a great opportunity to turn what could have been a significant loss to gardens into a valuable resource."[20]

Attaching birdhouses or signage stating "Woodpecker Tree" can augment a snag's dramatic and ornamental aspects. A special all-weather "Wildlife Tree" sign can be ordered.[21] Stumps can be used as benches or as flowerpot or birdbath holders. Woodpecker suet feeders or condos for tunnel-nesting solitary bees can be created by drilling holes. Slits can create bat and brown creeper homes. As supports for native vines, snags can attract ruby-throated hummingbirds and host butterflies. Stumps, snags, and compost and brush piles surrounded by nicely designed native plantings can be landscape features that are decorative as well as utilitarian. Unadorned and standing alone, snags suggest ancient and magical Orkney standing stones, stark reminders of our prehistoric heritage. "Wildlife trees offer a one-stop, natural habitat feature. In short, snags 'live on' as excellent wildlife trees for all to enjoy!"[22]

Fall is an ideal time to plant native shrubs, trees, and deciduous plants. The soil is still warm, and the cool autumn temperatures aren't as harsh as the summer heat. Watering and giving the newly planted roots the opportunity to grow enables the plants to get a head start on spring.

We read a lot about mindfulness. It is a state of active, open attention on the present when instead of letting one's life pass one by, one lives in the moment and awakens to experience. To incorporate mindfulness into spring and fall cleanup practices, midwestern landscapers and gardeners can practice blending their enjoyment of tidy yards and seasonal beauty with attentiveness to the needs of nature. For midwesterners interested in choosing native trees and shrubs for fall instead of nativars or introductions from Asia and Europe, we offer the following suggestions.

Shrubs

Nonnative:

AUTUMN OLIVE, JAPANESE SILVERBERRY. **Family:** Oleaster (Elaeagnaceae). **Genus:** *Elaeagnus* (*E. umbellata*). **Origin:** China, Japan, Korea; *CHERRY SILVERBERRY* (*E. multi-flora*); *RUSSIAN OLIVE* (*E. angustifolia*); *THORNY OLIVE* (*E. pungens*). **Height:** 20 feet. **Spread:** 30 feet. **Ornamental Attributes:** Closely related thorny large shrubs or small trees with silvery leaves, fragrant flowers, and red fruits. **Cultivation:** Full to part sun, dry to medium well-drained soil; tolerate tough conditions. Spread by suckers and seeds, create dense thickets, and displace native species. **Ecological Threat—All:** Classified as invasive in parts of the Midwest, except for cherry silverberry, which so far is only sporadically naturalized. **Zones:** 3–7.

Russian olive
(*Elaeagnus angustifolia*)

Native Alternatives:

SILVERBERRY. **Family:** Oleaster (Elaeagnaceae). **Genus:** *Elaeagnus* (*E. commutata*). **Height/Spread:** 3–8 feet. **Ornamental Attributes:** Small clusters of yellow flowers in summer with a heavy, sweet scent; silver leaves; red fruits. "The silverberry of the Midwest is a tall shrub that appears sprayed with aluminum paint." In fall each golden star-like flower "becomes a silver-dusted coral berry."[23] **Cultivation:** Full to part sun; dry to moist soil; tolerates poor and infertile soil due to its ability to fix nitrogen. **Zones:** 3–6; SILVER BUFFALOBERRY. **Genus:**

Silver buffaloberry (*Shepherdia argentea*)

Shepherdia (*S. argentea*). **Height:** 6–18 feet. **Spread:** 8–12 feet. **Ornamental Attributes:** Small yellow tubular flowers in late spring. Female plants produce red berries. "The blunt, lance-shaped, bright silver deciduous leaves of this upright thorny shrub reflect the sun and shimmer in the evening."[24] **Cultivation:** Full sun, light shade, moist or average soil. Nitrogen fixing. Dioecious. **Zones:** 3–7; RUSSET BUFFALOBERRY, CANADIAN BUFFALOBERRY (*S. canadensis*). **Height:** 6–9 feet. **Ornamental Attributes:** Shiny red fruit, leaf surfaces appear speckled. **Cultivation:** Sun, part shade, many soil conditions. **Note:** Endangered in Illinois, extirpated in Indiana. **Historical Note:** William Clark wrote in 1804 of the "deliciously flavoured . . . froot [*sic*]" called buffaloberry that "makes delitefull [*sic*] Tarts."[25] **Nature Note:** Native *Elaeagnus* species host 22 species of butterflies and moths. They have special value to native bees, their primary pollinators; provide ideal cover and nesting sites for birds. A source of essential fatty acids rarely found in fruits, their midsummer berries are a preferred food source for migrating birds and, into late winter, for many songbirds. **Zones:** 2–6.

More Native Alternatives:

AMERICAN STRAWBERRY BUSH, p. 241; AMERICAN WITCH HAZEL, p. 244; BAYBERRY, p. 232.

See Spring Shrubs for CHOKEBERRY SPP., p. 13; ELDERBERRY SPP., p. 29; MAPLELEAF and other native VIBURNUMS, p. 69; NINEBARK, p. 44.

See Summer Shrubs for DEVIL'S WALKING STICK, p. 123; FALSE INDIGO BUSH, p. 132; PRICKLY-ASH, p. 124.

See Summer Trees for ALLEGHENY CHINKAPIN, p. 171.

Russet buffaloberry (*Shepherdia canadensis*)

Nonnative:

BARBERRY. **Family:** Barberry (Berberidaceae). **Genus:** *Berberis.* **Note:** Thin, sharp needles make barberries "a plant you will NEVER want to hug!"[26] *JAPANESE BARBERRY (B. thunbergii).* **Origin:** Japan. **Height:** 3–6 feet. **Spread:** 4–5 feet. **Ornamental Attributes:** Thorny bushes; insignificant yellow flowers in April to May; insignificant red fall berries; red fall leaves. **Cultivation:** Full sun, part shade; dry to medium soil. Regular winter dieback requires pruning, which can be painful. Wear gloves. **Ecological Threat:** Classified as invasive and naturalized in midwestern states. It remains widely propagated and sold for landscaping. Birds transport seeds in their feces that can remain viable in the soil for ten years. The plants form dense monocultures where nothing else grows, competing with native woody and herbaceous plants, and the fallen leaves alter soil characteristics, enabling them to displace native plants.[27] **Cultivar/Variety Note:** "There are a shocking number of cultivars that are readily available in nearly every nursery, greenhouse, and garden center in the Midwest. This species and its cultivars are the bread and butter for many nurseries," write Weeks and Weeks.[28] The Canadian Food Inspection Agency regulates the import of certain cultivars of this species, as it is the alternate host of black stem rust.[29] Popular cultivars come in carmine, dark red, red, purple, cream, pink, yellow, chartreuse, and variegated, and as dwarfs, crowns, and pillars. Cultivars can scorch in summer heat and lose yellow and red/purple colors without full sun. "At this time, all the cultivars for a given invasive species are considered invasive."[30] Studies show that the barberry cultivars sold as "safe" alternatives to their invasive relatives are not safe, but remain invasive.[31] "You may do better to avoid planting these shrubs," writes Penelope O'Sullivan, "rather than to risk further spreading the species."[32] The Morton Arboretum is more direct, stating, "This Asian shrub is invasive and should not be planted."[33] **Lyme Disease Note:** Lyme disease–carrying deer ticks are 67 percent more likely to be in areas infested with Japanese barberry. Tick numbers drop by up to 80 percent with barberry removal;[34] *COMMON BARBERRY, EUROPEAN BARBERRY (B. vulgaris).* **Origin:** Europe. **Height:** 8–10 feet. Naturalized or invasive in the Midwest. **Interesting Fact:** In 1726, in Connecticut, common barberry became the first plant to win notoriety in America as an invader because it harbored wheat stem rust.[35] Now Connecticut and other states, including Michigan, prohibit it; *KOREAN BARBERRY (B. koreana).* **Origin:** Korea. Dangerous thorns. Excessive sucker growth makes it hard to control. Prohibited in Michigan. Invasive in Minnesota. **Zones:** 3–7; *MENTOR BARBERRY (B. × mentorensis [julianae × thunbergii]).* **Origin:** Eurasia. **Zones:** 5–7; **Disturbing Barberry Trend:** Efforts are underway to create "sterile" barberries. If this succeeds, additional landscapes will be dominated by Asian species that will further diminish the ability of North American butterflies to reproduce and of nesting birds to find caterpillars to feed their offspring. **Zones:** 4–8; *MAHONIA, HOLLYLEAVED BARBERRY, OREGON GRAPE-HOLLY.* **Genus:** *Mahonia (M. aquifolium,* syn. *Berberis aquifolium).* **Origin:** Pacific Northwest from British Columbia to northern California. "Widely used as an ornamental; reported as an escape from cultivation across the continent."[36] Prohibited in Michigan. **Zones:** 5–9.

Japanese barberry (*Berberis thunbergii*)

Bayberry (*Myrica pensylvanica*)

Native Alternatives:

BAYBERRY, NORTHERN BAYBERRY. **Family:** Bayberry (Myricaceae). **Genus:** *Morella* (*M. pensylvanica*, syn. *Myrica pensylvanica*). **Height/Spread:** 5–8 feet. **Ornamental Attributes:** Gray-green leaves turn burgundy in fall and persist through the winter. Clusters of showy, waxy, silvery-white berries remain on female plants all winter. Gray bark. All parts of the mostly deciduous shrub are fragrant. Looks great massed or grouped. **Cultivation:** Easily grown. Full sun to shade. Dry to medium, well-drained soil, tolerates poor soil and drought. Needs at least one male plant for pollination and fruit. Nitrogen fixing and salt tolerant. Useful for locations near roads that are salted in winter. **Note:** Endangered in Ohio. **Nature Note:** The high percentage of fat (50.3 percent) in bayberries enables the survival of migrating and overwintering birds,[37] often as emergency food. More than 85 bird species eat the berries, including gray catbird (p. 79), American robin (p. 62), great blue heron, vireos, tufted titmouse (p. 169), tree swallow (p. 55), ruby-crowned kinglet (p. 233), and palm warbler. The persistent fruits are especially favored by tree swallows and the yellow-rumped warbler, formerly known as myrtle and Audubon warbler (p. 183), with whom it has a special relationship, as the bird's specialized digestive enzymes break down the waxy coating on the fruit.[38] The shrub provides birds with important cover and nesting sites. Bayberry hosts 108 species of Lepidoptera (butterflies/moths) and is visited by many adult butterflies, including red-banded and banded hairstreaks (p. 210) and the Columbia silkmoth. **Zones:** 3–7.

　　LEATHERWOOD, EASTERN LEATHERWOOD. **Family:** Mezereum (Thymelaeaceae). **Genus:** *Dirca* (*D. palustris*). **Height/Spread:** 5–8 feet. **Historical Note:** This woodland shrub has been grown as a collector's plant for hundreds of years. **Ornamental Attributes:** Conspicuous and long-lasting early bell-shaped spring flowers. Among the first to leaf out in spring, its shiny green leaves are fuzzy beneath and held alternately on greenish-yellow stems; in fall they turn clear yellow. Single trunk, smooth gray bark. "Leatherwood never really attains tree size but always grows in tree form," writes Guy Sternberg. "Where garden scale is restricted, it gives the aesthetic equivalent of a tree in a small space."[39] It is used for mass plantings, but is "well suited for a formal setting where neatness counts," write Weeks

Ruby-crowned kinglet (*Regulus calendula*)

and Weeks.[40] **Cultivation:** Woodland-type shade; organically rich, moist to wet soils. **Nature Note:** Birds consume the fruits in May to June; also used for nesting. It hosts 1 species of Lepidoptera. **Zones:** 4–9.

AMERICAN BARBERRY. **Family:** Barberry (Berberidaceae). **Genus:** *Berberis* (*B. canadensis*). **Height:** 3–6 feet. **Spread:** 4–5 feet. **Ornamental Attributes:** Spectacular fall color. Looks like introduced barberries. Listed on a United States eradication program, although it is considered only a "potential" alternate wheat rust host. "This eradication program has not been discontinued, and we have the unusual case of one government agency committed to extirpate a rare species while also committed to protect it from harm, both at the same time. . . . Nationally, the eradication policy should be changed to exclude this species if it is to survive," writes plant expert Steven R. Hill.[41] **Nature Note:** The native barberry hosts 12 species of butterflies and moths. Birds and other wildlife seek its berries. **Endangerment Note:** Endangered in parts of the Midwest. **Zones:** 5–8.

American barberry (*Berberis canadensis*)

More Native Alternatives:

AMERICAN BEAUTYBERRY, p. 235; EASTERN BURNING BUSH, p. 240; SILVER-BERRY, p. 229; WINTERBERRY, p. 237.

See Spring Shrubs for CHOKEBERRY SPP., p. 13; FOTHERGILLA SPP., p. 27; GOLDEN CURRANT, p. 35; NINEBARK, p. 44; VIBURNUM SPP. (e.g., ARROW-WOOD and MAPLELEAF), p. 69.

See Summer Shrubs for AMERICAN BLACK CURRANT, p. 138; CAROLINA BUCK-THORN, p. 141; NEW JERSEY TEA, p. 134; SHRUBBY CINQUEFOIL, p. 129; ST. JOHN'S WORT SPP., p. 145; VIRGINIA SWEETSPIRE, p. 127.

See Winter Shrubs for AMERICAN HOLLY, p. 313; INKBERRY, p. 308.

Nonnative:

BEAUTYBERRY. **Family:** Mint (Lamiaceae). **Genus:** *Callicarpa.* **Origin:** Japan, China, Korea; *PURPLE BEAUTYBERRY* (*C. dichotoma*). **Height:** 2–4 feet. **Spread:** 3–5 feet. **Ornamental Attributes:** Lilac-violet fruits. Fruits best when grouped. **Cultivation:** Full sun best; moist well-drained soil; *JAPANESE BEAUTYBERRY* (*C. japonica*). **Note:** Naturalized in Kentucky. **Zones:** 5–8.

Japanese beautyberry (*Callicarpa japonica*)

American beautyberry (*Callicarpa americana*)

Native Alternatives:

AMERICAN BEAUTYBERRY, FRENCH MULBERRY. **Family:** Mint (Lamiaceae). **Genus:** *Callicarpa* (*C. americana*). **Height/Spread:** 3–6 feet. **Ornamental Attributes:** Deep pink flowers in spring. Clusters of spectacular glossy iridescent violet to purple berries in August to November. Yellow fall foliage. **Cultivation:** Easy to grow. Fruits best when planted in groups

and full sun in moist well-drained soil. In winter, it can be cut to the ground because it fruits on new growth. Native to southeastern United States but recommended by the Morton Arboretum for the Midwest on the basis of ornamental value, proven hardiness, availability, and freedom from serious problems. **Nature Note:** Flowers attract bees and butterflies. At least 10 species of overwintering and migrating songbirds eat its high-fat, late summer/fall berries, including American robin (p. 62), gray catbird (p. 79), northern cardinal (p. 61), brown thrasher (p. 219), and eastern towhee. Mammals eat the fruits. Crushed leaves can be used as a deterrent for mosquitoes and ticks. Hosts 1 species of Lepidoptera. **Zones:** 6–10.

Eastern towhee (*Pipilo erythrophthalmus*)

Coralberry (*Symphoricarpos orbiculatus*)

CORALBERRY, INDIAN CURRANT. Family: Honeysuckle (Caprifoliaceae). **Genus:** *Symphoricarpos* (*S. orbiculatus*). **Height:** 2–5 feet. **Spread:** 4–8 feet. **Ornamental Attributes:** A small slender shrub with arching stems resembles some cotoneasters; pink flowers in June to July; coral-red or "hot-pink" fall berries; delicate foliage, yellow fall color. "A planted row of coralberry along a drive is a striking sight in the dead of winter," write Weeks and Weeks.[42] **Cultivation:** Full to part sun, well-drained soil. Originally it was part of the oak savanna.

Zones: 4–7; SNOWBERRY (*S. albus*). **Height/ Spread:** 3–6 feet. **Ornamental Attributes:** Low-growing shrub with small pink-white flowers in June to July, delicate blue-green foliage, and snow-white fruits that persist through the winter. "One shrub with white fruits, the snowberry . . . is a treasure to lighten a shaded area," wrote Helen Van Pelt Wilson.[43] **Cultivation:** Sun to heavy shade. Dry, well-drained soils. Suckering habit helps stabilize slopes. **History:** On August 13, 1805, Meriwether Lewis observed a shrub bearing "a globular berry as large as a garden pea and as white as wax." In 1812, Thomas Jefferson reported he had planted the shrub and called it "the Snow-berry bush."[44] **Zones:** 3–7. **Coralberry and Snow-berry Nature Note:** Nectar and pollen attract

Snowberry (*Symphoricarpos albus*)

Winterberry (*Ilex verticillata*)

bees, wasps, and flies. Attract fruit-eating birds, including American robin (p. 62), black-capped chickadee (p. 322), and Northern cardinal (p. 61). Host 25 species of butterflies and moths, including the hummingbird clearwing (p. 72), the snowberry clearwing, and sulfur moths. The shrubs provide good cover to wildlife.

HOLLY. **Family:** Holly (Aquifoliaceae). **Genus:** *Ilex.* **Note:** "Hollies are wonderful staples of low-maintenance gardens."[45] All species of *Ilex* have male and female flowers on separate plants, and will produce fruit only if a male plant is available to pollinate the females. "One species can stand in as a pollinator for another," notes William Cullina;[46] WINTERBERRY, FIRE BUSH (*I. verticillata*). **Height/Spread:** 3–12 feet. Large shrub/small or medium-sized tree. **Ornamental Attributes:** Showy bright red berries in fall described by William Cullina as "fluorescent" and "spectacular" that persist through the winter into spring.[47] Bronze fall color. **Cultivation:** Easily grown, full sun to part shade. Found in moist soil but does well in medium soil, preferably acidic, and wet conditions. Females are showy when naturalized, massed, and used as borders or screens. To fruit, winterberries need a male that flowers at the same time they do, early-, mid-, or late-season. **Bird Note:** More than 20 species of birds eat the fruits. **Nativar Note:** Fruits of the true native species provide many migrating and over-wintering birds with high-fat emergency winter food. The large "superior" fruits some nativars produce may be too large for birds to eat. Some nurseries sell only single-sex nativars, eliminating all fruit production. Some nativar/cultivar fruits easily discolor. **Note:** Endangered in Iowa. Threatened in Arkansas. **Zones:** 3–9; POSSUMHAW, POSSUMHAW HOLLY (*I. decidua*). **Confusion Note:** Possumhaw is also the common name for *Viburnum nudum* var. *nudum*, see Spring Shrubs, p. 72. **Height/Spread:** 5–10 feet. Large shrub/small tree. **Ornamental Attributes:** Bright orange-red berries in autumn persist to spring. Glossy dark green leaves turn yellow in late fall. Berries and twiggy, horizontal branches provide winter interest. **Cultivation:** Sun best for fruits, wet to upland sites. Pollination can be by male possumhaw or American holly; sometimes it fruits without male pollination. Native to southern Illinois and Indiana. In Zone 5, place in a protected site. **Bird Note:** At least 49 species of birds eat the fruits. **Zones:** 5–9. *Ilex* **Nature Note:** Foliage provides warblers and water birds with cover and nesting sites. Ornamental and conspicuous fruits persist through the winter, providing emergency winter and early spring food to small mammals and local and

Possumhaw (*Ilex decidua*)

migratory birds, including Baltimore oriole (p. 167), bluebird (p. 61), blue jay (p. 79), gray catbird (p. 79), wood thrush (p. 175), cedar waxwing (p. 36), brown thrasher (p. 219), American robin (p. 62), rose-breasted grosbeak (p. 200), purple finch (p. 145), black-capped chickadee (p. 322), mourning dove, northern flicker (p. 99), red-bellied woodpecker (p. 55), northern cardinal (p. 61), and red-eyed vireo (p. 112). Special value to native bees. *Ilex* species host 39 species of moths and butterflies, including Henry's elfin butterfly (p. 93); nectar attracts butterflies.

More Native Holly Species:

See Winter Shrubs for AMERICAN HOLLY, p. 313; INKBERRY, p. 308.

More Native Alternatives:

AMERICAN STRAWBERRY BUSH, p. 241; BAYBERRY, p. 232; CORALBERRY, p. 236; LEATHERWOOD, p. 232; SILVERBERRY, p. 229.

More (Sometimes Edible) Fall-Fruiting Native Alternatives:

See Spring Shrubs for AMERICAN BLACK ELDERBERRY (yellow fall color), p. 29; AMERICAN BLADDERNUT (capsules filled with rattling seeds persist through winter;

yellow fall leaves), p. 41; CHOKEBERRY SPP. (red fall color and colorful berries), p. 13; DOGWOOD SPP. (red fall color), p. 48; ROSE SPP. (red, yellow fall color, colorful fruit), p. 60; SPICEBUSH (golden-yellow fall color and red berries), p. 22; VIBURNUM SPP. (red, purple fall color), p. 69; WAFER ASH (yellow fall color, papery seeds), p. 45.

See Summer Shrubs for ASHY AND OAKLEAF HYDRANGEA (flower-like seed-heads persist through fall/winter), p. 143, 144; BUTTONBUSH (bronze, burgundy, yellow fall color), p. 131; CLETHRA (orange or yellow fall color), p. 132; ST. JOHN'S WORT, p. 145.

See Spring Trees for CHOKECHERRY (red, orange fall color), p. 83.

See Winter Trees for RED CEDAR, p. 323.

Nonnative:

BURNING BUSH, WINGED EUONYMUS, WINGED WAHOO. **Family:** Bittersweet (Celastraceae). **Genus:** Spindletree, *Euonymus* (*E. alatus*). **Genus Note:** Nonnative species are easily confused with native species. **Origin:** China. **Height/Spread:** To 15 feet. **Ornamental Attributes:** Red or pinkish-red fall color, exaggerated corky stem wings when growing in sun. Insignificant red fruits. **Cultivation:** Full sun for red fall color, moist soil best, excellent drainage; tolerates a variety of soil types, very aggressive; naturalizes, creates thickets that can outcompete native plants and form a monoculture. "This species, it *seems,* is planted in every lawn in every town in the Midwest," write Weeks and Weeks.[48] "I have been shocked in recent

Burning bush
(*Euonymus alatus*)

years by the rapid takeover of invasive plant species in our woodlands in [Indiana]. I feel we are quietly but very effectively being taken over by a few species, including . . . burning bush!" writes Jeff Burbrink.[49] Burning bush "can seed itself" into nearby parks or woodlands "and overtake our native plants. Plant a different shrub with brilliant fall color," writes Penelope O'Sullivan.[50] For gardeners craving "a beautiful crimson-red stunner in your fall landscape," but rejecting the invasive burning bush, think about Virginia sweetspire, writes Jane Kirchner.[51] Burning bush is a shrub considered invasive that is spread by birds and animals that consume the fruit and then deposit seeds in other locations, spreading these species far from the sites where they were planted, notes the Morton Arboretum, which designates burning bush "Not recommended."[52] **Ecological Threat:** Classified as invasive in parts of the Midwest; ***DWARF-WINGED BURNING BUSH*** (*E. alatus* 'Compactus'). **Height/Spread:** 10 feet; ***WINGED SPINDLE TREE*** (*E. alatus* 'Odom' ***LITTLE MOSES*** and *E. alatus* 'Rudy Haag'). **Height/Spread:** 3–5 feet. "At this time, all the cultivars for a given invasive species are considered invasive."[53] Burning bush cultivars sold as "safe" alternatives produce fewer seeds but enough to remain invasive; ***EUROPEAN SPINDLETREE*** (*E. europaeus*). **Height/Spread:** 10–25 feet. Large shrub/small tree. **Ornamental Attributes:** Red fall leaves, conspicuous red fruits, orange seeds. **Ecological Threat:** Invasive in Chicago area; naturalized in parts of the Midwest. **Zones:** 4–8.

Native Alternatives:

EASTERN BURNING BUSH, EASTERN WAHOO, AMERICAN BURNING BUSH. **Family:** Bittersweet (Celastraceae). **Genus:** *Euonymus* (*E. atropurpureus*). **Height/Spread:** 5–10 feet. **Ornamental Attributes:** Looks like the exotic burning bush and has the same bright

Eastern burning bush
(*Euonymus atropurpureus*)

red fall color. Lime-green twigs bordered by corky lines provide winter interest. The distinctive, midautumn, showy, brilliantly colored, rosy-pink pods split to reveal scarlet-coated seeds and persist far into winter. "When planted with American witch hazel (*Hamamelis virginiana*) the late fall combination of yellow flowers and red popcorn fruit makes a brilliant display," write Sternberg and Wilson.[54] "In the 1914 edition of his horticultural encyclopedia, L. H. Bailey recommended this tree as having a splendid fall coloring," noted Patricia A. Taylor in 1996. "Obviously not too many people took note because it is rarely found in cultivation today."[55] **Note:** The Morton Arboretum recommends eastern burning bush for planting in the Midwest on the basis of ornamental value, proven hardiness, availability, and freedom from serious problems. **Cultivation:** Sun, shade; most soils. Tolerates pollution and black walnut tree toxicity. **Nature Note:** Fruits attract migrating and overwintering songbirds due to their high fat content. **Zones:** 3–7; AMERICAN STRAWBERRY BUSH, BURSTING-HEART, WAHOO (*E. americanus*). **Height:** 6-plus feet. **Spread:** 4 feet. **Ornamental Attributes:** Bright red fall leaves. Red, strawberry-like fruits open to reveal orange seeds. Conspicuous green stems. "A beautiful alternative" with "very interesting berries" to the invasive burning bush, which often plagues our wild areas, writes Alonso Abugattas, including American strawberry bush in "Top 13 Native Shrubs/Small Trees" as wildlife plants for homeowners.[56] **Cultivation:** Sun, shade tolerant, moist or medium soil. **Note:** Threatened in Illinois. Also see RUNNING STRAWBERRY BUSH in Summer Shrubs, p. 157. **Nature Note:** Nectar and pollen attract small bees and pollinating flies that, in turn, attract nesting birds. Wild turkey (p. 244), eastern bluebird (p. 61), northern cardinal (p. 61), American robin (p. 62), and northern mockingbird (p. 256) use the fruits as emergency winter food. Hosts 11 species of Lepidoptera (butterflies/moths); the caterpillars are important food for baby birds. **Zones:** 5–9.

American strawberry bush (*Euonymus americanus*)

Sumac spp.

SUMAC. **Family:** Sumac (Anacardiaceae). **Genus:** *Rhus.* **Genus Note:** Sumacs have outstanding, brilliant red, purple, or orange-red fall color, and pyramidal clusters of showy red fall fruits called drupes (female plants) persist through the winter. "Their early colors rank our sumac species among the elite trees of autumn . . . their blaze of fall color is splendid," write Guy Sternberg and Jim Wilson. "Most sumacs need only a sunny location and well-drained soil."[57] Crooked, leaning trunks and picturesque branches make them architecturally decorative in winter. Sumacs were once trees of the prairie-forest interface; they develop root sprouts as an adaptation to a fire-prone environment. Though spectacular groves and thickets are sumac's natural form, "individual specimens, if trained and restrained from suckering, make artistic small trees with sinuous limbs and graceful, leaning trunks."[58] For plants of both genders, choose or transplant from more than one clone. Sumacs are disease resistant and tolerate drought, salt, compacted soils, and black walnut tree toxicity. **Zones:** 3–9; **FRAGRANT SUMAC** (*R. aromatica* var. *aromatica*). **Height:** 2–6 feet. **Spread:** To 10 feet. **Ornamental Attributes:** Dense, low-growing, spreading shrub; useful as ornamental groundcover. Clusters of yellow flowers. Large red berries persist to March, and, unlike other sumacs, fragrant, three-lobed leaves turn orange, crimson, and purple in fall. This "a much maligned plant" that "is probably disparaged by many precisely because there is no challenge involved in having a shrub of almost year-round interest," writes Patricia A. Taylor, adding, "If you happen to have exposed banks or slopes on which nothing appears to grow, this is the plant for you."[59] **Cultivation:** Low maintenance. Full sun to part shade, dry to medium preferably acidic well-drained soil; spreads by root suckers. **Cultivar/Nativar Note:** Nativars created for low growth, such as *R. aromatica* 'Gro-Low', the self-pollinating clone of fragrant sumac, have greatly reduced fruit production.[60] A result is shortages of one of the preferred foods for birds.

Fragrant sumac (*Rhus aromatica*)

'Gro-Low' fragrant sumac's flowers and fruits "are of little ornamental value."[61] **Zones:** 3–9; SHINING SUMAC, WINGED SUMAC (*R. copallinum* var. *latifolia*). **Height:** 7–15 feet. **Spread:** 10–20 feet. **Ornamental Attributes:** Red or maroon fall drupes persist into winter. Flame-red fall foliage; SMOOTH SUMAC (*R. glabra*). **Height:** 9–12 feet. The dominant sumac of blackland prairies. **Ornamental Attributes:** Female plants produce showy, yellow-green flowers followed by pyramidal clusters of bright red, hairy drupes that persist through the winter. "Short, crooked, leaning trunks and picturesque branches."[62] Pinnately compound leaves become bright orange to scarlet in fall. **Cultivation:** Full sun, tolerant of poor, dry soils. Useful on slopes and for naturalizing. **Zones:** 3–9; STAGHORN SUMAC (*R. typhina*). **Height:** 5–25 feet. **Spread:** 15–20 feet. **Ornamental Attributes:** Showy yellowish-green clusters of flowers in July. Velvety red late-summer drupes persist into winter. Velvety hairs on young branches resemble velvety deer antlers; brilliant yellow/orange/red fall foliage. Spectacular

American crow (*Corvus brachyrhynchos*)

Wild turkey (*Meleagris gallopavo*)

groves and excellent screens can be created with these picturesquely shaped shrubs and trees. **Cultivation:** Full sun, tolerant of salt and dry conditions. **Sumac Control Note:** Keeping the true species short is achieved by winter pruning every few years as needed. **Sumac Nature Note:** Female plants need a male plant to produce fruit. More than 98 species of migrating and overwintering birds eat the high-fat sumac drupes as preferred food, and as emergency winter and early spring food, including eastern bluebird (p. 61), northern mockingbird (p. 256), American robin (p. 62), red-eyed vireo (p. 112), northern flicker (p. 99), purple finch (p. 145), wild turkey, American crow, brown thrasher (p. 219), gray catbird (p. 79), eastern towhee (p. 235), scarlet tanager, wood thrush (p. 175), and white-throated sparrow (p. 108). Sumac flowers attract native bees, honeybees (p. 19), and a variety of pollinating flies sought by nesting birds as food for nestlings. Small carpenter bees reproduce by creating tunnel-nests in the stems. Sumacs host 58 Lepidoptera species (butterflies/ moths), including the banded hairstreak (p. 210), spring azure (p. 95), summer azure (p. 128), and the luna moth (p. 54); birds eat the caterpillars and feed them to their offspring. Sumacs are nectar plants providing food for pollinators like bees and adult monarch butterflies (p. 124) throughout the season[63] and are one of the few reliable sources of nectar during a drought. Can be used as a part of conservation biological control. "In general, the ecological value of sumacs to wildlife is quite high," writes John Hilty.[64]

AMERICAN WITCH HAZEL, COMMON WITCH HAZEL. **Family:** Witch-hazel (Hamamelidaceae). **Genus:** *Hamamelis* (*H. virginiana*). **Height:** 20–30 feet. **Spread:** 15–20 feet. **Ornamental Attributes:** Multitrunked large shrub, small tree; showy, fragrant, yellow strap-like flowers in October and November provide late fall color when most trees and shrubs have lost their leaves; scalloped leaves turn gold or pale orange; branches can assume a zigzagging pattern. "This shrubby little tree is one of the most curious and interesting plants in our northern flora. When all other trees are making ready for winter, when its own leaves are yellow and falling, it bursts forth into abundant bloom," wrote Harriet L. Keeler.[65] "Although witch hazel blooms when temperatures are often quite cool, there are still enough

American witch hazel
(*Hamamelis virginiana*)

insects around to pollinate it. Then the plant literally halts the process, holding the pollen over the winter so that fertilization can occur in spring. The fruit then grows throughout the summer, finally maturing at the same time the plant is flowering," writes Karen Schik.[66] **Cultivation:** Full sun best for flowers, takes part shade; moist well-drained soil; tolerates drought, soil that is soggy or marshy for a long time, poor drainage, dry locations, and black walnut toxicity. The fruits release small black seeds explosively, sometimes hurling them 30 feet away from the parent tree. Good for naturalizing, massing, and borders. **Native American Note:** "To the North American Indians we undoubtedly owe the first knowledge of the efficacy of its bark for the curing of inflammations."[67] **Nature Note:** Hosts 63 species of butterflies and moths. Provides pollinating insects including bees with much-needed late-season pollen and nectar. Due to its location in various habitats, it provides a variety of birds and animals with food, nesting sites, and cover. American robin (p. 62), northern cardinal (p. 61), tufted titmouse (p. 169), dark-eyed junco (p. 322), and many other birds eat the seeds. **Zones:** 3–8.

More Native Alternatives:

AMERICAN BEAUTYBERRY, p. 235; WINTERBERRY, p. 237.

More Native Alternatives to Burning Bush with Brilliant Fall Color:

See Spring Shrubs for AMERICAN BLACK ELDERBERRY & RED ELDERBERRY (yellow fall color), pp. 29, 30; AMERICAN BLADDERNUT (yellow fall color, persistent bladder-like seedpods), p. 41; AMERICAN HAZELNUT (bright yellow, orange, red fall color), p. 102; AMERICAN SMOKETREE (red and purple fall color), p. 65; BLUEBERRY SPP. (brilliant red fall color), p. 27; NORTHERN BUSH HONEYSUCKLES (red, yellow fall color), p. 38; CHOKEBERRY SPP. (brilliant red fall color, colorful fruits), p. 13; DOGWOOD SPP. (red fall color), p. 48; FOTHERGILLA SPP. (red, orange, purple fall color), p. 27; NINEBARK (red and yellow fall color), p. 44; OZARK WITCH HAZEL (golden fall color), p. 75; RHODODENDRON, AZALEA SPP. (yellow, red fall color), p. 56; ROSE SPP. (red, orange, yellow, purple fall color), p. 60; SAND CHERRY (red fall color), p. 17; SASSAFRAS (orange, red, to almost pink fall color), p. 99; SERVICEBERRY SPP. (orange, red, yellow fall color), p. 20 (for a photograph of serviceberry in fall see p. 271); SPICEBUSH (golden-yellow fall color), p. 22; SWEETSHRUB (golden-yellow fall color), p. 19; VIBURNUM SPP. (red and purple fall color, colorful fruits), p. 69 (for a photograph of blackhaw in fall see p. 265); WAFER ASH (yellow fall color, papery seeds), p. 45.

See Summer Shrubs for AMERICAN BLACK CURRANT (crimson, yellow, gold, and deep purple fall color), p. 138; BOTTLEBRUSH BUCKEYE (yellow fall color), p. 130; BUTTONBUSH (bronze, burgundy, yellow fall color; showy seeds), p. 131; CAROLINA BUCKTHORN (yellow, orange fall color), p. 141; CLETHRA (yellow-orange fall color), p. 132; CURRANT SPP. (crimson, yellow, gold, and deep purple fall color), p. 35; DEVIL'S WALKING STICK (yellow/purple fall color), p. 123; FALSE INDIGO BUSH (yellow fall color), p. 132; FRANKLIN TREE (red, orange, purple fall color), p. 147; KALM'S ST. JOHN'S WORT (red fruit), p. 145; NEW JERSEY TEA (yellow leaves and winter twigs), p. 134; OAKLEAF HYDRANGEA (maroon, scarlet fall color), p. 144; STEEPLEBUSH (yellow fall color), p. 127; ST. JOHN'S WORT SPP. (yellow fall foliage, brown seed capsules), p. 145; VIRGINIA SWEETSPIRE (red, orange, gold fall color), p. 126; WHITE MEADOWSWEET (yellow fall color), p. 128.

See Winter Shrubs for AMERICAN HOLLY (red fruits), p. 313; REDOSIER DOGWOOD (red stems, red leaves), p. 310; JUNIPER SPP. (evergreen, dark blue berry-like cones), p. 306.

See Spring Trees for CAROLINA SILVERBELL (yellow fall leaves, showy fruits), p. 80; CHOKECHERRY (red, orange fall color, colorful fruits), p. 83; FLOWERING DOGWOOD (red fall leaves), p. 94; HAWTHORN SPP. (colorful fall leaves, fruits), p. 106; REDBUD (yellow fall color), p. 92; SASSAFRAS (orange, red, yellow fall color), p. 99; SERVICEBERRY SPP. (orange, red, yellow fall color), p. 77.

See Summer Trees for ALLEGHENY CHINKAPIN (yellow, purple fall leaves), p. 171; SOURWOOD (red fall leaves), p. 186.

See Winter Trees for ALDER SPP. (cones and catkins, yellow/yellow-red-tinged fall leaves), p. 316.

Nonnative:

COTONEASTER. **Family:** Rose (Rosaceae). **Genus:** *Cotoneaster.* **Origin:** Asia, Europe. **Ornamental Attributes:** Red or black berries. Colorful fall leaves. **Cultivation:** Full–part sun, medium soil; *PEKING COTONEASTER* (*C. acutifolius*). **Height/Spread:** 6–10 feet. **Ornamental Attributes:** Black fruit. Orange fall leaves. Small white flowers in spring. **Zones:** 4–7;

Cotoneaster spp.

CRANBERRY COTONEASTER (*C. apiculatus, C. coriaceus, C. franchetii, C. microphyllus, C. pannosus*). **Height:** 2–3 feet. **Ornamental Attributes:** Red berries. Bronze fall leaves. **Zones:** 4–8; *SIMONS' COTONEASTER* (*C. simonsii*). **Zones:** 6–9; *SHINY COTONEASTER* (*C. acutifolius* var. *lucidus*). **Zones:** 4–8; *SPREADING COTONEASTER* (*C. divaricatus*); *RED COTONEASTER, MANY-FLOWERED COTONEASTER* (*C. multiflorus*). Red cotoneaster is invasive in the Chicago area. Peking Cotoneaster is present in Wisconsin and a problem in the Chicago area. **Zones:** 5–7.

Native Alternatives:

AMERICAN BEAUTYBERRY, p. 235; BAYBERRY, p. 232; CORALBERRY, p. 236; SNOWBERRY, p. 236; WINTERBERRY, p. 237.

See also Native Alternatives to *BURNING BUSH,* p. 239.

More Native Alternatives:

See Spring Shrubs for AMERICAN SMOKETREE (purple fall color), p. 65; BLUEBERRY SPP. (spring flowers, red fall color), p. 27; CHOKEBERRY SPP. (white flowers, red fall foliage, colorful berries), p. 13; DOGWOOD SPP. (white flowers, red fall color, berries), p. 48; GOLDEN CURRANT (yellow, red-centered flowers), p. 35; NINEBARK (four-season interest), p. 44; ROSE SPP. (beautiful flowers, colorful fall foliage, red rose hips), p. 60; SCENTLESS MOCK ORANGE (sweet-scented white spring flowers), p. 46; SERVICE-BERRY SPP. (white flowers; red, orange, yellow fall foliage), p. 20; VIBURNUM SPP. (red, purple fall color; fall fruits), p. 69.

See Summer Shrubs for AMERICAN BLACK CURRANT (crimson, yellow, gold, and deep purple fall color), p. 138; NEW JERSEY TEA (black fruit), p. 134; ST. JOHN'S WORT SPP. (yellow fall foliage, brown seed capsules), p. 145.

See Winter Shrubs for AMERICAN HOLLY (red fruits), p. 313; CREEPING JUNIPER (blue fruits), p. 306; INKBERRY (black fruits), p. 308.

See Spring Trees for AMERICAN PLUM (red, orange, yellow fall color), p. 78; CHERRY SPP. (red fall color, summer fruits), p. 82.

Nonnative:

CUTLEAF STEPHANANDRA, LACE SHRUB. **Family:** Rose (Rosaceae). **Genus:** *Stephanandra* (*S. incisa, S. tanakae*). **Origin:** Japan. **Height:** 2 feet. **Spread:** 3–6 feet. Spreads by suckering. **Ornamental Attributes:** Maple-like leaves turn yellow in fall. **Cultivation:** Full sun to part shade. Moist well-drained soil. **Zones:** 4–7.

Native Alternatives:

FRAGRANT SUMAC, p. 242.

See Spring Shrubs for NORTHERN BUSH HONEYSUCKLE, p. 38; PASTURE ROSE, p. 61.

See Summer Shrubs for OAKLEAF HY-DRANGEA, p. 144; and for Vines/Groundcover see Native Alternatives to *WINTERCREEPER*, p. 152.

See Winter Trees for HAZEL ALDER, p. 317.

Cutleaf stephanandra (*Stephanandra incisa*)

Scarlet firethorn
(*Pyracantha coccinea*)

Nonnative:

DOGWOOD. See Spring Shrubs, p. 93.
    DOGWOOD, RED-STEMMED DOGWOODS. See Winter Shrubs, p. 309.
    HOLLY. See Winter Shrubs, p. 313.

Nonnative:

HONEYSUCKLE. See Spring Shrubs, p. 37.

Nonnative:

RHODODENDRON, AZALEA. See Spring Shrubs, p. 56.

Nonnative:

SCARLET FIRETHORN. **Family:** Rose (Rosaceae). **Genus:** *Firethorn* (*Pyracantha*) (*P. coccinea*). **Origin:** Europe, Asia. **Height/Spread:** 6–18 feet. **Ornamental Attributes:** Spiny evergreen shrub, long-lasting red berries. **Cultivation:** Full to part sun, medium soil, naturalizes. **Ecological Threat:** Naturalized in midwestern states. **Zones:** 6–9.

Native Alternatives:

AMERICAN BEAUTYBERRY, p. 235; AMERICAN MOUNTAIN ASH, p. 255; EASTERN BURNING BUSH, p. 240; POSSUMHAW, p. 237; SILVERBERRY, p. 229; SUMAC SPP., p. 242; WINTERBERRY, p. 237.
See Summer Shrubs for DEVIL'S WALKING STICK, p. 123; PRICKLYASH, p. 124.
See Winter Shrubs for AMERICAN HOLLY, p. 313.

Nonnative:

SMOKETREE, EUROPEAN SMOKETREE. See Spring Shrubs for *SMOKETREE,* p. 65.

Fall Trees

Nonnative:

ALDER. See Winter Trees, p. 316.

Nonnative:

ASPEN. See Summer Trees, p. 164.

Nonnative:

AUTUMN OLIVE, RUSSIAN OLIVE. See Fall Shrubs, p. 229.

Nonnative:

BIRCH. See Winter Trees, p. 320.

Nonnative:

BRADFORD PEAR. See Spring Trees, p. 76.

Nonnative:

HARRY LAUDER'S WALKING STICK. See Winter Shrubs, p. 311.

Japanese maple (*Acer palmatum*)

Nonnative:

MAPLE. Family: Soapberry (Sapindaceae). **Genus:** *Acer; AMUR MAPLE* (*A. tataricum* subsp. *ginnala,* syn. *A. ginnala*). **Origin:** China, Japan, Korea. **Height:** 10–20 feet. **Ornamental Attributes:** Multistemmed tall shrub or tree. Colorful fall leaves. **Cultivation:** Full sun, partial shade; moist well-drained soils. **Ecological Threat:** In 1996, the Brooklyn Botanic Garden found extensive wild populations in Illinois and Missouri.[68] Invasive or naturalized in midwestern states. Designated "Not recommended" by the Morton Arboretum.[69] **Zones:** 3–7; *FULL MOON MAPLE, DOWNY JAPANESE MAPLE* (*A. japonicum*). **Origin:** Japan. **Height/Spread:** 20–25 feet. **Ornamental Attributes:** Red fall color. **Cultivation:** Full to part sun; moist well-drained soil; naturalizes. "Needs copious water in warm summers or leaves will turn yellow and brown";[70] *HEDGE MAPLE, FIELD MAPLE* (*A. campestre*). **Origin:** Eurasia, Africa. **Ecological Threat:** Naturalized in some midwestern states. Designated "Not recommended" by the Morton Arboretum. **Zones:** 5–8; *JAPANESE MAPLE* (*A. palmatum*). **Origin:** Japan. **Height/Spread:** 10–25 feet. **Ornamental Attributes:** Its numerous cultivars have a variety of shapes and textures. Leaf colors vary from green all summer to brownish or red-to-maroon spring through fall, creating an impression of endless autumn. The trees can be pruned to resemble desired shapes, including umbrellas. **Cultivar Note:** Colored leaves, such as red, and weeping or other forms grafted to green-leaved root stock can produce green-leaved suckers that become the dominant foliage. **Ecological Threat:** Naturalized in midwestern states. **Cultivar Note:** There are more than 1,000 Japanese maple cultivars, including *A. palmatum* 'Osakazuki'. **Zones:** 5–8; *KOREAN MAPLE, PURPLE BLOOM MAPLE* (*A. pseudosieboldianum*). **Origin:** Korea. **Height/Spread:** 20 feet. **Zones:** 4–7; *MANCHURIAN SNAKEBARK MAPLE* (*A. tegmentosum*). **Origin:** Russia, China. **Height:** 20 feet. **Zones:** 4–8; *MIYABE MAPLE* (*A. miyabei*). **Origin:** Asia. **Height:** 40–50 feet. **Ornamental Attributes:** Yellow fall color. **Cultivation:** Full sun, moist well-drained soil. **Zones:** 4–8; *NIKKO MAPLE* (*A. nikoense*). **Origin:** Japan. **Height:** 20–30 feet. **Ornamental Attributes:** Red fall color. **Zones:** 5–8; *PAINTED MAPLE* (*A. pictum*). **Origin:** Japan, China. **Height/Spread:** 30–40 feet. **Ornamental Attributes:** Red or yellow fall color. **Zones:** 5–8; *PAPERBARK MAPLE* (*A. griseum*). **Origin:** China. **Height:** 15–30 feet. **Ornamental Attributes:** Exfoliating bark, red fall color. **Zones:** 5–8; *SNAKEBARK, JAPANESE STRIPED-BARK MAPLE* (*A. capillipes*). **Origin:** Japan. **Zones:** 5–7; *TATARIAN MAPLE, AMUR MAPLE* (*A. tataricum*). **Origin:** Europe and Asia. **Height:** 20–30 feet. **Ornamental Attributes:** Red, yellow fall color. Red samaras (seeds). **Cultivation:** Sun, part shade, most soils. **Ecological Threat:** Naturalized in a few midwestern states. **Zones:** 3–8; *THREE-FLOWER MAPLE* (*A. triflorum*). **Origin:** Asia. **Height:** 30 feet. **Zones:** 5–7; *TRIDENT MAPLE* (*A. buergerianum*). **Origin:** Japan, China. **Zones:** 5–8; **Ornamental Maple Note:** Maple species, native or nonnative, are threatened by the Asian longhorned beetle, accidentally introduced from China.

Native Alternatives:

MOUNTAIN MAPLE. **Family:** Maple (Aceraceae). **Genus:** *Acer* (*A. spicatum*). **Height/Spread:** 20–25 feet. **Ornamental Attributes:** Fragrant clusters of white flowers in May to June. Consistently brilliant red, yellow, or orange fall foliage. Maroon-purple bark; irregular, open silhouette. "It is very beautiful," wrote Alice Lounsberry. "The individual trees remain ever true to their colours and turn every year to the particular ones that they have chosen. A beautiful sight is to see two different maples standing closely together when one has changed to scarlet and the other to clear, bright yellow."[71] **Confusion Note:** Do not confuse Mountain Maple with the western species, Rocky Mountain Maple (*A. glabrum*). **Cultivation:** Easy to grow except in the shade. Moist well-drained soil. Sap used to make maple syrup. **Note:** Endangered in Kentucky. **Zones:** 2–7; STRIPED MAPLE, MOOSE-WOOD (*A. pensylvanicum*). **Height/Spread:** 15–30 feet. **Ornamental Attributes:** Pendulous chains of yellow flowers in spring become chains of long pale green samaras (fruits); graceful, uneven crown; branches and short trunk have smooth, green, longitudinally white-striped bark some liken to green-and-white candy canes; fall leaves turn striking lemon yellow; stems become bright red. "Mother Nature was surely in one of her jocund moods when she gave so many fine little touches to the striped maple," wrote Alice Lounsberry.[72] **Cultivation:** Light shade; well-drained soil, moist roots. Very slow growing understory tree. "Loves to hide itself under the shade of larger trees."[73] Can be grown as a shrub. **Life Span:** Up to 100 years. **Note:** Endangered in Ohio. **Zones:** 3–7. **Maple Nature Note:** See Summer Trees for MAPLE, p. 197.

See Summer Trees for BLACK MAPLE, RED MAPLE, and SUGAR MAPLE, p. 198; SILVER MAPLE and BOXELDER, p. 193.

Mountain maple
(*Acer spicatum*)

More Native Alternatives:

AMERICAN MOUNTAIN ASH, p. 255; SUMAC SPP., p. 242.

See Spring Trees for AMERICAN PLUM and other native plums, p. 78; CAROLINA SILVERBELL, p. 80; CHERRY SPP., p. 17; CRAB APPLE SPP., p. 89; CUCUMBER-TREE, p. 111; FLOWERING DOGWOOD, p. 94; FRINGE TREE, p. 105; HAWTHORN SPP., p. 106; PAWPAW, p. 113; REDBUD, p. 92; SERVICEBERRY SPP., p. 77; SNOW-BELL, p. 116; YELLOWWOOD, p. 96.

See Summer Trees for AMERICAN HORNBEAM, p. 182; BLACKGUM, p. 218; BLACKJACK OAK, p. 204; HOP HORNBEAM, p. 183; SOURWOOD, p. 186; STEWAR-TIA, p. 215.

See Fall Shrubs for AMERICAN WITCH HAZEL, p. 244; LEATHERWOOD, p. 232.

See Spring Shrubs for ALTERNATELEAF DOGWOOD, p. 49; AMERICAN SMOKE-TREE, p. 65; RED BUCKEYE, p. 33.

See Summer Shrubs for CAROLINA BUCKTHORN, p. 141; FRANKLIN TREE, p. 147.

Mountain ash (*Sorbus aucuparia*)

Nonnative:

MOUNTAIN ASH, EUROPEAN MOUNTAIN ASH, COMMON MOUNTAIN ASH.
Family: Rose (Rosaceae). **Genus:** *Sorbus* (*S. aucuparia*). **Other Species:** *S. maderensis, S. po-huashanensis* (syn. *S. amurensis*), and *S. kamtschatcensis.* **Origin:** Europe, Asia. **Height:** 20–40
feet. **Spread:** 8–20 feet. **Ornamental Attributes:** White flowers in May, pinnately compound
leaves. "In the autumn, the fall foliage of *S. aucuparia* is rather bland while the American species are often more colourful, especially *S. decora*."[74] Clusters of orange-red fall fruit; sometimes disease causes them to shrivel. **Cultivation:** Sun, well-drained moist acidic soil. Bacterial
fireblight can be a severe problem. **Ecological Threat:** Widely naturalized in the Midwest.
Zones: 3–6; *KOREAN MOUNTAIN ASH* (*S. alnifolia*). **Origin:** Japan, Korea, China.
Height: 40–50 feet. **Ornamental Attributes:** White flowers appear unpredictably in May, orange or yellow berries, yellow fall foliage. **Cultivation:** Full sun, well-drained soil. Short-lived
tree. **Zones:** 3–7. There are other less-well-known Asian species. Some are less hardy, others
are shrubs that tend to sucker. All are potentially invasive.

American mountain ash (*Sorbus americana*)

Native Alternatives:

AMERICAN MOUNTAIN ASH. **Family:** Rose (Rosaceae). **Genus:** *Sorbus* (*S. americana*, syn. *Pyrus americana*). **Height:** 15–20 feet. **Ornamental Attributes:** Showy white flowers in May. Pinnately compound leaves on bright red stalks turn red or golden-orange in fall. Bright coral-red berries (pomes) remain all winter. **Cultivation:** Sun to shade. Dry to moist soil. **Note:** Endangered in Illinois. **Zones:** 2–5; NORTHERN MOUNTAIN ASH, SHOWY MOUNTAIN ASH (*S. decora*). **Height:** 25–50 feet. **Ornamental Attributes:** Clusters of white spring flowers. Pinnately compound blue-green leaves turn yellow-orange to reddish-purple in fall. Branches low to the ground. Heavily drooping clusters of glossy red or orange berries in late summer to fall persist through the winter. **Cultivation:** Sun–shade. Any poor- to well-drained, wet, moist, to medium soil. **Note:** A northern species. Endangered in Ohio. Extirpated in Indiana. **Zones:** 3–9. **Emerald Ash Borer Note:** This pest does not affect mountain ash, pricklyash, and wafer ash because they are not members of the ash genus (*Fraxinus*). **Nature Note:** Native mountain ashes have special value to native bees; good additions to bee gardens. Beneficial flies and beetles visit for nectar or pollen; the trees host dagger and other small moths. The iron- and vitamin C-rich fruits are poisonous to people but serve as fall and emergency winter food for at least 14 species of birds, including ruffed grouse (p. 36), cedar waxwing (p. 36), pine grosbeak, evening grosbeak (p. 162), gray catbird (p. 79), brown thrasher (p. 219), eastern bluebird (p. 61), veery, and thrushes. These trees host 68 species of butterflies and moths. Along with wild cherry, sweetbay, American linden, tulip tree, birch, ash, cottonwood, and willow, mountain ash hosts the eastern tiger swallowtail butterfly (p. 18).

Leafcutting bee (*Megachilidae*)

Syrphid fly (*Eristalis* spp.)

PERSIMMON. Family: Ebony (Ebenaceae). **Genus:** *Diospyros* (*D. virginiana*). **Confusion Note:** Do not confuse with the Oriental persimmon (*Diospyros kaki*) native to China. **Height:** 35–60 feet; can reach 100 feet. **Spread:** 25–35 feet. **Ornamental Attributes:** Fragrant yellow or white flowers in spring. Large, orange, sweet, fall fruit becomes edible after the first frost. Yellow-green to brilliant orange-red fall leaves. Bumpy, black alligator bark. "As familiar indeed to the country boy as to the botanist is the persimmon," wrote Alice Lounsberry in 1901.[75] **Cultivation:** Sun to part shade, wide range of well-drained soils.

Adaptable to difficult soils; shrubby in poor soil, large tree in rich, moist soil. Hardier than the Asian species. Female needs a male pollen source to fruit. Low maintenance, tolerant of air pollution, drought, and black walnut tree toxicity.[76] **Life Span:** 60–80 years. **Zones:** 4–9. **Nature Note:** The major pollinators are long-tongued bees seeking nectar and pollen such as honeybees (p. 19), bumblebees (p. 61), little carpenter bees, digger bees, mason bees, leafcutting bees, and cuckoo bees. Pollen seekers include small halictid bees and syrphid flies. This tree is known to host 46 species of Lepidoptera (butterflies moths). The fruits are eaten by fox, raccoon, bear, box turtle, wild turkey (p. 244), bobwhite (p. 36), gray catbird (p. 79), cedar waxwing (p. 36), northern mockingbird, and pileated woodpecker.

Northern mockingbird (*Mimus polyglottos*)

Sumac (Chinese sumac) (*Rhus chinensis*)

Nonnative:

SUMAC, CHINESE SUMAC. **Family:** Sumac (Anacardiaceae). **Genus:** *Rhus* (*R. chinensis*). **Origin:** China, Japan. **Height:** 15–25 feet. **Spread:** 20–30 feet. **Ornamental Attributes:** White flowers in August to September; red fruits; fall foliage is sometimes colorful. **Cultivation:** Full to part sun, dry to medium soil. Naturalizes. **Zones:** 5–8.

Native Alternatives:

AMERICAN MOUNTAIN ASH, p. 255; AMERICAN WITCH HAZEL, p. 244; PERSIMMON, p. 256.

See Summer Trees for BLACKGUM, p. 218; HONEY LOCUST, p. 163; KENTUCKY COFFEE TREE, p. 159; OHIO BUCKEYE, p. 184; SUMAC SPP., p. 242.

Tree of heaven (*Ailanthus altissima*)

Nonnative:

TREE OF HEAVEN. **Family:** Quassia (Simaroubaceae). **Genus:** *Ailanthus* (*A. altissima*). **Origin:** China. **Height:** 40–80 feet. **Spread:** 30–60 feet. **Ornamental Attributes:** Pinnately compound leaves, showy fuzzy red or orange flowers and seeds; unremarkable fall color. "Broken stems smell of rancid peanut butter, and males reportedly smell worse than female trees."[77] **Cultivation:** Full to part sun, dry to medium soil. **Confusion Note:** Easily confused with native trees and shrubs like sumac and black walnut that have pinnately compound leaves. The Morton Arboretum designates it "Not recommended." **Ecological Threat:** Classified as invasive in several midwestern states. **Zones:** 4–8.

Tree of heaven
leaves and flowers
(*Ailanthus altissima*)

Native Alternatives:

OSAGE ORANGE. **Family:** Mulberry (Moraceae). **Genus:** *Maclura* (*M. pomifera*). **Height:** 50 feet. **Ornamental Attributes:** Large grapefruit-sized green fruits that turn golden yellow; twisted thorny branches, crooked trunk, and furrowed orange-tinted bark provide winter interest. Fall leaves turn golden yellow. "A very beautiful tree is the osage orange when it stands alone and its ripe golden balls of fruit gleam through its vividly green and lustrous leaves as though they were so many large oranges," wrote Alice Lounsberry.[78] For fruits, a male is needed for fertilization. "The penultimate hedge row plant for property lines," states Missouri Botanical Garden Plant Finder.[79] **Cultivation:** Easily grown. Full sun, part shade. Tolerates dry and wet soil and everything in between. **Life Span:** 75–300+ years. **Zones:** 4–9 **Pioneer Note:** Before the introduction of barbed wire it was used nationwide for fences. **Anachronistic Note:** Biologists believe that the large fruits evolved to be eaten and dispersed by the large herbivores, like brontotheres during the early Cenozoic and maintained by rhinos during the mid-Cenozoic, and then eaten by mastodons and other Pleistocene megafauna, which went

Osage orange (*Maclura pomifera*)

extinct about 13,000 years ago, Today, Osage orange is deemed an "extreme anachronism," writes Connie Barlow.[80] **Nature Note:** Birds including eastern bluebird (p. 61), raptors, and the ground-nesting bobwhite (p. 36), squirrels, and rabbits eat seeds (not the pulp); birds and mammals use the thorny branches for cover, nesting, and protection. It provides invaluable cover in open areas. The loggerhead shrike, which lacks talons to grasp prey while eating, would benefit from midwesterners choosing Osage oranges. This bird uses the thorns to impale its food and prefers it for nesting.

More Native Alternatives:

AMERICAN MOUNTAIN ASH, p. 255; PERSIMMON, p. 256; SUMAC SPP., p. 242.

See Spring Trees for FRINGE TREE, p. 105.

See Summer Trees for BLACK WALNUT, p. 220; HICKORY SPP., p. 221; HONEY LOCUST, p. 163; KENTUCKY COFFEE TREE, p. 159; OHIO BUCKEYE, p. 184.

See Fall Shrubs for AMERICAN WITCH HAZEL, p. 244.

Loggerhead shrike (*Lanius ludovicianus*)

More Native Trees:

Additional native trees, including some that can grow as large shrubs, with fall color and/or fruits:

See Spring Trees for AMERICAN HAZELNUT (bright yellow, orange, red fall color), p. 102; CAROLINA SILVERBELL (yellow fall leaves), p. 80; CATALPA SPP. (yellow fall leaves), p. 86; BLACK CHERRY, p. 82; CHOKECHERRY, p. 83; CRAB APPLE SPP. (red or red and yellow fall leaves), p. 89; REDBUD (yellow fall leaves), p. 92; FLOWERING DOGWOOD (red fall leaves, red berries), p. 94; FRINGE TREE (yellow fall leaves), p. 105; HAWTHORN SPP. (red, orange, yellow, purple fall leaves, colorful fruits), p. 106; MAGNOLIA SPP. (yellow fall leaves, red fruit), p. 110; PAWPAW (golden fall leaves), p. 113; PIN CHERRY (red, yellow, orange fall leaves), p. 83; PLUM SPP. (orange-red, red-yellow fall leaves), p. 78; SASSAFRAS (yellow, orange, red fall leaves, blue berries on bright red stems), p. 99; SERVICEBERRY SPP. (orange, red, yellow fall leaves), p. 77; SNOWBELL (yellow fall leaves), p. 116; YELLOW BUCKEYE (yellow, orange, or red fall leaves, nuts), p. 98; YELLOWWOOD (yellow fall leaves), p. 96.

See Summer Trees for ALLEGHENY CHINKAPIN (yellow, purple fall leaves), p. 171; AMERICAN BEECH (golden-brown fall leaves), p. 168; AMERICAN CHESTNUT (yellow fall leaves), p. 170; AMERICAN HORNBEAM (scarlet-orange and yellow fall leaves, papery fruit), p. 182; AMERICAN LARCH (golden-yellow fall leaves), p. 189; AMERICAN SYCAMORE (yellow fall leaves, "button balls"), p. 214; ASH SPP. (purple/golden fall color), p. 161; ASPEN SPP. (golden fall leaves), p. 165; BALD CYPRESS (copper fall leaves), p. 172; BLACKGUM (orange, yellow, and red fall leaves), p. 218; BLACK WALNUT (yellow fall leaves), p. 220; BOXELDER (yellow fall leaves, showy seed clusters), p. 193; COTTON-WOOD (yellow fall leaves), p. 166; ELM SPP. (yellow fall leaves), p. 176; HACKBERRY (yellow, yellow-brown fall leaves, purple berries), p. 174; HONEY LOCUST (golden fall leaves, long seedpods), p. 163: HOP HORNBEAM (yellow fall leaves, interesting fruits), p. 183; KENTUCKY COFFEE TREE (yellow fall color, showy pods), p. 159; MAPLE SPP. (red, yellow, orange fall leaves), p. 197; OAK SPP. (red, gold, golden-brown fall leaves, acorns), p. 202; OHIO BUCKEYE (red, orange, yellow fall leaves), p. 184; PECAN (yellow fall leaves), p. 222; SHAGBARK HICKORY (golden fall leaves, bright red spring flowers), p. 222; SOURWOOD (red leaves, showy seed capsules), p. 186; STEWARTIA (orange, scarlet fall leaves), p. 215; SWEETGUM (yellow, orange, red, crimson, burgundy, purple fall leaves, gumballs), p. 216; TULIP TREE (tulip-shaped yellow, gold leaves), p. 179.

See Winter Trees for ALDER SPP. (cones and catkins, yellow/yellow red-tinged fall leaves), p. 316; BIRCH SPP. (showy bark, golden fall leaves, catkins, cones), p. 320.

See Spring Shrubs for ALTERNATELEAF DOGWOOD (red and purple fall leaves), p. 49; AMERICAN BLADDERNUT (yellow fall leaves, rattling seed capsules), p. 41; AMERICAN SMOKETREE (yellow, orange, red and reddish-purple fall leaves), p. 65; CHOKEBERRY SPP. (red fall leaves), p. 13; OZARK WITCH HAZEL (golden-yellow fall leaves), p. 75; VIBURNUM SPP. (BLACKHAW, NANNYBERRY, RUSTY BLACKHAW VIBURNUMS) (red, purple fall leaves; colorful, sometimes persistent fruits), p. 69; WAFER ASH (yellow fall leaves, papery seeds), p. 45.

See Summer Shrubs for AMERICAN BLACK CURRANT (crimson, yellow, gold, and deep purple fall leaves), p. 138; BRAMBLES (raspberry, blackberry) (orange, red, or purple fall leaves), p. 139; CAROLINA BUCKTHORN (yellow fall leaves, colorful berries), p. 141; DEVIL'S WALKING STICK (yellow fall leaves), p. 123; MISSOURI GOOSEBERRY (yellow-orange to red then purple leaves in fall), p. 138.

See Winter Shrubs for AMERICAN HOLLY (red fruit), p. 313.

GALLERY OF SHRUBS AND TREES IN FALL

SHRUBS

American cranberrybush in fall

Arrowwood in fall

Black chokeberry in fall

Blackhaw in fall

Bottlebrush buckeye in fall

Downy hawthorn berries

Elderberry berries

Gray dogwood in fall

Ninebark in fall

Oakleaf hydrangea in fall

Prairie rose leaves and hips in fall

Red chokeberry in fall

Serviceberry in fall

Sumac spp. in fall
Also see p. 242

TREES

American elm in fall

American hazelnut
in fall

American hornbeam
in fall

American linden in fall

American sycamore tree in fall

Bald cypress in fall

Buckeye (Ohio buckeye) in fall

Bur oak leaves in fall

Canoe birch in fall

Fall: **Gallery of Trees** ✦ 279

Catalpa in fall

Chinkapin oak in fall

Cottonwood in fall

Fringe tree in fall

Hackberry in fall

Honey locust tree in fall

Kentucky coffee tree in fall

Maple tree in fall

Silver maple in fall

Sugar maple in fall

Oak trees in fall

Hill's oak leaves in fall

Red oak in fall

Scarlet oak in fall

Shagbark hickory in fall

Shumard oak leaves in fall

Swamp white oak in fall

Redbud tree in fall

River birch in fall

Sweetgum tree in fall

Tulip tree in fall

Washington hawthorn
berries in fall

White ash tree in fall

Yellowwood in fall

4

WINTER

W E MOSTLY THINK of how woody plants look in spring, summer, and fall when we decide to plant trees and shrubs. But woody plants also provide un-expected winter interest. It is the "fourth season" that showcases the gnarled limbs, twig and branch architecture, bark color and texture, persistent colorful fruits, leaves, or seeds, and dramatic silhouettes that characterize deciduous and evergreen shrubs and trees. Winter is an opportunity to observe the overlooked aesthetic and environmental characteristics of many woody plants that we planted for features admired in other seasons.

Midwestern Indians lived on food that the women collected during the summer and fall, but the men also went into the forests for game meat, fur, fuel, and wood. Winter remained a primary hunting season. When food was scarce, rose hips served as an emergency ration. Starvation was a common occurrence.[1] Agriculture became increasingly important with the arrival of Europeans, and dependence on the forest changed from hunting and gathering to trapping for the fur trade.[2] The advent of Euro-American westward expansion caused Native Americans to cede vast areas of land to the United States.

The Indians were long gone in 1843, when English traveler William Oliver de-scribed an Illinois winter. "Till about the middle of January the weather was very fine, with moderately frosty nights and clear sunshiny days; but about that time, winter commenced in earnest, and the northwest winds, with a temperature at zero, swept the prairie with a chilling blast, that made the bones of one's face ache. The trees might be heard through the night cracking from the effects of the frost."[3] It was

1914 when Eloise Butler wrote, "In winter, a more intimate acquaintance can be made with deciduous trees. For it is only after the leaves have fallen that the architecture of trees can be clearly discerned. A tree with its delicate tracery of leafless branches is a thing of beauty to eyes that are adjusted to see it."[4] "I enjoy the unique quality of winter," wrote Helen Van Pelt Wilson in 1978. "It is a season of short days and long thoughts. For me, this fourth season is full of peace and beauty. In winter [birds] are amusing companions and I can only suggest, to anyone who is lonely, that you invite the birds, and hours of exciting companionship will be yours. I know I can never read a book with any degree of concentration if I sit facing a window in view of the feeders here," said Wilson. "Of all seasons I love winter best."[5]

For me, one of the pleasures of winter is being cozy, reading, drinking hot tea, or engaging in other suitable indoor activities. The heated birdbath that I installed immediately outside a glass door provides a view of small groups of orange-breasted American robins (p. 62) assembling to enjoy this accessible source of scarce water. I get to hear and see small flocks of whistling red-footed, gray-, pink-, and blue-feathered doves choose my birdbath as their evening destination. Cardinals (p. 61), shrieking blue jays (p. 79), twittering goldfinches (p. 145), gentle juncos (p. 322), and red-bellied woodpeckers (p. 55) are some birds that fly through the cold seeking life-sustaining water. Thirsty squirrels visit too. From the safety of my warm retreat, I thank winter for giving me a tranquil and endearing view of ever-changing wildlife.

"Landscape designers rely heavily on conifers to provide accents in the winter landscape when so many other plants are drab and brown." But many deciduous plants have winter uses. "Species [of birch] with exfoliating bark provide lots of nooks and crannies in which insects hide during winter months, and thus supply woodpeckers with food when they need it most," writes Douglas Tallamy.[6] Shagbark hickory also has bark full of nooks and crannies. In winter, we are able to see the structural beauty of oaks. Amazing keystone species, oaks host "an astounding" number of species of Lepidoptera (butterflies/moths).[7] Unless a butterfly emerges on a rare warm day, we don't see it, as they hibernate during the winter. (See the introduction to Spring for more information.) Nor do we see chipmunks (p. 94) in winter, but we know that they are safe underground with seeds and acorns they stored. Gray squirrels eat acorns and cover them with earth, literally planting them. Raccoons, black bears, and deer eat acorns, digging through the snow to locate them. Native tree and shrub nuts are a vital source of winter food for woodland birds who peck holes through the shells to access the meat.

It is easier in winter to remove the invasive nonnative shrubs and trees that crowd oaks and other ecologically important trees. Putting cut woody material into piles creates brush piles that provide butterflies with overwintering sites, birds with shelter and nesting material, and fox, rabbit, squirrel, and amphibians with dens in nasty weather. Innumerable insects, including ants, consume dead woody species, and serve as food for woodpeckers and other wildlife. "Ants are integral to the life of a tree from the very beginning," Aaron M. Ellison notes. A seedling "that germinates from a seed that was lucky enough to land on the sweet, rich soil of an anthill will often get a head-start in the race for the canopy. So before putting ant baits around the wood-pile, remember that these little creatures, which in aggregate far outweigh all of Earth's vertebrates—including people—really do keep the world turning."[8]

The amount of native woody food, cover, and shelter for wildlife will depend on the size of your yard, but even the smallest property can usually hold some. "Small trees and shrubs that hold their fruits through the coldest month offer fine color accents for the winter garden, and also food for the birds whose bright plumage sparkles in the cold air," wrote Helen Van Pelt Wilson. "The choice of really handsome red-berried material for winter seems infinite. . . . Aside from the sheer beauty of their fruit and the rich tones of the early winter foliage, these are the trees and shrubs that attract the garden birds which devour the juicy fruits earlier in summer and fall, and the dried, somewhat bitter ones last. . . . In winter, in addition to berries, birds often feed on the 'cones' of alders, birches and sweet gums. When the wind strikes these, the seeds are blown onto the ground to the delight of goldfinches and others. . . . If you are planting a property, what an opportunity you have to develop winter beauty in your near view!" wrote Wilson."[9] Planning for spring planting brightens the dreary season of the year.

Winter may seem bleak, but the season has distinctive pleasures. Small events like checking for squirrels or birds while passing a window or dashing out for the morning newspapers provide visual opportunities. Appreciating a native tree or shrub's gnarled limbs, beautiful bark, or dramatic silhouette against a gray sky are rewarding aesthetic events. In winter, deciduous leaves do not interfere with observing wild creatures living beyond our door. Winter is harsh for man and beast, so the season is particularly rewarding when helping wildlife. Planting natural food sources enables birds and small mammals to eat independently of feeders, helpful sources that are sometimes erratic. Landscaping and gardening with native fruit-, nut-, and seed-bearing shrubs and trees is a practical method of helping vulnerable wildlife throughout the winter.

Those of us who permit native fall flowers and grasses to remain, leaf litter to accumulate around our trees and shrubs, and snags or "wildlife trees" to stand find winter a season when this foresight pays off. These renewable resources hold a wealth of insects, worms, and snails, bits of acorns and nuts, and native flower and grass seeds that provide vital food for squirrels and for doves, robins, woodpeckers, nuthatches, cardinals, juncos, and other tree- and ground-feeding birds. It is pleasurable to observe these creatures feeding. It feels particularly good knowing we are contributing to their survival. We hope our suggestions provide you with inspiration and ideas for choosing our beautiful native midwestern shrubs and trees for winter enjoyment.

Winter Shrubs

Nonnative:

ARBORVITAE, RUSSIAN ARBORVI-TAE, SIBERIAN CYPRESS, RUSSIAN CYPRESS. **Family:** Cypress (Cupressaceae). **Genus:** *Microbiota* (*M. decussata*). **Origin:** Russia. **Height:** 1–3 feet. **Spread:** 8–10 feet. **Ornamental Attributes:** Spreading evergreen foliage. **Cultivation:** Sun, well-drained soil. **Zones:** 3–7.

Native Alternatives:

Russian arborvitae (*Microbiota decussata*)

JUNIPER SPP.: COMMON JUNIPER. **Family:** Cypress (Cupressaceae). **Genus:** *Juniperus* (*J. communis* var. *depressa*). **Height:** To 3 feet. **Range Note:** Grows throughout the cool temperate Northern Hemisphere. **Ornamental Attributes:** Usually a spreading low shrub, rarely a small tree with an open irregular crown. Gray-blue-green evergreen foliage; blue-black cones with white bloom persist through winter. **Cultivation:** Sun, well-drained soil. Tolerates black walnut tree toxicity. **Note:** Endangered, threatened, or rare in parts of the Midwest. **Zones:** 4–7; CREEPING JUNIPER (*J. horizontalis*). **Height:** 1–3 feet. **Spread:** 20 feet. **Ornamental Attributes:** Spreading blue-green evergreen foliage; dark blue, berry-like cones with white bloom persist through winter. **Note:** Endangered or threatened in parts of the Midwest. **Cultivation:** Sun, well-drained soil. **Zones:** 2–6. **Juniper Nature Note:** Junipers host 43 species of butterflies and moths, including the olive hairstreak but-

Common juniper (*Juniperus communis* var. *depressa*)

terfly and the juniper hairstreak butterfly. The fatty, high-carbohydrate cones are lifesavers for about 54 species of birds[10] in winter and early spring when food is scarce, including northern cardinal (p. 61), cedar waxwing (p. 36), black-capped chickadee (p. 322), red and white-winged crossbills (p. 317), Cooper's hawk, blue jay (p. 79), yellow-bellied sapsucker (p. 79), common grackle, eastern kingbird (p. 55), brown thrasher (p. 219), gray catbird (p. 79), American robin (p. 62), dark-eyed junco (p. 322), wood thrush (p. 175), northern mockingbird (p. 256), prairie warbler (p. 200), pine warbler (p. 312), house finch, chipping sparrow (p. 51), song sparrow, field sparrow, and other native sparrows. White-footed mouse, black bear, gray fox, opossum, and eastern chipmunk (p. 94) also eat its fruits. Birds and small mammals use junipers for shelter and nesting sites.

Juniper hairstreak butterfly
(*Callophrys gryneus*)

Another Juniper:

See Winter Trees for RED CEDAR, p. 323.

Other Native Alternatives:

AMERICAN YEW, p. 314.
See Winter Trees for EASTERN WHITE PINE, p. 328; HEMLOCK, p. 325; VIRGINIA PINE, p. 329.

Song sparrow (*Melospiza melodia*)

Field sparrow (*Spizella pusilla*)

Boxwood spp.

Nonnative:

BARBERRY. See Fall Shrubs, p. 231.

Nonnative:

BOXWOOD, COMMON BOXWOOD, AMERI-CAN BOXWOOD. **Family:** Boxwood (Buxaceae). **Genus:** *Buxus* (*B. sempervirens*). **Origin:** Eurasia. **Height/Spread:** 5–12 feet. **Ornamental Attributes:** Erect broadleaf evergreen. **Cultivation:** Full to part sun, medium soil. Pesticides are used to fight insect pests and deadly boxwood blight. Boxwood naturalizes, needs sheltered locations, protection from strong wind, mulching, pruning, thinning, weed control. "Because they are broadleaved evergreens, boxwoods are subject to damage from winter desiccation as well as cold damage, both of which can lead to extensive browning."[11] Despite its name, this shrub is not native to America. Despite its ill-smelling foliage, it is ubiquitous and is considered America's most popular shrub. **Ecological Threat:** Naturalized in several midwestern states. There are many cultivars; *LITTLELEAF BOXWOOD, JAPANESE BOX-WOOD* (*B. microphylla*). **Height/Spread:** 4 feet; *KOREAN BOXWOOD* (*B. sinica* var. *insularis*). **Boxwood Ecological Threat:** Boxwood are failures as host plants for butterflies. The vast number of boxwood cultivars and species filling the landscape do their part to ensure North American butterflies lack reproductive sites. **Boxwood Zones:** 5–8.

Native Alternatives:

INKBERRY. **Family:** Holly (Aquifoliaceae). **Genus:** *Ilex* (*I. glabra*). **Height/Spread:** 3–8 feet. **Ornamental Attributes:** Hardier than boxwood, this erect broadleaf evergreen's glossy, green, leathery foliage looks good and remains all year; white flowers from March to June; persistent jet-black berries. **Cultivation:** Sun/shade, most soils, easy to grow. Pest free; withstands heavy pruning. Fruiting requires at least one male plant. Deer avoid it. **Bird Note:** Fruit attracts up to 49 bird species. **Nativar Note:** At this time, only female inkberry nativars are commercially available.[12] The shrubs need a male to produce fruit, so birds go hungry. **Nature Note:** See *Ilex* Nature Note, Fall Shrubs, p. 237. **Zones:** 4–9.

For more holly species, see AMERICAN HOLLY, p. 313. Also see Fall Shrubs for POS-SUMHAW, p. 237; WINTERBERRY, p. 237.

Inkberry (*Ilex glabra*)

Other Native Alternatives:

See Spring Shrubs for CHOKEBERRY SPP., p. 13; FOTHERGILLA SPP., p. 27.

See Summer Shrubs for ASHY HYDRANGEA, p. 143; OAKLEAF HYDRANGEA, p. 144; ST. JOHN'S WORT, p. 145.

See Fall Shrubs for AMERICAN BARBERRY, p. 231; BAYBERRY, p. 232; CORALBERRY, p. 236; SILVER-BERRY, other *Elaeagnus* species, p. 229; SNOWBERRY, p. 236.

Nonnative:

CHINESE JUNIPER. **Family:** Cypress (Cupressaceae). **Genus:** *Juniperus* (*J. chinensis*). **Origin:** China. **Height:** 10–12 feet. **Spread:** 3–4 feet. **Ornamental Attributes:** Evergreen shrub. White cones turn brown. **Cultivation:** Sun. Dry to medium well-drained soil. **Zones:** 3–9.

Native Alternatives:

AMERICAN YEW, p. 314.

See Winter Trees for AMERICAN ARBORVITAE, p. 319; EASTERN WHITE PINE, p. 327; HEMLOCK, p. 325; RED CEDAR, p. 323.

Chinese juniper (*Juniperus chinensis*)

Nonnative:

COTONEASTER. See Fall Shrubs, p. 246.

Nonnative:

DOGWOOD, RED-STEMMED DOGWOODS. **Family:** Dogwood (Cornaceae). **Genus:** *Cornus.* **Note:** Nonnative and native dogwoods have similar or even identical habits and names (indicating "red") that create confusion, even in the nursery industry. The following introduced species are multistemmed shrubs that produce suckers and white spring flowers. For colorful stems, sun and pruning are needed. **Cultivar Note:** Cultivars don't come true from seed. Variegated forms are less vigorous. **Species:** *BLOODTWIG DOGWOOD* (*C. sanguinea*). **Origin:** Europe. **Height/Spread:** 6–15 feet. **Ornamental Attributes:** Purple-black fruit; red fall color. **Cultivation:** Moist, well-drained soil.

Bloodtwig dogwood (*Cornus sanguinea*)

Zones: 5–7; *REDTWIG DOGWOOD, TATARIAN DOGWOOD, SIBERIAN DOG-WOOD* (*C. alba*). **Origin:** Asia, Siberia. **Height/Spread:** 6–10 feet. **Ornamental Attributes:** White berries; unreliable reddish-purple fall foliage. Leaves get brown spots. **Cultivation:** Dry to wet soil. This is the most susceptible of the red-stemmed dogwoods to insects and diseases. **Zones:** 3–8.

Native Alternatives:

REDOSIER DOGWOOD, AMERICAN DOGWOOD, RED STEM DOGWOOD, RED WILLOW, BLOODTWIG DOGWOOD. **Family:** Dogwood (Cornaceae). **Genus:** *Cornus* (*C. sericea* subsp. *sericea*, syn. *C. stolonifera*). **Height:** 3–10 feet. **Spread:** 7–10 feet. **Ornamental Attributes:** White flowers in May. White fruits in summer. Bright red stems remain showy all year. Looks great massed, makes a good hedge. Fall color ranges from yellow to a purplish red depending on the annual seasonal variations. "In a way, it's odd," writes Patricia A. Taylor. "Here is a shrub that is simply stunning when all decked out: creamy white flowers

Redosier dogwood (*Cornus sericea* subsp. *sericea* syn. *C. stolonifera*)

over a long period and wonderfully colorful fall foliage. And yet it is chiefly honored for its winter nakedness, when its bright red stems are handsome in leafless settings."[13] **Cultivation:** Best in sun and moist, well-drained soil high in organic matter but adapts to soil extremes. Drought tolerant. Adaptable, easy to grow. **Zones:** 2–7. **Nature Note:** See Spring Shrubs for DOGWOOD, p. 48. **Dogwood Cultivar/Nativar Note:** Redosier dogwood cultivars are susceptible to leaf and twig blights, scale, leaf miners, and bagworms, including 'Cardinal'; yellow twig dogwood ('Flaviramea', 'Silver and Gold'); and red twig dogwood ('Isanti', 'Farrow' ARCTIC FIRE™).

More Native Alternatives:

See Spring Shrubs for GRAY DOGWOOD, p. 49; SILKY DOGWOOD, p. 50 (dogwoods with red stems).

For More Dogwoods:

See Spring Shrubs for DOGWOOD, p. 48.

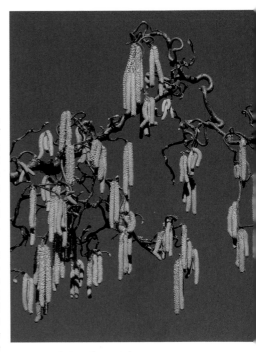

Nonnative:

HARRY LAUDER'S WALKING STICK, CONTORTED EUROPEAN FILBERT, CORKSCREW HAZEL. **Family:** Birch (Betulaceae). **Genus:** *Corylus* (*C. avellana* 'Contorta'). **Origin:** Europe. **Height:** 5–10 feet. **Spread:** 8–12 feet. **Ornamental Attributes:** Contorted branches. "Looks silly and contrived in its summer green," writes Penelope O'Sullivan.[14] **Cultivation:** Sun, part shade. Well-drained soil. Grafted plants (like this) need pruning to remove suckers. **Zones:** 4–8.

Another shrub noted for its contorted branches: ***CORKSCREW WILLOW.*** **Family:** Willow (Salicaceae). **Genus:** *Salix* (*S. matsudana* Koidzumi). **Origin:** China. **Height:** To 30 feet. **Spread:** 15 feet. **Ornamental Attributes:** Planted only for its contorted, twisted branches that are seen in winter; a "conversation piece." **Cultivation:** Full to part sun, consistently moist, well-drained soil. Short-lived tree with shallow roots that crack sidewalks. **Ecological Threat:** Naturalized in parts of the Midwest. **Zones:** 5–8.

Harry Lauder's walking stick
(*Corylus avellana* 'Contorta')

Native Alternatives:

DWARF CHINKAPIN OAK, DWARF CHINQUAPIN OAK, DWARF CHESTNUT OAK, SCRUB CHESTNUT OAK. **Family:** Beech (Fagaceae). **Genus:** *Quercus* (*Q. prinoides* var. *rufescens*). **Height:** 3–10 feet. Tree form may attain 20 feet. **Spread:** 8–12 feet. **Ornamental Attributes:** A unique slow-growing oak shrub or small tree. Interesting branch patterns; reliable producer of good-looking and wildlife-attracting acorns. "The tree can be used as a combination landscaping and wildlife plant. It is small enough and attractive enough to put into borders and gardens, where its leaves can turn a blazing orange-red before dropping in autumn. It can also be incorporated into a semi-wild area, where a grouping of several plants

Jack pine (*Pinus banksiana*)

Pine warbler (*Setophaga pinus*)

can quickly create an excellent wildlife habitat," writes Billy Bruce Winkles.[15] **Cultivation:** Sun and good well-drained soil for faster growth and best acorn production. Thrives in most soils, including sandy, rocky, and poor, but not in wet, clay, poorly drained, or alkaline soils. Acquire a small specimen to avoid injuring its long taproot. Lives 200–300 years. **Nature Note:** A prairie shrub, along with prairie willow and American plum, this oak provides the bobwhite quail (p. 36) with important low-growing woody cover from hawks. See OAK, Summer Trees, p. 202. **Note:** Critically imperiled in Indiana, imperiled in Nebraska, vulnerable in Iowa, possibly vulnerable in Missouri. **Zones:** 4–9.

JACK PINE. **Family:** Pine (Pinaceae). **Genus:** *Pinus* (*P. banksiana*). **Height:** 12–40 feet. **Ornamental Attributes:** Dwarf, shrubby, picturesque tree; contorted, gnarled trunk; windswept-looking irregular crown; somewhat twisted aromatic needles. "Jack Pine's irregular pattern of growth often provides it with a "bonsai" appearance."[16] This tree lends an architectural touch to the landscape. **Cultivation:** Extremely long-lived northern tree. Sun. Well-drained soil; grows well in dry and the poorest of soils. **Note:** Endangered or rare in parts of the Midwest. **Nature Note:** Important to nesting birds, including ground nesters like common nighthawks and vesper sparrows. In Michigan's sandy savannas, the endangered Kirtland's warbler nests at its base.[17] Native pines host 203 butterfly and moth species, including pine elfin butterfly, as well as the pine tree spur-throated grasshopper. Woodpeckers (pp. 55, 212), chickadees (p. 322), red-breasted (p. 322) and white-breasted nuthatches (p. 30), pine grosbeaks, dark-eyed juncos (p. 322), American goldfinches (p. 145), pine warblers, red and white-winged crossbills (p. 317), and mammals like red squirrels eat pine cone seeds. **Zones:** 2–6.

Other Native Alternatives:

See Spring Shrubs for ALTERNATELEAF DOGWOOD, p. 49; AMERICAN SMOKETREE, p. 65; MOUNTAIN LAUREL, p. 58; OZARK WITCH HAZEL, p. 75; PUSSY WILLOW, p. 53; RED BUCKEYE, p. 33; SCENTLESS MOCK ORANGE, p. 46.

See Summer Shrubs for DEVIL'S WALKING STICK, p. 123.

See Fall Shrubs for AMERICAN WITCH HAZEL, p. 244; SILVER BUFFALOBERRY, p. 229; STAGHORN SUMAC, p. 243.

See Spring Trees for AMERICAN HAZELNUT, p. 102; AMERICAN PLUM, p. 78; SERVICEBERRY SPP., p. 77.

See Summer Trees for AL-
LEGHENY CHINKAPIN, p. 171.
See Winter Trees for ALDER
SPP., p. 316.

Nonnative:

HOLLY, ENGLISH HOLLY.
Family: Holly (Aquifoliaceae). **Genus:** *Ilex* (*I. aquifolium*). **Origin:**
Europe, North Africa, Asia. **Height:**
To 50 feet. **Ornamental Attributes:**
Prickly-leaved, red-fruited evergreen tree. **Cultivation:** Full to part
sun; well-drained soil; naturalizes.
Advertised as a better ornamental
tree than American holly, but is less
winter hardy. **Note:** Fruiting requires at least one male plant. Birds

Holly (English holly) (*Ilex aquifolium*)

eat the fruits and spread the seeds. **Zones:** 7–9; *JAPANESE HOLLY* (*I. crenata*). **Origin:** Japan. **Height:** 4–10 feet. **Ornamental Attributes:** Red fall berries. **Ecological Threat:** Naturalized in Ohio. **Zones:** 5–8.

Native Alternatives:

AMERICAN HOLLY. **Family:** Holly (Aquifo-
liaceae). **Genus:** *Ilex* (*I. opaca* var. *opaca*). **Height:**
15–25 feet. **Spread:** 10–15 feet. **Ornamental Attributes:** Prickly-leaved, red-fruited evergreen tree.
"From the standpoint of berries, American holly
is particularly desirable, because its glory is a
winter matter. An evergreen, it dots itself with
red in late November and at Christmas time becomes the very symbol of the season."[18] **Note:**
Fruiting requires at least one male plant. **Anachronistic Note:** Are hollies "still defending against
mastodons?" writes Connie Barlow, noting their
prickly leaves are well above the reach of contemporary eaters, like deer.[19] **Cultivation:** Full to
part sun; well-drained soil. "American holly is
more adaptable to our colder environs than first
thought. It is best, however, to plant it in a protected area away from harsh winds."[20] Deer avoid
it. **Bird Note:** American holly berries are the "favorite with 45 species of birds."[21] **Nature Note:**
See *Ilex* Nature Note in Fall Shrubs, p. 237. **Life
Span:** 100–150 years. **Zones:** 5–9.

American holly (*Ilex opaca* var. *opaca*)

More Native Holly Species:

INKBERRY, p. 308.
   See Fall Shrubs for POSSUMHAW, p. 237; WINTERBERRY, p. 237.

More Native Alternatives:

See Fall Shrubs for AMERICAN BARBERRY, p. 231; AMERICAN BEAUTYBERRY, p. 235; AMERICAN STRAWBERRY BUSH, p. 241; BAYBERRY, p. 232; BURNING BUSH (native species), p. 240; LEATHERWOOD, p. 232; SUMAC SPP., p. 242.

Nonnative:

JAPANESE YEW. **Family:** Yew (Taxaceae). **Genus:** *Taxus* (*T. cuspidata*). **Popular hybrid:** *T. × media.* **Origin:** Japan. **Height:** 10–20 feet. **Spread:** 15–25 feet. **Ornamental Attributes:** Spreading evergreen shrub; female produces cones with a fleshy red cup around the seed. **Cultivation:** Sun, part shade, dry to medium well-drained

Japanese yew (*Taxus cuspidata*)

soil. **Ecological Threat:** Naturalized in midwestern states. Its widespread planting contributes to its becoming potentially invasive. **Zones:** 4–7.

Native Alternative:

AMERICAN YEW, CANADA YEW. **Family:** Yew (Taxaceae). **Genus:** *Taxus* (*T. canadensis*). **Height:** 3–8 feet. **Spread:** 6–10 feet. **Ornamental Attributes:** Spreading to somewhat upright evergreen shrub with dense green needles; female produces cones with a fleshy red cup around the seed. "American yew is the hardiest of all yews, yet the eastern and central North American native has been little exploited in ornamental horticulture," writes C. Colston Burrell, who calls it "an underutilized native species."[22] Yews are very tolerant of heavy pruning or shearing as new growth develops on old wood. If not pruned, most eventually attain tree size after many years of growth. **Cultivation:** Sun, shade; well-drained soil; pest free but

a favorite of deer. **Note:** Endangered in Indiana, threatened in Kentucky. **Nature Note:** Grouse, cedar waxwings (p. 36), American robins (p. 62), blue jays (p. 79), northern cardinals (p. 61), and squirrels eat the fruit. Dense evergreen foliage provides excellent shelter and nest sites for many species of birds and also chipmunks (p. 94). **Zones:** 2–7.

American yew (*Taxus canadensis*)

More Native Alternatives:

COMMON JUNIPER, p. 306; CREEPING JUNIPER, p. 306; INKBERRY, p. 308.
   See Winter Trees for AMERICAN ARBORVITAE, p. 319; EASTERN WHITE PINE, p. 327; HEMLOCK, p. 325.

Mugo pine (*Pinus mugo*)

Nonnative:

MUGO PINE. **Family:** Pine (Pinaceae). **Genus:** *Pinus* (*P. mugo*). **Origin:** Europe. **Height:** 4–10 feet. **Spread:** 15–25 feet. **Ornamental Attributes:** Mounding, spreading evergreen shrub. **Cultivation:** Sun, well-drained soil. **Zones:** 3–7.

Native Alternatives:

AMERICAN YEW, p. 314.
   See Winter Trees for EASTERN WHITE PINE, p. 328; VIRGINIA PINE, p. 329.

Nonnative:

ORIENTAL PHOTINIA. See Spring Shrubs, p. 47.

Nonnative:

PUSSY WILLOW. See Spring Shrubs, p. 52.

Nonnative:

SCARLET FIRETHORN. See Fall Shrubs, p. 249.

More Native Shrubs with Winter Interest:

See Spring Shrubs for AMERICAN BLADDERNUT, p. 41; AMERICAN SMOKETREE, p. 65; CHOKEBERRY SPP., p. 13; DOGWOOD SPP. (INCLUDING ALTERNATELEAF DOGWOOD), p. 48; FOTHERGILLA SPP., p. 27; NINEBARK, p. 44; NORTHERN BUSH HONEYSUCKLE, p. 38; OZARK WITCH HAZEL, p. 75; PUSSY WILLOW & OTHER NATIVE WILLOWS, p. 53; RED BUCKEYE, p. 33; ROSE SPP., p. 60; SCENT-LESS MOCK ORANGE, p. 46; SERVICEBERRY, p. 20; VIBURNUM SPP., p. 69; WAFER ASH, p. 45.

See Summer Shrubs for BUTTONBUSH, p. 131; CLETHRA, p. 132; FRANKLIN TREE, p. 147; HYDRANGEA SPP., p. 143; NEW JERSEY TEA, p. 134; RUNNING STRAWBERRY BUSH, p. 157; ST. JOHN'S WORT SPP., p. 145.

See Fall Shrubs for AMERICAN WITCH HAZEL, p. 244; BAYBERRY, p. 232; CORAL-BERRY, p. 236; EASTERN BURNING BUSH, p. 240; POSSUMHAW HOLLY, p. 237; SILVER BUFFALOBERRY, p. 229; SNOWBERRY, p. 236; SUMAC SPP., p. 242; WIN-TERBERRY, p. 237.

See Spring Trees for AMERICAN HAZELNUT, p. 102; CAROLINA SILVERBELL, p. 80; FRINGE TREE, p. 105; SERVICEBERRY, p. 77.

See Summer Trees for ALLEGHENY CHINKAPIN, p. 171.

See Winter Trees for ALDER SPP., p. 316.

Winter Trees

Nonnative:

ALDER, BLACK ALDER, COMMON AL-DER, EUROPEAN ALDER. **Family:** Birch (Betulaceae). **Genus:** *Alnus* (*A. glutinosa*). **Origin:** Europe, Africa, Asia. **Height:** 40–60 feet. **Spread:** 20–40 feet. **Ornamental Attributes:** Gummy young twigs and leaves, brown, purple flowers in March to April, glossy dark green leaves, persistent woody female cones, drooping male catkins. **Cultivation:** Full to part sun, medium to wet soil; naturalizes. **Ecological Threat:** Invasive in some midwestern states. The Morton Arboretum designates it "Not recommended." **Zones:** 3–7.

Native Alternatives:

ALDER, SPECKLED ALDER, GRAY AL-DER. **Family:** Birch (Betulaceae). **Genus:** *Alnus.* (*A. incana* subsp. *rugosa*). **Height:** 20–35 feet. **Spread:** 10–15 feet. Often a good-sized tree,

Black Alder (*Alnus glutinosa*)

sometimes a large shrub. **Ornamental Attributes:** Purplish-red flowers in March to April. Quilted green leaves turn yellow in fall. Persistent cones and catkins and crooked, leggy picturesque trunks provide winter interest. **Cultivation:** Full sun to shade, medium to wet soil. Fast growing. Tolerates black walnut tree toxicity. **Note:** Endangered in Illinois. **Zones:** 2–7; HAZEL ALDER, BROOKSIDE ALDER, SMOOTH ALDER (*A. serrulata*). **Height:** 12–20 feet. A multiply trunked, suckering shrub or small tree commonly found at the edge of water; picturesque habit, shiny gray-brown bark, purple spring flowers, yellow red-tinged fall leaves. **Zones:** 4–8; GREEN ALDER, NORTHERN ALDER, MOUNTAIN ALDER (*A. viridis* subsp. *crispa*). **Height:** 12–36 feet. **Cultivation:** Part shade, shade, wet soil. Northern midwestern species. Nitrogen-fixing—thrives on nutrient-poor sites.[23]

Alder Nature Note: Alder species host 255 species of moths and butterflies, including orange sulphur (p. 101), eastern tiger swallowtail (p. 18), giant swallowtail (p. 45), green comma butterfly (p. 103); also beetles and some aphids that attract carnivorous harvester butterfly caterpillars. Ruffed grouse (p. 36), American woodcock, rusty grackle, swamp sparrow, American goldfinch (p. 145), common redpoll (p. 54), white-winged crossbill, pine siskin (p. 54), blue jay (p. 79), great blue heron, scarlet tanager, evening grosbeak (p. 162), warblers, and woodland jumping mouse eat alder seeds, buds, or catkins and use the trees for cover and nesting.

More Native Alternatives:

CANOE BIRCH, p. 320; RIVER BIRCH, p. 320.

See Spring Shrubs for PUSSY WILLOW, p. 53.

See Spring Trees for FRINGE TREE, p. 105.

Alder (speckled alder) (*Alnus incana* subsp. *rugosa*)

American woodcock (*Scolopax minor*)

White-winged crossbill (*Loxia leucoptera*)

Swamp sparrow (*Melospiza georgiana*)

Chinese arborvitae (*Platycladus orientalis*)

Nonnative:

ARBORVITAE, ORIENTAL ARBORVITAE, CHINESE ARBORVITAE. **Family:** Cypress (Cupressaceae). **Genus:** *Platycladus* (*P. orientalis*, syn. *Thuja orientalis*). **Origin:** China, North Korea, Russia. **Height:** 25–45 feet. **Spread:** 10–20 feet. **Ornamental Attributes:** Green evergreen foliage. **Cultivation:** Full to part sun, medium soil. **Zones:** 6–9.

Native Alternatives:

AMERICAN ARBORVITAE, WHITE CEDAR, EASTERN ARBORVITAE, EASTERN OR NORTHERN WHITE CEDAR. **Family:** Cypress (*Cupressacae*). **Genus:** *Thuja* (*T. occidentalis*). **Confusion Note:** Do not confuse with western arborvitae or western redcedar (*T. plicata*) from western United States. **Height:** 40–50 feet. **Spread:** 6–20 feet. **Ornamental Attributes:** Distinctive cedar fragrance. Columnar dark, evergreen, flat, fan-like branches and dense awl-like leaves that are soft to the touch. Persistent cones and catkins, crooked leggy picturesque trunks, and red-brown bark create winter interest. Widely used as an ornamental tree, it retains its lower branches and adapts well to mass plantings, natural screen, and trimmed hedges. It is planted in residential landscapes, parks, and cemeteries where it is a symbol of eternal life.[24] **Cultivation:** Sun to shade. Prefers moist, well-drained, limestone-derived, neutral or slightly alkaline soils. New branches develop from concealed buds in the branch crotches, so withstands heavy pruning and shearing, preferably in early spring or midsummer. Slow growing, requires practically no maintenance. Tolerates black walnut tree toxicity. **Life Span:** Lives 400 years. **Nature Note:** Hosts 50 species of butterflies and moths. Supports other beneficial insects, including ants, plant bugs, and beetles, many eaten by American robin (p. 62), pine siskin (p. 54), common redpoll (p. 54), junco (p. 322), northern cardinal (p. 61), black-capped chickadee (p. 322), evening grosbeak (p. 162), and American tree sparrow, along with red squirrel, which also eats the cones or seeds. Used for nesting by migrating birds like Cape May warbler, blackburnian warbler (p. 326), and ruby-crowned kinglet (p. 233). Where plentiful, ovenbirds use it as cover to nest on the ground. It is used as shelter by migra-

Cape May warbler (*Setophaga tigrina*)

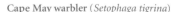

Black-throated green warbler
(*Setophaga virens*)

Magnolia warbler (*Setophaga magnolia*)

American arborvitae (*Thuja occidentalis*)

tory songbirds like wood thrush (p. 175), northern parula (p. 167), black-throated green, black-and-white, and magnolia warblers, and white-throated sparrow. Provides important wildlife habitat, including cover for birds and deer during severe winters. **Note:** This tree is a northern species that is endangered or threatened in midwestern states at the edges of its range. **Zones:** 3–7; HEMLOCK, p. 325.

Nonnative:

ASPEN. See Summer Trees, p. 164.

Nonnative:

AUTUMN OLIVE, RUSSIAN OLIVE. For both, see Fall Shrubs, p. 229.

Nonnative:

BEECH. See Summer Trees, p. 168.

Nonnative:

European white birch (*Betula pendula*)

BIRCH: EUROPEAN WHITE BIRCH, EUROPEAN BIRCH, SILVER BIRCH, WEEPING WHITE BIRCH. **Family:** Birch (Betulaceae). **Genus:** *Betula* (*B. pendula*). **Origin:** Europe, Asia Minor. **Height:** 30–40 feet. **Spread:** 15–30 feet. **Ornamental Attributes:** Persistent catkins and cones, exfoliating white bark resembling the native canoe birch. **Cultivation:** Full to part sun, medium to wet soil. **Ecological Threat:** Naturalized in the Midwest. **Zones:** 2–6; *WHITE BIRCH, DOWNY BIRCH* (*B. pubescens* subsp. *pubescens*). Naturalized in the Midwest; *ASIAN WHITE BIRCH* (*B. platyphylla* including var. *japonica*). **Height:** 40–50 feet. **Spread:** 15–25 feet. **Ornamental Attributes:** Yellow fall foliage, white, nonexfoliating bark. **Cultivation:** Full sun, moist well-drained soil. **Zones:** 5–8; *WHITE BARKED HIMALAYAN BIRCH* (*B. utilis* including *B. utilis* var. *jacquemontii*). **Origin:** Himalayas. **Height:** 30–40 feet. **Note:** The Morton Arboretum designates it "Not recommended." **Zones:** 5–6. **Asian and European Birch Disease Note:** "European and Asian species and cultivars of birch are very susceptible to bronze birch borer, even if trees are healthy and vigorous."[25]

Native Alternatives:

BIRCH: CANOE BIRCH, PAPER BIRCH **Family:** Birch (Betulaceae). **Genus:** *Betula* (*B. papyrifera* var. *papyrifera*). **Note:** Catkins and cones persist through the winter. Old birches may re-sprout, a survival technique developed in the forests during fire season. **Height:** 50–70 feet for single-trunked trees; multitrunked trees are shorter. **Spread:** 25–45 feet. **Ornamental Attributes:** Golden fall leaves. "The whitest bark of all the birches."[26] Exfoliating bark reveals orange-brown inner bark. **Cultivation:** Well-drained soil, tolerates a wide range of soil types; more resistant to borers than most birches. **Native American Note:** Used for birch bark canoes, wigwams, syrup, and trading. **Nature Note:** Northernmost populations of the luna moth (p. 54) most often utilize this birch as a host plant.[27] **Life Span:** 100–140 years. **Zones:** 2–6; GRAY BIRCH, AMERICAN WHITE BIRCH, OLD FIELD BIRCH (*B. populifolia*). **Height:** 35–50 feet. **Ornamental Attributes:** Narrow, columnar, single- or multitrunked tree; slender branches reach nearly to the ground; white, nonexfoliating bark; yellow fall color. "It is delicate and beautiful with leaves almost as tremulous as those of the aspen."[28] **Cultivation:** Sun to shade, dry to wet soil. **Note:** Endangered in Indiana. **Life Span:** About 50 years. **Zones:** 3–6; RIVER BIRCH (*B. nigra*). **Height/Spread:** 40–60 feet. **Ornamental Attributes:** Reddish-brown exfoliating bark, yellow fall color. "Through the winter the river birch has an open, feathery look which is very attractive."[29] **Cultivation:** Full sun, part shade; average, medium to wet soils. Tolerates dry soil, poor drainage. Easily grown. River birch is perhaps the most culturally adaptable and heat tolerant of the birches. **Zones:** 4–9; SWEET BIRCH, BLACK BIRCH, CHERRY BIRCH (*B. lenta*). **Height:** 40–60 feet. **Ornamental Attributes:** Mostly single stemmed with smooth, aromatic charcoal-gray bark. "Toothed, oval leaves are pleated and turn clear yellow in autumn. Use the tree as a specimen, shade tree, tall screen, or to create an airy grove."[30] Local people "formerly made in the season quite a little money with their birch stills" wrote Alice Lounsberry in 1900.[31] **Life Span:** 150–250 years. **Zones:** 4–7; YELLOW BIRCH, GRAY BIRCH (*B. alleghaniensis* var. *alleghaniensis;* syn. *B. lutea*). **Height:** 50 feet; can grow taller. **Spread:** 20–30 feet. **Ornamental Attributes:** Aromatic tree with twigs that smell and taste like wintergreen, showy catkins, and blazing yellow fall color. "The bark of the yellow birch, however, is one that should attract the attention of all; for it is particularly unique and beautiful. It is golden with a silver sheen and the separating shreds curl about it like the ribbon decorations of some fantastic lady."[32] **Cultivation:** Sun, light shade, moist well-drained soil, some protection from wind. **Note:** Endangered in Illinois. **Life Span:** 150–300 years. **Zones:** 3–7. **Native Birch Pest Note:** Native species of white-barked birch, such as paper (*B. papyrifera*) and gray (*B. populifolia*), evolved with the borers, and healthy trees are much more resistant than the nonnatives. Native non-white-barked species

Canoe birch (*Betula papyrifera* var. *papyrifera*)
Also see p. 279

River birch (*Betula nigra*)
Also see p. 297

Compton tortoiseshell butterfly (*Nymphalis vaualbum*)

also have significant resistance to bronze birch borers. Yellow birch (*B. alleghaniensis*) and sweet birch (*B. lenta*) are also generally resistant to bronze birch borer unless stressed, and river birch (*B. nigra*) appears to be immune.[33] Sweet, river, and yellow birches are tolerant of black walnut toxicity. **Birch Nature Note:** Native species host 413 butterfly and moth species, including red-spotted purple (p. 18), viceroy (p. 54), Compton tortoiseshell, green comma (p. 103), imperial and luna moths (p. 54), eastern tiger swallowtail butterfly (p. 18), cecropia (p. 18) and polyphemus moths (p. 211), duskywing butterflies (e.g., dreamy duskywing), and white-marked tussock moth. "If you plant silverbell, oaks, birches, willows or black cherry in your yard, you may attract the spectacular prometha moth."[34] Along with American elm, aspen, willows, hackberry, and red mulberry, canoe birch is a host plant for the mourning cloak butterfly (p. 62). "Birches are excellent sources of food for wildlife," writes Douglas Tallamy. "Not only do they support several hundred species of moths and butterflies, they also produce seeds and flower buds that are important for songbirds, small mammals, grouse and turkeys. Species with exfoliating bark provide lots of nooks and crannies in which insects hide during winter months, and thus supply woodpeckers with food when they need it most."[35] The bark is used to make nests by the Philadelphia vireo and black-throated green warbler (p. 319). River birch attracts more than 35 species of birds to its seeds, flower buds, and insects on the foliage,[36] including red-breasted nuthatch, black-capped chickadee, dark-eyed junco, common redpoll (p. 54), cedar waxwing (p. 36), fox sparrow, pine siskin (p. 54), American goldfinch (p. 145), American tree swallow, and woodpeckers (pp. 55, 212). Red-tailed hawks and other birds, squirrels, and other wild animals use birches for nesting, den habitat, and/or cover. The yellow-bellied sapsucker (p. 79) drills holes—later accessed by ruby-throated hummingbirds (p. 91)—into canoe birch bark for the sap.

Red-breasted nuthatch (*Sitta canadensis*)

Black-capped chickadee (*Poecile atricapillus*)

Fox sparrow (*Passerella iliaca*)

Dark-eyed junco (*Junco hyemalis*)

More Native Alternatives:

See Summer Trees for ASPEN, p. 165.
   See Fall Trees for STRIPED MAPLE, p. 252.

Nonnative:

BLADDERNUT. See Spring Shrubs, p. 15.

Nonnative:

CEDAR, JAPANESE CEDAR. **Family:** Cypress (Cupressaceae). **Genus:** *Cryptomeria* (*C. japonica*). **Origin:** Japan, China. **Height:** 50–60 feet. **Spread:** 20–30 feet. **Ornamental Attributes:** Evergreen. **Cultivation:** Full sun; medium soil. It needs consistently moist soils and protection from drying winter winds. **Zones:** 5–9.

Native Alternatives:

RED CEDAR, EASTERN RED CEDAR. **Family:** Cypress (Cupressaceae). **Genus:** *Juniperus* (*J. virginiana* var. *virginiana*). **Height:** Slow growing but can grow to tree size, 30–40 or more feet. **Spread:** 8–15 feet. **Ornamental Attributes:** Columnar, aromatic evergreen with a single trunk and exfoliating scented bark. Gray-green, blue-green, light or dark green sharp pointed awl-shaped foliage. Female trees produce copious ethereally pale, silver-coated, berry-like blue cones that remain over the winter; the cones also create gin's characteristic flavor. **Cultivation:** Best in full sun, average to humus-rich, well-drained soil. "This tough, underappreciated tree tolerates drought, heat, wind, salt, alkaline soil, acidic soil, and moderate air pollution."[37] Quite salt tolerant, can be used near roads, driveways, and sidewalks. Adaptive to difficult conditions, it serves as a windbreak, a living snow fence, and an easily trimmed hedge. Pruning to retain or correct shape or size should be done before new growth starts in the spring. "When I see a juniper pruned into cloud forms with foliage puffs at the branch tips, I marvel at how much one plant can suffer for looks' sake and still flourish," writes Penelope O'Sullivan, noting she is impressed by "their resilience."[38] Cedar rusts "do not seriously damage the red cedar,"[39] but do harm apples and hawthorns. Disease prevention entails preventing crowding

Japanese cedar (*Cryptomeria japonica*)

Red cedar (*Juniperus virginiana* **var.** *virginiana*)

and providing lots of sun. Red cedar can be aggressive in grassland ecosystems that are not managed by controlled burns or mowing; they are naturally landscaping derelict roadsides near big cities. Tolerates black walnut tree toxicity. **Life Span:** 150–300 years. **Bird Note:** This cedar is popular with cedar waxwings (p. 36). **Nature Note:** See JUNIPER, p. 306. **Zones:** 2–9.

More Native Alternatives:

AMERICAN ARBORVITAE, p. 319; HEMLOCK, p. 325.
See Winter Shrubs for AMERICAN YEW, p. 314; COMMON JUNIPER, p. 306.

Nonnative:

CHINESE CATALPA. See Spring Trees, p. 85.

Nonnative:

CRAB APPLE. See Spring Trees, p. 89.

Nonnative:

DOGWOOD. See Spring Shrubs, p. 93.

Nonnative:

EMPRESS TREE. See Spring Trees, p. 96.

Nonnative:

ENGLISH HOLLY. See Winter Shrubs, p. 313.

Nonnative:

FALSE CYPRESS, JAPANESE FALSE CYPRESS. **Family:** Cypress (Cupressaceae). **Genus:** *Chamaecyparis* (*C. pisifera*). **Origin:** Japan. **Height:** 50–70 feet. **Spread:** 10–20 feet. **Ornamental Attributes:** Evergreen stays green throughout winter; yellowish-brown cones. **Cultivation:** Full sun, medium soil; *HINOKI CYPRESS* (*C. obtusa*). Same description. **Zones:** 4–8.

Native Alternatives:

AMERICAN ARBORVITAE, p. 319; BALSAM FIR, p. 330; HEMLOCK, p. 325; PINE SPP., p. 327; RED CEDAR, p. 323.

False cypress (*Chamaecyparis pisifera*)

Nonnative:

GINKGO. See Summer Trees, p. 178.

Nonnative:

HAWTHORN. See Spring Trees, p. 105

Nonnative:

HEMLOCK: JAPANESE HEMLOCK. **Family:** Pine (Pinaceae). **Genus:** *Tsuga* (*T. diversifolia*). **Origin:** Japan. **Height:** 30–40 feet. **Spread:** 15–20 feet. **Ornamental Attributes:** Green-needled evergreen, brown cones. **Cultivation:** Full to part shade, medium soil. **Zones:** 4–7.

Japanese hemlock (*Tsuga diversifolia*)

Native Alternative:

HEMLOCK: CANADIAN HEMLOCK, EASTERN HEMLOCK. **Family:** Pine (Pinaceae). **Genus:** *Tsuga* (*T. canadensis*). **Height:** 40–70 feet. **Spread:** 25–35 feet. **Ornamental Attributes:** Straight-trunked, graceful pyramidal tree; short dark green needles with silvery undersides; horizontal, feathery branches often droop to the ground; can be trimmed as a hedge. "The hemlock has been much planted as an ornamental tree and has in cultivation produced new varieties, but none of them is so free and graceful in its growth as the wild tree."[40] **Cultivation:** Shade, part shade. Moist, medium well-drained soil. A tiny Asian insect, hemlock wooly adelgid, that secretes white wax as it feeds on sap, has spread into the Midwest. **Life Span:** 450–800 years. **Zones:** 3–7. **Nature Note:** Hemlocks provide important habitat, shelter, and winter cover for many wildlife species. The tree hosts 92 species of butterflies and moths, including the Columbia silkmoth. More than 35 species of birds eat the seeds, including black-capped chickadee (p. 322), red and white-winged crossbills (p. 317), dark-eyed junco (p. 322), veery, blue jay (p. 79), American goldfinch (p. 145), warblers, and pine siskin (p. 54), which clings to branch tips and hangs upside down to pick at seeds. Red squirrel and white-footed and woodland deer mice also eat the seeds. In warm weather, ruby-throated hummingbirds (p. 91) seek spiders and their prey among the branches. Black-throated blue warblers (p. 326), black-throated green

Hemlock (*Tsuga canadensis*)

Black-throated blue warbler (*Setophaga caerulescens*)

Blackburnian warbler (*Setophaga fusca*)

warblers (p. 319), blackburnian warblers, and magnolia warblers (p. 319) seek hemlocks for nesting. Ruffed grouse (p. 36), wild turkey (p. 244), owls, and other roosting birds use the trees for shelter and cover. Bears may den in large hollow trees; cubs climb them if feeling threatened. "It's a pity that no remnant populations of this aristocratic tree have been found in Illinois," writes John Hilty.[41]

Another Native Alternative:

BALSAM FIR, p. 330.

Nonnative:

HORNBEAM. See Summer Trees, p. 182.

Nonnative:

HORSE CHESTNUT. See Summer Trees, p. 184.

Nonnative:

JUNIPER, CHINESE JUNIPER (tree form). For image see *CHINESE JUNIPER* in Winter Shrubs, p. 309. **Family:** Cypress (Cupressaceae). **Genus:** *Juniperus* (*J. chinensis*). **Origin:** China, Japan. **Height:** 40–60 feet. **Spread:** 20–40 feet. There are many shrub cultivars. **Ornamental Attributes:** Green-needled evergreen. Brown cones in summer. **Cultivation:** Full sun, medium soil. Fast grower. "Be careful with chinensis, they often get too big and can overwhelm a landscape."[42] **Zones:** 3–9.

Native Alternatives:

HEMLOCK, p. 325; PINE SPP., p. 327; RED CEDAR, p. 323.

Nonnative:

PINE: AUSTRIAN PINE, EUROPEAN BLACK PINE. **Family:** Pine (Pinaceae). **Genus:** *Pinus* (*P. nigra*). **Origin:** Europe. **Height:** 40–60 feet. **Spread:** 20–40 feet. **Ornamental Attributes:** Green-needled evergreen, brown cones. **Cultivation:** Full sun; deep, moist, well-drained soil. Very susceptible to the pine wilt nematode (roundworm) that quickly kills the tree. **Ecological Threat:** Invasive with isolated distribution in Michigan; naturalized in midwestern states. The Morton Arboretum designates Austrian pine "Not recommended."[43] **Zones:** 4–7; *JAPANESE BLACK PINE* (*P. thunbergii*). **Origin:** Japan, South Korea. **Height:** 20–60 feet. **Ornamental Attributes:** Green-needled evergreen. New shoots require pruning to retain desired shape. **Cultivation:** Full sun; medium soil; naturalizes. **Zones:** 5–8; *JAPANESE RED PINE* (*P. densiflora*). **Origin:** China, Korea, Russia, Japan. **Ornamental Attributes:** Flat-topped. Needles may yellow in winter. **Cultivation:** Salt intolerant. **Zones:** 3–7; *JAPANESE WHITE PINE* (*P. parviflora*). **Origin:** Japan. **Height:** 40 feet. **Cultivation:** Full sun; medium soil. Neither flowers nor fruit are ornamentally significant. The shaggy gray bark is not particularly outstanding. **Zones:** 5–7; *SCOTCH PINE, SCOTS PINE* (*P. sylvestris*). **Origin:** Asia, Europe. **Height:** 50 feet. **Ornamental Attributes:** Twisted and bluish needles look like Virginia pine. Weak branches can break in the wind. **Cultivation:** Sun; well-drained soil; very susceptible to the deadly pine wilt nematode. **Ecological Threat:** Invasive in some midwestern states. **Zones:** 3–7; *SWISS STONE PINE* (*P. cembra*). **Origin:** Europe. **Height:** 30–40 feet. **Ornamental Attributes:** Green needled evergreen, brown cones. **Cultivation:** Full sun; medium soil. **Ecological Threat:** Invasive in the Midwest. **Zones:** 4–7; *DOUGLAS FIR, ROCKY MOUNTAIN DOUGLAS FIR.* **Genus:** *Pseudotsuga* (*P. menziesii* var. *glauca*). **Origin:** Native to the western United States, where it benefits regional wildlife like pine white butterflies. In the Midwest, "It will not function as a native."[44] **Height:** Usually 75–100 feet. **Ornamental Attributes:** Bluish-green needles, pendulous cones. **Cultivation:** Part shade; moist or dry soil. **Ecological Threat:** Naturalized in Minnesota. **Zones:** 4–6.

Austrian pine (*Pinus nigra*)

Native Alternatives:

EASTERN WHITE PINE, WHITE PINE. Family: Pine (Pinaceae). **Pine Note:** "About the great there is a simplicity, and somehow we are sensible of this when we stand before these grave inhabitants of the forests the pines," wrote Alice Lounsberry. "They have lived long on the globe."[45] **Genus:** *Pinus* (*P. strobus*). **Height:** 50–80 feet, grows taller in the wild. **Spread:** 20

Eastern white pine
(*Pinus strobus*)

feet. **Ornamental Attributes:** Bundles of soft, flexible, long, slender, blue-green to silver-green needles. Flowers are small yellow cones. Fruits are large elongated resinous brown cones that hold seeds. Oval, pyramidal shape. "This is a tall and stately pine that is justifiably popular," writes John Hilty.[46] **Cultivation:** Full sun, tolerates light shade; prefers good, well-drained acidic soil and protection from west wind. Tolerates dry and wet soil; intolerant of salt. Fast growing. Can be sheared and grown as a hedge. **Note:** Rare in Indiana. **Life Span:** 200–450 years. **Zones:** 3–8; JACK PINE. See Winter Shrubs, p. 312; LOBLOLLY PINE, BULL PINE, ROSEMARY PINE, OLDFIELD PINE (*P. taeda*). **Height:** 60 feet. **Ornamental Attributes:** Large, resinous, fragrant tree; gray scaly bark; yellow-green to dark green needles; reddish-brown cones. "Raw charm, beautiful bark."[47] **Cultivation:** Full sun; moist, dry, and difficult sites. A southern pine, fire exclusion helped it compete with other pines; now it is successfully grown in the Midwest where planted along the periphery of its natural range. **Life Span:** 100–300 years. **Zones:** 6–9; PITCH PINE (*P. rigida*). **Height:** 40–70 feet. **Ornamental Attributes:** Irregular

Red pine (*Pinus resinosa*)

form; twisting, gnarled, drooping branches; scaly, black bark tinged with red or purple; stiff, yellow-green needles turn dark green. Becomes dwarfed on exposed sites. Pitch pine is uniquely ornamental. **Cultivation:** Sun; dry, poor to wet soils; salt tolerant. **Zones:** 4–7; RED PINE, CANADIAN PINE, NORWAY PINE (*P. resinosa*). **Height:** 50–80 feet. **Spread:** 20–25 feet. **Ornamental Attributes:** Needles remain green through winter; brown cones develop in summer. "A picturesque tree, it is to the clear, bright colour of the bark of its trunk that this species of pine owes its name of red pine."[48] **Cultivation:** Full sun; dry, medium, moist soil. "It grows rapidly and can sustain itself in soil where many others would die from a lack of nourishment."[49] Used ornamentally and also as windbreaks to reduce home heating/cooling costs. **Note:** Endangered in Illinois. **Name Note:** Named "Norway" by mistake, it is native to the United States. **Zones:** 2–5; SHORTLEAF PINE, YELLOW PINE, SPRUCE PINE (*P. echinata*). **Height:** 50–100 feet. **Ornamental Attributes:** Long, clear trunk covered by plates of broad, flat, reddish-brown bark; broad, open crown; tufts of bright green needles. **Cultivation:** Sun; moist to dry soil. **Note:** Endangered in Illinois. **Life Span:** 200–300 years. **Zones:** 6–9; VIRGINIA PINE, JERSEY PINE, SCRUB PINE (*P. virginiana*). **Height:** 15–40 feet. Often a shrub. **Ornamental Attributes:** Gnarled, scrubby, twisted trunk, irregular silhouette, reddish-brown trunk, prickly cones. "But who shall say that its rugged, irregular growth does not present beauty in another than the conventional form?"[50] **Cultivation:** Sun; dry and moist, poor soil; grows where few other plants will. Drought tolerant. **Life Span:** 100–200 years. **Zones:** 4–8. *Pinus* **Nature Note:** The trees host 203 Lepidoptera species, including the frosted elfin butterfly, eastern pine elfin butterfly, northern and southern pine sphinx, pine devil moth, and the imperial moth, which prefers white pine. Pines host the pine tree cricket, pine tree spur-throated grasshopper, and sawflies, whose larvae enable the survival of eastern bluebirds and chickadees, which rely on them to feed early spring babies. Animals seeking pine cones for their nourishing seeds include red, gray, and southern flying squirrels, chipmunks (p. 94), voles, wild turkey (p. 244), bobwhite (p. 36), mourning dove, red-bellied woodpecker (p. 55), brown creeper, red- and white-breasted nuthatches (pp. 322, 30), pine grosbeak, dark-eyed junco (p. 322), common redpoll (p. 54), American goldfinch (p. 145), purple finch (p. 145), red and white-winged crossbills (p. 317), pine warbler (p. 312), and Carolina wren. Pine siskins (p. 54) can be seen clinging to branch tips and hanging upside down to pick at seeds. Eastern white pine cone seeds are favorites of black-capped chickadees (p. 322) and yellow-bellied sapsuckers. Pine's excellent cover lures blue-headed vireo, pine warbler (p. 312), yellow-throated warbler (p. 330), black-throated green warbler (p. 319), American crow (p. 244), bald eagle, and several hawks for nesting. Evening grosbeaks (p. 162) use pines for roosting, as do various owls. Provide nesting sites as well for many birds, including woodpeckers, common grackles, mourning doves, chickadees, and nuthatches.

Imperial moth (*Eacles imperialis*)

Frosted elfin butterfly (*Callophrys irus*)

Yellow-throated warbler
(*Setophaga dominica*)

BALSAM FIR. Genus: *Abies* (*A. balsamea*). Height: 45–75 feet. Spread: 25 feet. Ornamental Attributes: Spire-like shape, fragrant flowers, bluish-purple cones, and loss of lower branches give it an interesting appearance. An attractive landscape plant used as screening and shade and to reduce temperature in the area it covers. Soft, fragrant needles, once used to stuff pillows, make it a favorite Christmas tree. Cultivation: Sun to shade; moist, well-drained soil. *Abies* Nature Note: Hosts 117 species of butterflies and moths. Provides significant cover for wildlife, nest sites, and food for birds and mammals. Zones: 3–5.

Nonnative:

PLANE TREE. See Summer Trees, p. 213.

Nonnative:

POPLAR. See *ASPEN,* Summer Trees, p. 164.

Nonnative:

SPRUCE: NORWAY SPRUCE, EUROPEAN SPRUCE. Family: Pine (Pinaceae). Genus: *Picea* (*P. abies*). Origin: Europe. Height: 40–60 feet. Spread: 25–30 feet. Ornamental Attributes: Evergreen tree, brown cones; tends to lose lower branches. An alien conifer pushed by the ornamental plant industry. Cultivation: Full sun; medium soil, disease susceptible. Ecological threat: Naturalized in the Midwest. Zones: 2–7; *SERBIAN SPRUCE* (*P. omorika*). Origin: Balkans. Similar to Norway spruce in size, appearance, and cultivation requirements. Zones: 4–7; *ORIENTAL SPRUCE, CAUCASIAN SPRUCE* (*P. orientalis*). Origin: Turkey. Height: 50–75 feet. Ornamental Attributes: Looks like Norway spruce. Zones: 4–8; *COLORADO SPRUCE, COLORADO BLUE SPRUCE* (*P. pungens*). Origin: Mountains of west Wyoming and east Idaho to Arizona and New Mexico. Height: 40–60 feet. Ornamental Attributes: Green to silver-blue needles. Outside of its native range, such as in the Midwest, due to its susceptibility to diseases, insects, and mites, it is full of dead branches, loses lower branches with age, and generally looks ill and unsightly. Those planted in the Midwest are declining.[51] "It seems every suburban yard has to have at least one of the blue-needled cultivars studding a bed of burgundy- and chartreuse-leaved shrubs (preferably ones that bloom hot pink)," providing an "optically painful" visual experience that risks turning "our residential landscapes into ersatz amusement parks," writes William Cullina.[52] Cultivation: Full sun,

Norway spruce
(*Picea abies*)

part shade; most soils. In the Midwest, this tree is intolerant of wet soil, heat, pollution, and high humidity. **Wildlife Value:** In its native western region, this North American tree provides benefits to wildlife; but in the Midwest, the benefits it provides to wildlife are few.[53] **Ecological Threat:** Naturalized in Minnesota. **Zones:** 3–7.

Native Alternatives:

WHITE SPRUCE. **Family:** Pine (Pinaceae). **Genus:** *Picea* (*P. glauca*). **Height:** 40–60 feet; can reach 100 feet. **Spread:** 40 feet. **Ornamental Attributes:** Frosted appearance from wax-coated blue-green needles; compact and regular branching, lower branches sweep the ground; upper crown holds small spruce cones. **Cultivation:** Best in northern half of the United States. Full sun best. Takes shade. Moist, acidic loam; tolerant of many soil types. "Of the three [native spruce] species [i.e., black, red, and white], white spruce is by far the most amenable to landscaper use over most of our area," writes Guy Sternberg. "White spruce, unlike the others is somewhat drought-resistant and can be grown on almost any reasonable planting site. All three species tolerate wind, cold, sun and shade. White spruce is one of the toughest conifers—most unusual for a spruce—and it does well even in windbreak plantings on the Great Plains."[54] Deer resistant; salt and drought tolerant. Excellent shelter tree for wildlife.

White spruce (*Picea glauca*)

Historical Fact: During the last Ice Age, the vast white spruce forest covering the Great Plains followed the retreating ice northward;[55] BLACK SPRUCE (*P. mariana*). **Height:** 30–60 feet. **Ornamental Attributes:** Narrow, spire-like shape. Descending branches with upturned ends hold dark, bluish-green needles. Lower limbs sweep the ground. **Cultivation:** Sun to shade. Wet to medium acidic soils. Slow growing. Not genetically equipped to handle heat and drought; RED SPRUCE (*P. rubens*). Needs its natural mountain habitat replicated to do well. **Zones:** These three species can be cultivated from the northern limits of tree growth in Zones 2–6.[56] **Nature Note:** Spruce twigs, leaves, seeds, and insects that live on the tree bark and foliage are important wildlife food for birds, including black-capped chickadee (p. 322), red-breasted (p. 322) and white-breasted nuthatches (p. 30), dark-eyed junco (p. 322), and pine grosbeak (actually a finch) and evening grosbeak (p. 162); the trees provide these and other birds with valuable roosting, hiding, and nesting sites. The trees host 156 species of butterflies and moths, including the Columbia silkmoth. Hummingbirds (p. 91) visit their branches seeking spiders and their prey.

More Native Alternatives:

AMERICAN ARBORVITAE, p. 319; HEMLOCK, p. 221; PINE SPP., p. 328; RED CEDAR, p. 323.

For More Native Trees with Winter Interest:

See Spring Trees for AMERICAN HAZELNUT (flower buds, shape), p. 102; AMERICAN PLUM & OTHER PLUM SPP. (short, crooked trunk; scaly black bark; and spreading, sometimes thorny branches), p. 78; CAROLINA SILVERBELL (persistent showy four-winged brown fruit; exfoliating bark; branches low to the ground), p. 80; CATALPA (pods/branches, distinctive and dramatic winter silhouette), p. 86; CHOKECHERRY (beautiful buds and twigs), p. 83; CRAB APPLE SPP. (dramatic shape, decorative bark), p. 89; FLOWERING DOGWOOD (horizontal branches, interesting bark texture, fruits), p. 94; FRINGE TREE (thick twiggy form, shape), p. 105; HAWTHORN SPP. (interesting shapes; dense, intricate branch patterns; bark; many have thorns; colorful fruit eaten by overwintering birds), p. 106; REDBUD (arching limbs, clinging seedpods), p. 92; SASSAFRAS (deeply furrowed bark), p. 99; SERVICEBERRY SPP. (graceful shape, silver-gray bark), p. 20; YELLOW BUCKEYE (stout, picturesque branches sweep the ground; exfoliating bark), p. 98; YELLOWWOOD (attractive gray bark), p. 96.

See Summer Trees for ALLEGHENY CHINKAPIN (multitrunked), p. 171; AMERICAN BEECH (striking silhouette; golden-brown leaves persist through winter; smooth, silvery, steel-gray bark; prickly husks), p. 168; AMERICAN HORNBEAM (sinuous, twisted trunks and branches; handsome winter shape), p. 182; AMERICAN SYCAMORE (showy bark, "button balls"), p. 214; ASPEN (beautiful bark), p. 165; BITTERNUT HICKORY (highly conspicuous yellow winter buds), p. 221; BLACKGUM (gray scaly bark; horizontal, pagoda-like limbs), p. 218; BOXELDER (twisted growth habit, persistent showy seed clusters), p. 193; COTTONWOOD (imposing tree, ridged bark), p. 166; ELM SPP. (beautiful bark, attractive shapes), p. 176; HACKBERRY (vase-shaped, elm-like shade tree; rough, corky bark; fruits that birds eat in winter), p. 174; HICKORY SPP. (interesting shapes, bark), p. 221; HONEY LOCUST (long, twisted pods; beautiful bark, thorns, shape), p. 163; KENTUCKY COFFEE TREE (showy pods, beautiful bark, stout twigs, unique look), p. 159; MAPLE SPP. (eccentric to uniformly branching), p. 196; OAK SPP. (spectacular trees, striking silhouettes, interesting bark; some hold their leaves), p. 202; OHIO BUCKEYE (prominent buds through the winter; flaky bark), p. 184; RED MULBERRY (develops interesting shape), p. 195; SOURWOOD (crooked stems, silver-gray seed capsules), p. 186; SWEETGUM (spiky brown seed balls), p. 216; TULIP TREE (tall, imposing tree), p. 179; WALNUT (interesting shape), p. 220.

See Fall Trees for MOUNTAIN ASH SPP. (colorful fruit persists over winter), p. 255; MOUNTAIN MAPLE (interesting silhouette), p. 252; OSAGE ORANGE (twisted thorny branches, crooked trunk, furrowed orange-tinted bark), p. 259; STRIPED MAPLE (smooth, green, longitudinally white-striped bark on branches and trunk), p. 252.

For More Native Shrubs with Winter Interest:

See Spring Shrubs for ALTERNATELEAF DOGWOOD (striking silhouette), p. 49; AMERICAN BLADDERNUT (rattling bladder-like seedpods resemble Chinese lanterns; deep green twigs), p. 41; AMERICAN SMOKETREE (interesting shape), p. 65; CHOKEBERRY SPP. (colorful berries persist through winter, providing birds with food), p. 13; MAPLELEAF VIBURNUM (black berries persist through winter), p. 71; MOUNTAIN LAUREL (twisted trunk, evergreen leaves), p. 58; NINEBARK (persistent seed capsules, exfoliating bark), p. 44; OZARK WITCH HAZEL (picturesque winter branching structure, extremely fragrant clusters of fringe-like flowers January to April), p. 75; PRAIRIE WILLOW (wand-like yellow-brown to red stems), p. 53; PURPLEFLOWERING RASPBERRY (exfoliating bark), p. 62; RED BUCKEYE (coarse, open structure; light brown, flaky bark), p. 33; VIBURNUM SPP. (bold structure, persistent fruits eaten by birds), p. 69; WAFER ASH (papery seeds), p. 45.

See Summer Shrubs for BOTTLEBRUSH BUCKEYE (elegant curving branch structure), p. 130; BUTTONBUSH (persistent red fruits), p. 131; CLETHRA (brown capsules look like peppercorns and persist through winter), p. 132; DEVIL'S WALKING STICK (striking silhouette, coarse branches, dramatic prickles), p. 123; FALSE INDIGO BUSH (persistent pods), p. 132; LEADPLANT (seeds persist through winter), p. 133; ST. JOHN'S WORT (persistent seeds, exfoliating bark), p. 145; WILD HYDRANGEA (brown flowers persist through winter), p. 143.

See Fall Shrubs for BAYBERRY (persistent showy, waxy, silvery-white fruits eaten by birds; gray bark), p. 232; EASTERN BURNING BUSH (lime-green twigs, corky lines, brilliantly colored pods and seeds persist into winter), p. 240; POSSUMHAW HOLLY (bright orange-red berries eaten by birds; twiggy, horizontal branches), p. 237; SILVER BUFFALOBERRY (thorns, smooth brown bark, silver branches), p. 229; SUMAC SPP. (persistent dark red fruits eaten by birds, dramatic shapes, heights varying from groundcover to 25 feet), p. 242.

See Winter Shrubs for AMERICAN HOLLY (red fruits eaten by birds, prickly evergreen leaves), p. 313; AMERICAN YEW (evergreen), p. 314.

GALLERY OF SHRUBS AND TREES IN WINTER

SHRUBS

Ashy hydrangea in winter

Oakleaf hydrangea
in winter

Black chokeberry in winter

Red chokeberry in winter

Shrubby St. John's wort
in winter

Prairie rose hips
in winter

Serviceberry in winter

TREES

American beech in winter

American elm in winter

American witch hazel in winter

Catalpa in winter

Cottonwood
in winter

Kentucky coffee tree in winter

Oak trees in winter

Sweetgum in winter

Tulip tree in winter

Bur oak in winter

Red maple in winter

American sycamore in winter

Honey locust in winter

Yellowwood in winter

Washington hawthorn
in winter

Redbud in winter

NOTES

Preface

1. Neil Soderstrom, quoting Douglas Tallamy, "Which Trees and Shrubs to Plant? Douglas Tallamy's Newest Study," *About Town,* Spring 2015, http://www.abouttown.us/index.php/all -abouttown-articles/bulding-and-home/1259-Which-Trees-and-Shrubs-to-Plant-Douglas -Tallamys-Newest-Study (page discontinued).

2. Douglas Tallamy, "Lepidopteran Use of Native & Alien Ornamental Plants," University of Delaware website, accessed July 30, 2016, http://udel.edu/~dtallamy/host/index.html; also see Ben Team, "What Kind of Birds Eat Caterpillars?" Mom.me, accessed July 30, 2016, http: //animals.mom.me/kind-birds-eat-caterpillars-9422.html.

3. Genevieve Schmidt, "The Planting Pyramid: Adding Wildlife Value to Your Garden," *Find Native Plants,* March 6, 2014, http://findnativeplants.com/the-planting-pyramid-adding -wildlife-value-to-your-garden/.

4. "Monarch Butterfly Numbers Up, But Total Still Down 90%, Says Texas A&M Prof," *Gilmer Mirror,* February 18, 2016, http://www.gilmermirror.com/view/full_story/27092561 /article-Monarch-Butterfly-Numbers-Up--But-Total-Still-Down-90--Says-Texas-A-M-Prof; "American Goldfinch, . . . possibly has declined recently in some areas," *Audubon Guide to North American Birds,* https://www.audubon.org/field-guide/bird/american-goldfinch; Mel White, "North American Birds Declining as Threats Mount: Global warming, habitat loss, wind turbines, and cats are factors," *National Geographic,* June 21, 2013, http://news .nationalgeographic.com/news/2013/06/130621-threats-against-birds-cats-wind-turbines -climate-change-habitat-loss-science-united-states/.

5. Douglas Tallamy, "A Call For Backyard Biodiversity," *American Forests,* Autumn 2009, https://www.americanforests.org/magazine/article/backyard-biodiversity/; Soderstrom, quoting Tallamy, "Which Trees and Shrubs to Plant?"

6. *Greenacres: Landscaping with Native Plants,* US EPA, last updated February 21, 2016, https://archive.epa.gov/greenacres/web/html/.

7. Gary Wade et al., *Native Plants for Georgia Part III: Wildflowers,* UGA Extension Publication B 987-3, reviewed December 31, 2014, http://extension.uga.edu/publications/detail.cfm ?number=B987-3.

8. Ginny Stibolt, "Doug Tallamy!," Native Plants and Wildlife Gardens, 2012, http: //nativeplantwildlifegarden.com/doug-tallamy/ (site discontinued; relaunched as blog).

9. Katrina Marland, "The Birds and the Bees . . . And the Bats," *Loose Leaf* (American Forests blog), June 21, 2012, http://www.americanforests.org/blog/birds-bees-and-bats/; Melinda Housholder, "Batty for Urban Wildlife," *Loose Leaf* (American Forests blog), May 15, 2012, http://www.americanforests.org/blog/batty-for-urban-wildlife/.

10. Stibolt, "Doug Tallamy!"

11. Soderstrom, quoting Tallamy, "Which Trees and Shrubs to Plant?"

How to Use This Book

1. See USDA PLANTS Database, Frequently Asked Questions: "What do you mean by native and introduced? . . . At PLANTS we use Introduced since it is widely known rather than the similar term naturalized," http://plants.usda.gov/faq.html#native; USDA NRCS, "Introduced,

Invasive, and Noxious Plants: Introduced Plants of the PLANTS Floristic Area," USDA PLANTS Database, https://plants.usda.gov/java/noxiousDriver.

2. The United States National Arboretum, "What Is a Native Plant, Anyway?," USDA US National Arboretum: Gardens & Horticulture, last updated May 13, 2002, http://www.usna .usda.gov/Gardens/faqs/nativefaq2.html.

3. USDA Natural Resources Conservation Service Connecticut, "Native, Invasive, and Other Plant-Related Definitions," accessed July 30, 2016, http://www.nrcs.usda.gov/wps/portal /nrcs/detail/ct/technical/ecoscience/invasive/?cid=nrcs142p2_011124.

4. The Morton Arboretum, *Plants Tolerant of Black Walnut Toxicity*, 2014, https://www .mortonarb.org/trees-plants/tree-and-plant-advice/horticulture-care/plants-tolerant-black -walnut-toxicity.

5. Christopher J. Starbuck, *Selecting Landscape Plants: Uncommon Trees for Specimen Planting*, University of Missouri Extension, 2008, http://extension.missouri.edu/p/G6810.

6. Virginia Big Tree Program, "Lifespans of Common Trees in Virginia," Virginia Tech, 2016, http://bigtree.cnre.vt.edu/lifespan.html; Eastern OLDLIST, database of maximum tree ages for eastern North America, 2013, http://www.ldeo.columbia.edu/~adk/oldlisteast/.

7. Ellen Sousa, "Developing Sterile Invasives . . . Why Bother?," Native Plants and Wildlife Gardens, http://nativeplantwildlifegarden.com/developing-sterile-invasives-why-bother/ (site discontinued; relaunched as blog); Tiffany M. Knight, Kayri Havens, and Pati Vitt, "Will the Use of Less Fecund Cultivars Reduce the Invasiveness of Perennial Plants?" *BioScience* 61, no. 10 (October 2011), http://bioscience.oxfordjournals.org/content/61/10/816.abstract; Timothy M. Abbey, ed., *Alternatives for Invasive Ornamental Plant Species*, Connecticut Agricultural Experiment Station for the Connecticut Invasive Plant Working Group, September 2004, http://www .ct.gov/caes/lib/caes/documents/special_features/nativealternatives.pdf, 1. Studies to create sterile plants are ongoing. See Harold Pellett, "Landscape Plant Development Center's Breeding Project—Status," North Carolina State University Cooperative Extension, updated November 23, 2009, http://www.ces.ncsu.edu/fletcher/programs/nursery/metria/metria12/pellett/.

8. Soderstrom, quoting Tallamy, "Which Trees and Shrubs to Plant?"

9. Climate of Chicago, http://en.wikipedia.org/wiki/Climate_of_Chicago.

10. The United States National Arboretum, USDA Plant Hardiness Zone Map, last updated July 13, 2016, http://www.usna.usda.gov/Hardzone/.

11. Minnesota Department of Natural Resources, "Minnesota, Iowa, Wisconsin, Michigan, Ohio, New York, Illinois, Indiana, Kentucky, Tennessee, Missouri, and Arkansas in the Eastern Broadleaf Forest Province (EBF) or the Eastern Deciduous Forests Plant Province or Regional Vegetation Type," http://www.dnr.state.mn.us/ecs/222/index.html; C. Colston Burrell, *Native Alternatives to Invasive Plants* (New York: Brooklyn Botanic Garden, 2006), 8, 9.

12. University of Minnesota Extension, "Trees and Shrubs: Diseases, Insects and Other Problems," SULIS: Sustainable Urban Landscape Information Series, accessed July 30, 2016, http://www.extension.umn.edu/garden/landscaping/maint/tree_disease.html.

13. William Cullina, *Native Trees, Shrubs, and Vines* (Boston: Houghton Mifflin Harcourt, 2002), 29.

14. Janna Beckerman and B. Rosie Lerner, "Disease-Resistant Annuals and Perennials in the Landscape," Purdue University, Purdue Extension, August 2009, https://www.extension .purdue.edu/extmedia/BP/ID-414-W.pdf.

15. "Nativars: Where Do They Fit In?," Wild Ones, reprinted from *Wild Ones Journal* 26, no. 5 (November/December 2013), special section, http://www.wildones.org/wp-content /uploads/2011/12/Nativars-Statement.pdf.

Introduction

1. Christopher Brickell and Trevor Cole, eds., *The American Horticultural Society Encyclopedia of Plants & Flowers* (New York: DK Publishing, 2002), 62, 114.

2. Leah Zerbe, "Never Plant Butterfly Bush Again—Avoid This Invasive Species" (interview with Douglas Tallamy), Rodale's Organic Life, April 1, 2015, http://www.rodalesorganiclife.com /garden/3-reasons-never-plant-butterfly-bush-again.

3. LauraTangley, "Chickadees Show Why Birds Need Native Trees," *National Wildlife Federation's Blog,* April 28, 2015, http://blog.nwf.org/2015/04/chickadees-show-why-birds-need -native-trees/.

4. Mary Anne Borge, "Butterflybush—Are There Better Alternatives?," The Natural Web, September 11, 2013, quoting Jim P. Brock and Kenn Kaufman's *Field Guide to Butterflies of North America.* This is adapted from an article that appeared in the Summer 2012 issue of *Butterfly Gardener,* a publication of the North American Butterfly Association, https://the -natural-web.org/2013/09/11/butterflybush-are-there-better-alternatives/.

5. Borge, "Butterflybush—Are There Better Alternatives?"

6. USDA NRCS, "Introduced, Invasive, and Noxious Plants: Introduced Plants of the PLANTS Floristic Area," USDA PLANTS Database, http://plants.usda.gov/java/noxiousDriver.

7. *Greenacres: Landscaping with Native Plants,* US EPA, last updated February 21, 2016, https://archive.epa.gov/greenacres/web/html/.

8. Emily Grebenstein, "Escape of the Invasives: Top Six Invasive Plant Species in the United States," *Smithsonian Insider,* April 19, 2013, http://insider.si.edu/2013/04/top-six -invasive-plant-species-in-the-united-states/.

9. Eastern Illinois University, "Invasive Plant Species," *Landscaping and Restoration Using Illinois Native Plant Species,* accessed July 30, 2016, http://castle.eiu.edu/~n_plants/invasives .html.

10. Tallamy, quoted by Zerbe, "Never Plant Butterfly Bush Again." Also see Center for Biological Diversity, "The Extinction Crisis": "Of the more than 300,000 known species of plants, the IUCN [International Union for Conservation of Nature] has evaluated only 12,914 species, finding that about 68 percent of evaluated plant species are threatened with extinction"; accessed July 30, 2016, http://www.biologicaldiversity.org/programs/biodiversity/elements_of _biodiversity/extinction_crisis/.

11. S. Williams, "Mitigating Lyme Disease Risk through Control of an Invasive Plant Species," USDA, 2014, http://portal.nifa.usda.gov/web/crisprojectpages/0224920-mitigating-lyme -disease-risk-through-control-of-an-invasive-plant-species.html.

12. Diana Yates, "What's in Your Landscape? Plants Can Alter West Nile Virus," Illinois News Bureau, July 1, 2015, https://news.illinois.edu/blog/view/6367/236766, referencing Allison Gardner et al., "Asymmetric Effects of Native and Exotic Invasive Shrubs on Ecology of the West NILE Virus Vector *Culex Pipiens.*"

13. Sarah Hayden Reichard and Peter White, "Horticulture as a Pathway of Invasive Plant Introductions in the United States," *BioScience* 51, no. 2 (February 2001): 103–13, http://labs .bio.uothe%20United%20States.htm.

14. Gary Wade et al., *Native Plants for Georgia Part III: Wildflowers,* UGA Extension Publication B 987-3, reviewed December 31, 2014, http://extension.uga.edu/publications/detail .cfm?number=B987-3#title1.

15. Laura Tangley, "Why Birds Need Native Trees," *National Wildlife Federation's Blog,* January 15, 2015, quoting Douglas Tallamy, https://www.nwf.org/News-and-Magazines/National -Wildlife/Birds/Archives/2015/Chickadees-And-Native-Trees.aspx.

16. Reichard and White, "Horticulture as a Pathway of Invasive Plant Introductions."

17. Elizabeth D. Brusati, Douglas E. Johnson, and Joseph DiTomaso, "Predicting Invasive Plants in California," *California Agriculture* 68, no. 3 (July–September 2014): 89–95, doi:10.3733 /ca.v068n03p89.

18. Reichard and White, "Horticulture as a Pathway of Invasive Plant Introductions." The economic cost of invasive plants in natural areas, agriculture, and gardens was estimated in 1999 to be $35 billion per year. In 2009, the economic costs of invasive weeds for federal, state, and local governments was estimated to be $125 billion per year—a statistic said to be "rising

quickly." Cory Ritterbusch, "Invasive Species," PrairieWorks, February 23, 2009, http://www .prairieworksinc.com/category/invasive-species/.

19. Anthony DePalma, "Unwanted Guests: Invasive Species Infiltrate the Garden State," *New Jersery Monthly,* July 14, 2015, http://njmonthly.com/articles/jersey-living/unwanted -guests-invasive-species-infiltrate-garden-state/. Also see the summary of the discussion of the Illinois Invasive Plant Species Council Meeting, November 12, 2013, regarding listing the Callery pear (*Pyrus calleryana*) as an invasive species: "There was much discussion about the nomination form for Callery pear. In particular, the form did not present adequate informa- tion on the economic value of Callery pear to Illinois. . . . The Callery pear species represents an average of 8–10 percent of most growers' business in Illinois, and a whopping 20 percent of sales for at least 3 or 4 businesses. For most growers and garden centers, it's in their top five species in terms of sales, and for a good majority, it's in their top two. . . . This species is of particular importance in plantings near or under powerlines, since it is stays small enough to allow it to be planted in these scenarios. Several attendees expressed support for a market- driven approach for Callery pear instead of a regulatory. If the public is further educated on the potential of Callery pear to escape and become invasive, then demand will go down for the plant. There was general consensus that [the council] should not pursue regulation for Callery Pear." "Invasive Species Corner," *The Harbinger: News-letter of the Illinois Native Plant Society,* Fall 2013, http://www.ill-inps.org/images/pub/Harbinger_Vol30_No4_Fall2013.pdf.

20. USDA PLANTS Database, "Introduced, Invasive, and Noxious Plants: Introduced Plants of the PLANTS Floristic Area," https://plants.usda.gov/java/noxiousDriver.

21. Stephanie Yao, "Longer Marketing Time Increases the Risk of Naturalization by Horti- cultural Plants," United States Department of Agriculture, Agricultural Research Service, Feb- ruary 24, 2009, http://www.ars.usda.gov/is/pr/2009/090224.htm.

22. Theresa M. Culley and Nicole A. Hardiman, "The Beginning of a New Invasive Plant: A History of the Ornamental Callery Pear in the United States," *BioScience* 57, no. 11 (Decem- ber 2011): 956–64, http://bioscience.oxfordjournals.org/content/57/11/956.full. Choosing a cultivar of a nonnative invasive plant doesn't imply it won't be invasive. "Cultivars themselves may escape and form invasive populations" and "may cross-fertilize with related native or introduced species nearby. Genetically distinct cultivars may cross-fertilize with one another. Self-sterile cultivars" like Callery pear and purple loosestrife "can successfully cross-fertilize. The rootstock of grafted individuals can potentially sprout and reproduce by crossing with the upper scion" such as Callery (Bradford) pear. "Alternatively, the rootstock itself can be- come invasive, as is the case for the multiflora rose . . . which was originally used as rootstock for cultivated roses and planted as a living fence. Finally, some cultivars may be preadapted for invasion because of horticulturally desirable traits selected during their development (e.g., abundant flowering, environmental tolerance) as well as innate traits developed in their native habitat (e.g., allelopathy)."

23. Ellen Sousa, "Developing Sterile Invasives . . . Why Bother?" Native Plants and Wildlife Gardens, http://nativeplantwildlifegarden.com/developing-sterile-invasives-why-bother/ (site discontinued; relaunched as blog); Tiffany M. Knight, Kayri Havens, and Pati Vitt, "Will the Use of Less Fecund Cultivars Reduce the Invasiveness of Perennial Plants?" *BioScience* 61, no. 10 (October 2011): 816–22, http://bioscience.oxfordjournals.org/content/61/10/816; Timothy M. Abbey, ed., *Alternatives for Invasive Ornamental Plant Species,* Connecticut Agricultural Ex- periment Station for the Connecticut Invasive Plant Working Group, September 2004, http: //www.ct.gov/caes/lib/caes/documents/special_features/nativealternatives.pdf, 1.

24. Ronald L. Stuckey and Theodore M. Barkley, "Weeds in North America," in *Flora of North America,* vol. 1, chap. 8 (2007), http://www.floranorthamerica.org/Volume/V01 /Chapter08.

25. Elizabeth Kolbert, *The Sixth Extinction: An Unnatural History* (New York: Henry Holt, 2014), 211. "Still, today, Americans often deliberately import 'foreign varieties' they think might prove 'useful or interesting.' Garden catalogs are filled with non-native plants."

26. Douglas W. Tallamy, *Bringing Nature Home: How Native Plants Sustain Wildlife in Our Gardens* (Portland, OR: Timber Press, 2007), 9, 10, 14.

27. Douglas Tallamy, "A Call for Backyard Biodiversity," *American Forests* 115, no. 3 (Autumn 2009): 24, http://www.americanforests.org/magazine/article/backyard-biodiversity/.

28. Tallamy, *Bringing Nature Home*, 87.

29. Ibid., 111.

30. Bill Hopkins, "Native Plants for Butterfly Gardens," Native Plant Society of Texas, February 22, 2014, http://npsot.org/wp/story/2014/4971/.

31. Stephen W. Kress, "The Interlaced Biology of Birds and Plants," in *Bird Gardens: Welcoming Wild Birds to Your Yard*, ed. Stephen W. Kress, 21st-Century Gardening Series Handbook no. 156 (Brooklyn, NY: Brooklyn Botanic Garden, 1998), 10.

32. Susan Tweit, "Turn Your Yard into a Winter Refueling Spot for Birds," *Audubon Magazine*, January–February 2013, http://www.audubon.org/magazine/january-february-2013/turn-your-yard-winter-refueling-spot.

33. Conserve Lake County, e-mail, August 26, 2014.

34. Rick Darke and Doug Tallamy, *The Living Landscape: Designing for Beauty and Biodiversity in the Home Garden* (Portland, OR: Timber Press, 2014), 104.

35. Tallamy, *Bringing Nature Home*, 44.

36. Mariette Nowak, for the Wisconsin Society for Ornithology, *Beyond the Birdfeeder: Creating a Bird-Friendly Yard with Native Wisconsin Plants*, Wild Ones, updated February 2013, http://www.wildones.org/wp-content/uploads/2011/12/birdsc-brochure-2013-02.pdf.

37. Tangley, "Why Birds Need Native Trees," quoting Douglas Tallamy. Tangley, "Why Birds Need Native Trees." Also see Neil Soderstrom, quoting Douglas Tallamy, "Which Trees and Shrubs to Plant? Douglas Tallamy's Newest Study," *About Town*, Spring 2015, http://www.abouttown.us/index.php/all-abouttown-articles/bulding-and-home/1259-Which-Trees-and-Shrubs-to-Plant-Douglas-Tallamys-Newest-Study (page discontinued).

38. Tangley, "Chickadees Show Why Birds Need Native Trees."

39. Tallamy, *Bringing Nature Home*, 54.

40. "Hummingbirds Eating Insects," The Wild Bird Store, accessed July 30, 2016, http://wildbirdsonlinc.com/articles_hummingbirds_eating_insects.html. Insects eaten by hummingbirds include small beetles, true bugs, weevils, flies, gnats, mosquitoes, aphids, mites, leafhoppers, flying ants, and parasitic wasps. Their favorite insect food source is the spider and harvestmen (daddy long legs). Some ornithologists estimate that spiders are between 60 percent and 80 percent of their diet.

41. Insects eaten by cardinals include beetles, grasshoppers, leafhoppers, caterpillars, and stinkbugs.

42. "Plant Natives to Feed the Birds," Choose Natives: Plant for Life, August 21, 2014, http://choosenatives.org/tag/baby-birds-are-fed-caterpillars/. Insects eaten by chickadees include aphids, whitefly, scale, caterpillars, ants, and earwigs.

43. Mariette Nowak, "Creating a Bird-Friendly Yard with Native Plants: Birds and Plants—An Ancient Collaboration," Wild Ones, last updated December 1, 2011, http://www.wildones.org/learn/native-plants-natural-landscaping/creating-a-bird-friendly-yard/.

44. Tallamy, "Call for Backyard Biodiversity."

45. Michael Snyder, "Why Are Some Trees Pollinated by Wind And Some by Insects?," *Northern Woodlands*, Spring 2009, http://northernwoodlands.org/articles/article/why_are_some_trees_pollinated_by_wind_and_some_by_insects. Insect-pollinated trees include basswood, cherries, black locust, catalpa, tulip tree, and the willows.

46. Soderstrom, quoting Tallamy, "Which Trees and Shrubs to Plant?"

47. "Nativars: Where Do They Fit In?," Wild Ones, reprinted from *Wild Ones Journal* 26, no. 5 (November/December 2013), special section, http://www.wildones.org/wp-content/uploads/2011/12/Nativars-Statement.pdf.

48. Soderstrom, quoting Tallamy, "Which Trees and Shrubs to Plant?"

49. Sue Sweeney, "The Nativar Dilemma," Native Plants and Wildlife Gardens, 2011–12, http://nativeplantwildlifegarden.com/the-nativar-dilemma/ (site discontinued; relaunched as blog). Also see Douglas Tallamy, quoted in "Nativars: Where Do They Fit In?"; Mariette Nowak, "What's the Problem? Nativars," *Wild Ones Journal* 27, no. 1 (January/February 2014): 12, http://www.wildones.org/download/Journold/2014Vol27No1%20Journal.pdf.

50. Soderstrom, quoting Tallamy, "Which Trees and Shrubs to Plant?"

51. Vincent Vizachero, "Native Cultivars—Good, Bad, and Ugly," Native Plants and Wildlife Gardens, 2011–14, http://nativeplantwildlifegarden.com/native-cultivars-good-bad-and-ugly/ (site discontinued; relaunched as blog).

52. Ibid.

53. Rene Ebersole, "How to Buy Native Plants: Knowing native plants are your garden's best option is one thing. Finding them can be quite another," *Audubon*, July 19, 2013, http://www.audubon.org/news/how-buy-native-plants.

54. Soderstrom, quoting Tallamy, "Which Trees and Shrubs to Plant?"

55. Ibid.

Chapter 1: Spring

1. Kelly Kindscher, *Edible Wild Plants of the Prairie: An Ethnobotanical Guide* (Lawrence: University Press of Kansas, 1987): chokecherry, 180, 181 (also plum, crab apple); wild plum, 171, 172, also sand cherry, 173; serviceberry, 29, 30; wild rose, 201.

2. Eliza W. Farnham, *Life in Prairie Land* (1846; repr., Champaign: University of Illinois Press, 1988), 129, 134, 138, 139.

3. Alice Lounsberry, *A Guide to the Trees,* illus. Mrs. Ellis Rowan (New York: Frederick A. Stokes, 1900), 269.

4. Neil Soderstrom, quoting Douglas Tallamy, "Which Trees and Shrubs to Plant? Douglas Tallamy's Newest Study," *About Town,* Spring 2015, http://www.abouttown.us/index.php/all-abouttown-articles/bulding-and-home/1259-Which-Trees-and-Shrubs-to-Plant-Douglas-Tallamys-Newest-Study (page discontinued).

5. Indigos and clovers (pea family) are some species upon which eastern tailed-blue, frosted elfin, and gray hairstreak butterflies lay their eggs. Ozark swallowtail and black swallowtail butterflies lay their eggs on native parsley family plants like golden Alexanders and yellow pimpernel.

6. Sally S. Weeks and Harmon P. Weeks Jr., *Shrubs and Woody Vines of Indiana and the Midwest: Identification, Wildlife Values, and Landscaping Use* (West Lafayette, IN: Purdue University Press, 2012), 116.

7. "Plant Profiles: Chokeberry, Black," Chicago Botanic Garden, accessed July 1, 2016, http://www.chicagobotanic.org/plantinfo/chokeberry_black.

8. *Aronia prunifolia* is the agreed-upon species name of Swink and Wilhelm in *Plants of the Chicago Region* (1994) and Voss in *Michigan Flora* (1985), and since they are regional, the authors follow their views.

9. Terry L. Ettinger, "Recommended Shrubs: Chokeberry," Terry L. Ettinger Horticulture Consulting Services, accessed July 1, 2016, http://www.tlehcs.com/recommended%20plants/shrubs/aronia.htm.

10. "Aronia (black chokeberry)—Plant Description and Habitat," University of Maine Cooperative Extension, accessed July 1, 2016, http://umaine.edu/agriculture/home/aronia/plant-description-and-habitat/.

11. Michael A. Dirr, *Dirr's Hardy Trees and Shrubs: An Illustrated Encyclopedia* (Portland, OR: Timber Press, 1997), 299.

12. Weeks and Weeks, *Shrubs and Woody Vines,* 168–69; Sally S. Weeks, Harmon P. Weeks Jr., and George R. Parker, *Native Trees of the Midwest: Identification, Wildlife Values, and Landscaping Use* (West Lafayette, IN: Purdue University Press, 2010), 170.

13. A. D. Webster, *Hardy Ornamental Flowering Trees and Shrubs,* 2nd ed. (London: Hicks, Wilkinson & Sears, 1893, 1897), http://www.gutenberg.org/files/10852/10852-h/10852-h.htm.

14. William Cullina, *Native Trees, Shrubs, and Vines: A Guide to Using, Growing, and Propagating North American Woody Plants* (Boston: Houghton Mifflin, 2002), 64.

15. Mariette Nowak for the Wisconsin Society for Ornithology, *Beyond the Birdfeeder: Creating a Bird-Friendly Yard with Native Wisconsin Plants,* Hoy Audobon Society, 2003, http://www.hoyaudubon.org/documents/birdscaping.pdf. Nowak is the author of *Birdscaping in the Midwest: A Guide to Gardening with Native Plants to Attract Birds* (Madison: University of Wisconsin Press, 2012).

16. "*Lindera benzoin* (L.) Blume—Northern spicebush, Spicebush, Wild allspice," NPIN: Native Plant Database, Lady Bird Johnson Wildflower Center, record modified October 27, 2013, http://www.wildflower.org/plants/result.php?id_plant=LIBE3.

17. Jason Sheets, "April Plant of the Month: *Lindera benzoin,* Spicebush," New York Restoration Project, April 3, 2015, https://www.nyrp.org/blog/april-plant-of-the-month-lindera-benzoin-spicebush/.

18. Patricia A. Taylor, *Easy Care Native Plants: A Guide to Selecting and Using Beautiful Ameri-can Flowers, Shrubs, and Trees in Gardens and Landscape*s (New York: Henry Holt, 1996), 146.

19. Ibid.

20. "Berries and Brambles," Chicago Botanic Garden, accessed July 1, 2016, http://www.chicagobotanic.org/plantinfo/berries_and_brambles.

21. Penelope O'Sullivan, *The Homeowner's Complete Tree and Shrub Handbook* (North Adams, MA: Storey Publishing, 2007), 70.

22. Helen Van Pelt Wilson and Léonie Bell, *The Fragrant Year: Scented Plants for Your Garden and Your House* (New York: William Morrow, 1967), 184.

23. John Hilty, "Common Elderberry," in "Trees, Shrubs, and Woody Vines of Illinois," Illinois Wildflowers, acccessed July 1, 2016, http://www.illinoiswildflowers.info/trees/plants/cm_elder.htm.

24. O'Sullivan, *Homeowner's Complete Tree and Shrub Handbook,* 200.

25. Ibid.

26. Guy Sternberg and Jim Wilson, *Landscaping with Native Trees: The Northeast, Midwest, Midsouth and Southeast Edition* (Shelburne, VT: Chapters, 1995), 50–51.

27. O'Sullivan, *Homeowner's Complete Tree and Shrub Handbook,* 230.

28. Green Deane, "Foraging for Forsythia," Eat the Weeds, accessed July 1, 2016, http://www.eattheweeds.com/foraging-for-forsythia-2/.

29. "Clove Currant: *Ribes odoratum,* or *Ribes aureum,*" A Way to Garden, May 12, 2013, http://awaytogarden.com/the-clove-currant-ribes-odoratum-or-ribes-aureum/.

30. Wilson and Bell, *Fragrant Year,* 33.

31. "Forbidden Fruit 2: State by State Legality of Gooseberry and Currant Berry (Laws regarding plants in the *Ribes* genus), The Greener Grass Farm, February 8, 2015, https://thegreenergrassfarm.com/2015/02/08/forbidden-fruit-2-state-by-state-legality-of-gooseberry-and-currant-berry-laws-regarding-plants-in-the-ribes-genus/.

32. Nowak, *Beyond the Birdfeeder.*

33. "Forest Songbirds and Invasive-Plant Management," Forest Preserve District of DuPage County, accessed July 1, 2016, http://www.weftecasia.com/DuPage_Plants_and_Wildlife/Birds/Songbirds/Forest_Songbirds_and_Invasive-Plant_Management.aspx?ekfrm=363.

34. "Invasive Plants in the Chicago Region," Chicago Botanic Garden, accessed July 1, 2016, http://www.chicagobotanic.org/research/identifying_threats/invasive.

35. Weeks and Weeks, *Shrubs and Woody Vines,* 104, 105.

36. Melissa Howard, "Lilacs: History and Culture," accessed July 1, 2016, https://suite.io/melissa-howard/8d72gd.

37. Cullina, *Native Trees, Shrubs, and Vines,* 257.

38. Ibid.

39. C. Colston Burrell, *Native Alternatives to Invasive Plants* (Brooklyn, NY: Brooklyn Botanic Garden, 2006), 109.

40. Heike Morales, "Calligrapha spiraeae, Ninebark beetle," 2012, http://www.epcc.edu /Biology/Documents/Poster_DrW/Chihuaha_Desert_Life/Insecta/Calligrapha_spiraeae.pdf; Ted C. MacRae, "Beetle Botanists," Beetles in the Bush, June 14, 2012, https://beetlesinthebush .wordpress.com/2012/06/14/beetle-botanists/.

41. "Ninebark," *Better Homes and Gardens,* 2016, http://www.bhg.com/gardening/plant -dictionary/shrub/ninebark/. Author and native plant specialist Mariette Nowak writes she "never saw excessive leaf beetle damage" on the green-leaved natives. "Nativars: What's the Problem?" *Wild Ones Journal* 27, no. 1 (January/February 2014): 12, http://www.wildones.org /download/Journold/2014Vol27No1%20Journal.pdf. A study showed that as much as 10 percent of the foliage can be damaged by insects before a gardener would even notice. Douglas W. Tallamy, *Bringing Nature Home: How Native Plants Sustain Wildlife in Our Gardens* (Portland, OR: Timber Press, 2007), 91.

42. Emily G. Tenczar and Vera A. Krischik, "Effects of New Cultivars of Ninebark on Feeding and Ovipositional Behavior of the Specialist Ninebark Beetle, Calligrapha spiraeae (Coleoptera: Chrysomelidae)," *Horticultural Science* 42, no. 6 (2007): 1396–99, http://cues.cfans .umn.edu/old/krischiklab/pubs/Tenczar_Krischik_2007nb.pdf.

43. "Ninebark 'Little Devil'" in "Shrubs Boast Blooms, Pest Resistance," Preen, 2016, http: //www.preen.com/articles/new-shrubs-blooms-pest-resistance.

44. "Diablo Ninebark . . . Mold Problems?" GardenWeb, May 22, 2008, http://forums2 .gardenweb.com/discussions/1587623/diablo-ninebark-mold-problems.

45. Wilson and Bell, *Fragrant Year,* 86. Reference to Mrs. Wilder, author of *The Fragrant Path.*

46. Dirr, *Dirr's Hardy Trees and Shrubs,* 224.

47. Invasive Plant Species Assessment Working Group, "Blunt-leaved Privet, *Ligustrum obtusifolium,*" Invasive Plant Species Fact Sheet, Indiana Department of National Resources, accessed July 1, 2016, https://secure.in.gov/dnr/files/Blunt_Leaved_Privet.pdf.

48. Tiffany M. Knight, Kayri Havens, and Pati Vitt, "Will the Use of Less Fecund Cultivars Reduce the Invasiveness of Perennial Plants?" *BioScience* 61, no. 10 (October 2011): 816–22, http://bioscience.oxfordjournals.org/content/61/10/816http://bioscience.oxfordjournals.org/ content/61/10/816.

49. Burrell, *Native Alternatives to Invasive Plants,* 15.

50. Weeks and Weeks, *Shrubs and Woody Vines,* 132, 133.

51. Sternberg and Wilson, *Landscaping with Native Trees,* 89.

52. Herb Wilson, "Birding: Researchers Find That Migrating Birds Prefer Native Plants over Invasives, The Higher Fat Content of Native Plants Is a Crucial Source of Energy," *Portland Press Herald,* September 6, 2015, http://www.pressherald.com/2015/09/06/birding-researchers -find-that-migrating-birds-prefer-native-plants-over-invasives/.

53. Sternberg and Wilson, *Landscaping with Native Trees,* 89.

54. Alice Lounsberry, *Southern Wild Flowers and Trees,* illus. Mrs. Ellis Rowan (New York: Frederick A. Stokes, 1901), 111.

55. Ibid.

56. Ibid.

57. Johnny Caryopsis, "The Biology of Pussy Willows," *Nature North,* Spring, http://www .naturenorth.com/spring/flora/pwillow/Fpwillw1.html.

58. Tallamy, *Bringing Nature Home,* 101, 131.

59. David K. Parshall, Horace B. Davidson, and John T. Watts, *Common Butterflies and Skippers of Ohio* (Columbus: Ohio Department of Natural Resources, Division of Wildlife, 2006), 35; 2009 and 2013 editions have been published.

60. Mark P. Widrlechner, Sharon K. Dragula, and Richard A. Larson, "Exploring the Deciduous Azaleas and Elepidote Rhododendrons of the Midwestern United States," *Journal of the*

American Rhododendron Society 47, no. 3 (1993), http://www.rhododendron.org/v47n3p153 .htm; http://scholar.lib.vt.edu/ejournals/JARS/v47n3/v47n3-widrlechner.htm.

61. Tallamy, *Bringing Nature Home,* 62, 63.

62. Sternberg and Wilson, *Landscaping with Native Trees,* 256.

63. William Bartram, *Travels of William Bartram,* ed. Mark Van Doren (1791; repr., New York: Dover, 1955), 264.

64. Taylor, *Easy Care Native Plants,* 150.

65. Ibid., 157.

66. Weeks and Weeks, *Shrubs and Woody Vines,* 32, 33.

67. John Hilty, "Pasture Rose," in "Prairie Wildflowers of Illinois," Illinois Wildflowers, accessed July 1, 2016, http://www.illinoiswildflowers.info/prairie/plantx/pasture_rosex.htm.

68. Alan Windham and Frank Hale, "Observations on Rose Rosette Disease," http://www .newenglandgrows.org/pdfs/ho_WindhamRoseRosette.pdf.

69. Daniel Wovcha and Robert Dana, "Minnesota Profile: Prairie Wild Rose (*Rosa arkansana*)," *Minnesota Conservation Volunteer,* Minnesota Department of Natural Resources, accessed January 8, 2016, http://files.dnr.state.mn.us/eco/mcbs/publications/mcv_magazine _prairie_wild_rose_rosa_arkansana.pdf.

70. Kindscher, "Rosa arkansana," in *Edible Wild Plants of the Prairie,* 201.

71. Wilson and Bell, *Fragrant Year,* 142.

72. Ibid.

73. O'Sullivan, *Homeowner's Complete Tree and Shrub Handbook,* 190.

74. Sternberg and Wilson, *Landscaping with Native Trees,* 96, 97.

75. "Cotinus coggygria - Scop.," Plants for a Future, accessed July 1, 2016, http://www.pfaf .org/user/Plant.aspx?LatinName=Cotinus+coggygria.

76. Cullina, *Native Trees, Shrubs, and Vines,* 102.

77. Edward F. Gilman and Dennis G. Watson, "Cotinus obovatus: American Smoketree," University of Florida IFAS Extension, Southern Trees Fact Sheets, accessed January 8, 2016, https://edis.ifas.ufl.edu/st208.

78. Sternberg and Wilson, *Landscaping with Native Trees,* 96.

79. Billy Bruce Winkles, "American Smoketree," Tree Trail, http://www.treetrail.net /american_smoketree.html.

80. "American Highbush Cranberry," *Botany Blog, Plants of the Northeastern U.S.,* July 30, 2010, http://botany.thismia.com/2010/.

81. Timothy M. Abbey, ed., *Alternatives for Invasive Ornamental Plant Species,* Connecticut Agricultural Experiment Station for the Connecticut Invasive Plant Working Group, September 2004, http://www.ct.gov/caes/lib/caes/documents/special_features/nativealternatives.pdf.

82. Taylor, *Easy Care Native Plants,* 165.

83. Weeks and Weeks, *Shrubs and Woody Vines,* 78.

84. Ibid., 88.

85. Lounsberry, *Southern Wild Flowers and Trees,* 479.

86. Weeks and Weeks, *Shrubs and Woody Vines,* 88, 89.

87. Taylor, *Easy Care Native Plants,* 165.

88. Weeks and Weeks, *Shrubs and Woody Vines,* 90.

89. Ibid., 80.

90. Ibid., 92.

91. For more plants with high fat content, see "Native Plants for Birds," Fiddlehead Creek Farm and Native Plant Nursery, last updated March 2011, http://fiddleheadcreek.com/wp-content /uploads/2012/01/Fiddlehead-Creek-Bird-NY-Native-Plant-List-March-2011-for-web.pdf.

92. "March's Plant of the Month: Mapleleaf Viburnum," Fiddlehead Creek Native Plant Nursery, March 6, 2011, http://fiddleheadcreek.com/marchs-plant-of-month-mapleleaf/.

93. Cindy Gilberg, "Native Witch Hazel in Winter," *Healthy Planet,* December 29, 2012, http://thehealthyplanet.com/2012/12/native-witch-hazel-in-winter/.

94. Ibid.

95. Dirr, *Dirr's Hardy Trees and Shrubs,* 315.

96. Rebecca Williams, "Why Are Spruce Trees in the Midwest Declining?," News for Michigan, February 23, 2016, http://michiganradio.org/post/why-are-spruce-trees-midwest-declining #stream/0.

97. "'Stop the Spread!' of Invasive Callery Pear Tree Hybrids: Help Columbia Manage the Threat of Invasive Callery Pear Tree Hybrids," Columbia Parks and Recreation, City of Columbia, Missouri, accessed July 1, 2016, http://www.gocolumbiamo.com/ParksandRec/Parks_and _Facilities/stopthespread.php.

98. Durant Ashmore, "The Curse of the Bradford Pear," *GreenvilleOnline,* March 29, 2016, http://www.greenvilleonline.com/story/life/2016/03/21/curse-bradford-pear/82070210/.

99. Lounsberry, *Guide to the Trees,* 269.

100. Cullina, *Native Trees, Shrubs, and Vines,* 45.

101. Janet Allen, "Cultivars and Hybrids of Native Plants," *Stewardship Garden,* accessed July 1, 2016, http://www.ourhabitatgarden.org/plants/cultivars.html.

102. "Plant Finder: Rainbow Pillar Serviceberry," Chalet Landscape, Nursery, Garden Center (Wilmette, IL), accessed July 1, 2016, http://plants.chaletnursery.com/12120004/Plant/3116.

103. Arthur Lee Jacobson, "Serviceberry Trees," accessed July 1, 2016, http://www.arthurleej .com/a-serviceberries.html.

104. Weeks, Weeks, and Parker, *Native Trees of the Midwest,* 170.

105. Sternberg and Wilson, *Landscaping with Native Trees,* 194.

106. Kindscher, "Prunus americana," in *Edible Wild Plants of the Prairie,* 171.

107. Lounsberry, *Guide to the Trees,* 161.

108. Cullina, *Native Trees, Shrubs, and Vines,* 201.

109. Sternberg and Wilson, *Landscaping with Native Trees,* 122.

110. Taylor, *Easy Care Native Plants,* 125.

111. Tallamy, *Bringing Nature Home,* 101.

112. Dirr, *Dirr's Hardy Trees and Shrubs,* 296.

113. "Sakura—What I Missed Most away from Japan," *Hamadayama Life,* accessed July 1, 2016, http://www.ocada.jp/life/sakura2.php.

114. G. D. Palmer, "Life Expectancy of Ornamental Cherry Trees," SFGate, accessed July 1, 2016, http://homeguides.sfgate.com/life-expectancy-ornamental-cherry-trees-59577.html.

115. Weeks, Weeks, and Parker, *Native Trees of the Midwest,* 170.

116. Virginia Barlow, "Chokecherry, Prunus virginiana," *Northern Woodlands,* October 21, 2008, http://northernwoodlands.org/articles/article/chokecherry_prunus_virginiana.

117. Lounsberry, *Southern Wild Flowers and Trees,* 253.

118. Tallamy, *Bringing Nature Home,* 101.

119. John Hilty, "Wild Black Cherry," in "Trees, Shrubs, and Woody Vines of Illinois," Illinois Wildflowers, accessed July 1, 2016, http://www.illinoiswildflowers.info/trees/plants/wb _cherry.htm.

120. Barlow, "Chokecherry, Prunus virginiana."

121. Kindscher, *Edible Wild Plants of the Prairie,* 180.

122. Webster, "Prunus," in *Hardy Ornamental Flowering Trees and Shrubs,* http://www .gutenberg.org/files/10852/10852-h/10852-h.htm.

123. Henry Hoare, *Flowering Trees and Shrubs* (London: Arthur L. Humphreys, 1902), 17–18.

124. Lounsberry, *Guide to the Trees,* 196.

125. Ibid.

126. Sue Sweeney, "The Monday Garden: Catalpa: Great American and Invader?" *Ontario Trees and Shrubs,* no. 162 (May 1, 2005), http://ontariotrees.com/mondaygarden/article.php ?id=162.

127. Laura G. Jull, "Trees to Avoid Planting in the Midwest and Some Excellent Alternatives," Michigan State University Diagnostic Services, accessed July 1, 2016, http://www.pestid .msu.edu/wp-content/uploads/2014/07/Trees-to-avoidf623.pdf.

128. O'Sullivan, *Homeowner's Complete Tree and Shrub Handbook*, 283.

129. Wilson and Bell, *Fragrant Year*, 94.

130. Martha E. Hellander, *The Wild Gardener: The Life and Selected Writings of Eloise Butler* (St. Cloud, MN: North Star Press of St. Cloud, 1992). Quotes appear at pp. 179, xii, 59.

131. Harriet L. Keeler, "Rose Family, Crab Apple," in *Our Native Trees and How to Identify Them*, 2nd ed. (New York: Charles Scribner's Sons, 1900), 133.

132. Lounsberry, *Guide to the Trees*, 159.

133. John Hilty, "Prairie Crab Apple," in "Trees, Shrubs, and Woody Vines of Illinois," Illinois Wildflowers, accessed July 1, 2016, http://www.illinoiswildflowers.info/trees/plants/prairie_crab.html.

134. Lounsberry, *Southern Wild Flowers and Trees*, 246.

135. Lounsberry, *Guide to the Trees*, 113.

136. Sternberg and Wilson, *Landscaping with Native Trees*, 83.

137. Cullina, *Native Trees, Shrubs, and Vines*, 84.

138. Douglas Tallamy, quoted by Soderstram, "Which Trees and Shrubs to Plant?"

139. Douglas Tallamy, quoted by Donna Cottingham, "Creating a Butterfly Garden," Virginia Department of Game and Inland Fisheries, accessed January 8, 2016, http://www.dgif.virginia.gov/habitat/butterfly-garden.asp.

140. Cullina, *Native Trees, Shrubs, and Vines*, 97.

141. Sternberg and Wilson, *Landscaping with Native Trees*, 91.

142. Tallamy, *Bringing Nature Home*, 102.

143. Weeks, Weeks, and Parker, *Native Trees of the Midwest*, 268.

144. Lounsberry, *Guide to the Trees*, 210; Lounsberry, *Southern Wild Flowers and Trees*, 264.

145. Lounsberry, *Guide to the Trees*, 147.

146. Keeler, "Laurel Family, Sassafras," in *Our Native Trees*, 230.

147. Ibid., 263.

148. Burrell, *Native Alternatives to Invasive Plants*, 51.

149. Weeks, Weeks, and Parker, *Native Trees of the Midwest*, 226.

150. Alonso Abugattas, "Top '10' Lists of Wildlife Plants," Prince William Conservation Alliance, accessed July 1, 2016, http://www.pwconserve.org/plants/alonso_top10.pdf.

151. Wilson and Bell, *Fragrant Year*, 96.

152. Sternberg and Wilson, *Landscaping with Native Trees*, 225.

153. J. C. Huntley, "Black Locust," USDA Forest Service Northeastern Area, accessed July 1, 2016, http://na.fs.fed.us/pubs/silvics_manual/volume_2/robinia/pseudoacacia.htm.

154. Wilson and Bell, *Fragrant Year*, 96.

155. Sweeney, "Monday Garden: Catalpa."

156. Lounsberry, *Southern Wild Flowers and Trees*, 117.

157. Weeks and Weeks, *Shrubs and Woody Vines*, 138.

158. Kindscher, "Corylus americana," in *Edible Wild Plants of the Prairie*, 100.

159. Sternberg and Wilson, *Landscaping with Native Trees*, 85.

160. Wilson and Bell, *Fragrant Year*, 98.

161. Jull, "Trees to Avoid."

162. Keeler, "Rose Family, Hawthorn," in *Our Native Trees*, 148, 152.

163. "The Writings of Eloise Butler: Hawthorn of World Fame through Poetry and Prose of England, Virginian Waterleaf, White Lily and Geranium Featured in June," *Minneapolis Sunday Tribune*, June 4, 1911, reprinted in http://www.friendsofeloisebutler.org/pages/history/ebwriting/tribune60411.html.

164. Sternberg and Wilson, *Landscaping with Native Trees*, 99, 100.

165. Keeler, "Rose Family, Hawthorn," 146.

166. Sternberg and Wilson, *Landscaping with Native Trees*, 98, 99.

167. Cullina, *Native Trees, Shrubs, and Vines*, 105.

168. Helen Van Pelt Wilson, *Color for Your Winter Yard and Garden with Flowers, Berries, Birds, and Trees* (New York: Charles Scribner's Sons, 1979), 80, 81, 123.

169. Connie C. Barlow, *The Ghosts of Evolution: Nonsensical Fruit, Missing Partners, and Other Ecological Anachronisms* (New York: Basic Books, 2000), 162–68.

170. Sternberg and Wilson, *Landscaping with Native Trees,* 99.

171. John Hilty, "Waxy-Fruited Hawthorn," in "Trees, Shrubs, and Woody Vines of Illinois," Illinois Wildflowers, accessed July 1, 2016, http://www.illinoiswildflowers.info/trees/plants/wf _hawthorn.htm.

172. Taylor, *Easy Care Native Plants,* 127–28.

173. Ibid.

174. Ibid., 126; quoting Richard Johnson, curator of the Caroline Dorman Nature Preserve when listing easy-care native plants.

175. Keeler, "Magnolia Family," in *Our Native Trees,* 14.

176. Wilson and Bell, *Fragrant Year,* 95.

177. Barlow, *Ghosts of Evolution,* 93.

178. Cullina, *Native Trees, Shrubs, and Vines,* 56.

179. Barlow, *Ghosts of Evolution,* 214, 105.

180. Cullina, *Native Trees, Shrubs, and Vines,* 239–40.

181. Weeks, Weeks, and Parker, *Native Trees of the Midwest,* 310.

182. Ibid.

183. Burrell, *Native Alternatives to Invasive Plants,* 50.

184. Cullina, *Native Trees, Shrubs, and Vines,* 229.

Chapter 2: Summer

1. William McClain, "Mysteries of the Trail-Marker Trees," *Illinois Steward* 15, no. 2 (Summer 2006), http://web.extension.illinois.edu/illinoissteward/openissue.cfm?IssueID=59.

2. "Land, Water, and Forest," Indians of the Midwest, accessed July 10, 2016, http://publications.newberry.org/indiansofthemidwest/the-homeland-its-use/land-water-and -forest/.

3. "Explorers and Missionaries, 1673–1698," in *Prairie State: Impressions of Illinois, 1673– 1967, by Travelers and Other Observers,* comp. and ed. Paul M. Angle (Chicago: University of Chicago Press, 1968), 5.

4. John Bakeless, "The Wild Middle West," referencing journals of Robert Rogers (1883), pp. 190, 199, 201, in *America as Seen by Its First Explorers: The Eyes of Discovery* (New York: Dover, 1989), 300, 301.

5. Jim Robbins, "Future Landscapes, Viewed from the Past," quoting Shari Gardner, Science Times, *New York Times,* January 26, 2016.

6. Douglas W. Tallamy, *Bringing Nature Home: How Native Plants Sustain Wildlife in Our Gardens* (Portland, OR: Timber Press, 2007), 130.

7. William Cullina, *Native Trees, Shrubs, and Vines: A Guide to Using, Growing, and Propagating North American Woody Plants* (Boston: Houghton Mifflin, 2002), 205.

8. Cathy Lockman, "1,000 Tree Project Plants Seeds, Good Deeds," Illinois Farm Bureau Partners, August 13, 2012, http://ilfbpartners.com/tree-project-plants-seeds-good-deeds/, quoting Tom Sisulak, the originator of the 1,000 Tree Planting Project, an all-volunteer effort to plant 1,000 trees on one day every fall in the village of Riverside.

9. C. Colston Burrell, *Native Alternatives to Invasive Plants* (Brooklyn, NY: Brooklyn Botanic Garden, 2006), 37.

10. Connie Barlow, *The Ghosts of Evolution: Nonsensical Fruit, Missing Partners, and Other Ecological Anachronisms* (New York: Basic Books, 2000), 165–67.

11. Patricia A. Taylor, *Easy Care Native Plants: A Guide to Selecting and Using Beautiful American Flowers, Shrubs, and Trees in Gardens and Landscapes* (New York: Henry Holt, 1996), 150.

12. Sally S. Weeks and Harmon P. Weeks Jr., *Shrubs and Woody Vines of Indiana and the Midwest: Identification, Wildlife Values, and Landscaping Use* (West Lafayette, IN: Purdue University Press, 2012), 158.

13. Ibid., 226.

14. Ibid., 224.

15. Penelope O'Sullivan, *The Homeowner's Complete Tree and Shrub Handbook* (North Adams, MA: Storey Publishing, 2007), 183.

16. Tallamy, *Bringing Nature Home,* 95. Buddleia hosts only the buddleia budworm moth, whose worms "crumple all the vegetative tips and stunt plant growth. Not native, probably a native of Mexico," states Jerry Powell as quoted by Bob Patterson, http://bugguide.net/node/view/365382.

17. Leah Zerbe, "Never Plant Butterfly Bush Again: Avoid This Invasive Species," quoting Douglas Tallamy, *Rodale's OrganicLife,* April 1, 2015, http://www.rodalenews.com/butterfly-bush-bad.

18. American Institute of Biological Sciences, "'Non-invasive' Cultivar? Buyer Beware," *ScienceDaily,* October 11, 2011, www.sciencedaily.com/releases/2011/10/111007073214.htm; Tiffany M. Knight, Kayri Havens, and Pati Vitt, "Will the Use of Less Fecund Cultivars Reduce the Invasiveness of Perennial Plants?" *BioScience* 61, no. 10 (October 2011): 816–22, http://bioscience.oxfordjournals.org/content/61/10/816. Also see Mark H. Brand, Jonathan M. Lehrer, and Jessica D. Lubell, "Fecundity of Japanese Barberry (*Berberis thunbergii*) Cultivars and Their Ability to Invade a Deciduous Woodland," *Invasive Plant Science and Management* 5, no. 4 (2012): 464–76, doi: http://dx.doi.org/10.1614/IPSM-D-12-00029.1, http://www.bioone.org/doi/abs/10.1614/IPSM-D-12-00029.1. When plants were allowed to mature for 4 to 5 years beyond the first evaluation time, cultivars exhibited significant increases in fruits per plant. Plants that initially appeared to be fruitless produced fruits also.

19. Cullina, *Native Trees, Shrubs, and Vines,* 39.

20. Catherine Siddall, "*Aesculus parviflora,* Bottlebrush Buckeye," North American Native Plant Society, accessed July 10, 2016, http://www.nanps.org/index.php/gardening/native-plants-to-know/131-aesculus-parviflora-bottlebrush-buckeye.

21. Tallamy, *Bringing Nature Home,* 98.

22. Alonso Abugattas, Oaks, "Top '10' Lists of Wildlife Plants," Conserve Prince William, accessed July 10, 2016, http://www.pwconserve.org/plants/alonso_top10.pdf.

23. Weeks and Weeks, *Shrubs and Woody Vines,* 34, 35.

24. Cullina, *Native Trees, Shrubs, and Vines,* 95.

25. Burrell, *Native Alternatives to Invasive Plants,* 63.

26. John Hilty, "False Indigo," in "Trees, Shrubs, and Woody Vines of Illinois," Illinois Wildflowers, accessed July 10, 2016, http://www.illinoiswildflowers.info/trees/plants/false_indigo.htm.

27. Taylor, *Easy Care Native Plants,* 140.

28. "*Ribes alpinum,*" Missouri Botanical Garden Plant Finder, accessed July 10, 2016, http://www.missouribotanicalgarden.org/PlantFinder/PlantFinderDetails.aspx?kempercode=r740.

29. Weeks and Weeks, *Shrubs and Woody Vines,* 182, 183.

30. Michael Knudson, "American Black Currant," United States Department of Agriculture, Natural Resources Conservation Service Plant Guide, April 2010, http://plants.usda.gov/plantguide/pdf/pg_riam2.pdf.

31. Weeks and Weeks, *Shrubs and Woody Vines,* 188, 189.

32. Mariette Nowak for the Wisconsin Society for Ornithology, "Midsummer Berries," in *Beyond the Birdfeeder: Creating a Bird-Friendly Yard with Native Wisconsin Plants,* 2003, Hoy Audubon Society, http://www.hoyaudubon.org/documents/birdscaping.pdf; "Wild Blackberry," Trees and Plants, The Morton Arboretum, accessed July 15, 2016, http://www.mortonarb.org/trees-plants/tree-plant-descriptions/wild-blackberry.

33. Weeks and Weeks, *Shrubs and Woody Vines,* 380.

34. "Forest Songbirds and Invasive-Plant Management," Forest Preserve District of DuPage County, accessed July 15, 2016, http://www.dupageforest.org/DuPage_Plants_and_Wildlife /Birds/Songbirds/Forest_Songbirds_and_Invasive-Plant_Management.aspx?ekfrm=363.

35. "Common Buckthorn (Not Recommended)," Trees and Plants, The Morton Arboretum, accessed July 15, 2016, http://www.mortonarb.org/trees-plants/tree-plant-descriptions /common-buckthorn-not-recommended.

36. Knight, Havens, and Vitt, "Will the Use of Less Fecund Cultivars Reduce the Invasiveness of Perennial Plants?"

37. Burrell, *Native Alternatives to Invasive Plants*, 107.

38. Guy Sternberg and Jim Wilson, *Landscaping with Native Trees: The Northeast, Midwest, Midsouth and Southeast Edition* (Shelburne, VT: Chapters, 1995), 256.

39. G. Clarke Nuttall, *Beautiful Flowering Shrubs* (London: Cassell, 1905), 230, quoting Mrs. Earl, author of *Potpourri from a Surrey Garden*.

40. Taylor, *Easy Care Native Plants*, 147.

41. Ibid.

42. O'Sullivan, *Homeowner's Complete Tree and Shrub Handbook*, 244.

43. Weeks and Weeks, *Shrubs and Woody Vines*, 62.

44. Cullina, *Native Trees, Shrubs, and Vines*, 136.

45. John Hilty, "Wild Hydrangea, *Hydrangea arborescens*," in "Woodland Wildflowers of Illinois," Illinois Wildflowers, accessed July 10, 2015, http://www.illinoiswildflowers.info /woodland/plants/hydrangea.htm.

46. William Bartram, *Travels of William Bartram*, ed. Mark Van Doren (1791; repr., New York: Dover, 1955), 254, 273, 308. (America was then an unbroken tapestry of native plant species. The plants Bartram identified in the southeast are also native to the Midwest.)

47. O'Sullivan, *Homeowner's Complete Tree and Shrub Handbook*, 241.

48. Weeks and Weeks, *Shrubs and Woody Vines*, 64.

49. Emily DeBolt, "September's Plant of the Month: Crimson-eyed Rose Mallow," Fiddlehead Creek Native Plant Nursery, August 28, 2012, http://fiddleheadcreek.com/septembers -plant-of-the-month/.

50. Taylor, *Easy Care Native Plants*, 124.

51. O'Sullivan, *Homeowner's Complete Tree and Shrub Handbook*, 232.

52. "*Franklinia alatamaha*," NPIN: Native Plant Database, Lady Bird Johnson Wildflower Center, record modified February 1, 2008, http://www.wildflower.org/plants/result.php?id _plant=FRAL.

53. William Wiesenborn, "Tamarisk," in *Invasive Plants: Weeds of the Global Garden*, ed. John M. Randall and Janet Marinelli (Brooklyn, NY: Brooklyn Botanic Garden, 1996), 43.

54. Weeks and Weeks, *Shrubs and Woody Vines*, 384.

55. O'Sullivan, *Homeowner's Complete Tree and Shrub Handbook*, 227.

56. Weeks and Weeks, *Shrubs and Woody Vines*, 384. Cultivar number cites Michael A. Dirr (1998).

57. Knight, Havens, and Vitt, "Will the Use of Less Fecund Cultivars Reduce the Invasiveness of Perennial Plants?"; e-mail from Kayri Havens, November 22, 2013.

58. Tallamy, *Bringing Nature Home*, 102.

59. "Invasive Plants in Pennsylvania—Cork-trees: *Phellodendron japonicum* Maxim., *P. amurense* Rupr. and *P. lavallei* Dode.," Pennsylvania Department of Conservation and Natural Resources, accessed July 15, 2016, http://www.dcnr.state.pa.us/cs/groups/public/documents /document/dcnr_010285.pdf.

60. Michael A. Dirr, *Dirr's Hardy Trees and Shrubs: An Illustrated Encyclopedia* (Portland, OR: Timber Press, 1997), 266.

61. Dani Simons, "Amur Corktree," Plant Conservation Alliance's Alien Plant Working Group: LEAST WANTED, last updated July 7, 2009, http://www.nps.gov/plants/alien/fact /pham1.htm.

62. Bruce Marlin, "Amur Cork Tree—*Phellodendron amurense*," accessed July 15, 2016, http://www.cirrusimage.com/tree_Amur_cork.htm; Holly K. Ober, "The Value of Oaks to Wildlife," University of Florida IFAS Extension Electronic Data Information Source, revised April 2014, http://edis.ifas.ufl.edu/uw292;"Weed of the Week: Amur Corktree," USDA Forest Service, Invasive Plants website, February 19, 2005, http://www.na.fs.fed.us/fhp/invasive_plants /weeds/amur-corktree.pdf.

63. Alice Lounsberry, *Southern Wild Flowers and Trees*, illus. Mrs. Ellis Rowan (New York: Frederick A. Stokes, 1901), 263.

64. Barlow, *Ghosts of Evolution*, 129–33, 214.

65. Tina Casagrand, "Millions of Ash Trees Are Dying, Creating Huge Headaches for Cities," *National Geographic,* December 4, 2014, http://news.nationalgeographic.com/news/2014/12 /141202-emerald-ash-borer-forestry-trees-environment/.

66. Gary W. Watson, ed., *Selecting and Planting Trees,* The Morton Arboretum, 2015, https: //www.mortonarb.org/files/15CTP_Tree%20Selection%20Planting_BRCH_ReaderSpread _0331_sm-1.pdf.

67. Casagrand, "Millions of Ash Trees Are Dying."

68. "Woodpecker Watch," Vermont Invasives, accessed July 15, 2016, http://www.vtinvasives .org/group/woodpecker-watch.

69. Sternberg and Wilson, *Landscaping with Native Trees*, 116–17.

70. Alice Lounsberry, *A Guide to the Trees,* illus. Mrs. Ellis Rowan (New York: Frederick A. Stokes, 1900), 209, 210.

71. Barlow, *Ghosts of Evolution*, 41, 49, 168.

72. Ibid., 41, 49, 168.

73. "Honey-locust," Trees and Plants, The Morton Arboretum, accessed July 15, 2016, http: //www.mortonarb.org/trees-plants/tree-plant-descriptions/honey-locust.

74. Christina D. Wood, "'A Most Dangerous Tree': The Lombardy Poplar in Landscape Gardening," *Arnoldia* 54, no. 1 (Winter 1994): 24–30, http://arnoldia.arboretum.harvard.edu /pdf/articles/904.pdf.

75. Ibid.

76. Burrell, *Native Alternatives to Invasive Plants*, 40.

77. "Quaking Aspen," National Wildlife Federation, accessed July 15, 2016, http://www.nwf .org/Wildlife/Wildlife-Library/Plants/Quaking-Aspen.aspx.

78. Lounsberry, *Southern Wild Flowers and Trees*, 113.

79. Aaron Bergdahl, "Cottonwood Canker Fungi," in *Biennial Forest Health Report, North Dakota 2013–2014,* p. 20, North Dakota Forest Service, January 26, 2015, https://www.ag.ndsu .edu/ndfs/documents/biennial-forest-health-report-nd-2013-14.pdf.

80. David K. Parshall, Horace B. Davidson, and John T. Watts, *Common Butterflies and Skippers of Ohio* (Columbus: Ohio Department of Natural Resources, 2004), 35.

81. E. D. Nauman, "The Nesting Habits of the Baltimore Oriole," *Wilson Bulletin,* December 1930, 295–96, http://www.avibirds.com/pdf/N/Noordelijke%20troepiaal2.pdf.

82. Lounsberry, *Guide to the Trees,* 175.

83. Harriet L. Keeler, "Beech," in *Our Native Trees* (New York: Charles Scribner's Sons, 1900), 382.

84. Helen Van Pelt Wilson, *Color for Your Winter Yard and Garden with Flowers, Berries, Birds, and Trees* (New York: Charles Scribner's Sons, 1979), 106–7.

85. "Chinese Chestnut *Castanea mollissima*," Ohio Department of Natural Resources Division of Forestry, Common Ohio Trees, http://forestry.ohiodnr.gov/chinesechestnut.

86. Ibid.

87. Lounsberry, *Southern Wild Flowers and Trees*, 131.

88. Tallamy, *Bringing Nature Home*, 66.

89. Bernd Heinrich, "Revitalizing Our Forests," *New York Times,* December 20, 2013, http: //www.nytimes.com/2013/12/21/opinion/revitalizing-our-forests.html?_r=0.

90. "*Castanea pumila,*" NPIN: Native Plant Database, Lady Bird Johnson Wildflower Center, record modified November 12, 2015, http://www.wildflower.org/plants/result.php?id_plant =CAPU9.

91. Lounsberry, *Southern Wild Flowers and Trees,* 121.

92. Seth Harper, "Horticultural Bottom Ten—Chicago Edition," *The Museum* (blog), last updated September 2, 2015, http://www.naturemuseum.org/the-museum/blog.

93. David W. French, Mark E. Ascerno, and Ward C. Stienstra, "The Dutch Elm Disease," Minnesota Extension Service, accessed January 11, 2016, https://www.mda.state.mn.us/news /publications/pestsplants/plantdiseases/theded.pdf.

94. Dirr, *Dirr's Hardy Trees and Shrubs,* 85.

95. Cullina, *Native Trees, Shrubs, and Vines,* 248.

96. slimwhitman, "Anyone had a 'certified male' Ginkgo produce fruit?" GardenWeb, October 12, 2009, http://forums2.gardenweb.com/discussions/1726485/anyone-had-a-certified -male-ginkgo-produce-fruit.

97. Frank S. Santamour et al., "Checklist of Cultivated Ginkgo," *Journal of Arbori- culture* 9, no. 3 (March 1983): 88, joa.isa-arbor.com/request.asp?JournalID=1&ArticleID =1872&.

98. Tom Kimmerer, "Ginkgo Trees Are Lovely—Let's Stop Planting Them," Planet Experts, October 20, 2014, http://www.planetexperts.com/ginkgo-trees-urban-biodiversity/.

99. Rick Darke and Douglas Tallamy, *The Living Landscape: Designing for Beauty and Bio- diversity in the Home Garden* (Portland, OR: Timber Press, 2014), 106.

100. Lounsberry, *Guide to the Trees,* 187.

101. Tallamy, *Bringing Nature Home,* 101.

102. Donna Cottingham, "Creating a Butterfly Garden," Virginia Department of Game and Inland Fisheries, quoting Douglas Tallamy, http://www.dgif.virginia.gov/habitat/butterfly -garden.asp.

103. Dirr, *Dirr's Hardy Trees and Shrubs,* 74.

104. Lounsberry, *Southern Wild Flowers and Trees,* 116.

105. Lounsberry, *Guide to the Trees,* 171.

106. Laura G. Jull, "Trees to Avoid Planting in the Midwest and Some Excellent Alterna- tives," Michigan State University Diagnostic Services, accessed July 1, 2016, http://www.pestid .msu.edu/wp-content/uploads/2014/07/Trees-to-avoidf623.pdf.

107. Lounsberry, *Southern Wild Flowers and Trees,* 133.

108. Steve D. Wratten et al., "Recent Advances in Conservation Biological Control of Arthro- pods by Arthropods," *Biological Control,* special issue (May 2008), http://www.landislab.ent .msu.edu/pdf/Landis%20PDF%20Collection/8.Jonsson.Wratten.Landis.Gurr.2008.Recent %20advances%20in%20conservation.pdf. Conservation biological control (CBC) aims at im- proving the efficacy of natural enemies and can contribute to safer and more effective biological control practices.

109. "Japanese Beetle," Pest Products, accessed July 15, 2016, http://www.pestproducts.com /japanesebeetle.htm.

110. Caitlin Reinartz, "Native Tree Spotlight: In Defense of Box Elder," Urban Ecology Center, March 2013, http://urbanecologycenter.org/blog/native-tree-spotlight-in-defense-of -box-elder.html.

111. Nowak, *Beyond the Birdfeeder.*

112. Harper, "Horticultural Bottom Ten—Chicago Edition."

113. "Norway Maple (*Acer platanoides*)," Introduced Species Summary Project, last ed- ited February 17, 2003, http://www.columbia.edu/itc/cerc/danoff-burg/invasion_bio/inv_spp _summ/Acer_platanoides.html.

114. "Norway Maple, *Acer platanoides* L.," The Pennsylvania Flora Project of Morris Arbo- retum, updated November 2011, http://paflora.org/original/pdf/INV-Fact%20Sheets/Acer %20platanoides.pdf 2 of 3.

115. Knight, Havens, and Vitt, "Will the Use of Less Fecund Cultivars Reduce the Invasiveness of Perennial Plants?"

116. "Invasive Trees and Plants," The Morton Arboretum, accessed July 10, 2016, http://www.mortonarb.org/trees-plants/tree-and-plant-advice/horticulture-care/invasive-trees-and-plants.

117. Sternberg and Wilson, *Landscaping with Native Trees*, 38, 39.

118. David Beaulieu, "Best Maple Trees for Fall Color," *About Home*, updated April 7, 2016, http://landscaping.about.com/cs/fallfoliagetrees/a/fall_foliage7.htm.

119. "Seedless Maples," Midwest Gardening, accessed July 15, 2016, http://midwestgardentips.com/seedless_maples.html.

120. Tom Ogren, "How Female Trees & Shrubs in Modern Landscape Are Affecting Our Air Quality," *Awareness Magazine*, March/April 2000, http://www.awarenessmag.com/marapro/mao_how_female_trees.html; Thomas Leo Ogren, "Proximity Allergy, Hay Fever and Asthma Caused by Landscape Trees and Shrubs," Allergy-Free Gardening, 2016, http://www.allergyfree-gardening.com/articles/57-proximity-allergy-hay-fever-and-asthma-caused-by-landscape-trees-and-shrubs.html.

121. Jeff Behar, "Allergic Rhinitis (Hay Fever): Causes, Treatments and More!" Muscle Mag Fitness, 2016, http://www.musclemagfitness.com/disease-and-conditions/allergies/allergic-rhinitis-hay-fever-causes-treatments-and-more.html.

122. Doreen Cubie, "Choosing a Tree for Your Yard? Go Native: Natives Support Local Wildlife and Tend to Be Better Behaved Than Exotics," quoting Mary Pat Rowan and Kurt Reinhart, National Wildlife Federation, October 1, 2003, https://www.nwf.org/News-and-Magazines/National-Wildlife/Gardening/Archives/2003/Choosing-a-Native-Tree-for-Your-Yard.aspx.

123. Gus Raeker and Mike Stambaugh, "Too Much Sugar!" *Missouri Conservationist Magazine*, June 2004, Missouri Department of Conservation, last revised November 16, 2010, http://mdc.mo.gov/conmag/2004/03/too-much-sugar?page=0,0.

124. John E. Lloyd and Jeffrey Hahn, "Bronze Birch Borer and Twolined Chestnut Borer in Minnesota," University of Minnesota Extension, 2016, http://www.extension.umn.edu/garden/insects/find/bronze-birch-borer/.

125. Tallamy, *Bringing Nature Home*, 126.

126. Billy Bruce Winkles, "Dwarf Chestnut Oak (*Quercus prinoides*)," Tree Trail, accessed July 15, 2016, http://www.treetrail.net/quercus_prinoides.html.

127. Alonso Abugattas, Oaks, "Top '10' Lists of Wildlife Plants," Conserve Prince William, accessed July 15, 2016, http://www.pwconserve.org/plants/alonso_top10.pdf.

128. Ober, "Value of Oaks to Wildlife."

129. Sternberg and Wilson, *Landscaping with Native Trees*, 203.

130. Lounsberry, *Guide to the Trees*, 133.

131. John Madson, *Tallgrass Prairie* (Nashville, TN: Falcon Press, 1993), 17.

132. Sally S. Weeks, Harmon P. Weeks Jr., and George R. Parker, *Native Trees of the Midwest: Identification, Wildlife Value, and Landscaping Use* (West Lafayette, IN: Purdue University Press, 2010), 196.

133. Ibid., 202.

134. Beaulieu, "Best Maple Trees for Fall Color."

135. "Fall Color Guide," Forest Resources AgResearch and Education Center, University of Tennessee Institute for Agriculture, accessed July 15, 2016, http://forestry.tennessee.edu/leafid.htm.

136. Lounsberry, *Guide to the Trees*, 243.

137. Harriet L. Keeler, "White Oak," in *Our Native Trees*, 330.

138. Wilson, *Color for Your Winter Yard and Garden*, 109.

139. "*Quercus lyrata*," NPIN: Native Plant Database, Lady Bird Johnson Wildflower Center, record modified November 6, 2015, http://www.wildflower.org/plants/result.php?id_plant=QULY.

140. Weeks, Weeks, and Parker, *Native Trees of the Midwest,* 208.

141. Tricia Drevets, "How To Cook, Eat And Even Make Coffee With Acorns," Off The Grid News, accessed July 15, 2016, http://www.offthegridnews.com/off-grid-foods/how-to-cook-eat-and-even-make-coffee-with-acorns/.

142. Pete Wilton, "Birds Time Breeding to Hit 'Peak Caterpillar,'" *Oxford Science Blog,* May 25, 2015, http://phys.org/news/2015-05-birds-peak-caterpillar.html.

143. Tallamy, *Bringing Nature Home,* 127–30.

144. Ibid.

145. Debra Breton, "Caterpillar: It's What's for Dinner," quoting Douglas Tallamy, Cornell Lab of Ornithology, Nest Watch, August 2013, http://nestwatch.org/connect/news/caterpillar-its-whats-for-dinner/.

146. Parshall, Davidson, and Watts, *Common Butterflies and Skippers of Ohio,* 17.

147. Tallamy, *Bringing Nature Home,* 101, 102.

148. John Hilty, "Moth Caterpillars Feeding on Oaks (Quercus spp.)," Illinois Wildflowers, accessed July 15, 2016, http://www.illinoiswildflowers.info/trees/tables/table98.htm.

149. Monika Maeckle, "Here They Come! Monarch and Other Butterflies Passing Through, Laying Eggs and Sipping Nectar," *Rivard Report,* posted on March 17, 2012, http://therivardreport.com/here-they-come-monarch-and-other-butterflies-passing-through-laying-eggs-and-sipping-nectar/.

150. Ober, "Value of Oaks to Wildlife."

151. Bob Thomas, "Blue Jay: Acorn Planters," Loyola University Center for Environmental Communication, January 12, 2010, http://loyno.edu/lucec/natural-history-writings/blue-jay-acorn-planters; *John M. Harper, Richard B. Standiford, and John W. LeBlanc, "Jays Plant Acorns,"* University of California Oak Woodland Management, 2016, *http://ucanr.edu/sites/oak_range/Oak_Articles_On_Line/Oak_Woodland_Wildlife/Jays_Plant_Acorns/;* Cornell Lab of Ornithology, "Blue Jay," All about Birds, 2015, http://www.allaboutbirds.org/guide/blue_jay/lifehistory.

152. Sternberg and Wilson, *Landscaping with Native Trees,* 185.

153. Lounsberry, *Southern Wild Flowers and Trees,* 337–38.

154. "*Stewartia ovata,*" Missouri Botanical Garden Plant Finder, accessed July 15, 2016, http://www.missouribotanicalgarden.org/PlantFinder/PlantFinderDetails.aspx?kempercode=a911.

155. Tallamy, *Bringing Nature Home,* 102.

156. "Tupelo," Trees and Plants, The Morton Arboretum, accessed July 15, 2016, http://www.mortonarb.org/trees-plants/tree-plant-descriptions/tupelo.

157. Lounsberry, *Southern Wild Flowers and Trees,* 99, 100.

158. Steiner, *Landscaping with Native Plants of Wisconsin,* 176.

159. Tallamy, *Bringing Nature Home,* 160.

160. Ibid.

161. Sternberg and Wilson, *Landscaping with Native Trees,* 132.

162. Ibid.

163. "Royal Walnut Moth," Butterflies and Moths of North America, accessed July 15, 2016, http://www.butterfliesandmoths.org/species/Citheronia-regalis.

164. Tallamy, *Bringing Nature Home,* 147.

165. "About Light Pollution," Firefly, accessed July 15, 2016, http://www.firefly.org/light-pollution.html. Fireflies typically won't make an appearance where there are bright ambient lights, such as full moon evenings.

166. Tallamy, *Bringing Nature Home,* 147.

167. Harriet L. Keeler, "Shellbark Hickory," in *Our Native Trees,* 284.

168. Harriet L. Keeler, "Pignut," in *Our Native Trees,* 292.

169. Alvar Núñez Cabeza de Vaca, *Adventures in the Unknown Interior of America,* trans. and ed. Cyclone Covey (Albuquerque: University of New Mexico Press, 1983), 69.

170. Sue Pike, "Shagbark Hickory Are Easy to Identify in the Spring," *SeacoastOnline,* May 6, 2010, http://www.seacoastonline.com/articles/20100506-LIFE-5060347.

Chapter 3: Fall

1. Patricia K. Ourada, "The Menominee Indians: A History" (PhD diss., University of Oklahoma, 1973), 12.

2. William E. McClain, "Prairie Establishment and Landscaping," Illinois Department of Natural Resources, Natural Heritage Technical Publication #2, 1997, 4, quoting Father Antoine Hennepin's description of a bison hunt in 1679, from John Gilmary Shea's 1880 translation.

3. Eliza W. Farnham, *Life in Prairie Land* (1846; repr., Champaign: University of Illinois Press, 1988), 108–9.

4. Sara Stein, *Noah's Garden: Restoring the Ecology of Our Own Back Yards* (Boston: Houghton Mifflin, 1993), 57.

5. "Weed of the Week: Callery Pear / Bradford Pear," USDA Forest Service, Forest Health Staff, Invasive Plants, September 26, 2005, http://www.na.fs.fed.us/fhp/invasive_plants/weeds /callery_pear.pdf.

6. Matt Estep, "Why Is Red Fall Color Nearly Absent in Northern Europe but Prevalent in North America?," Appalachian State University Department of Biology, Fall 2015, http://biology .appstate.edu/fall-colors/why-red-fall-color-nearly-absent-northern-europe-prevalent-north -america. Reasons include east-west running mountains (the Alps) that prevent the southerly migration of species during the glaciers that intermittently covered the northern temperate zone, the elimination of insect pests, and the elimination of evolutionary selective pressures to produce red leaves.

7. Stephanie Reitz, "Taming the Rampant Burning Bush—UConn Shrub Has Color but No Seeds," *Boston Globe*, August 22, 2011, http://article.wn.com/view/2011/08/22/Taming_the _rampant_burning_bush/#/related_news.

8. Colin Poitras, "UConn Scientist Develops Sterile Variety of Invasive Plant," *UConn Today*, August 19, 2011, http://today.uconn.edu/blog/2011/08/uconn-scientist-develops-sterile-variety -of-invasive-plant-2/.

9. Ibid.

10. Ellen Sousa, "Developing Sterile Invasives . . . Why Bother?" Native Plants and Wildlife Gardens, http://nativeplantwildlifegarden.com/developing-sterile-invasives-why-bother/ (site discontinued).

11. Tiffany M. Knight, Kayri Havens, and Pati Vitt, "Will the Use of Less Fecund Cultivars Reduce the Invasiveness of Perennial Plants?" *BioScience* 61, no. 10 (October 2011): http: //bioscience.oxfordjournals.org/content/61/10/816.abstract.

12. Douglas W. Tallamy, *Bringing Nature Home: How Native Plants Sustain Wildlife in Our Gardens* (Portland, OR: Timber Press, 2007), 53, 54.

13. Laura Tangley, "Why Birds Need Native Trees," National Wildlife Federation, January 15, 2015, https://www.nwf.org/News-and-Magazines/National-Wildlife/Birds/Archives/2015 /Chickadees-And-Native-Trees.aspx.

14. Ibid.

15. Terry W. Johnson, "Out My Backdoor: Make Your Yard a Pit Stop for Southbound Migrants," Georgia Wild, September 6, 2013, http://www.georgiawildlife.com/node/3425.

16. M. E. Hutchins, "Attracting Wildlife to Your Backyard," Alabama Cooperative Extension System, November 1996, http://www.aces.edu/pubs/docs/A/ANR-0778/.

17. "Snags for Wildlife," Connecticut Department of Energy and Environmental Protection, revised December 1999, http://www.ct.gov/deep/cwp/view.asp?A=2723&Q=326090.

18. M. S. Sargent and K. S. Carter, "Homes for Wildlife," in *Managing Michigan's Wildlife: A Landowner's Guide*, ed. Sargent and Carter (East Lansing: Michigan United Conservation Clubs, 1999), http://www.michigandnr.com/publications/pdfs/huntingwildlifehabitat/landowners _guide/habitat_mgmt/backyard/Homes_for_Wildlife.htm.

19. "Snags—The Wildlife Tree," *Living with Wildlife*, Washington Department of Fish and Wildlife, 2011, http://wdfw.wa.gov/living/snags/; Richard and Diane Van Vleck, "Snags in the

Home Habitat," Personal Pages, *The Home Habitat,* accessed January 8, 2016, http://www
.americanartifacts.com/smma/per/snag.htm.

20. James Gagliardi, "A Second Life for a Tree," *Smithsonian Gardens,* February 17, 2014,
https://smithsoniangardens.wordpress.com/2014/02/17/a-second-life-for-a-dead-tree/.

21. Aluminum signs identifying a snag as a wildlife tree are available for sale by the Nature
Store of the Cavity Conservation Initiative, whose mission is to encourage the retention of
dead and dying trees for their ecological value to habitats, especially for birds that nest in tree
cavities as well as all wildlife species that rely on such trees: http://cavityconservation.com
/nature-store-2.

22. "Snags—The Wildlife Tree."

23. Helen Van Pelt Wilson and Léonie Bell, *The Fragrant Year: Scented Plants for Your Garden and Your House* (New York: William Morrow, 1967), 98.

24. C. Colston Burrell, *Native Alternatives to Invasive Plants* (Brooklyn, NY: Brooklyn Botanic Garden, 2006), 79.

25. Kelly Kindscher, *Edible Wild Plants of the Prairie: An Ethnobotanical Guide* (Lawrence:
University Press of Kansas, 1987), 211.

26. James Kohut, "Never Hug A Barberry: Exposing the Thorny, Spiny Truth," Northscaping.
com, accessed January 8, 2016, http://www.northscaping.com/IZArticles/IS-0118.

27. Japanese barberry Fact Sheet, NH Department of Agriculture, Markets, and Food,
accessed July 15, 2016, http://agriculture.nh.gov/publications-forms/documents/japanese
-barberry.pdf.

28. Sally S. Weeks and Harmon P. Weeks Jr., *Shrubs and Woody Vines of Indiana and the
Midwest: Identification, Wildlife Values, and Landscaping Use* (West Lafayette, IN: Purdue Uni-
versity Press, 2012), 376, quoting Michael A. Dirr and Charles W. Heuser Jr. in *The Reference
Manual of Woody Plant Propagation* (2006).

29. "Japanese Barberry," Ontario's Invading Species Awareness Program, accessed July 16,
2016, http://www.invadingspecies.com/invaders/plants-terrestrial/japanese-barberry/.

30. Timothy M. Abbey, ed., *Alternatives for Invasive Ornamental Plant Species,* Connecticut
Agricultural Experiment Station for the Connecticut Invasive Plant Working Group, September 2004, 1: "At this time, all the cultivars for a given invasive species are considered invasive";
http://www.ct.gov/caes/lib/caes/documents/special_features/nativealternatives.pdf.

31. Knight, Havens, and Vitt, "Will the Use of Less Fecund Cultivars Reduce the Invasiveness of Perennial Plants?"

32. Penelope O'Sullivan, *The Homeowner's Complete Tree and Shrub Handbook* (North
Adams, MA: Storey Publishing, 2007), 178.

33. " Japanese barberry," Trees and Plants, The Morton Arboretum, accessed July 16, 2016,
http://www.mortonarb.org/trees-plants/tree-plant-descriptions/japanese-barberry.

34. Hilary Smith, "Japanese Barberry: A Ticking Time Bomb," *Adirondack Daily Enterprise,*
September 18, 2012, http://www.adirondackdailyenterprise.com/page/content.detail/id/532935
/Japanese-barberry—a-ticking-time-bomb.html?nav=5144.

35. Sylvan Ramsey Kaufman and Wallace Kaufman, *Invasive Plants,* 2nd ed. (Mechanics-
burg, PA: Stackpole Books, 2012), 17.

36. "*Mahonia aquifolium,*" NPIN: Native Plant Database, Lady Bird Johnson Wildflower
Center, record modified March 2, 2016, http://www.wildflower.org/plants/result.php?id_plant
=maaq2.

37. Susan Tweit, "Turn Your Yard into a Winter Refueling Spot for Birds," *Audubon Magazine,* January–February 2013, http://www.audubon.org/magazine/january-february-2013/turn
-your-yard-winter-refueling-spot.

38. "Wax Myrtle (Morella cerifera)," *Bolivar Naturally,* 2016, http://www.houstonaudubon
.org/default.aspx?act=newsletter.aspx&newsletterid=1701&category=Natives&MenuGroup
=NB&&AspxAutoDetectCookieSupport=1.

39. Guy Sternberg and Jim Wilson, *Landscaping with Native Trees: The Northeast, Midwest,
Midsouth and Southeast Edition* (Shelburne, VT: Chapters, 1995), 255.

40. Weeks and Weeks, *Shrubs and Woody Vines*, 142.

41. Steven R. Hill, "Conservation Assessment for American Barberry (*Berberis canadensis*) Mill.," USDA Forest Service, Eastern Region, March 7, 2003, http://www.fs.usda.gov/Internet /FSE_DOCUMENTS/fsm91_054157.pdf.

42. Weeks and Weeks, *Shrubs and Woody Vines*, 76.

43. Helen Van Pelt Wilson, *Color for Your Winter Yard and Garden with Flowers, Berries, Birds, and Trees* (New York: Charles Scribner's Sons, 1978), 88–89.

44. Joseph Mussulman, quoting Lewis and Jefferson, "Snowberry, Symphoricarpos albus," Discovering Lewis and Clark, June 2004, http://www.lewis-clark.org/article/1926?ArticleID =1926.

45. Patricia A. Taylor, *Easy Care Native Plants* (New York: Henry Holt, 1996), 148.

46. William Cullina, *Native Trees, Shrubs, and Vines: A Guide to Using, Growing, and Propagating North American Woody Plants* (Boston: Houghton Mifflin, 2002), 140.

47. Ibid., 142.

48. Weeks and Weeks, *Shrubs and Woody Vines*, 362.

49. Jeff Burbrink, "Invasive Plants Are Taking Over the Woodlands," *Goshen News*, October 13, 2015, http://www.goshennews.com/news/lifestyles/invasive-plants-are-taking-over-the -woodlands/article_afe0bc4b-012f-5678-b9f1-0847584b56ea.html.

50. O'Sullivan, *Homeowner's Complete Tree and Shrub Handbook*, 227.

51. Jane Kirchner, "Native Shrubs for Fall Color and Wildlife Benefit," *National Wildlife Federation's Blog*, October 15, 2013, http://blog.nwf.org/2013/10/native-shrubs-for-fall-color -and-wildlife-benefits/.

52. "Invasive Trees and Plants," The Morton Arboretum, 2016, http://www.mortonarb.org /trees-plants/tree-and-plant-advice/horticulture-care/invasive-trees-and-plants.

53. Knight, Havens, and Vitt, "Will the Use of Less Fecund Cultivars Reduce the Invasiveness of Perennial Plants?"

54. Sternberg and Wilson, *Landscaping with Native Trees*, 104, 105.

55. Taylor, *Easy Care Native Plants*, 123.

56. Alonso Abugattas, Oaks, "Top '10' Lists of Wildlife Plants," Conserve Prince William, accessed July 15, 2016, http://www.pwconserve.org/plants/alonso_top10.pdf.

57. Sternberg and Wilson, *Landscaping with Native Trees*, 222, 223.

58. Ibid., 222, 223.

59. Taylor, *Easy Care Native Plants*, 160, quoting Chris Graham of Ontario's Royal Botanical Garden.

60. Mariette Nowak, "Nativars: What's the Problem?" *Wild Ones Journal*, January/February 2014, 12, http://www.wildones.org/download/Journold/2014Vol27No1%20Journal.pdf.

61. Terry L. Ettinger, "Recommended Shrubs—'Gro-low' Fragrant Sumac," Terry L. Ettinger Horticulture Consulting Services, accessed July 16, 2016, http://www.tlehcs.com/Recommended %20Plants/Shrubs/grolow.htm.

62. "*Rhus glabra*," NPIN: Native Plant Database, Lady Bird Johnson Wildflower Center, accessed July 25, 2016, http://www.wildflower.org/plants/result.php?id_plant=RHGL.

63. "Monarch Memories Last a Lifetime," WildOnes, accessed July 16, 2016, http://www .wildones.org/wp-content/uploads/2012/12/WFM-Gardening-Press-Release-Part-1.pdf.

64. John Hilty, "Winged Sumac," in "Trees, Shrubs, and Woody Vines of Illinois," Illinois Wildflowers, accessed July 16, 2016, http://www.illinoiswildflowers.info/trees/plants/winged _sumac.htm.

65. Harriet L. Keeler, "Witch Hazel," in *Our Native Trees and How to Identify Them*, 2nd ed. (New York: Charles Scribner's Sons, 1900), 158.

66. Karen Schik, "Which Hazel Is It?" Friends of the Mississippi River, 2016, http://www .fmr.org/mississippi/phenology/witch_hazel-2010-10.

67. Ibid.

68. John E. Ebinger, "Amur Maple," in *Invasive Plants: Weeds of the Global Garden*, ed. John M. Randall and Janet Marinelli (Brooklyn, NY: Brooklyn Botanic Garden, 1996), 25.

69. "Amur maple (Not recommended)," Trees and Plants, The Morton Arboretum, accessed July 16, 2016, http://www.mortonarb.org/trees-plants/tree-plant-descriptions/amur-maple-not-recommended.

70. Wilson, *Color for Your Winter Yard and Garden*, 121.

71. Alice Lounsberry, *A Guide to the Trees*, illus. Mrs. Ellis Rowan (New York: Frederick A. Stokes, 1900), 202, 203, 204.

72. Ibid., 201.

73. Ibid., 202.

74. Todd Boland, "Mountain-ash—A Multifaceted Tree," September 24, 2011, Dave's Garden, http://davesgarden.com/guides/articles/view/2114/.

75. Alice Lounsberry, *Southern Wild Flowers and Trees*, illus. Mrs. Ellis Rowan (New York: Frederick A. Stokes, 1901), 414.

76. Ibid., 100–101.

77. Edward F. Gilman and Dennis G. Watson, "*Ailanthus altissima*, Tree-of-Heaven," US Forest Service Fact Sheet ST-67, November 1993, http://hort.ufl.edu/database/documents/pdf/tree_fact_sheets/ailalta.pdf.

78. Lounsberry, *Southern Wild Flowers and Trees*, 144.

79. "*Maclura pomifera*," Missouri Botanical Garden Plant Finder, http://www.missouribotanicalgarden.org/PlantFinder/PlantFinderDetails.aspx?kempercode=a879.

80. Connie Barlow, *The Ghosts of Evolution: Nonsensical Fruit, Missing Partners, and Other Ecological Anachronisms* (New York: Basic Books, 2000), 181–83.

Chapter 4: Winter

1. Robert Downes, "The Indians in Winter," Northern Express, March 14, 2011, referencing *The Huron: Farmers of the North*, by Bruce Tribber and the Ojibwa captive John Tanner, http://www.northernexpress.com/michigan/article-5543-the-indians-in-winter.html.

2. Robert E. Bieder, *Native American Communities in Wisconsin, 1600–1960: A Study of Tradition and Change* (Madison: University of Wisconsin Press, 1995), 62.

3. William Oliver, *Eight Months in Illinois–With Information to Immigrants* (1843; repr., Carbondale: Southern Illinois University Press, 2002), 81.

4. Martha E. Hellander, *Wild Gardener: The Life and Selected Writings of Eloise Butler* (St. Cloud, MN: North Star Press of St. Cloud, 1992), 160, 161, quoting from *Annals of a Wild Garden*, c. 1914.

5. Helen Van Pelt Wilson, *Color for Your Winter Yard and Garden with Flowers, Berries, Birds, and Trees* (New York: Charles Scribner's Sons, 1978), xi, xii, xiii, 109, 19.

6. Douglas W. Tallamy, *Bringing Nature Home: How Native Plants Sustain Wildlife in Our Gardens* (Portland, OR: Timber Press, 2007), 143, 138.

7. Tallamy, *Bringing Nature Home*, 126, 128. In 2007, 517 Lepidoptera species that oaks support had been identified. As additional species were identified, the number grew to 534. See Selected Bibliography and Resources, p. 000. "Best Bets: What to Plant," Bringing Nature Home, http://www.bringingnaturehome.net/what-to-plant.html; "Lepidopteran Use of Native & Alien Ornamental Plants," http://udel.edu/~dtallamy/host/.

8. Aaron M. Ellison, "Ants and Trees: A Lifelong Relationship," *American Forests*, Winter 2014, http://www.americanforests.org/magazine/article/ants-and-trees-a-lifelong-relationship/.

9. Wilson, *Color for Your Winter Yard and Garden*, 79, 80, 109.

10. Mariette Nowak for the Wisconsin Society for Ornithology, *Beyond the Birdfeeder: Creating a Bird-Friendly Yard with Native Wisconsin Plants*, 2003, Hoy Audobon Society, http://www.hoyaudubon.org/documents/birdscaping.pdf.

11. Bert Cregg and Jan Byrne, "Winter Injury or Boxwood Blight?" Michigan State University Extension, May 1, 2015, http://msue.anr.msu.edu/news/winter_injury_or_boxwood_blight.

12. Vincent Vizachero, "Native Cultivars—Good, Bad, and Ugly," 2011–14, http://nativeplantwildlifegarden.com/native-cultivars-good-bad-and-ugly/ (site discontinued).

13. Patricia A. Taylor, *Easy Care Native Plants* (New York: Henry Holt, 1996), 145.

14. Penelope O'Sullivan, *The Homeowner's Complete Tree and Shrub Handbook* (North Adams, MA: Storey Publishing, 2007), 67.

15. Billy Bruce Winkles, "Dwarf Chestnut Oak," Tree Trail, accessed July 17, 2016, http://www.treetrail.net/quercus_prinoides.html.

16. John Hilty, "Jack Pine," in "Trees, Shrubs, and Woody Vines of Illinois," Illinois Wildflowers, accessed July 17, 2016, http://www.illinoiswildflowers.info/trees/plants/jack_pine.htm.

17. "Kirtland's Warbler, Working Together to Save a Special Bird, Managing the Forest for the Kirtland's Warbler," U.S. Fish and Wildlife Service Endangered Species, accessed January 13, 2016, http://www.fws.gov/midwest/endangered/birds/Kirtland/kiwamgmt.html.

18. Wilson, *Color for Your Winter Yard and Garden,* 83.

19. Connie Barlow, *The Ghosts of Evolution: Nonsensical Fruit, Missing Partners, and Other Ecological Anachronisms* (New York: Basic Books, 2000), 162–68.

20. Sally S. Weeks, Harmon P. Weeks Jr., and George R. Parker, *Native Trees of the Midwest: Identification, Wildlife Values, and Landscaping Use* (West Lafayette, IN: Purdue University Press, 2010), 286.

21. Wilson, *Color for Your Winter Yard and Garden,* 97.

22. C. Colston Burrell, "American Yew," How Stuff Works, April 23, 2007, http://home.howstuffworks.com/american-yew.htm; and C. Colston Burrell, Native Alternatives to Invasive Plants (Brooklyn, NY: Brooklyn Botanic Garden, 2006), 121.

23. "*Alnus viridis,*" NPIN: Native Plant Database, Lady Bird Johnson Wildflower Center, record modified September 30, 2015, http://www.wildflower.org/plants/result.php?id_plant=ALVI5.

24. "BWSR Featured Plant: Northern White Cedar," Minnesota Board of Water and Soil Resources, April 26, 2012, http://www.bwsr.state.mn.us/news/webnews/april2012/plant.pdf.

25. John E. Lloyd and Jeffrey Hahn, "Bronze Birch Borer and Twolined Chestnut Borer in Minnesota," University of Minnesota Extension, 2016, http://www.extension.umn.edu/garden/insects/find/bronze-birch-borer/.

26. Wilson, *Color for Your Winter Yard and Garden,* 106.

27. Donald W. Hall, "Featured Creatures: Luna Moth," University of Florida Entomology and Nematology, last revised May 2012, http://entnemdept.ufl.edu/creatures/misc/moths/luna_moth.htm.

28. Alice Lounsberry, *A Guide to the Trees,* illus. Mrs. Ellis Rowan (New York: Frederick A. Stokes, 1900), 276.

29. Alice Lounsberry, *Southern Wild Flowers and Trees,* illus. Mrs. Ellis Rowan (New York: Frederick A. Stokes, 1901), 118.

30. Burrell, *Native Alternatives to Invasive Plants,* 41.

31. Lounsberry, *Southern Wild Flowers and Trees,* 119.

32. Lounsberry, *Guide to the Trees,* 179.

33. Lloyd and Hahn, "Bronze Birch Borer."

34. Tallamy, *Bringing Nature Home,* 101.

35. Ibid., 138.

36. The Morton Arboretum, *Trees and Shrubs That Attract Birds* (2002), pamphlet available on request.

37. Burrell, *Native Alternatives to Invasive Plants,* 28.

38. O'Sullivan, *Homeowner's Complete Tree and Shrub Handbook,* 260.

39. Guy Sternberg and Jim Wilson, *Landscaping with Native Trees: The Northeast, Midwest, Midsouth and Southeast Edition* (Shelburne, VT: Chapters, 1995), 134.

40. Lounsberry, *Guide to the Trees,* 227.

41. John Hilty, "Eastern Hemlock," http://www.illinoiswildflowers.info/trees/plants/east _hemlock.htm.

42. Bert Cregg, quoting Justin "Chub" Harper, "Conifer Corner," *The Michigan Landscape*, September/October 2004, 34, http://www.hrt.msu.edu/uploads/535/78626/cedars.pdf.

43. "Austrian Pine (Not Recommended)," Trees and Plants, The Morton Arboretum, accessed July 16, 2016, http://www.mortonarb.org/trees-plants/tree-plant-descriptions/austrian -pine-not-recommended.

44. Tallamy, *Bringing Nature Home*, 60.

45. Lounsberry, *Guide to the Trees*, 246.

46. John Hilty, "Eastern White Pine," in "Trees, Shrubs, and Woody Vines of Illinois," Illinois Wildflowers, http://www.illinoiswildflowers.info/trees/plants/white_pine.htm.

47. O'Sullivan, *Homeowner's Complete Tree and Shrub Handbook*, 303.

48. Lounsberry, *Guide to the Trees*, 249, 251.

49. Ibid., 256.

50. Ibid., 251.

51. Rebecca Williams, "Why Are Spruce Trees in the Midwest Declining?," News for Michigan, February 23, 2016, http://michiganradio.org/post/why-are-spruce-trees-midwest -declining#stream/0.

52. William Cullina, *Native Trees, Shrubs, and Vines: A Guide to Using, Growing, and Propagating North American Woody Plants* (Boston: Houghton Mifflin, 2002), 188.

53. Ibid., 62, 153.

54. Sternberg and Wilson, *Landscaping with Native Trees*, 166, 167.

55. Earl J. S. Rook, "*Larix laricina*, Tamarack," in *Flora, Fauna, Earth, and Sky . . . The Natural History of the Northwoods*, last updated August 18, 2004, http://www.rook.org/earl/bwca /nature/trees/larixlar.html.

56. Sternberg and Wilson, *Landscaping with Native Trees*, 166, 167.

GLOSSARY

Alien species: "With respect to a particular ecosystem, any species, including its seeds, eggs, spores, or other biological material capable of propagating that species, that is not native to that ecosystem" (Federal Laws and Regulations, Executive Order 13112, 1999). See also Nonnative.

Caterpillar: The larval stage for Lepidoptera (butterflies, moths). Lepidoptera life stages are egg to caterpillar/larva to pupa/chrysalis to adult. Most caterpillars feed on foliage of "host plants," which generally are native to the region.

Catkin: Flowers in the form of a slim elongated cluster of scaly bracts. Also called ament.

Cloning: The process of producing an organism that is an exact replica of another using the original organism's DNA. The major disadvantage is reduction of the genetic diversity that enables healthy natural selection. See also Cultivar.

Cultivar: An abbreviation for a cultivated variety, as opposed to a variety. See also Variety. These are plants that are selected and/or bred by humans based on one or more specific traits, such as flower or leaf shape or color, growth habit, disease resistance, or less susceptibility to a particular disease (but not all diseases), and that then are propagated in a way that maintains those traits. Most cultivars of native ornamental plants are created by one of two methods, selection or hybridization. In selection, a plant is propagated to preserve an atypical appearance or behavior. In hybridization, the plant is the offspring of two different species or varieties. Some cultivars are hybrids that naturally created themselves, but most cultivars are created by plant breeders. Creation is followed by propagation. About 70 percent of ornamental cultivars are propagated not by seed, but asexually, by cloning. Methods of cloning include cuttings, division, tissue culture, budding, and grafting. Cloning ensures the "offspring" will be genetically identical. Cultivars tend to retain the characteristics of the parent for just one generation; many cultivar seeds don't produce the selected characteristics. When checking labels, note that the Cultivated Plant Code states that for the cultivar's full scientific name, the part of the name that indicates the cultivar itself follows the genus name and the species name and is set off by single quotation marks or preceded by the abbreviation "cv." Cultivars of invasive plants, such as Burning Bush 'Compacta' (*Euonymus alatus* 'Compactus') are invasive. For cultivars of native plants, see Nativar.

Deciduous: A plant that loses all its leaves at the end of the growing season. The leaves of most deciduous plants reveal their real color in fall when they start to go dormant for the winter and there is no more chlorophyll to keep the leaves green.

Dioecious plants: Plants for which male and female reproductive organs are on separate plants, as opposed to monoecious.

Drupe: A fleshy fruit, such as a peach, plum, or cherry, usually having a single hard stone that encloses a seed. Also called "stone fruit."

Dry: Low soil water.

Eastern United States: States east of the Mississippi River.

Ecosystem: A complete community of living organisms and the nonliving materials of their surroundings.

Endangered: Describes plant and animal species in danger of becoming extinct throughout all or a significant part of their natural range.

Environment: The sum of all external factors (air, water, minerals, organisms) surrounding and having an influence on the survival, development, and evolution of an organism.

Evergreen: A plant that holds green leaves, either broadleaf or needles, throughout the year. When a leaf falls off, it is replaced by a new one. Some plants are evergreen in the south, but semievergreen or deciduous in the colder north.

Exfoliating: Having peeling or flaking bark.

Exotic: Foreign, nonnative, alien, nonindigenous, from another part of the world, as opposed to native or indigenous. See also Nonnative.

Extinct: Describes a plant or animal species that no longer lives on earth in its natural habitat.

Extirpation: Local extinction, when a species ceases to exist in a specific geographical area, though it still exists elsewhere. Local extinctions may be followed by a replacement or reintroduction of the species taken from other locations.

Fauna: Animal life, as opposed to flora, which is plant life.

Fecund: Fertile. Producing or capable of producing seeds, fruits, offspring. Not sterile. Plants that produce even a few seeds or fruits are not sterile.

Fka: Formerly known as.

Flora: Plant life, as opposed to fauna, which is animal life.

Flower: In the popular sense, the bloom or blossom of a plant; the showy portion, usually of a different color, shape, and texture from the foliage. Flower-producing plants include grasses, shrubs, and trees.

Foliage: Plant's leaves.

Granivorous birds: Birds that eat seeds.

Herbaceous plants: Plants with nonwoody stems whose above-ground growth usually dies back in winter in the temperate zone.

Honey plant: See Special Value to Bees.

Host plant: The plants, generally native, upon or near which female moths, skippers, and butterflies and other insects lay their eggs, and upon which the larvae or caterpillars feed. Specialist insects are very selective about their host plants, herbaceous and woody. E.g., milkweeds are the sole plant genus used by monarch butterflies for reproduction; their sole host plants. Generalist insects have more choices.

Hybrid: The offspring of two animals or plants of different breeds, varieties, species, or genera which can be produced naturally or through human manipulation for specific genetic characteristics. The hybrid origin of two species that hybridized or interbred naturally in the wild is indicated by an "×," as in *Amelanchier × grandiflora*, commonly known as apple serviceberry, a naturally occurring hybrid of *A. arborea* and *A. laevis*. Man-made hybrids have the genus name, then "×," then its given name enclosed within single quotes, as in *Coreopsis ×* 'Moonbeam', which is a cultivar of hybrid origin. Hybrids bred for disease resistance can be less susceptible to a particular disease (but not all diseases).

Insectivorous birds: Birds that eat insects.

Introduced species: "'Introduction' means the intentional or unintentional escape, release, dissemination, or placement of a species into an ecosystem as a result of human activity" (Federal Laws and Regulations, Executive Order 13112, 1999). USDA PLANTS defines introduced (or naturalized) species as plants that escaped cultivation *and* are established in the wild and reproducing spontaneously without human help. "These plants are introduced to some part of the PLANTS Floristic Area, though they may be native in other parts. While many are harmless or beneficial, others that are not already invasive or noxious have a high potential to become so in all or part of their range. In general, introduced plants are likely to invade or become noxious since they lack co-evolved competitors and natural enemies to control their populations" ("Introduced Plants of the PLANTS Floristic Area," https://plants.usda.gov/java/noxiousDriver). PLANTS' state and county distribution maps show the distribution of native and naturalized populations only, not planted or horticultural populations. Plants growing in yards, along streets, or planted in other settings are not included unless they have escaped cultivation and are established in the wild and reproducing spontaneously without the aid of humankind (http://plants.usda.gov/faq.html#native).

Invasive species: This term lacks a standard definition; it has many. Federal Laws and Regulations, Executive Order 13112, 1999, states: "'Invasive species' means an alien species whose introduction does or is likely to cause economic or environmental harm or harm to human health." The horticulture industry introduced about 50 percent of invasive plants for landscaping purposes. Immigrants brought others to use as medicine, cooking herbs, and food and in small manufacturing. Government agencies introduced some for wildlife and habitat and for erosion control. Others were introduced accidentally in ballast, shipping material, or agricultural crops. Once introduced, invasive species are difficult or impossible to remove. Cultivars for a given invasive species are considered invasive. Studies show that cultivars of popular nonnative invasive plants that are sold as "safe" alternatives to their invasive relatives are not safe, but remain invasive.

Larva: A distinct juvenile form that many animals, including insects and amphibians, undergo before metamorphosis into adults. Larvae appear in a variety of forms. The larval forms of the various insects are called caterpillars, grubs, maggots, and nymphs.

Lepidoptera: A large order of insects comprising the butterflies, moths, and skippers that as adults usually have four broad scaly wings and that as larvae are caterpillars.

Metamorphosis: In biology, a profound change in form from one stage to the next in the life history of an organism, as from the caterpillar to the pupa and from the pupa to the adult butterfly.

Migrating birds: The many species of birds, including warblers and hummingbirds, that engage in the regular seasonal movement, most often north and south along a flyway, that may include many thousands of miles, between breeding and winter grounds.

Monoculture: Plants with the same patterns of growth resulting from genetic similarity. Monocultures covering large areas greatly decrease plant and animal biodiversity. Nonnative invasive trees (e.g., Bradford pear) and shrubs (e.g., Japanese barberry) turn natural areas into monocultures.

Monoecious plants: Plants for which both male and female reproductive organs are on the same plant, as opposed to dioecious, in which they are on separate plants.

Nativar: Term used for a cultivar of a native plant species, as compared to a "straight" or "true" native species. Concerns regarding the use of nativars include the loss of genetic diversity that occurs by replacing true native species with clones and the inability of wildlife to recognize or access plants with characteristics not found in nature. An example of a nativar of redbud is *Cercis canadensis* 'Forest Pansy' (or *Cercis canadensis* cv. Forest Pansy). Also see Cultivar.

Native plant: "'Native species' means, with respect to a particular ecosystem, a species that, other than as a result of an introduction, historically occurred or currently occurs in that ecosystem" (Federal Laws and Regulations, Executive Order 13112, 1999). Arguing that native status accrues from origin, evolution, and functionality, Douglas Tallamy created this definition: "A plant or animal that has evolved in a given place over a period of time sufficient to develop complex and essential relationships with the physical environment and other organisms in a given ecological community" (Rick Darke and Doug Tallamy, *The Living Landscape: Designing for Beauty and Biodiversity in the Home Garden* [Portland, OR: Timber Press, 2014], 93).

Naturalized plant: Naturalized horticultural plants are nonnative plants that escape gardens and are able to survive independent of cultivation. Invasive plants are naturalized species that invade natural areas, displace native plants, and alter ecosystem functions. A federal study found that the longer nonnative horticultural plants are sold, the greater the risk of naturalization and invasiveness (Stephanie Yao, "Longer Marketing Time Increases the Risk of Naturalization by Horticultural Plants," USDA Agricultural Research Service, February 24, 2009, http://www.ars.usda.gov/is/pr/2009/090224.htm). A species can be defined as both a naturalized and an invasive plant.

Nonnative: An organism is considered nonnative when it has been introduced by humans to a location outside its native or natural range. In North America, nonnative plants are often from Europe or Asia. Nonnative plants can also be introduced from different geological regions in the same continent, such as a Colorado blue spruce grown in the Midwest. Plants that are not native are variously called introduced, nonnative, exotic, alien, foreign, adventive, or nonindigenous species. The introduction can be either accidental or intentional, as in ornamental garden and landscape plants.

Oligolecty: Used in pollination ecology to refer to bees that exhibit a specialized, narrow preference for pollen sources, typically for a single genus of flowering plants. The specialist insect is an oligolege.

Pemmican: A mixture of fat and meat, often with added berries, created by Native Americans as a high-energy food for use by winter hunters.

Pesticide: A substance or mixture of substances used to kill insects, plants, birds, mammals, and fish. A pesticide may be a chemical substance, biological agent (such as a virus or bacteria), antimicrobial, disinfectant, or device. Pesticides are poisons potentially toxic to humans and other animals and have been linked to animal deformities and human diseases. The definition often includes herbicides.

Perennial: A plant that lives more than two years, as opposed to an annual, a plant that completes its life cycle in one year and reproduces by seeds.

Pheromones: Any of a variety of substances secreted by many animal species that alter the behavior of individuals of the same species. Sex-attractant pheromones, secreted by a male or female to attract the opposite sex, are widespread among insects. It has been found that the leaves of red oak give off a volatile aldehyde that stimulates the female polyphemus moth to release a male-attracting pheromone.

Pollination: The act of transferring pollen grains from the male anther of a flower to the female stigma to achieve fertilization. The goal of every living organism, including plants, is to create offspring for the next generation. One of the ways that plants can produce offspring is by making fruit/seeds. Seeds contain the genetic information to produce a new plant. Seeds can only be produced when pollen is transferred between flowers of the same species. A self-pollinating plant can fertilize itself. A cross-pollinating plant needs a pollinator.

Pollinator: A biotic agent or vector, such as an animal, insect, wind, or water, that transfers pollen from plant to plant to achieve pollination. Pollinators include ants, bats, bees, beetles, birds, butterflies, flies, moths, wasps, and other animals.

Rare: At risk.

Safe: Noninvasive plants. "We suggest that only female sterile cultivars that cannot reproduce asexually should be considered 'safe' and noninvasive. Marketing less fecund cultivars as 'safe' is premature at this time, and further research is necessary to determine the potential invasiveness of different cultivars" (Tiffany M. Knight, Kayri Havens, and Pati Vitt, "Will the Use of Less Fecund Cultivars Reduce the Invasiveness of Perennial Plants?" *BioScience* 61, no. 10 (October 2011): 816–22, http://bioscience.oxfordjournals.org/content/61/10/816).

Samara: Winged seeds.

Semievergreen: Plants that retain all or some of their leaves in fall or into winter.

Shrub: Woody perennial usually with multiple stems. Trees and shrubs sometimes overlap.

Special Value to Bees: Identified by beekeepers and pollination biologists as an important pollen or nectar source (honey plant) for bees.

Specialist: See Oligolecty. Some butterflies are specialists in their choice of host plants, be they herbaceous or woody.

Species: "A group of organisms all of which have a high degree of physical and genetic similarity, generally interbreed only among themselves, and show persistent differences from members of allied groups of organisms" (Federal Laws and Regulations, Executive Order 13112, 1999).

Sterile: Not fertile; infertile. See Fecund.

Straight: See Nativar.

Subspecies: See Variety.

Sucker: A shoot from a parent's underground stem that creates a new root.

Supports Conservation Biological Control: A status achieved by a plant that attracts predatory or parasitoid insects that prey upon pest insects.

Taproot: Primary descending root.

Thicket: A colony of a species.

Threatened: A plant or animals species that is likely to become endangered in the immediate or foreseeable future throughout all or a significant part of its natural range.

Tolerant: Capable of enduring.

Tree: Woody perennial at least 20 feet tall with one main stem. The categories of trees and shrubs sometimes overlap.

True: See Nativar.

USDA PLANTS: United States Department of Agriculture Natural Resources Conservation Service PLANTS Database.

Variety: A variety (abbreviated as v. or var.), in contrast to a cultivar, is a minor natural and consistent variation (flower color, size) of the original species, and is able to be propagated by seed. The name of a variety is presented differently than a cultivar name. Rather than being presented in single quotes, it is italicized and in lowercase—just like the species name, which it follows. An example is Chokecherry: *Prunus virginiana* var. *virginiana* (see p. 83), which is the variety that is native to the Midwest. More extreme variations are designated subspecies (abbreviated ssp.).

Weed: The word derives for Old English for "grass" or "herb." In Europe in the Middle Ages, the meaning changed to a wild plant that grows where it is not wanted, especially in a cultivated field. Names including "weed" given to some native flowers by immigrants persist to this day. In contemporary North America "weed" can mean a nonnative and/ or invasive species, such as buckthorn or Bradford pear. Some use "weed" in reference to native plants like the sugar maple, which, in the Midwest, because of humans' disruption of the fire cycle, takes over woodlands by creating sugar maple monocultures and preventing reproduction by other important native species, like oaks and hickories.

Woody plant: Plant having a woody base that does not die down each year.

SELECTED BIBLIOGRAPHY
AND RESOURCES

Published Sources

Adelman, Charlotte, and Bernard L. Schwartz. *The Midwestern Native Garden: Native Alternatives to Nonnative Flowers and Plants—An Illustrated Guide*. Athens: Ohio University Press, 2011.

Bates, John. *Trailside Botany: 101 Favorite Trees, Shrubs and Wildflowers in the Upper Midwest*. Duluth, MN: Pfeifer-Hamilton, 1995.

Burrell, C. Colston. *Native Alternatives to Invasive Plants*. Brooklyn, NY: Brooklyn Botanic Garden, 2006.

Cullina, William. *Native Trees, Shrubs, and Vines: A Guide to Using, Growing, and Propagating North American Woody Plants*. Boston: Houghton Mifflin, 2002.

Czarapata, Elizabeth J. *Invasive Plants of the Upper Midwest: An Illustrated Guide to Their Identification and Control*. Madison: University of Wisconsin Press, 2005.

Darke, Rick, and Doug Tallamy. *The Living Landscape: Designing for Beauty and Biodiversity in the Home Garden*. Portland, OR: Timber Press, 2014. Note: See chapter 5, Jim McCormac's "Selected Plants for the Midwest and Mountain States," 345.

Grese, Robert E., ed. *The Native Landscape Reader*. Boston: University of Massachusetts Press in association with Library of American Landscape History, 2011.

Harper-Lore, Bonnie, and Maggie Wilson, eds. *Roadside Use of Native Plants*. Washington, DC: Island Press, 2000.

Harstad, Carolyn. *Go Native! Gardening with Native Plants and Wildflowers in the Lower Midwest*. Bloomington: Indiana University Press, 1999.

Hightshoe, Gary L. *Native Trees, Shrubs, and Vines for Urban and Rural America: A Planting Design Manual for Environmental Designers*. New York: Van Nostrand Reinhold, 1988.

Holm, Heather N. *Pollinators of Native Plants: Attract, Observe and Identify Pollinators and Beneficial Insects with Native Plants*. Minnetonka, MN: Pollination Press, 2014

Hill, Patricia. *Design Your Natural Midwest Garden*. Madison, WI: Trails Books, 2008.

Jenkins, Virginia Scott. *The Lawn: A History of an American Obsession*. Washington, DC: Smithsonian Institution Press, 1994.

Johnson, Lorraine, ed. *Landscaping with Native Plants*. 4th ed. Appleton, WI: Wild Ones, 2004.

Kaufman, Kenn, Jeff Sayre, and Kimberly Kaufman. *Kaufman Field Guide to Nature of the Midwest*. Boston: Houghton Mifflin Harcourt, 2015.

Kindscher, Kelly. *Edible Wild Plants of the Prairie: An Ethnobotanical Guide*. Lawrence: University Press of Kansas, 1987.

———. *Medicinal Wild Plants of the Prairie*. Lawrence: University Press of Kansas, 1992.

Kline, Christopher. *Butterfly Gardening with Native Plants: How to Attract and Identify Butterflies—Midwestern Edition*. Sugar Grove, OH: Beery Ridge Publishing, 2012.

Little, Elbert L. *National Audubon Society Field Guide to Trees: Eastern Region*. New York: Alfred A. Knopf, 1980.

Marinelli, Janet, ed. *Going Native: Biodiversity in Our Own Backyards.* Brooklyn, NY: Brooklyn Botanic Garden, 1994.

Nowak, Mariette. *Birdscaping in the Midwest: A Guide to Gardening with Native Plants to Attract Birds.* Madison: University of Wisconsin Press, 2012.

Nowakowski, Keith Gerard. *Native Plants in the Home Landscape: For the Upper Midwest.* Urbana: University of Illinois Extension, 2004.

Opler, Paul A. *A Field Guide to Eastern Butterflies.* Peterson Field Guide Series. New York: Houghton Mifflin, 1998.

Ottensen, Carole. *The Native Plant Primer: Trees, Shrubs, and Wildflowers for Natural Gardens.* New York: Harmony Books, 1995.

Packard, Steven, and Cornelia F. Mutel, eds. *The Tallgrass Restoration Handbook: For Prairies, Savannas, and Woodlands.* Washington, DC: Island Press, 1996.

Parshall, David K., and Jim Davidson. *Common Butterflies and Skippers of Ohio.* Columbus: Ohio Department of Natural Resources, Division of Wildlife, 2013.

Peterson, Roger Tory. *Peterson First Guide to Birds of North America.* Boston: Houghton Mifflin, 1986.

Peterson, Roger Tory, Janet Wehr, and George Petrides. *A Field Guide to Eastern Trees: Eastern United States and Canada, Including the Midwest.* Boston: Houghton Mifflin, 1998.

Randall, John M., and Janet Marinelli, eds. *Invasive Plants: Weeds of the Global Garden.* Brooklyn, NY: Brooklyn Botanic Garden, 1996.

Roberts, Edith A., and Elsa Rehmann. *American Plants for American Gardens.* 1929. Reprinted with a foreword by Darrel G. Morrison. Athens: University of Georgia Press, 1996.

Stein, Sara. *Noah's Garden: Restoring the Ecology of Our Own Back Yards.* Boston: Houghton Mifflin, 1993.

Sternberg, Guy, and Jim Wilson. *Landscaping with Native Trees: The Northeast, Midwest, Midsouth and Southeast Edition.* Shelburne, VT: Chapters, 1995.

Tallamy, Douglas W. *Bringing Nature Home: How Native Plants Sustain Wildlife in Our Gardens.* Portland, OR: Timber Press, 2007.

———. *Bringing Nature Home: How You Can Sustain Wildlife with Native Plants.* Updated and expanded ed., with a foreword by Rick Darke. Portland, OR: Timber Press, 2009.

Taylor, Patricia A. *Easy Care Native Plants: A Guide to Selecting and Using Beautiful American Flowers, Shrubs, and Trees in Gardens and Landscapes.* New York: Henry Holt, 1996.

Thompson, Bill, III. *Midwestern Birds: Backyard Guide—Watching, Feeding, Landscaping, Nurturing.* Minneapolis, MN: Cool Springs Press, 2013.

Wagner, David L. *Caterpillars of Eastern North America.* Princeton Field Guides. Princeton, NJ: Princeton University Press, 2005.

Wasowski, Sally, with Andy Wasowski. *Requiem for a Lawnmower and Other Essays on Easy Gardening with Native Plants.* Dallas: Taylor Publishing, 1992.

Weeks, Sally S., and Harmon P. Weeks Jr. *Shrubs and Woody Vines of Indiana and the Midwest: Identification, Wildlife Values, and Landscaping Use.* West Lafayette, IN: Purdue University Press, 2012.

Weeks, Sally S., Harmon P. Weeks Jr., and George R. Parker. *Native Trees of the Midwest: Identification, Wildlife Values, and Landscaping Use.* West Lafayette, IN: Purdue University Press, 2010.

Whitman, Ann H., ed. *Familiar Birds of North America: Eastern Region.* National Audubon Society Pocket Guide. New York: Alfred A. Knopf, 1987.

———, ed. *Familiar Trees of North America: Eastern Region.* National Audubon Society Pocket Guide. New York: Alfred A. Knopf, 1986.

Wild Ones Journal (Wild Ones, PO Box 1274, Appleton, WI 54912, 1-920-730-3986; toll free at 877-FYI-WILD (877-394-9453); info@for-wild.org; http://www.for-wild.org/.

Wilson, James D. *Common Birds of North America: An Expanded Guidebook.* Midwest Edition. Minocqua, WI: Willow Creek Press, 2001.

Wilson, William H. W. *Landscaping with Wildflowers and Native Plants*. San Francisco: Ortho Books, 1984.

Xerces Society. *Attracting Native Pollinators: Protecting North America's Bees and Butterflies*. North Adams, MA: Storey Publishing, 2011.

Selected Resources

Note: The abundance of native plant sellers and nature-oriented organizations is too vast to list. Here are some useful site-finding resources.

A. Regional Native Plant Sellers

Note: Native plant purveyors provide wonderful plants, inspiration, and catalogs with much useful information. The following resources can help locate native plant sellers.

1. *Find Native Plants,* http://findnativeplants.com/midwest/. Native plant nurseries and landscapers of Illinois, Indiana, Iowa, Michigan, Minnesota, Missouri, Ohio, Wisconsin, and Canada.

2. Grand Prairie Friends, *Prairie Nurseries,* http://grandprairiefriends.org/nurseries.php. Online resource for locating native plant sellers in Illinois, Indiana, Iowa, Kentucky, Michigan, Minnesota, Missouri, and Wisconsin.

3. Missouri Prairie Foundation, *Grow Native!* http://grownative.org/resource-guide /plants. Resource Guide: Plants, Landscape Architects: Missouri, southern Illinois, eastern Kansas, and northern Arkansas.

4. Indiana Native Plant and Wildflower Society, "Sources of Indiana Native Plants," http: //www.inpaws.org/landscaping/sources-of-indiana-native-plants/.

5. Iowa DNR: http://www.iowadnr.gov/Conservation/Forestry/State-Forest-Nursery, http://www.iowadnr.gov/Conservation/Wildlife-Landowner-Assistance.

6. Kansas Native Plant Society, Plant & Seed Sources, http://www.kansasnativeplantsociety .org/plant_seed_sources.php.

7. Lady Bird Johnson Wildflower Center—National Suppliers Directory, http://www .wildflower.org/suppliers/. (Also lists organizations and their native plant sales.)

8. Michigan Native Plant Producers Association, http://mnppa.org/.

9. (Michigan) Wildflower Association of Michigan—Landscaping with native plants, http://www.wildflowersmich.org/index.php?menu=8.

10. Minnesota DNR, Native plant suppliers and landscapers in Minnesota http://www .dnr.state.mn.us/gardens/nativeplants/suppliers.html.

11. Minnesota DNR, Native plant nurseries and consultants outside of Minnesota, http: //files.dnr.state.mn.us/assistance/backyard/gardens/native_plant/suppliers_outofstate.pdf.

12. Ohio Native Plant Nurseries and Resources, http://findnativeplants.com/midwest /ohionative-plants/.

13. Ohio State University Extension, Vendors and Mail Order Companies, http://webgarden .osu.edu/native.html.

14. PlantNative—Native Plant Nursery Directory (list of native plant nurseries and sources of native plants, broken down by state), http://www.plantnative.org/national_nursery_dir _main.htm.

15. Ultimate Guide to Finding Native Plants, http://www.ecosystemgardening.com/finding -native-plants.html. Online resource for locating regional and state native plant sellers in Illinois, Indiana, Iowa, Michigan, Minnesota, Missouri, Ohio, Wisconsin.

16. Wisconsin Native Plant Nurseries and Resources, http://findnativeplants.com/midwest /wisconsin-native-plants/.

17. Native Plant Nurseries in Wisconsin (Wisconsin DNR), http://dnr.wi.gov/files/pdf /pubs/er/er0698.pdf.

18. *Woodlands and Prairie Magazine,* "Mrs. Woods' Guide to Sources of Native Seeds, Trees and Plants," http://www.woodlandsandprairies.com/resource-nativeplantnurseries.htm.

B. Native and Nonnative Plant Identification

1. Illinois Native Plant Guide, USDA Natural Resources Conservation Guide Illinois, http://www.nrcs.usda.gov/wps/portal/nrcs/detail/il/plantsanimals/?cid=nrcs141p2_030715 #speci.2. Illinois Wildflowers, Trees, Shrubs, & Woody Vines and other categories of plants, http://www.illinoiswildflowers.info/index.htm. Also: Links to Other Websites, http://www .illinoiswildflowers.info/files/linksx.htm.

3. Lady Bird Johnson Wildflower Center—Native Plant Information Network (NPIN), http://www.wildflower.org/; also see http://www.wildflower.org/explore/.

4. Minnesota Seasons. Descriptions, information about plants and trees. http://www .minnesotaseasons.com/Plants/Index/Trees.html.

5. Missouri Botanic Garden Plant Finder, http://www.missouribotanicalgarden.org /plantfinder/plantfindersearch.aspx.

6. The Morton Arboretum, Native Shrubs of the Midwest for the Home Landscape, http: //www.mortonarb.org/files/Native-Shrubs-Midwest.pdf.

7. Ravine and Bluff Vegetation of the Chicago Region, Lake Michigan Watershed Ecosystem Partnership, http://www.greatlakes.org/document.doc?id=1382.

8. Shrubs of the Chicago Region, Volunteer Stewardship Network—Chicago Wilderness, http://fieldguides.fieldmuseum.org/sites/default/files/rapid-color-guides-pdfs/385_1.pdf.

9. USDA Natural Resources Conservation Service PLANTS Database, http://plants.usda .gov/. Search this database by common name, scientific name, plant family, or genus. Determine if a plant is native (N) or introduced (I) (naturalized), check map for distribution, and access other information provided by the site, including links to other sites.

C. Landscaping with Native Plants

1. Timothy M. Abbey, ed., *Alternatives for Invasive Ornamental Plant Species* (Connecticut Agricultural Experiment Station for the Connecticut Invasive Plant Working Group, 9-2004), http://www.ct.gov/caes/lib/caes/documents/special_features/nativealternatives.pdf.

2. Bringing Nature Home, http://www.bringingnaturehome.net/. This site supports the lecture series and book *Bringing Nature Home* by University of Delaware professor Doug Tallamy.

3. Dyck Arboretum, http://dyckarboretum.org/landscaping-with-native-plants/.

4. Finding Alternatives to Invasive Ornamental Plants in New York, http://www.nyis.info /user_uploads/files/Alvey%20Alt%20to%20Inv%20Orn%20Spp.pdf.

5. How to Use Native Plants for Landscaping and Restoration in Minnesota, http://files .dnr.state.mn.us/assistance/backyard/gardens/native_plant/nativelandscaping.pdf.

6.. Lady Bird Johnson Wildflower Center: Native Plant Information Network (NPIN), http://www.wildflower.org/collections/. Also, "Recommended Species by State" and "Recommended Species by Canadian Province" in the NPIN Special Collections section. Also, propagation protocols and deer-resistant native plants and Botanical Glossary, Drought Resources Center, How To Articles, Image Gallery, Mr. Smarty Plants, Research Literature, Native Plant Database, Step By Step Guides.

7. Landscaping with Native Plants, Greenacres, US EPA, 2016, https://archive.epa.gov /greenacres/web/html/chap1.html; https://archive.epa.gov/greenacres/web/html/index-2.html.

8. National Wildlife Federation: Garden for Wildlife, http://www.nwf.org/How-to-Help /Garden-for-Wildlife/Gardening-Tips/Using-Native-Plants/Midwest.aspx. Programs include Certified Wildlife Habitats; Top Ten Native Plants for the Midwest.

9. Missouri Botanical Garden, *Native Landscaping Manual: A Guide to Native Landscaping in Missouri,* http://www.missouribotanicalgarden.org/visit/family-of-attractions/shaw-nature -reserve/gardens-gardening-at-shaw-nature-reserve/native-landscaping-for-the-home -gardener/native-landscaping-manual.aspx.

10. The United States National Arboretum, "Kick the Invasive Exotic Gardening Habit with Great Native Plant Alternatives," last updated March 18, 2005, http://www.usna.usda.gov /Gardens/faqs/InvasivesAlternatives.html.

11. Wild Ones: Native Plants, Natural Landscapes, http://www.wildones.org/, http://www .wildones.org/learn/native-plants-natural-landscaping/.

12. Stephanie Yao, "Longer Marketing Time Increases the Risk of Naturalization by Horticultural Plants." USDA Agricultural Research Service, February 24, 2009, http://www.ars .usda.gov/is/pr/2009/090224.htm.

D. Butterflies, Moths, Other Insects, and More

1. Butterflies and Moths of North America, http://www.butterfliesandmoths.org/. Click on "Species Search" on the "Learn" menu to find a specific butterfly or moth species by name. Click on "Regional Checklists" and select your state and/or county to learn whether the insect frequents your area. Access the website for information on host plants and nectar preferences, photos of the butterfly or moth and caterpillar, descriptions of habitats, and life histories. Or if you wish information about a specific butterfly or moth, click on its name.

2. Butterflies of America: Interactive Listing of American Butterflies, http://www .butterfliesofamerica.com/intro.htm.

3. Illinois Wildflowers (Dr. John Hilty): Plant-Feeding Insect Database, http://www .illinoiswildflowers.info/plant_insects/database.html.

4. Jeff's Nature Home Page (Jeffrey S. Pippen), http://www.jeffpippen.com/.

5. Lady Bird Johnson Wildflower Center: Special Collections, under "National Collections," Butterflies and Moths of North America—Plants that are valuable to moths and butterflies; Value to Beneficial Insects, Special Value to Native Bees, Bumble Bees, and Honey Bees. Provides Nesting Materials/Structure for Native Bees. Supports Conservation Biological Control, http://www.wildflower.org/collections/.

E. Butterflies, Moths, and Other Insects

1. Lepidopterists' Society, http://www.lepsoc.org/internet_resources.php.

2. North American Butterfly Association (NABA), http://www.naba.org/. Butterfly Gardening: Regional Butterfly Garden Guides; NABA Chapters.

3. USDA Forest Service: Celebrating Wildflowers, http://www.fs.fed.us/wildflowers/aboutus .shtml.

4. Xerces Society for Invertebrate Conservation, http://www.xerces.org/.

F. Birding and Ornithology—Resources

1. Bird Education Network (BEN), http://birdeducation.org/resources.htm.

2. Bird Clubs in North America, American Birding Association (ABA), https://aba.org /resources/birdclubs.html.

G. Invasive Plants—Resources

1. USDA Forest Service: Celebrating Wildflowers, http://www.fs.fed.us/wildflowers/aboutus .shtml.

2. Chicago Botanic Garden Invasive Plants in the Chicago Region, http://www .chicagobotanic.org/research/conservation/invasive/chicago/; http://www.chicagobotanic.org /research/identifying_threats/invasive.

3. City of Chicago Guide to Land-Based Invasive Plants, http://www.cityofchicago.org /content/dam/city/depts/bacp/environmentdocs/landbasedinvasiveplantbrochure2011.pdf.

4. EDDMAPS (Early Detection and Distribution Mapping System), www.eddmaps.org; http://www.eddmaps.org/Species/.

5. Environmental Literacy Council (database—Search for Resources by State), http://www .enviroliteracy.org/article.php/40.html.

6. Global Compendium of Weeds, http://www.hear.org/gcw/.

7. Holden Arboretum Invasive Species (Ohio), http://www.holdenarb.org/education /Invasivespecies.asp.

8. Illinois, USDA Forest Service, Forest Invasive Plant Resource Center, http://na.fs.fed.us /spfo/invasiveplants/states/il.asp.

9. Indiana, USDA Forest Service, Forest Invasive Plant Resource Center, http://na.fs.fed .us/spfo/invasiveplants/states/in.asp; Invasive Exotic Plants in Indiana Natural Areas, http: //www.in.gov/dnr/naturepreserve/6346.htm.

10. Invasive.org: Invasive and Exotic Species Profiles & State, Regional and National Lists, http://www.invasive.org/species.cfm.

11. Invasive Plant Atlas of the United States: http://www.invasiveplantatlas.org/; http://www .invasiveplantatlas.org/shrubs.html; http://www.invasiveplantatlas.org/vines.html; http://www.invasiveplantatlas.org/trees.html.

12. Michigan, USDA Forest Service, Forest Invasive Plant Resource Center, http://na.fs.fed .us/spfo/invasiveplants/states/mi.asp.

13. The Morton Arboretum, Invasive Trees and Plants, http://www.mortonarb.org/trees -plants/tree-and-plant-advice/horticulture-care/invasive-trees-and-plants.

14. National Environmental Coalition on Invasive Species (NECIS), http://www.necis.net/.

15. National Invasive Species Information Center. Its "iMapInvasives" facilitates early de- tection by "citizen scientists." http://www.landscope.org/explore/threats/invasives/.

16. Plant Conservation Alliance, http://www.nps.gov/plants/alien/factmain.htm.

17. Plant Conservation Alliance's Alien Plant Working Group, "Least Wanted: Alien Plant Invaders of Natural Areas—Fact Sheets, http://www.nps.gov/plants/alien/fact.htm.

18. The United States National Arboretum, http://www.usna.usda.gov/Gardens/faqs /nativefaq2.html.

19. University of Wisconsin invasive species photo gallery, http://dnr.wi.gov/topic/invasives /photos/; Invasive Plants of Wisconsin, https://www.uwgb.edu/Biodiversity/herbarium/invasive _species/invasive_plants01.htm.

20. USDA National Agricultural Library, National Invasive Species Information Center (NISIC). "Gateway to invasive species information; covering Federal, State, local, and inter- national sources." http://www.invasivespeciesinfo.gov/plants/main.shtml.

21. USDA Natural Resources Conservation Service PLANTS Database: Introduced, Inva- sive, and Noxious Plants, https://plants.usda.gov/java/noxiousDriver.

22. USDA PLANTS Database: This database can be searched by common or scientific name, plant family or genus. A native plant is "N." An introduced (or naturalized plant) is "I." An introduced plant may also be invasive. Also: maps and links to other sites. http://plants .usda.gov.

23. US Forest Service Northeastern Area, http://www.na.fs.fed.us/fhp/invasive_plants/; http://na.fs.fed.us/fhp/invasive_plants/weeds/.

24. Weeds Gone Wild, Alien Plant Invaders of Natural Areas, http://www.nps.gov/plants /alien/index.htm.

H. Compilations of Naturalized or Invasive Plant Lists

1. Midwest Invasive Plant Network (MIPN)—Compilation of Midwestern States' Invasive Plant Lists, http://www.mipn.org/plantlist/.

2. National Association of Invasive Plant Councils, http://www.na-ipc.org/.

3. USDA PLANTS Database: Search database by common name, scientific name, plant family or genus. N = native plant. I = introduced – naturalized plant). Note: Introduced plants are often invasive. Maps and links to other sites. http://plants.usda.gov.

4. USDA PLANTS—Introduced, Invasive, and Noxious Plants, http://plants.usda.gov/java /noxiousDriver.

I. Threatened and Endangered Species

1. Center for Plant Conservation (CPC), Missouri Botanical Garden, "Dedicated solely to preventing the extinction of U.S. native plants." http://www.missouribotanicalgarden.org/media/fact-pages/center-for-plant-conservation.aspx

2. Lady Bird Johnson Wildflower Center: Threatened & Endangered Species—A database of plants that have Threatened or Endangered status with the U.S. Fish & Wildlife Service, http://www.wildflower.org/collections/.

3. USFWS: Endangered Species Program in the Upper Midwest, http://www.fws.gov/midwest/endangered/; http://www.fws.gov/midwest/endangered/plants/.

4. USDA PLANTS Database—Threatened and Endangered, https://plants.usda.gov/threat.html.

J. Compilations of Native Plant Societies

1. Center for Plant Conservation—Lists of State Native Plant Societies, http://www.centerforplantconservation.org/Links/plantlinks.asp#NativePlantSocieties

2. Find Native Plants: Illinois, Indiana, Iowa, Michigan, Minnesota, Missouri, Ohio, Wisconsin and Canada: Native Plant Organizations. (Also: Where to See Native Plants, Native Plant Calendar of Events, Articles, Recommended Native Plant Books for the Midwest and Great Plains), http://findnativeplants.com/midwest/illinois-native-plants/.

3. Lady Bird Johnson Wildflower Center— National Organizations Directory, http://www.wildflower.org/organizations/.

4. North American Native Plant Society. Native plant society links, http://www.nanps.org/; http://www.nanps.org/index.php/resources/native-plant-societies.

5. USDA Forest Service, Celebrating Wildflowers: Links to Native Plant Societies, Botanical Gardens and Arboreta, and Conservation Organizations plus data on gardening with native plants, invasive plants, butterfly, bee and other pollinators, and native alternatives to nonnative plants. http://www.fs.fed.us/wildflowers/links.shtml.

6. Wild Ones: Native Plants, Natural Landscapes. Appleton, WI. This Midwest-based native plant organization has 52 chapters in 12 states. Phone: 1-920-730-3986; toll-free: 877-FYI-WILD (877-394-9453); e-mail: info@wildones.org; website: http://www.wildones.org/.

K. Blogs about Native Plant Landscaping

1. *Going Native, My Journey from Traditional to Native Plant Suburban Landscaping,* http://nativeplantconvert.blogspot.com/

2. *Humane Gardener,* http://www.humanegardener.com/

3. *Native Plants and Wildlife Gardens!* http://nativeplantwildlifegarden.com/

4. *Native Plants, National Wildlife Federation,* http://blog.nwf.org/tags/native-plants/; *Garden for Wildlife, National Wildlife Federation,* http://www.nwf.org/How-to-Help/Garden-for-Wildlife/Gardening-Tips/Using-Native-Plants.aspx.

5. *Ohio Birds and Biodiversity,* http://jimmccormac.blogspot.com/.

6. *Restoring the Landscape with Native Plants,* http://www.restoringthelandscape.com/.

7. *Kentucky Native Plant and Wildlife,* http://kentuckynativeplantandwildlife.blogspot.com/.

8. *Native Plants Forum,* www.gardenweb.com/forums/natives.

9. Wild Ones, Native Plant Blogs, http://www.wildones.org/resources/native-plant-blogs/.

L. Native Woody Species in Descending Order of Lepidoptera Productivity

To sustain local butterflies, moths, and birds when gardening and landscaping, plant a wide diversity of native plant species. Plant tall native trees in your property's corners and around the borders, surround them with densely planted smaller trees and shrubs, and place native grasses and flowers in front. Create areas of woody and herbaceous species. Natives host Lepidoptera (butterflies and moths). Layers provide birds with cover and nesting sites.

Douglas Tallamy conducted a ground breaking "attempt to categorize native and alien plant genera in terms of their ability to support insect herbivores and, by inference, overall biodiversity. We did this by ranking all native plant genera (woody and herbaceous) in terms of the number of Lepidoptera species recorded using them as host plants. Our hope is that this ranking will be used as one of the criteria for plant selections in managed and unmanaged landscapes by restoration ecologists, landscape architects and designers, land managers, and homeowners" (Lepidopteran Use of Native & Alien Ornamental Plants, http://udel .edu/~dtallamy/host/index.html).

The following lists, derived from Tallamy's rankings, set out Lepidoptera productivity by common and genus name for Large Native Trees; Small Native Trees, Shrubs, Vines; and Native Herbaceous Species.

LARGE NATIVE TREES

Oak (*Quercus*)—Host 534 Lepidoptera species. Black cherry (*Prunus*)—456 species. Willow (*Salix*)—455 species. Birch (*Betula*)—413 species. Poplar, cottonwood, aspen (*Populus*)—368 species. Maple, boxelder (*Acer*)—285 species. Elm (*Ulmus*)—213 species. Pines (*Pinus*)—203 species. Hickory (*Carya*)—200 species. Spruce (*Picea*)—156 species. Basswood/linden (*Tilia*)—150 species. Ash (*Fraxinus*)—50 species. Walnut, butternut (*Juglans*)—130 species. Beech (*Fagus*)—126 species. Chestnut (*Castanea*)—125 species. Tamarack, larch (*Larix*)—121 species. Fir (*Abies*)—117 species. Hemlock (*Tsuga*)—92 species. Mountain ash (*Sorbus*)—68 species. Black locust (*Robinia*)—72 species. White cedar, American arborvitae (*Thuja*)—50 species. Honeylocust (*Gleditsia*)—46 species. Persimmon (*Diospyros*)—45 species. Sycamore (*Platanus*)—45 species. Hackberry (*Celtis*)—43 species. Juniper, eastern red cedar (*Juniperus*)—42 species. Sweetgum (*Liquidambar*)—35 species. Buckeye (*Aesculus*)—32 species. Blackgum, sourgum, tupelo (*Nyssa*)—26 species. Tulip tree, tulip/yelow poplar (*Liriodendron*)—21 species. Pawpaw (*Asimina*)—12 species. Mulberry (*Morus*)—9 species. Catalpa (*Catalpa*)—8 species. Osage orange (*Maclura*)—8 species. Kentucky coffee tree (*Gymnocla*)—5 species.

SMALL NATIVE TREES, SHRUBS, VINES

Oak, dwarf chinkapin (*Quercus*)—Host 534 Lepidoptera species. Cherry, plum (*Prunus*)—456 species. Willow (*Salix*)—455 species. Birch (*Betula*)—413 species. Crab apple (*Malus*)—311 species. Blueberry, cranberry (*Vaccinium*)—288 species. Blackberry, raspberry (*Rubus*)—163 species. Hawthorn (*Crataegus*)—159 species. Alder (*Alnus*)—156 species. Rose (*Rosa*)—139 species. American hazelnut, filbert (*Corylus*)—131 species. Serviceberry, Juneberry, shadbush (*Amelanchier*)—124 species. Dogwood, bunchberry (*Cornus*)—118 species. Fir, balsam (*Abies*)—117 species. Bayberry (*Myrica*)—108 species. Viburnum (*Viburnum*)—104 species. Spirea, meadowsweet (*Spiraea*)—89 species. Gooseberry, currant (*Ribes*)—99 species. Hop hornbeam, ironwood (*Ostrya*)—94 species. Meadowsweet/spirea (*Spiraea*)—89 species. Grape (*Vitis*)—79 species. American hornbeam, ironwood, musclewood, blue beech (*Carpinus*) —68 species. Mountain ash (*Sorbus*)—68 species. Sweet fern (*Comptonia*)—64 species. Witch hazel (*Hamameli*)—63 species. Sumac (*Rhus*)—58 species. Azalea, rhododendron (*Rhododendron*)—51 species. White cedar, American arborvitae (*Thuja*)—50 species. New Jersey tea (*Ceanothu*)—45 species. Huckleberry, dangleberry (*Gaylussacia*)—44 species. Elderberry (*Sambucus*)—42 species. Juniper/common, creeping (*Juniperus*)—42 species. Ninebark (*Physocarpus*)—41 species. Sassafras (*Sassafras*)—38 species. Winterberry, holly, inkberry (*Ilex*)—39 species. Honeysuckle (*Lonicera*)—37 species. Bottlebrush buckeye (*Aesculus*)—32 species. Mountain-laurel (*Kalmia*)—32 species. Virginia creeper, woodbine (*Parthenocissus*)—32 species. Chokeberry (*Photinia*)—29 species. Snowberry (*Symphoricarpos*)—25 species. Buffaloberry (*Shepherdia*)—22 species. Magnolia, sweetbay (*Magnolia*)—21 species. Buttonbush (*Cephalanthus*)—19 species. Redbud (*Leguminosae*)—19 species. Sourwood (*Oxydendrum*)—14 species. American barberry (*Berberis*)—12 species. Pawpaw (*Asimina*)—12 species. (Native) Buckthorn (*Frangula*)—11 species. (Native) Burning bush, wahoo (*Euonymous*)—11 species. Spicebush (*Lindera*)—11 species. (Native) Buckthorn (*Rhamnus*)—10 species. Clethra, summersweet, sweetpepperbush (*Clethra*)—10 species. Fringetree (*Chionanthus*)—8 species. Yew (*Taxus*)—8 species. Bittersweet (*Celastrus*)—7 species. Labrador tea (*Ledum*)—7 species. Silverbell (*Halesia*)—7 species. Trumpetcreeper, trumpet vine (*Campsis*)—7 species. Clematis, leather flower (*Clematis*)—6 species. Wafer ash, hoptree (*Ptelea*)—6 species. Pricklyash (*Zanthoxyl*)—6 species. Bush honeysuckle (*Diervilla*)—5 species. Hydrangea (*Hydrangea*)—5 species. Smoketree (*Cotinus*)—5 species. Swamp loosestrife (*Decodon*)—5 species. Buckthorn bully, bumelia (*Sideroxylon*)—4 species. Mistletoe (*Phoradendron*)—4 species. Scentless mock-orange (*Philadelphus*)—4 species. Sweetshrub (*Calycanth*)—2 species. Snowberry, eastern teaberry, wintergreen (*Gaultheria*)—2 species. Bladdernut (*Staphylea*)—2 species. American beautyberry (*Callicarpa*)—1 species. Leatherwood (*Dirca*)—1 species. Mountain camellia, silky camellia (*Stewartia*)—1 species. The following host no known species: Allegheny vine (*Adlumia*), Dwarf mistletoe (*Arceuthobium*). Supplejack (*Berchemia*).Yellowwood (*Cladrastis*). Crowberry (*Empetrum*). Sweetspire (*Itea*). Snowbell (*Styrax*). Yellowroot (*Xanthorhiza*).

NATIVE HERBACEOUS SPECIES

Goldenrod (*Solidago*) Host 115 species. Aster (*Symphyotrichum, Eurybia, Doellingeria*)—115 species. Sunflower (*Helianthus*)—73 species. Joe pye, boneset (*Eupatorium*)—42 species. Morning glory (*Ipomoea*)—39 species. Sedges (*Carex*)—36 species. Honeysuckle (*Lonicera*)—36 species. Lupine (*Lupinus*)—33 species. Violet (*Viola*)—29 species. Geranium (*Geranium*)—23 species. Black-eyed Susan, brown-eyed Susan, orange coneflower (*Rudbeckia*)—17 species. Iris (*Iris*)—17 species. Evening primrose, sundrops (*Oenothera*)—16 species. Milkweed (*Asclepias*)—12 species (including the monarch butterfly). Verbena (*Verbena*)—11 species. Beardtongue (*Penstemon*)—8 species. Phlox (*Phlox*)—8 species. Bee balm (*Monarda*)—7 species. Veronica (*Veronica*)—6 species. Little bluestem (*Schizachyrium*) (native grass)—6 species. Cardinal flower, great blue lobelia (*Lobelia*)—4 species. **Data Note:** Douglas Tallamy wrote, "We restricted our search to moths and butterflies that develop on plant genera occurring naturally or planted ornamentally in the mid-Atlantic region of North America. We supplemented larval host associations and ranges described in [various studies] with records from over 400 sources in the primary literature and occasionally with our own field collections." **Authors' Note:** Most of the plants featured in this book are included in "Selected Plants for the Midwest and Mountain States" by Jim McCormac in *The Living Landscape* by Rick Darke and Doug Tallamy.

We used the following source materials:

Bringing Nature Home, http://www.bringingnaturehome.net/what-to-plant.html.
Lepidopteran Use of Native & Alien Ornamental Plants, http://udel.edu/~dtallamy/host /index.html.

ILLUSTRATION AND
PHOTOGRAPHY CREDITS

Birds

American crow (*Corvus brachyrhynchos*) by Louis Agassiz Fuertes
American goldfinch (*Spinus tristis)* courtesy of Bob Hines, US Fish and Wildlife Service
American redstart (*Setophaga ruticilla*) by Louis Agassiz Fuertes
American robin (*Turdus migratorius*) by Louis Agassiz Fuertes
American woodcock (*Scolopax minor*) by Louis Agassiz Fuertes
Baltimore oriole (*Icterus galbula*) by Louis Agassiz Fuertes
Blackburnian warbler (*Setophaga fusca*) by Louis Agassiz Fuertes
Blackcapped chickadee (*Poecile atricapillus*) by Louis Agassiz Fuertes
Black-throated blue warbler (*Setophaga caerulescens*) by Louis Agassiz Fuertes
Black-throated green warbler (*Setophaga virens*) by Louis Agassiz Fuertes
Blue jay (*Cyanocitta cristata*) by Louis Agassiz Fuertes
Bobwhite quail (*Colinus virginianus*) by Louis Agassiz Fuertes
Brown thrasher (*Toxostoma rufum*) by Louis Agassiz Fuertes
Cape May warbler (*Setophaga tigrina*) by Louis Agassiz Fuertes
Cedar Waxwing (*Bombycilla cedrorum*) by Louis Agassiz Fuertes
Chipping sparrow (*Spizella passerina*) by Louis Agassiz Fuertes
Common redpoll (*Acanthis flammea*) by Louis Agassiz Fuertes
Dark-eyed junco (*Junco hyemalis*) by Louis Agassiz Fuertes
Eastern bluebird (*Sialia sialis*) by Louis Agassiz Fuertes
Eastern kingbird (*Tyrannus tyrannus*) by Louis Agassiz Fuertes
Eastern towhee (*Pipilo erythrophthalmus*) by Louis Agassiz Fuertes
Evening grosbeak (*Coccothraustes vespertinus*) by Louis Agassiz Fuertes
Field sparrow (*Spizella pusilla*) by Allan Brooks
Fox sparrow (*Passerella iliaca*) by Allan Brooks
Gray catbird (*Dumetella carolinensis*) by Louis Agassiz Fuertes
Hooded warbler (*Setophaga citrina*) by Louis Agassiz Fuertes
House wren (*Troglodytes aedon*) by Louis Agassiz Fuertes
Loggerhead shrike (*Lanius ludovicianus*) by Louis Agassiz Fuertes
Magnolia warbler (*Setophaga magnolia*) by Louis Agassiz Fuertes
Northern cardinal (*Cardinalis cardinalis*) by Louis Agassiz Fuertes
Northern flicker (*Colaptes auratus*) by Louis Agassiz Fuertes
Northern mockingbird (*Mimus polyglottos*) by Louis Agassiz Fuertes
Northern parula warbler (*Setophaga americana)* by Louis Agassiz Fuertes
Pine siskin (*Carduelis pinus*) by Louis Agassiz Fuertes

Pine warbler (*Setophaga pinus*) by Louis Agassiz Fuertes
Prairie warbler (*Setophaga discolor*) by Louis Agassiz Fuertes
Purple finch (*Haemorhous purpureus*) by Louis Agassiz Fuertes
Red-breasted nuthatch (*Sitta canadensis*) courtesy of Cephas
Red-eyed vireo (*Vireo olivaceus*) by Louis Agassiz Fuertes
Red-bellied woodpecker (*Melanerpes carolinus*) released into the public domain by
    Ken Thomas
Red-headed woodpecker (*Melanerpes erythrocephalus*) by Louis Agassiz Fuertes
Red-winged blackbird (*Agelaius phoeniceus*) by Louis Agassiz Fuertes
Rose-breasted grosbeak (*Pheucticus ludovicianus*) by Louis Agassiz Fuertes
Ruby-crowned kinglet (*Regulus calendula*) by Louis Agassiz Fuertes
Ruby-throated hummingbird (*Archilochus colubris*) by Louis Agassiz Fuertes
Ruffed grouse (*Bonasa umbellus*) by Louis Agassiz Fuertes
Song sparrow (*Melospiza melodia*) by Allan Brooks
Sparrow hawk aka American kestrel (*Falco sparverius*) by Louis Agassiz Fuertes
Swamp sparrow (*Melospiza georgiana*) by Allan Brooks
Tree swallow (*Tachycineta bicolor*) by Louis Agassiz Fuertes
Tufted titmouse (*Baeolophus bicolor*) by Louis Agassiz Fuertes
White-breasted nuthatch (*Sitta carolinensis*) by Louis Agassiz Fuertes
White-throated sparrow (*Zonotrichia albicollis*) by Louis Agassiz Fuertes
White-winged crossbill (*Loxia leucoptera*) by Louis Agassiz Fuertes
Wild turkey (*Meleagris gallopavo*) by Louis Agassiz Fuertes
Wood duck (*Aix sponsa*) by Louis Agassiz Fuertes
Wood thrush (*Hylocichla mustelina*) by Louis Agassiz Fuertes
Yellow-bellied sapsucker (*Sphyrapicus varius*) by Louis Agassiz Fuertes
Yellow-rumped warbler (*Setophaga coronata*) by Louis Agassiz Fuertes
Yellow warbler (*Setophaga petechia*) by Louis Agassiz Fuertes
Yellow-throated warbler (*Setophaga dominica*) by Louis Agassiz Fuertes

Butterflies and Moths

Acadian hairstreak butterfly (*Satyrium acadica*) courtesy of Tom Peterson of Fermilab
American snout butterfly (*Libytheana carinenta*) used with the permission of © Jeffrey Pippen
Banded hairstreak butterfly (*Satyrium calanus*) used with the permission of © Jeffrey Pippen
Cecropia moth (*Hyalophora cecropia*) courtesy of Tom Peterson of Fermilab
Clouded sulphur butterfly (*Colias philodice*) used with the permission of © Jeffrey Pippen
Columbia silkmoth (*Hyalophora columbia*) courtesy of Lavaltrois
Common buckeye butterfly (*Junonia coenia*) © Bernard L. Schwartz
Compton tortoiseshell butterfly (*Nymphalis vaualbum*) courtesy of D. Gordon E. Robertson
Coral hairstreak butterfly (*Satyrium titus*) used with the permission of © Jeffrey Pippen
Eastern comma butterfly (*Polygonia comma*) used with the permission of © Jeffrey Pippen
Eastern tiger swallowtail butterfly (*Papilio glaucus*) used with the permission of © Jeffrey
    Pippen
Edwards' hairstreak butterfly (*Satyrium edwardsii*) used with the permission of © Jeffrey
    Pippen
Frosted elfin butterfly (*Callophrys irus*) used with the permission of © Jeffrey Pippen
Giant swallowtail butterfly (*Papilio cresphontes*) used with permission of © Jeffrey Pippen

Gorgone checkerspot butterfly (*Chlosyne gorgone*) courtesy of Whitney Cranshaw, Colorado State University, Bugwood.org

Great ash sphinx moth (*Sphinx chersis*) courtesy of Joseph Berger, Bugwood.org

Green comma butterfly (*Polygonia faunus*) used with permission of © Jeffrey Pippen

Hackberry emperor butterfly (*Asterocampa celtis*) used with the permission of © Jeffrey Pippen

Henry's elfin butterfly (*Callophrys henrici*) courtesy of Megan McCarty

Hoary edge butterfly (*Achalarus lyciades*) courtesy of Jerry A. Payne, USDA Agricultural Research Service, Bugwood.org

Horace's duskywing butterfly (*Erynnis horatius*) used with the permission of © Jeffrey Pippen

Hummingbird clearwing moth (*Hemaris thysbe*) used with the permission of © Jeffrey Pippen

Imperial moth (*Eacles imperialis*) released into the public domain by its author, Lizmillea

Io moth (*Automeris io*) used with the permission of © Jeffrey Pippen

Juniper hairstreak butterfly (*Callophrys gryneus*) used with the permission of © Jeffrey Pippen

Juvenal's duskywing skipper (*Erynnis juvenalis*) used with the permission of © Jeffrey Pippen

Karner blue butterfly (*Lycaeides melissa samuelis*) used with the permission of © Jeffrey Pippen

Locust underwing moth (*Euparthenos nubilis*) used with the permission of © Jeffrey Pippen

Luna moth (*Actias luna*) used with the permission of © Jeffrey Pippen

Marine blue butterfly (*Leptotes marina*) © Bernard L. Schwartz

Monarch butterfly (*Danaus plexippus*) on purple coneflower © Bernard L. Schwartz

Monarch butterfly caterpillar (*Danaus plexippus*) © Bernard L. Schwartz

Mourning cloak butterfly (*Nymphalis antiopa*) used with the permission of © Jeffrey Pippen

Northern broken dash butterfly (*Wallengrenia egeremet*) used with the permission of © Jeffrey Pippen

Oak hairstreak butterfly (*Satyrium favonius*) used with the permission of © Jeffrey Pippen

Orange sulphur butterfly (*Colias eurytheme*) on a purple coneflower © Bernard L. Schwartz

Painted lady butterfly (*Vanessa cardui*) released into the public domain by Tbc

Pandora sphinx moth (*Eumorpha pandorus*) courtesy Edward L. Manigault, Clemson University Donated Collection, Bugwood.org

Pawpaw sphinx moth (*Dolba hyloens*) courtesy of the NPS

Peck's skipper (*Polites peckius*) used with the permission of © Jeffrey Pippen

Pipevine swallowtail butterfly (*Battus philenor*) released into the public domain by Ryan Kaldari

Polyphemus moth (*Antheraea polyphemus*) used with the permission of © Jeffrey Pippen

Promethea silkworm caterpillar (*Callosamia promethea*) courtesy of John H. Ghent, USDA Forest Service, Bugwood.org

Question mark butterfly (*Polygonia interrogationis*) used with the permission of © Jeffrey Pippen

Red admiral butterfly (*Vanessa atalanta*) © Bernard L. Schwartz

Red-spotted purple butterfly (*Limenitis arthemis*) used with the permission of © Jeffrey Pippen

Rose hooktip moth (*Oreta rosea*) used with the permission of © Jeffrey Pippen

Rosy maple moth (*Dryocampa rubicunda*) used with the permission of © Jeffrey Pippen

Silver-spotted skipper (*Epargyreus clarus*) used with the permission of © Jeffrey Pippen

Sleepy duskywing skipper (*Erynnis brizo*) used with the permission of © Jeffrey Pippen

Southern dogface butterfly (*Zerene cesonia*) used with the permission of © Jeffrey Pippen

Spicebush swallowtail butterfly (*Papilio troilus*) used with the permission of © Jeffrey Pippen
Spring azure butterfly (*Celastrina ladon*) used with the permission of © Jeffrey Pippen
Striped hairstreak butterfly (*Satyrium liparops*) courtesy of Fvlamoen
Summer azure butterfly (*Celastrina neglecta*) used with the permission of © Jeffrey Pippen
Tulip tree silkmoth (*Callosamia angulifera*) used with the permission of © Jeffrey Pippen
Viceroy butterfly (*Limenitis archippus*) used with the permission of © Jeffrey Pippen
White-lined sphinx moth (*Hyles lineata*) courtesy of J. Pinta
White M hairstreak butterfly (*Parrhasius m-album*) used with the permission of © Jeffrey Pippen
Zebra swallowtail butterfly (*Eurytides marcellus*) released into the public domain by its author, Dave Pape

Insects

Andrena spp. courtesy of Joseph Berger, Bugwood.org
Andrenid bee (Andrenidae) courtesy of Cherly Moorehead, Bugwood.org
Bee fly (Bombyliidae) © Bernard L. Schwartz
Bumblebees (*Bombus* spp.) © Bernard L. Schwartz
Flower fly (Syrphidae) courtesy of Whitney Cranshaw, Colorado State University, Bugwood.org
Green leaf katydid (*Microcentrum rhombifolium*) released into the public domain by its author, I, Ltshears
Honeybee (*Apis mellifera*) © Bernard L. Schwartz
Leafcutting bee (Megachilidae) courtesy of Jack Dykinga, USDA Agricultural Research Service, Bugwood.org
Leafhopper (*Cicadellidae* spp.) courtesy of Susan Ellis, Bugwood.org
Orchard mason bee (*Osmia lignaria*) USDA photo by Jack Dykinga
Syrphid fly (*Eristalis* spp.) courtesy of Susan Ellis, Bugwood.org
Tumbling flower beetle (*Tomoxia* spp.) courtesy of Beatriz Moisset

Mammals

Eastern chipmunk (*Tamias striatus*) by Louis Agassiz Fuertes

Shrubs and Trees (Spring)

Abelia, hardy (*Abelia mosanensis*) courtesy of Michael Wolf
American bladdernut (*Staphylea trifolia*) © Bernard L. Schwartz
American cranberrybush flowers (*Viburnum opulus* var. *americanum*) © Bernard L. Schwartz
American cranberrybush shrub (*Viburnum opulus* var. *americanum*) © Bernard L. Schwartz
American black elderberry (*Sambucus canadensis*) © Bernard L. Schwartz
American fly honeysuckle (*Lonicera canadensis*) courtesy of Rob Routledge, Sault College, Bugwood.org
American hazelnut (*Corylus americana* var. *indehiscens*) © Bernard L. Schwartz
American plum (*Prunus americana*) courtesy of Homer Edward Price
American smoketree (*Cotinus obovatus*) © Bernard L. Schwartz
American snowbell (*Styrax americanus*) courtesy of Robert H. Mohlenbrock @ USDA-NRCS PLANTS Database/USDA SCS, *Southern Wetland Flora: Field Office Illustrated Guide to Plant Species* (1991)

American wisteria (*Wisteria frutescens*) © Bernard L. Schwartz

Amur maackia (*Maackia amurensis*) courtesy of Bruce Martin of Morton Arboretum

Arrowwood viburnum (*Viburnum dentatum* var. *dentatum*) © Bernard L. Schwartz

Beautybush (*Kolkwitzia amabilis*) courtesy of KENPEI

Black cherry (*Prunus serotina* var. *serotina*) © Bernard L. Schwartz

Black cherry leaves and flowers (*Prunus serotina* var. *serotina*) © Bernard L. Schwartz

Black chokeberry (*Photinia melanocarpa*) © Bernard L. Schwartz

Black locust leaves and flowers (*Robinia pseudoacacia*) © Bernard L. Schwartz

Black willow (*Salix nigra*) © Bernard L. Schwartz

Bladdernut (*Staphylea pinnata*) from Jacob Sturm, *Deutschlands Flora in Abbildungen* (1796)

Bradford pear (*Pyrus calleryana* 'Bradford') © Bernard L. Schwartz

Bridalwreath spirea (*Spiraea prunifolia*) from Philipp Franz von Siebold and Joseph Gerhard Zuccarini, *Flora Japonica, Sectio Prima* (1870)

Carolina silverbell (*Halesia carolina*) courtesy of Kurt Sturber

Catalpa tree (*Catalpa speciosa*) © Bernard L. Schwartz

Catalpa tree flowers (*Catalpa speciosa*) © Bernard L. Schwartz

Chinese catalpa (*Catalpa ovata*) released into the public domain by Peter Coxhead

Chinese fringe tree (*Chionanthus retusus*) courtesy of KENPEI

Chinese redbud (*Cercis chinensis*) courtsey of Fanghong

Clove currant (*Ribes odoratum*) courtesy of Stan Shebs

Common serviceberry bush (*Amelanchier arborea* var. *arborea*) © Bernard L. Schwartz

Common serviceberry flowers (*Amelanchier arborea* var. *arborea*) © Bernard L. Schwartz

Cornelian cherry (*Cornus mas*) © Bernard L. Schwartz

Cornelian cherry flowers (*Cornus mas*) © Bernard L. Schwartz

Cucumbertree (*Magnolia acuminata*) from Mary Vaux Walcott, *Wild Flowers of North America* (Washington, DC: Smithsonian Institution, 1925)

Daphne (*Daphne mezereum*) from Franz Eugen Köhler, *Köhler's Medizinal-Pflanzen* (1897)

Dogwood (*Cornus kousa*) from Philipp Franz von Siebold and Joseph Gerhard Zuccarini, *Flora Japonica, Sectio Prima* (1870)

Downy arrowwood (*Viburnum rafinesqueanum*) © Bernard L. Schwartz

Downy hawthorn (*Crataegus mollis*) from the National Geographic Society, 1915–24

Dwarf fothergilla (*Fothergilla gardenii*) © Bernard L. Schwartz

Dwarf fothergilla flowers (*Fothergilla gardenii*) © Bernard L. Schwartz

Eastern redbud (*Cercis canadensis* var. *canadensis*) © Bernard L. Schwartz

Empress tree (*Paulownia tomentosa*) from Philipp Franz von Siebold and Joseph Gerhard Zuccarini, *Flora Japonica, Sectio Prima* (1870)

English hawthorn (*Crataegus laevigata*) from Otto Wilhelm Thomé, *Flora von Deutschland, Österreich und der Schweiz* (1885)

European cranberry bush (*Viburnum opulus*) released into the public domain by Wouter Hagens

European elderberry (*Sambucus nigra*) courtesy of H. Zell

European privet (*Ligustrum vulgare*) © Bernard L. Schwartz

Flame azalea (*Rhododendron calendulaceum*) used with the permission of © Darrell Kromm of Reeseville Ridge Nursery, Reeseville, WI

Flowering almond (*Prunus glandulosa*) courtesy of Dalgial

Flowering dogwood flowers (*Cornus florida*) © Bernard L. Schwartz

Flowering dogwood tree (*Cornus florida*) © Bernard L. Schwartz

Forsythia (*Forsythia*) © Bernard L. Schwartz

Forsythia flowers (*Forsythia*) © Bernard L. Schwartz

Fringe tree (*Chionanthus virginicus*) © Bernard L. Schwartz

Fringe tree flowers (*Chionanthus virginicus*) © Bernard L. Schwartz

Gray dogwood (*Cornus racemosa*) © Bernard L. Schwartz

Highbush blueberry (*Vaccinium corymbosum*) courtesy of Kurt Stuber

Honeysuckle (*Lonicera maackii*) © Bernard L. Schwartz

Japanese flowering cherry (*Prunus serrulata*) courtsey of Kropsoq

Japanese flowering quince (*Chaenomeles japonica*) © Bernard L. Schwartz

Japanese kerria, Japanese rose (*Kerria japonica*) from Philipp Franz von Siebold and Joseph Gerhard Zuccarini, *Flora Japonica, Sectio Prima* (1870)

Japanese snowbell (*Styrax japonicus*) courtesy of Richard Webb, self-employed horticulturist, Bugwood.org.

Jetbead (*Rhodotypos scandens*) courtesy of Leslie J. Mehrhoff, University of Connecticut, Bugwood.org

Korean rhododendron (*Rhododendron mucronulatum*) released into the public domain by Daderot

Lilac (*Syringa vulgaris*) © Bernard L. Schwartz

Magnolia tree (*Magnolia*) © Bernard L. Schwartz

Mountain laurel (*Kalmia latifolia*) courtesy of Vlmastra

Nearly Wild rose (*Rosa* x 'Nearly Wild') © Bernard L. Schwartz

Ninebark flowers (*Physocarpus opulifolius*) © Bernard L. Schwartz

Ninebark shrub (*Physocarpus opulifolius*) © Bernard L. Schwartz

Northern bush honeysuckle (*Diervilla lonicera*) used with the permission of © Darrel Kromm of Reeseville Ridge Nursery, Reeseville, WI

Oriental photinia (*Photinia villosa*) courtesy of KENPEI

Ozark witch hazel (*Hamamelis vernalis*) © Bernard L. Schwartz

Pawpaw flower (*Asimia triloba*) © Bernard L. Schwartz

Pawpaw tree (*Asimia triloba*) © Bernard L. Schwartz

Pin cherry (*Prunus pensylvanica* var. *pensylvanica*) from *Curtis's Botanical Magazine,* vol. 139 (1913)

Possumhaw (*Viburnum nudum* var. *nudum*) released into the public domain by its author, Chhe

Prairie crab apple (*Malus ioensis* var. *ioensis*) © Bernard L. Schwartz

Prairie rose (*Rosa arkansana*) © Bernard L. Schwartz

Purpleflowering raspberry (*Rubus odoratus* var. *odoratus*) © Bernard L. Schwartz

Pussy willow, goat willow (*Salix caprea*) from Otto Wilhelm Thomé, *Flora von Deutschland, Österreich und der Schweiz* (1885)

Pussy willow (*Salix discolor*) © Bernard L. Schwartz

Red buckeye (*Aesculus pavia* var. *pavia*) © Bernard L. Schwartz

Red buckeye flowers (*Aesculus pavia* var. *pavia*) © Bernard L. Schwartz

Red chokeberry (*Photinia pyrifolia*) © Bernard L. Schwartz

Red chokeberry flowers (*Photinia pyrifolia*) © Bernard L. Schwartz

Roughleaf dogwood (*Cornus drummondii*) released into the public domain by John Knouse

Sand cherry (*Prunus pumila* var. *pumila*) courtesy of Rob Routledge, Sault College, Bugwood.org

Sargent crab apple (*Malus sargentii*) © Bernard L. Schwartz

Scotch broom (*Cytisus scoparius*) by Franz Eugen Köhler, *Köhler's Medizinal-Pflanzen* (1897)

Siberian peashrub (*Caragana arborescens*) by artist Pierre-Joseph Redouté (1759–1840)

Slender deutzia (*Deutzia gracilis*) in the public domain (US government photograph)

Smoketree (*Cotinus coggygria*) © Bernard L. Schwartz

Spicebush flowers (*Lindera benzoin*) courtesy of SB Johnny

Sweet mockorange (*Philadelphus coronarius*) used with the permission of © Darrel Kromm of Reeseville Ridge Nursery, Reeseville, WI

Sweetshrub (*Calycanthus floridus*) © Bernard L. Schwartz

Twinberry honeysuckle (*Lonicera involucrata*) from *Curtis's Botanical Magazine,* vol. 140 (1914)

Umbrella-tree (*Magnolia tripetala*) released into the public domain by Masebrock

Washington hawthorn (*Crataegus phaenopyrum*) © Bernard L. Schwartz

Weeping willow (*Salix babylonica*) © Bernard L. Schwartz

Weigela (*Weigela floribunda*) © Bernard L. Schwartz

Winter hazel (*Corylopsis glabrescens*) courtesy of Denis Prévôt

Yellow buckeye (*Aesculus flava)* © Bernard L. Schwartz

Yellowwood (*Cladrastis kentukea*) © Bernard L. Schwartz

Yellowwood flowers (*Cladrastis kentukea*) © Bernard L. Schwartz

Shrubs and Trees (Summer)

Adam's needle (*Yucca filamentosa*) © Bernard L. Schwartz

Alpine currant (*Ribes alpinum*) from Carl Axel Magnus Lindman, *Bilder ur Nordens Flora* (1901–5)

American aspen (*Populus tremuloides*) courtesy of USDA-NRCS PLANTS Database/D. E. Herman et al., *North Dakota Tree Handbook* (1996)

American aspen (*Populus tremuloides*) © Bernard L. Schwartz

American beech (*Fagus grandifolia*) © Bernard L. Schwartz

American beech leaves (*Fagus grandifolia*) © Bernard L. Schwartz

American black currant (*Ribes americanum*) used with the premission of © Darrel Kromm of Reeseville Ridge Nursery, Reeseville, WI

American chestnut (*Castanea dentata*) released into the public domain by Daderot

American elm (*Ulmus americana*) © Bernard L. Schwartz

American elm leaves (*Ulmus americana*) © Bernard L. Schwartz

American hornbeam (*Carpinus caroliniana*) © Bernard L. Schwartz

American hornbeam leaves (*Carpinus caroliniana*) © Bernard L. Schwartz

American linden leaves (*Tilia americana*) © Bernard L. Schwartz

American linden tree (*Tilia americana*) © Bernard L. Schwartz

American sycamore leaves (*Platanus occidentalis*) © Bernard L. Schwartz

American sycamore tree (*Platanus occidentalis*) © Bernard L. Schwartz

Amur cork tree (*Phellodendron amurense*) courtesy of Bruce Marlin, Morton Arboretum

Angelica tree (*Aralia elata*) © Bernard L. Schwartz

Ashy hydrangea (*Hydrangea cinerea*) © Bernard L. Schwartz

Aspen (European aspen) (*Populus tremula*) from Carl Axel Magnus Lindman, *Bilder ur Nordens Flora* (1901–5)

Bald cypress (*Taxodium distichum*) © Bernard L. Schwartz

Bald cypress needles (*Taxodium distichum*) © Bernard L. Schwartz

Bearberry (*Arctostaphylos uva-ursi*) courtesy of Sten Prose

Beech (European beech) (*Fagus sylvatica*) from Franz Eugen Köhler, *Köhler's Medizinal-Pflanzen* (1887)

Blackgum (*Nyssa sylvatica*) courtesy of Bostonian13

Blackgum leaves and fruit (*Nyssa sylvatica*) courtesy of Matthew C. Perry of the USGS

Black maple (*Acer nigrum*) © Bernard L. Schwartz

Black maple leaves (*Acer nigrum*) © Bernard L. Schwartz

Black walnut nuts and leaves (*Juglans nigra)* © Bernard L. Schwartz

Black walnut tree (*Juglans nigra*) © Bernard L. Schwartz

Bottlebrush buckeye (*Aesculus parviflora*) © Bernard L. Schwartz

Boxelder (*Acer negundo*) courtesy of USDA

Bur oak (*Quercus macrocarpa*) © Bernard L. Schwartz

Bur oak leaves and acorns (*Quercus macrocarpa*) © Bernard L. Schwartz

Butterfly bush (*Buddleja davidii*) © Bernard L. Schwartz

Butterfly shrub (shrubby cinquefoil) (*Potentilla fruticosa*) © Bernard L. Schwartz

Buttonbush (*Cephalanthus occidentalis*) courtesy of BotBln

Buttonbush sp. courtesy of Sten Porse

Carolina buckthorn (*Frangula caroliniana*) released into the public domain by its author, Masebrock

Chaste tree (*Vitex agnus-castus* var. *agnus-castus*) released into the public domain by Mario Bernasconi

Chestnut (Chinese Chestnut) (*Castanea mollissima*) courtesy of Jerry A. Payne, USDA Agricultural Research Service, Bugwood.org

Chinese elm (*Ulmus parvifolia*) released into the public domain by Ronnie Nijboer

Chinkapin oak (*Quercus muehlenbergii*) © Bernard L. Schwartz

Chinkapin oak leaves (*Quercus muehlenbergii*) © Bernard L. Schwartz

Clethra (sweetpepper bush) (*Clethra alnifolia*) courtesy of H. Zell

Climbing hydrangea (*Hydrangea anomala* subsp. *petiolaris*) released into the public domain by Fepup

Common buckthorn (*Frangula cathartica*) from Carl Axel Magnus Lindman, *Bilder ur Nordens Flora* (1901–5)

Cottonwood leaves (*Populus deltoides*) © Bernard L. Schwartz

Cottonwood tree (*Populus deltoides*) © Bernard L. Schwartz

Dawn redwood (*Metasequoia glyptostroboides*) released into the public domain by GatesofHell

Devil's walking stick (*Aralia spinosa*) courtesy of James H. Miller & Ted Bodner, Southern Weed Science Society, Bugwood.org

Dutchman's pipe (*Aristolochia tomentosa*) © Bernard L. Schwartz

False indigo bush (*Amorpha fruticosa*) courtesy of Jennifer Anderson @ USDA-NRCS PLANTS Database

Flowering ash (*Fraxinus ornus*) courtesy of Jean-Pol Grandmont

Ginkgo (*Ginkgo biloba*) © Bernard L. Schwartz

Golden rain tree (*Koelreuteria paniculata*) courtesy of Sten Porse

Hackberry leaves (*Celtis occidentalis*) © Bernard L. Schwartz

Hackberry tree (*Celtis occidentalis*) © Bernard L. Schwartz

Hickory (*Carya*) © Bernard L. Schwartz

Honey locust leaves (*Gleditsia triacanthos*) © Bernard L. Schwartz

Honey locust tree (*Gleditsia triacanthos*) © Bernard L. Schwartz

Hornbeam (European hornbeam) (*Carpinus betulus*) © Bernard L. Schwartz

Horse chestnut tree (*Aesculus hippocastanum*) © Bernard L. Schwartz

Hydrangea arborescens 'Annabelle' © Bernard L. Schwartz

Japanese lilac tree (*Syringa reticulata*) © Bernard L. Schwartz

Japanese pagoda tree (*Styphnolobium japonicum*) © Bernard L. Schwartz

Japanese spirea (*Spiraea japonica* var. *fortunei*) © Bernard L. Schwartz

Katsura tree (*Cercidiphyllum japonicum*) © Bernard L. Schwartz

Kentucky coffee tree (*Gymnocladus dioicus*) © Bernard L. Schwartz

Kentucky coffee tree leaves and seeds (*Gymnocladus dioicus*) © Bernard L. Schwartz

Korean evodia (*Tetradium daniellii*) courtesy of Dalgial

Leadplant (*Amorpha canescens*) © Bernard L. Schwartz

Littleleaf linden (*Tilia cordata*) © Bernard L. Schwartz

Mallow (Crimsoneyed rose mallow) (*Hibiscus moscheutos*) courtesy of Robert H. Mohlen-brock @ USDA-NRCS PLANTS Database

Mallow hedge (*Hibiscus*) © Bernard L. Schwartz

Mimosa (silk tree) (*Albizia julibrissin*) released into the public domain by Cmapm

Missouri gooseberry (*Ribes missouriense*) courtesy of Eric in SF

Mulberry tree (*Morus alba*) from Francisco Manuel Blanco, *Flora de Filipinas* (1880–83)

New Jersey tea (*Ceanothus americanus*) used with the permission of © Prairie Moon Nursery

Norway maple (*Acer platanoides*) © Bernard L. Schwartz

Norway maple leaves (*Acer platanoides*) © Bernard L. Schwartz

Oak (English oak) (*Quercus robur*) © Bernard L. Schwartz

Oak (English oak) leaves (*Quercus robur*) © Bernard L. Schwartz

Oakleaf hydrangea (*Hydrangea quercifolia*) © Bernard L. Schwartz

Ohio buckeye (*Aesculus glabra* var. *glabra*) © Bernard L. Schwartz

Ohio buckeye flowers and leaves (*Aesculus glabra* var. *glabra*) © Bernard L. Schwartz

Plane tree (*Platanus hybrida*) © Bernard L. Schwartz

Pricklyash (*Zanthoxylum americanum*) © Bernard L. Schwartz

Red maple (*Acer rubrum*) © Bernard L. Schwartz

Red maple leaves (*Acer rubrum*) © Bernard L. Schwartz

Red mulberry (*Morus rubra*) by Ellis Rowan (artist, 1847–1922).

Red oak (*Quercus rubra*) © Bernard L. Schwartz

Red oak leaves (*Quercus rubra* var. *rubra*) © Bernard L. Schwartz

Rose of Sharon (*Hibiscus syriacus*) © Bernard L. Schwartz

Seven-son flower (*Heptacodium miconioides*) released into the public domain by Pipi69e

Shagbark hickory leaves (*Carya ovata*) © Bernard L. Schwartz

Shagbark hickory tree (*Carya ovata*) © Bernard L. Schwartz

Shrubby St. John's wort (*Hypericum prolificum*) © Bernard L. Schwartz

Silver maple (*Acer saccharinum*) © Bernard L. Schwartz

Silver maple leaves (*Acer saccharinum*) © Bernard L. Schwartz

Sourwood (*Oxydendrum arboreum*) released into the public domain by its author, Jim Conrad

Steeplebush (*Spiraea tomentosa*) by Mary Vaux Walcott, *Wild Flowers of North America* (Washington, DC: Smithsonian Institution, 1925)

Stewartia (Japanese stewartia) (*Stewartia pseudocamellia*) courtesy of KENPEI

Stewartia (*Stewartia ovata*) released into the public domain by Bbwinkles

Sugar maple (*Acer saccharum*) © Bernard L. Schwartz

Sugar maple leaves (*Acer saccharum*) © Bernard L. Schwartz

Swamp white oak (*Quercus bicolor*) © Bernard L. Schwartz

Swamp white oak leaves (*Quercus bicolor*) © Bernard L. Schwartz

Sweetgum (Oriental sweetgum) (*Liquidambar orientalis*) from Franz Eugen Köhler, *Köhler's Medizinal-Pflanzen* (1897)

Sweetgum (*Liquidambar styraciflua*) © Bernard L. Schwartz

Sweetgum leaves and fruits (*Liquidambar styraciflua*) © Bernard L. Schwartz

Sycamore maple (*Acer pseudoplatanus*) from Johan Carl Krauss, *Afbeeldingen der fraaiste, meest uitheemsche boomen en heesters* (1802)

Symplocos spp. from Philipp Franz von Siebold and Joseph Gerhard Zuccarini, *Flora Japonica, Sectio Prima* (1870)

Tamarix spp. courtesy of Jerzy Opioła

Trumpet vine (*Campsis radicans*) © Bernard L. Schwartz

Tulip tree (*Liriodendron chinense*) © Bernard L. Schwartz

Tulip tree leaves (*Liriodendron chinense*) © Bernard L. Schwartz

Virginia creeper (*Parthenocissus quinquefolia*) © Bernard L. Schwartz

Virginia sweetspire (*Itea virginica*) courtesy of SB Johnny

Walnut (English walnut) (*Juglans regia*) courtesy of Georg Slickers

White ash (*Fraxinus americana*) © Bernard L. Schwartz

White ash leaves (*Fraxinus americana*) © Bernard L. Schwartz

White meadowsweet (*Spiraea alba* var. *alba*) courtesy of Robert H. Mohlenbrock @ USDA-NRCS PLANTS Database

White oak (*Quercus alba*) © Bernard L. Schwartz

White oak leaves (*Quercus alba*) © Bernard L. Schwartz

Wineberry (*Rubus phoenicolasius*) courtesy of Qwert1234

Wintercreeper (*Euonymus fortunei*) on an American elm tree © Bernard L. Schwartz

Shrubs and Trees (Fall)

American barberry (*Berberis canadensis*) used with the permission of © Paul L. Redfearn Jr., Missouri State University

American beautyberry (*Callicarpa americana*) © Bernard L. Schwartz

American mountain ash (*Sorbus americana*) courtesy of Fungus Guy

American strawberry bush (*Euonymus americanus*) courtesy of James H. Miller & Ted Bodner, Southern Weed Science Society, Bugwood.org

American witch hazel (*Hamamelis virginiana*) from Franz Eugen Köhler, *Köhler's Medizinal-Pflanzen* (1897)

Bayberry (*Myrica pensylvanica*) in fall © Bernard L. Schwartz

Burning bush (*Euonymus alatus*) © Bernard L. Schwartz

Coralberry (*Symphoricarpos orbiculatus*) used with the permission of © Prairie Moon Nursery

Cotoneaster spp. from Jacob Sturm, *Deutschlands Flora in Abbildunge* (1796)

Cutleaf stephanandra (*Stephanandra incisa*) courtesy of Qwert123

Eastern burning bush (*Euonymus atropurpureus*) used with the premission of © Darrel Kromm of Reeseville Ridge Nursery, Reeseville, WI

Fragrant sumac (*Rhus aromatica*) © Bernard L. Schwartz

Japanese barberry (*Berberis thunbergii*) © Bernard L. Schwartz

Japanese beautyberry (*Callicarpa japonica*) © Bernard L. Schwartz

Japanese maple (*Acer palmatum*) © Bernard L. Schwartz

Mountain ash (*Sorbus aucuparia*) courtesy of Andreas Steinhoff

Mountain maple (*Acer spicatum*) from F. André Michaux, *The North American sylva, or A description of the forest trees of the United States, Canada and Nova Scotia . . .* (1819)

Osage orange (*Maclura pomifera*) courtesy of H. Zell

Possumhaw (*Ilex decidua*) from the USDA

Russet buffaloberry (*Shepherdia canadensis*) courtesy of Robert Flogaus-Faust

Russian olive (*Elaeagnus angustifolia*) © Bernard L. Schwartz

Scarlet firethorn (*Pyracantha coccinea*) courtesy of Brosen
Silver buffaloberry (*Shepherdia argentea*) courtesy of Julia Adamson, photographer in the Saskatoon area
Snowberry (*Symphoricarpos albus*) © Bernard L. Schwartz
Sumac (Chinese sumac) (*Rhus chinensis*) courtesy of KENPEI
Sumac spp. © Bernard L. Schwartz
Tree of heaven (*Ailanthus altissima*) © Bernard L. Schwartz
Tree of heaven leaves and flowers (*Ailanthus altissima*) © Bernard L. Schwartz
Winterberry (*Ilex verticillata*) courtesy of Rob Routledge, Sault College, Bugwood.org

Shrubs in Fall Gallery

American cranberrybush in fall © Bernard L. Schwartz
Arrowwood in fall © Bernard L. Schwartz
Black chokeberry in fall © Bernard L. Schwartz
Blackhaw in fall © Bernard L. Schwartz
Bottlebrush buckeye in fall © Bernard L. Schwartz
Downy hawthorn berries © Bernard L. Schwartz
Elderberry berries © Bernard L. Schwartz
Gray dogwood in fall © Bernard L. Schwartz
Ninebark in fall © Bernard L. Schwartz
Oakleaf hydrangea in fall © Bernard L. Schwartz
Prairie rose leaves and hips in fall © Bernard L. Schwartz
Red chokeberry in fall © Bernard L. Schwartz
Serviceberry in fall © Bernard L. Schwartz
Sumac spp. in fall © Bernard L. Schwartz

Trees in Fall Gallery

American elm in fall © Bernard L. Schwartz
American hazelnut in fall © Bernard L. Schwartz
American hornbeam in fall © Bernard L. Schwartz
American linden in fall © Bernard L. Schwartz
American sycamore tree in fall © Bernard L. Schwartz
Bald cypress in fall © Bernard L. Schwartz
Buckeye (Ohio buckeye) in fall © Bernard L. Schwartz
Bur oak leaves in fall © Bernard L. Schwartz
Canoe birch in fall © Bernard L. Schwartz
Catalpa in fall © Bernard L. Schwartz
Chinkapin oak in fall © Bernard L. Schwartz
Cottonwood in fall © Bernard L. Schwartz
Fringe tree in fall © Bernard L. Schwartz
Hackberry in fall © Bernard L. Schwartz
Hill's oak leaves in fall © Bernard L. Schwartz
Honey locust in fall © Bernard L. Schwartz
Kentucky coffee tree in fall © Bernard L. Schwartz
Maple in fall © Bernard L. Schwartz
Oak spp. in fall © Bernard L. Schwartz

Redbud tree in fall © Bernard L. Schwartz
Red oak tree in fall © Bernard L. Schwartz
River birch in fall © Bernard L. Schwartz
Scarlet oak in fall © Bernard L. Schwartz
Shagbark hickory in fall © Bernard L. Schwartz
Shumard oak leaves in fall © Bernard L. Schwartz
Silver maple in fall © Bernard L. Schwartz
Sugar maple in fall © Bernard L. Schwartz
Swamp white oak in fall © Bernard L. Schwartz
Sweetgum tree in fall © Bernard L. Schwartz
Tulip tree in fall © Bernard L. Schwartz
Washington hawthorn berries in fall © Bernard L. Schwartz
White ash tree in fall © Bernard L. Schwartz
Yellowwood in fall © Bernard L. Schwartz

Shrubs and Trees (Winter)

Alder (black alder) (*Alnus glutinosa*) courtesy of Bruce Martin, Morton Arboretum
Alder (speckled alder) (*Alnus incana* subsp. *rugosa*) from Carl Axel Magnus Lindman, *Bilder ur Nordens Flora* (1901–5)
American arborvitae (*Thuja occidentalis*) © Bernard L. Schwartz
American holly (*Ilex opaca* var. *opaca*) courtesy of James H. Miller & Ted Bodner, Southern Weed Science Society, Bugwood.org
American yew (*Taxus canadensis*) © Bernard L. Schwartz
Austrian pine (*Pinus nigra*) © Bernard L. Schwartz
Bloodtwig dogwood (*Cornus sanguinea*) © Bernard L. Schwartz
Boxwood spp. © Bernard L. Schwartz
Canoe birch (*Betula papyrifera* var. *papyrifera*)© Bernard L. Schwartz
Chinese arborvitae (*Platycladus orientalis*) courtesy of Bruce Martin, Morton Arboretum
Chinese juniper (*Juniperus chinensis*) courtesy of Fanghong
Common juniper (*Juniperus communis* var. *depressa*) courtesy of Chris Cant
Eastern white pine (*Pinus strobus*) courtesy of USFWS
European white birch (*Betula pendula*) © Bernard L. Schwartz
False cypress (*Chamaecyparis pisifera*) courtesy of Bruce Martin, Morton Arboretum
Harry Lauder's walking stick (*Corylus avellana* 'Contorta') courtesy of Schnobby
Hemlock (*Tsuga canadensis*) © Bernard L. Schwartz
Holly (English holly) (*Ilex aquifolium*) courtesy of Erich Ferdinand
Inkberry (*Ilex glabra*) courtesy of James H. Miller, USDA Forest Service, Bugwood.org
Jack pine (*Pinus banksiana*) courtesy of USDA-NRCS PLANTS Database/D. E. Herman et al., *North Dakota Tree Handbook* (1996)
Japanese cedar (*Cryptomeria japonica*) from Philipp Franz von Siebold and Joseph Gerhard Zuccarini, *Flora Japonica, Sectio Prima* (1870)
Japanese hemlock (*Tsuga diversifolia*) courtesy of Sten Porse
Japanese yew (*Taxus cuspidata*) courtesy Kurt Stuber
Mugo pine (*Pinus mugo*) © Bernard L. Schwartz
Norway spruce (*Picea abies*) © Bernard L. Schwartz
Red cedar (*Juniperus virginiana* var. *virginiana*) © Bernard L. Schwartz
Redosier dogwood (*Cornus sericea* subsp. *sericea* syn. *C. stolonifera*) © Bernard L. Schwartz

Red pine (*Pinus resinosa*) courtesy of USFWS
River birch (*Betula nigra*) © Bernard L. Schwartz
Russian arborvitae (*Microbiota decussata*) courtesy of Kym
White spruce (*Picea glauca*) courtesy of USDA-NRCS PLANTS Database/D. E. Herman et al.,
    North Dakota Tree Handbook (1996)

Shrubs in Winter Gallery

Ashy hydrangea in winter © Bernard L. Schwartz
Black chokeberry in winter © Bernard L. Schwartz
Oakleaf hydrangea in winter © Bernard L. Schwartz
Prairie rose hips in winter © Bernard L. Schwartz
Red chokeberry in winter © Bernard L. Schwartz
Serviceberry in winter © Bernard L. Schwartz
Shrubby St. John's wort in winter © Bernard L. Schwartz

Trees in Winter Gallery

American beech in winter © Bernard L. Schwartz
American elm in winter © Bernard L. Schwartz
American witch hazel in winter © Bernard L. Schwartz
American sycamore in winter © Bernard L. Schwartz
Bur oak in winter © Bernard L. Schwartz
Catalpa in winter © Bernard L. Schwartz
Cottonwood in winter © Bernard L. Schwartz
Honey locust in winter © Bernard L. Schwartz
Kentucky coffee tree in winter © Bernard L. Schwartz
Oak trees in winter © Bernard L. Schwartz
Redbud in winter © Bernard L. Schwartz
Red maple in winter © Bernard L. Schwartz
Redosier dogwood in winter © Bernard L. Schwartz
Sweetgum in winter © Bernard L. Schwartz
American sycamore in winter © Bernard L. Schwartz
Tulip tree in winter © Bernard L. Schwartz
Washington hawthorn in winter © Bernard L. Schwartz
Yellowwood in winter © Bernard L. Schwartz

INDEX

COLOR KEY

Green: Native plants

Red: Nonnative plants

Note: The first entry is the location of the image and/or the description or reference.

ABELIA, 13

Abugattas, Alonso, 131, 202, 241

ADAM'S NEEDLE, 125

Air and water quality/flooding, 2, 3

ALDER, 316

ALDER, 316–17, 55, 118, 168, 246, 260, 305, 313, 394

ALDER BUCKTHORN. See GLOSSY BUCKTHORN

ALDERLEAF BUCKTHORN, 141

ALLEGHENY CHINKAPIN, 171, 125, 230, 246, 260, 313, 316, 332

ALLEGHENY SERVICEBERRY, 77

ALLSPICE BUSH. *See* SPICEBUSH

ALPINE CURRANT, 137

ALTERNATELEAF DOGWOOD, 49, 81, 85, 93, 114, 148, 253, 260, 312, 316, 334

ALTHAEA. See ROSE OF SHARON

AMERICAN ALDER BUCKTHORN. *See* ALDERLEAF BUCKTHORN

AMERICAN AMPELOPSIS. *See* HEARTLEAF PEPPERVINE

AMERICAN ARBORVITAE, 318–19, 52, 142, 309, 315, 324, 332, 394

AMERICAN ASPEN, 165, 118

AMERICAN BARBERRY, 233, 42, 139, 377

AMERICAN BASSWOOD. *See* AMERICAN LINDEN

AMERICAN BEAUTYBERRY, 235, 40, 147–48, 234, 245, 247, 250, 314, 395

AMERICAN BEECH, 168–69, 88, 101, 159, 171, 180, 200, 210, 212, 221, 225, 228, 260, 332; AMERICAN BEECH IN WINTER, 342

AMERICAN BLACK CURRANT, 138, 23, 36, 40, 42, 63, 142, 151, 234, 246, 248, 260, 369

AMERICAN BLACK ELDERBERRY, 29–30, 238, 246; ELDERBERRY BERRIES, 266

AMERICAN BLADDERNUT, 41, 15, 16, 45–46, 81, 85, 95, 105, 117, 187, 238, 246, 260, 316, 334, 395

AMERICAN BOXWOOD. See BOXWOOD

AMERICAN BURNING BUSH. *See* EASTERN BURNING BUSH

AMERICAN CHESTNUT, 170–71, 210, 260

AMERICAN CRAB APPLE, 89

AMERICAN CRANBERRYBUSH, 69, 52, 142; AMERICAN CRANBERRYBUSH IN FALL, 262

AMERICAN ELM, 176–/8, 16/, 174, 201, 322; AMERICAN ELM IN FALL, 274; AMERICAN ELM IN WINTER, 343. *See also* ELM

AMERICAN FILBERT. *See* AMERICAN HAZELNUT

AMERICAN FLY HONEYSUCKLE, 38, 41, 128, 146

AMERICAN GOOSEBERRY, 139

AMERICAN HACKBERRY. *See* HACKBERRY

AMERICAN HAZELNUT, 102, 52, 55, 75, 102, 105, 118, 142, 171, 260, 312, 316, 332, 344, 394; AMERICAN HAZELNUT IN FALL, 274; AMERICAN HAZELNUT IN WINTER, 344

AMERICAN HOLLY, 313, 52, 234, 237–38, 246, 248, 250, 260, 308, 334

AMERICAN HOP HORNBEAM. *See* HOP HORNBEAM

AMERICAN HORNBEAM, 182–85, 81, 178, 187–88, 212, 253, 260, 332, 394; AMERICAN HORNBEAM IN FALL, 275

AMERICAN HYDRANGEA. *See* ASHY
HYDRANGEA
AMERICAN LARCH, 189, 173, 260
AMERICAN LINDEN, 190–91, 81, 88, 101, 181,
187, 189, 255; AMERICAN LINDEN IN
FALL, 275
AMERICAN MOUNTAIN ASH, 255, 81,
149, 159, 164, 181, 194, 253, 255, 257, 259
AMERICAN PLANETREE. *See* AMERI-
CAN SYCAMORE
AMERICAN PLUM, 78, 11, 15, 16, 19, 21, 24,
31, 36, 45, 47, 63, 67, 74–75, 78, 80, 84, 248,
253, 312, 332
AMERICAN RED RASPBERRY, 139
AMERICAN RHODODENDRON. *See*
ROSEBAY RHODODENDRON
AMERICAN SMOKETREE, 65–66, 15, 45, 81,
85, 93, 95, 114, 142, 246, 248, 253, 260, 312,
316, 334, 365
AMERICAN SNOWBELL, 116–17
AMERICAN STRAWBERRY BUSH, 241,
157, 230, 238, 314
AMERICAN SYCAMORE, 214, 159, 193, 260,
332; AMERICAN SYCAMORE IN
FALL, 276; AMERICAN SYCAMORE
IN WINTER, 352
AMERICAN WHITE BIRCH. *See* GRAY
BIRCH
AMERICAN WILD RED CHERRY. *See*
CHOKECHERRY
AMERICAN WISTERIA, 43, 75, 156–57
AMERICAN WITCH HAZEL, 244–45, 75,
230, 241, 253, 257, 259–60, 312, 316;
AMERICAN WITCH HAZEL IN
WINTER, 344
AMERICAN YEW, 314, 52, 142, 307, 309, 315,
324, 334, 379
AMUR CHERRY, 81
AMUR CHOKECHERRY. See AMUR
CHERRY
AMUR CORK TREE, 158, 189, 371
AMUR HONEYSUCKLE, 37
AMUR MAACKIA. See MAACKIA
AMUR MAPLE, 251, 76, 149, 377–78
Anachronistic plants, 107, 113, 124, 159, 163–64,
179, 259, 313
AMUR PEPPERVINE. See PORCELAIN-
BERRY VINE
ANGEL-FRUITED STUARTIA. *See*
STEWARTIA
ANGELICA TREE, 123, 185
ANGELICA TREE. *See* DEVIL'S WALK-
ING STICK

ANNABELLE HYDRANGEA, 143
Ants, 18, 87, 211, 304–5
APPALACHIAN MOCK-ORANGE. *See*
SCENTLESS MOCK ORANGE
APPLE SERVICEBERRY, 77, 382
ARALIA. *See* DEVIL'S WALKING STICK
ARBORVITAE, 306–7, 318
ARBORVITAE. *See* AMERICAN
ARBORVITAE
ARKANSAS ROSE. *See* PRAIRIE ROSE
'ARNOLD'S RED' (TATARIAN HONEY-
SUCKLE), 37
ARROWWOOD VIBURNUM, 70, 73; AR-
ROWWOOD IN FALL, 263
ASH, 161
ASH, 161–62, 21, 28, 45–46, 52, 67, 81, 85, 93, 95,
105, 114, 117, 124–25, 149, 151, 159, 167, 179,
181, 194, 221, 226, 239, 246, 253–57, 259–60,
300, 316, 334, 371, 378, 394–95; WHITE
ASH TREE IN FALL, 300
ASHLEAF MAPLE. *See* BOXELDER
ASHY HYDRANGEA, 143, 120, 149, 309;
ASHY HYDRANGEA IN WINTER,
336
ASIAN BUSH HONEYSUCKLE. See
HONEYSUCKLE
ASIAN WHITE BIRCH, 320
ASIATIC DOGWOOD, 93
ASPEN, 164, 215, 250, 319, 330
ASPEN, 165, 11, 118, 166–67, 176, 201, 211, 260,
320, 322–23, 330, 332, 371, 394
ATLANTIC NINEBARK. *See* NINEBARK
AUSTRIAN PINE, 327
AUTUMN OLIVE, 229, 3, 15, 76, 168, 250, 319
AZALEA. See RHODODENDRON,
AZALEA
AZALEA, 56–58, 14, 21, 25, 33, 41, 45, 129, 139,
144, 180, 246, 394

BABYLON WEEPING WILLOW. See
WEEPING WILLOW
BALD CYPRESS, 172–73, 190, 218, 260; BALD
CYPRESS IN FALL, 277
BALM OF GILEAD. *See* BALSAM
POPLAR
BALSAM FIR, 330, 324
BALSAM POPLAR, 165
BARBERRY, 231, 3, 33, 40, 42, 140–42, 225–26,
308–9, 314, 369, 376–77, 383, 394
BARBERRY. *See* AMERICAN BARBERRY
BASKET OAK. *See* SWAMP CHESTNUT
OAK
BASSWOOD. *See* LINDEN

BAYBERRY, 232, 52, 73, 142, 157, 180, 230, 238, 247, 309, 314, 316, 334, 394
BAY WILLOW. See LAUREL WILLOW
BEAKED HAZELNUT, 102
BEARBERRY, 156–57, 28, 58
BEAUTYBERRY, 234, 125
BEAUTYBUSH, 15
BEECH, 168
BEECH. *See* AMERICAN BEECH
BEE TREE. *See* AMERICAN LINDEN; WHITE BASSWOOD
BELL'S HONEYSUCKLE. See SHOWY FLY HONEYSUCKLE
BICOLOR OAK. *See* SWAMP WHITE OAK
BIGFRUIT HAWTHORN, 107
BIGLEAF HYDRANGEA. See FRENCH HYDRANGEA
BIGLEAF LINDEN, 190
BIGLEAF MAGNOLIA, 110, 181, 187, 192, 194
BIGLEAF SNOWBELL, 117
BIGTOOTH ASPEN, 165
BIGTREE PLUM. *See* MEXICAN PLUM
BIRCH, 320, 169
BIRCH, 320, 168; CANOE BIRCH IN FALL, 279; RIVER BIRCH IN FALL, 297
BIRD CHERRY. *See* PIN CHERRY
Birds
    American crow, 244, 30, 51, 212, 220, 223, 330
    American goldfinch, 145, 55, 103, 128, 132, 134, 180, 183, 199, 312, 322, 325, 329, 357
    American kestrel, 55
    American redstart, 89, 54, 112
    American robin, 62, 12, 14, 19, 21, 23, 30, 36, 39, 51, 73, 75, 79, 88, 91, 99, 108, 112, 132, 154–55, 175, 184, 201, 219, 232, 235, 237–38, 241, 244–45, 304, 307, 314, 318
    American woodcock, 317
    Baltimore oriole, 167, 19, 21, 51, 91, 139, 154–55, 178–79, 201, 238, 371
    Blackburnian warbler, 326, 318
    Black-capped chickadee, 322, 14, 28, 54, 55, 199, 237, 318, 325
    Black-throated blue warbler, 325–26, 167
    Black-throated green warbler, 319, 322, 325, 330
    Blue jay, 79, 28, 36, 73, 91, 103, 112, 154, 169, 171, 212, 238, 304, 307, 314, 317, 325, 374
    Bobwhite quail, 36, 51, 62, 93, 134, 146, 154–55, 212, 223, 312
    Brown thrasher, 219, 12, 14, 19, 21, 30, 36, 51, 61–62, 108, 139, 154, 175, 212, 235, 238, 244, 255, 307
    Cape May warbler, 318

Cedar waxwing, 36, 14, 19, 21, 30, 51, 62, 73, 106, 108, 154, 175, 238, 255–56, 307, 314, 322, 324
Chipping sparrow, 51, 145, 307
Common redpoll, 54, 55, 73, 317–18, 322, 329
Dark-eyed junco, 322, 55, 75, 145, 214, 245, 307, 325, 329, 332
Downy woodpecker, 55
Eastern bluebird, 61, 19, 21, 30, 51, 73, 91, 94, 99, 154, 212, 241, 244, 255, 259, 329
Eastern kingbird, 55, 19, 22, 51, 108, 132, 139, 154, 201, 307
Eastern towhee, 235
Evening grosbeak, 162, 51, 139, 255, 317–18, 330, 332
Field sparrow, 307, 128, 145
Fox sparrow, 322, 55, 106, 108, 145
Golden kinglet, 30, 54
Gray catbird, 79, 19, 21, 23, 28, 30, 41, 51, 55, 62, 73, 91, 99, 139, 154, 175, 184, 201, 232, 235, 238, 244, 255–56, 307
Great crested flycatcher, 22, 51, 112
Hooded warbler, 99
House wren, 28
Loggerhead shrike, 259, 108
Magnolia warbler, 319, 326
Northern cardinal, 61, 14, 19, 21, 30, 36, 39, 41, 51, 73, 75, 91, 93, 108, 139, 154, 162, 175, 180, 183–84, 235, 237–38, 241, 245, 307, 314, 318
Northern flicker, 99, 14, 19, 51, 91, 112, 175, 199, 201, 219, 238, 244
Northern mockingbird, 256, 19, 21, 22, 51, 73, 91, 154, 175, 244, 244, 307
Northern parula warbler, 167
Orchard oriole, 91
Pine siskin, 54, 55, 189, 317–18, 322, 325, 329
Pine warbler, 312, 307, 329
Prairie warbler, 200, 307
Prothonotary warbler, 55
Purple finch, 145, 51, 62, 91, 108, 154–55, 162, 167, 169, 180, 184, 199, 214, 238, 244, 329
Red-bellied woodpecker, 55
Red-breasted nuthatch, 322, 30, 55, 154, 162, 200, 212, 220–21, 312, 329, 333
Red-eyed vireo, 112, 22–23, 30, 125, 238, 244
Red-headed woodpecker, 212, 19, 30, 51, 99, 103, 154, 214
Red-winged blackbird, 55, 28, 128, 146
Rose-breasted grosbeak, 200, 19, 21, 51, 62, 73, 93, 108, 139, 238
Ruby-crowned kinglet, 233, 30, 54, 232
Ruby-throated hummingbird, 91, 18, 21, 33, 35, 38–39, 58, 80, 88, 91, 98, 101, 130, 132, 134, 139, 146–47, 155, 159, 228, 322, 325

Birds (*cont.*)

Ruffed grouse, 36, 51, 55, 103, 106, 108, 112, 165, 169, 183, 199, 212, 255, 317, 326

Rusty grackle, 55

Song sparrow, 307, 51, 91, 145

Sparrow hawk, 55

Swamp sparrow, 317

Tree swallow, 55, 51, 232, 322

Tufted titmouse, 169, 21, 51, 75, 91, 134, 154, 212, 232, 245

Warbling vireo, 55

White-breasted nuthatch, 30, 154, 162, 169, 212, 220–21, 312, 329, 333

White-throated sparrow, 108, 19, 23, 54, 91, 139, 244

White-winged crossbill, 317, 307, 312, 325, 329

Wild turkey, 244, 39, 51, 94, 99, 103, 105, 112, 113, 134, 154, 162, 169, 171, 173, 175, 199, 212, 219, 220, 223, 241, 256, 326, 329

Willow flycatcher, 55

Wood duck, 162, 51, 55, 146, 169, 173, 183, 192, 199, 201, 212, 214, 223

Wood thrush, 175, 14, 19, 21, 22, 23, 30, 39, 41, 51, 61, 73, 99, 108, 139, 154, 169, 183, 219, 238, 244, 307, 319

Yellow-bellied sapsucker, 79, 51, 55, 91, 154, 169, 175, 180, 221, 228, 307, 322, 329

Yellow-breasted chat, 91

Yellow-rumped warbler, 183, 232

Yellow-shafted flicker, 51

Yellow-throated warbler, 330, 173

Yellow warbler, 89, 54–55, 128, 167

BITTERNUT HICKORY, 221, 332

BLACK ALDER. See ALDER

BLACK ASH, 161

BLACK BIRCH. *See* SWEET BIRCH

BLACK CHERRY, 82, 18–19, 112, 178, 180–81, 185, 187, 209, 211, 260, 322, 366, 394

BLACK CHOKEBERRY, 13, 40; BLACK CHOKEBERRY IN FALL, 264; BLACK CHOKEBERRY IN WINTER, 337

BLACK ELDERBERRY. See ELDERBERRY

BLACKGUM, 218, 81, 159, 164, 178, 180, 185, 192, 200, 253, 257, 260, 332, 394

BLACKHAW, 70–72, 52, 81, 85, 93, 114, 246, 260; BLACKHAW IN FALL, 265

BLACK HAWTHORN. *See* DOUGLAS HAWTHORN

BLACK HICKORY, 221–22

BLACK HUCKLEBERRY, 28, 40, 157

BLACKJACK OAK, 204, 211, 253

BLACK JETBEAD. See JETBEAD

BLACK LOCUST, 100–101, 92, 361, 367, 394

BLACK MAPLE, 199, 252

BLACK MULBERRY, 195, 200

BLACK OAK, 204–7, 201, 209, 211

BLACK POPLAR, 164

BLACK POPLAR. *See* SWAMP COTTONWOOD

BLACK RASPBERRY, 139

BLACK SPRUCE, 332

BLACK TUPELO. *See* BLACKGUM

BLACK TWINBERRY. *See* TWINBERRY HONEYSUCKLE

BLACK WALNUT, 220–21, xii, 21, 22, 30, 39, 41, 43–44, 49–50, 53, 62, 70–72, 75, 78, 80, 83–84, 92, 94, 98–100, 102, 105, 108, 111, 114, 124–25, 134, 143, 145, 153–55, 159, 163–64, 169–70, 176, 179–80, 182, 185, 193, 200, 204, 206–8, 212, 214, 218, 223, 241–42, 245, 256, 258–60, 306, 317–18, 322, 324, 358

BLACK WILLOW, 118–19, 55, 167, 201

BLADDERNUT, 15, 323

BLOODTWIG DOGWOOD, 309–10

BLOODTWIG DOGWOOD. *See* REDOSIER DOGWOOD

BLUE ASH, 161

BLUE BEECH. *See* AMERICAN HORNBEAM

BLUEBERRY, 27–28, 20–21, 25, 38–39, 58, 139, 151, 157, 246, 248, 394

BLUE-FRUITED DOGWOOD. *See* SILKY DOGWOOD

BLUE HAW. *See* RUSTY BLACKHAW

BLUNT-LEAVED PRIVET. See BORDER PRIVET

BORDER PRIVET, 48

BORDERS, 129

BORDERS, vii, 5, 13, 50, 102, 130, 133, 143, 225, 227, 237, 245, 311, 393. *See also* HEDGES

BOTTLEBRUSH BUCKEYE, 130–31, 33, 99, 125, 137, 150, 185, 246, 334, 369, 394; BOTTLEBRUSH BUCKEYE IN FALL, 266

BOXELDER, 193, 199, 260, 332, 394

BOXWOOD, 308, vii, 141

BRADFORD PEAR, 76, 20, 146, 184, 186, 250, 366, 375, 383, 386

BRAMBLE, 139

BRIDALWREATH SPIREA. See SPIREA

BROOKSIDE ALDER. *See* HAZEL ALDER

BUCKEYE, OHIO, 184–85; YELLOW, 98

BUCKTHORN, 140–41, 6, 37, 125, 169

BUDDLEJALEAF VIBURNUM, 68

BUFFALO BELLOWS. *See* LEADPLANT

BUFFALOBERRY. See SILVERBERRY
BUFFALO CURRANT. See GOLDEN CURRANT
BULL PINE. See LOBLOLLY PINE
BUMALD SPIREA, 126, 67
BUNCHBERRY DOGWOOD, 157
BURNING BUSH, 239–40, vii, 14, 21, 27, 77, 141, 144, 146, 225–26, 234, 247, 250, 314, 316, 334
BUR OAK, 202–4, 208–11; BUR OAK LEAVES IN FALL, 279; BUR OAK IN WINTER, 350
Burrell, C. Colston, 44, 49, 99, 118, 123, 132, 141, 314, 358, 363, 368, 376, 379
BURR OAK. See BUR OAK
BURSTING-HEART. See AMERICAN STRAWBERRY BUSH
BUSH CLOVER. See SHRUBBY LESPEDEZA
Butler, Eloise, 89, 106, 304
Butterflies
    Acadian hairstreak butterfly, 54
    Banded hairstreak butterfly, 210, 223
    Clouded sulphur butterfly, 101
    Common buckeye butterfly, 33
    Compton tortoiseshell butterfly, 322
    Coral hairstreak butterfly, 18
    Eastern comma butterfly, 177
    Eastern tiger swallowtail butterfly, 18, 22, 112, 124, 167, 183, 255
    Edwards' hairstreak, 210, 211
    Frosted elfin butterfly, 329
    Giant swallowtail butterfly, 45, 125
    Gorgone checkerspot butterfly, 130
    Green comma butterfly, 103, 317
    Hackberry emperor butterfly, 176
    Henry's elfin, 93, 18, 30, 73, 92, 139, 238
    Hoary edge butterfly, 135
    Horace's duskywing butterfly, 210, 211
    Juniper hairstreak butterfly, 307
    Juvenal's duskywing skipper, 102
    Karner blue butterfly, 128, 127
    Marine blue butterfly, 43
    Monarch butterfly, 124, 54, 127, 133, 167, 244, 357, 382, 395
    Monarch butterfly caterpillar, 124
    Mourning cloak butterfly, 62, 167, 176, 201, 322
    Northern broken dash butterfly, 135
    Oak hairstreak butterfly, 211
    Orange sulphur butterfly, 101
    Painted lady butterfly, 132
    Peck's skipper, 135, 73, 134
    Pipevine swallowtail butterfly, 156
    Question mark butterfly, 176
    Red admiral butterfly, 191–92
    Red-spotted purple butterfly, 18, 102–3
    Silver-spotted skipper, 101, 43, 132, 154, 155, 164, 192
    Sleepy duskywing skipper, 210
    Southern dogface butterfly, 133
    Spicebush swallowtail butterfly, 22, 125, 179
    Spring azure butterfly, 95, 38, 134
    Striped hairstreak butterfly, 18, 108
    Summer azure butterfly, 128, 127
    Viceroy butterfly, 54, 167
    White M hairstreak butterfly, 211
    Zebra swallowtail butterfly, 114
BUTTERFLY BUSH, 129, 2, 121, 128, 132–36, 359, 369
BUTTERFLY SHRUB, 129–30, 23, 36, 42, 63, 122, 137
BUTTERNUT, 220, 394
BUTTONBUSH, 131, 45
BUTTONWOOD. See AMERICAN SYCAMORE

CABBAGE ROSE, 60
CALIFORNIA PRIVET, 48
CALLERY PEAR. See BRADFORD PEAR
CANADA YEW. See AMERICAN YEW
CANADIAN BUFFALOBERRY. See RUSSET BUFFALOBERRY
CANADIAN HEMLOCK, 325
CANADIAN PINE. See RED PINE
CANADIAN PLUM, 79
CANOE BIRCH, 320, 176, 317; CANOE BIRCH IN FALL, 279
CAROLINA ALLSPICE. See SWEETSHRUB
CAROLINA BUCKTHORN, 141, 149, 234, 246, 253, 260
CAROLINA FALSE BUCKTHORN. See CAROLINA BUCKTHORN
CAROLINA ROSE. See PASTURE ROSE
CAROLINA SILVERBELL, 80, 21, 24, 36, 45, 63, 66, 73, 75, 84, 92–93, 95, 101, 105, 114, 117, 129, 246, 253, 260, 316, 332
CATALPA, 85, 170, 323
CATALPA, 86–88, 80, 101, 180, 181, 185, 187, 188, 192, 193, 194, 195, 201, 260, 333, 394; CATALPA IN FALL, 280; CATALPA IN WINTER, 345
CATAWBA RHODODENDRON, 57
CAUCASIAN LINDEN, 190
CAUCASIAN SPRUCE. See ORIENTAL SPRUCE

Cavity-nesting mammals and birds, 87, 192, 199, 212, 376

CEDAR, 323, 149

CEDAR, 323, 52, 121, 142, 207, 239, 307, 309, 318, 324, 326, 332, 394

CHASTE TREE, 136

CHERRY, 16, 81–82, 17, 21, 115, 146, 170, 215, 229

CHERRY, 17–19, 82–84, 11, 24, 25, 28, 31, 33, 36, 45, 46, 53, 63, 66, 73, 74, 79, 80, 93, 95, 101, 112, 141, 142, 157, 170, 178, 179, 180, 181, 185, 187, 198, 209, 211, 239, 246, 248, 253, 255, 260, 322, 381, 386, 394

CHERRY, PLUM, 81–82, 17, 115, 180, 394

CHERRY, PLUM, ALMOND, 16–17, 82, 115

CHERRYBARK OAK, 209

CHERRY BIRCH. *See* SWEET BIRCH

CHERRY SILVERBERRY, 229

CHESTNUT, 170

CHESTNUT, 170–71, 122, 212, 260, 311, 394

CHESTNUT OAK, 204, 209, 311, 373, 379

Chicago Botanic Garden, 13, 27, 66, 391

CHICKASAW PLUM, 79

CHINESE ARBORVITAE. See ARBORVITAE

CHINESE ASH, 161

CHINESE BUCKTHORN, 140

CHINESE BUTTONBUSH, 131

CHINESE CATALPA, 85, 324

CHINESE CHESTNUT. See CHESTNUT

CHINESE ELM, 173–74

CHINESE FRINGE TREE. See FRINGE TREE

CHINESE JUNIPER, 309, 326

CHINESE PLUM. See FLOWERING ALMOND

CHINESE PRIVET, 48

CHINESE REDBUD. See REDBUD

CHINESE SUMAC. See SUMAC

CHINESE TULIP TREE, 219

CHINESE WISTERIA, 43, 75

CHINESE WITCH HAZEL, 74

CHINKAPIN OAK, 204–5, 24, 55, 142, 311; CHINKAPIN OAK IN FALL, 281

CHINQUAPIN OAK. *See* CHINKAPIN OAK

CHOCOLATE VINE. See FIVE LEAF AKEBIA

CHOKEBERRY, 13–14, 15, 21, 24, 25, 28, 31, 33, 36, 39, 40, 41, 45, 46, 47, 52, 63, 64, 67, 73, 74, 83, 139, 142, 144, 230, 234, 239, 248, 260, 264, 309, 316, 334, 362, 394; BLACK CHOKEBERRY IN FALL, 264; BLACK CHOKEBERRY IN WINTER, 337; RED CHOKEBERRY IN FALL, 261, 269; RED CHOKEBERRY IN WINTER, 338

CHOKECHERRY, 83, 11, 13, 19, 36, 45, 46, 63, 66, 73, 74, 75, 83, 142, 239, 246, 248, 260, 316, 332, 362, 366, 386

CIGAR TREE. *See* NORTHERN CATALPA

CLETHRA, 132, 122, 128, 137, 142, 146, 149–50, 239, 246, 316, 334, 395

CLIMBING EUONYMUS. See WINTERCREEPER

CLIMBING HYDRANGEA, 153

CLIMBING HYDRANGEA, 153

CLIMBING PRAIRIE ROSE. *See* CLIMBING ROSE

CLIMBING ROSE, 60

CLOVE CURRANT. *See* GOLDEN CURRANT

COASTAL SWEETPEPPER BUSH. *See* CLETHRA

COCKSPUR HAWTHORN. *See* COCKSPUR THORN

COCKSPUR THORN, 106

COFFEETREE. *See* KENTUCKY COFFEE TREE

COLORADO BLUE SPRUCE. See COLORADO SPRUCE

COLORADO SPRUCE, 330

COMMON ALDER. See ALDER

COMMON BARBERRY, 231

COMMON BEECH. See BEECH

COMMON BLACKBERRY, 139

COMMON BOXWOOD. See BOXWOOD

COMMON BRIAR ROSE, 60

COMMON BUCKTHORN. See EUROPEAN BUCKTHORN

COMMON CHOKECHERRY. *See* CHOKECHERRY

COMMON ELM. See ENGLISH ELM

COMMON FILBERT. See FILBERT

COMMON FLOWERING QUINCE, 31

COMMON HACKBERRY. *See* HACKBERRY

COMMON HAWTHORN. See HAWTHORN; ONESEED HAWTHORN

COMMON HORNBEAM. See HORNBEAM

COMMON HORSE CHESTNUT. See HORSE CHESTNUT

COMMON JUNEBERRY. *See* COMMON SERVICEBERRY

COMMON JUNIPER, 306, 315, 324

COMMON LILAC. See LILAC

COMMON MOUNTAIN ASH. *See MOUNTAIN ASH*

COMMON PRIVET. *See EUROPEAN PRIVET*

COMMON PRICKLYASH. *See PRICKLYASH*

COMMON SERVICEBERRY, 77

COMMON SNOWBALL VIBURNUM. See EUROPEAN CRANBERRY BUSH

COMMON SPICEBUSH. *See SPICEBUSH*

COMMON WITCH HAZEL. *See AMERICAN WITCH HAZEL*

CONTORTED EUROPEAN FILBERT. See HARRY LAUDER'S WALKING STICK

CONTORTED EUROPEAN HAZEL, 311

COPENHAGEN HAWTHORN, 106, 24

COPPER BEECH, 168

CORALBERRY, 236, 238, 247, 309, 316

CORAL HONEYSUCKLE, 155

CORK ELM. *See ROCK ELM; WINGED ELM*

CORKSCREW HAZEL. See HARRY LAUDER'S WALKING STICK

CORKSCREW WILLOW, 118, 311

CORNELIAN CHERRY, 21–24

CORNELIAN CHERRY DOGWOOD. See CORNELIAN CHERRY

COTONEASTER, 246–47, 141, 309

COTTONWOOD, 166–67, 88, 118, 164, 178–79, 201, 218, 255, 260, 332, 371, 394; COTTONWOOD IN FALL, 282; COTTONWOOD IN WINTER, 345

COW OAK. *See SWAMP CHESTNUT OAK*

CRAB APPLE, 89

CRAB APPLE, 89–91, 92 11, 21, 80, 84, 95, 106, 108, 114, 122, 194, 394

CRACK WILLOW, 118

CRANBERRY, 28, 139, 157

CRANBERRY COTONEASTER, 247

CRANBERRY VIBURNUM. See EUROPEAN CRANBERRY BUSH

CREEPING DOGWOOD. *See BUNCHBERRY DOGWOOD*

CREEPING JUNIPER, 306, 157, 248, 315

CREEPING SAND CHERRY, 17, 157

Crevices, nooks, crannies in bark/trees, 12, 162, 228, 304, 322

CRIMEAN LINDEN. See CAUCASIAN LINDEN

CRIMSONEYED ROSEMALLOW. *See MALLOW*

CRIMSON WEIGELA. *See WEIGELA*

CUCUMBER MAGNOLIA. *See CUCUMBERTREE*

CUCUMBERTREE, 111, 80, 84, 253

Cullina, William, xiii, 43, 66, 77, 92, 94, 107, 113, 116, 122, 130, 134, 143, 176, 237, 331, 358, 363, 365–70, 372, 377, 380, 387

Cultivars. *See Nativars/cultivars*

CULTIVATED CURRANT, 137

CURLY WILLOW. See CORKSCREW WILLOW

CURRANT, 137

CURRANT, 35, 138–39, 25, 31, 33, 36, 39–42, 45–46, 52, 63–64, 139, 142, 151, 234, 236, 246, 248, 260

CUSTARD APPLE. *See PAWPAW*

CUTLEAF STEPHANANDRA, 248

DAHURIAN BUCKTHORN. See COMMON BUCKTHORN

DAMASK ROSE, 60

DANGLEBERRY. See BLACK HUCKLEBERRY

DAPHNE, 24–25

DAWN REDWOOD, 172

Dead, dying trees. *See Snags*

DECUMARIA. *See CLIMBING HYDRANGEA*

DEERBERRY, 139, 28, 36, 39, 42, 58

DEUTZIA, 25

DEVIL'S SHOESTRINGS. *See LEADPLANT*

DEVIL'S WALKING STICK, 123

DEWBERRY, 139

Dirr, Michael A., 16, 47, 76, 81, 158, 174, 182

DOG BANANA. *See PAWPAW*

DOG ROSE. See COMMON BRIAR

DOGWOOD, 93, 309–10, 21, 28, 249, 324

DOGWOOD, 48–51, 94–95, 310–11, 157, 21, 24, 28, 36, 39, 45, 52, 73, 80, 81, 84, 85, 92, 93, 94, 95, 101, 114, 139, 141, 142, 148, 151, 157, 187, 194, 218, 226, 239, 246, 248, 253, 260, 267, 316, 332, 334, 394; GRAY DOGWOOD IN FALL, 267

DOTTED HAWTHORN, 107

DOUBLEFILE VIBURNUM. See JAPANESE SNOWBALL VIBURNUM

DOUGLAS FIR, 327

DOUGLAS HAWTHORN, 107

DOWNY ARROWWOOD, 71

DOWNY BIRCH. See WHITE BIRCH

DOWNY CHERRY. See NANKING CHERRY

DOWNY HAWTHORN, 106, 114; DOWNY HAWTHORN BERRIES, 266

DOWNY JAPANESE MAPLE. See FULL MOON MAPLE

DOWNY POPLAR. *See* SWAMP COTTONWOOD

DRUMMOND'S DOGWOOD. *See* ROUGHLEAF DOGWOOD

DUTCHMAN'S PIPE, 156

DWARF BUSH HONEYSUCKLE. *See* NORTHERN BUSH HONEYSUCKLE

DWARF CHESTNUT. *See* ALLEGHENY CHINKAPIN

DWARF CHESTNUT OAK. *See* DWARF CHINKAPIN OAK

DWARF CHINKAPIN OAK, 311

DWARF CHINQUAPIN OAK. *See* DWARF CHINKAPIN OAK

DWARF FOTHERGILLA. *See* FOTHERGILLA

DWARF HONEYSUCKLE, 37

DWARF KOREAN LILAC. See MEYER LILAC

DWARF SERVICEBERRY. *See* RUNNING SERVICEBERRY

DWARF-WINGED BURNING BUSH, 240

DWARF WITCHALDER. *See* FOTHERGILLA

EARLY AZALEA, 57

EARLY WILD ROSE. *See* SMOOTH ROSE

EASTERN ARBORVITAE. *See* AMERICAN ARBORVITAE

EASTERN BLACK CURRANT. *See* AMERICAN BLACK CURRANT

EASTERN BURNING BUSH, 240–41, 234, 250, 316, 334

Eastern chipmunk, 94, 30, 36, 125, 192, 199, 307

EASTERN COTTONWOOD. *See* COTTONWOOD

EASTERN HEMLOCK. *See* CANADIAN HEMLOCK

EASTERN LARCH. *See* AMERICAN LARCH

EASTERN LEATHERWOOD. *See* LEATHERWOOD

EASTERN REDBUD. *See* REDBUD

EASTERN RED CEDAR. *See* RED CEDAR

EASTERN SAND CHERRY. *See* CREEPING SAND CHERRY

EASTERN SWEETSHRUB. *See* SWEETSHRUB

EASTERN SYCAMORE. *See* AMERICAN SYCAMORE

EASTERN WAHOO. *See* EASTERN BURNING BUSH

EASTERN WHITE CEDAR. *See* AMERICAN ARBORVITAE

EASTERN WHITE PINE, 327, 178, 315

ELDERBERRY, 29, 68

ELDERBERRY, 29–30, 14, 15, 39, 45, 52, 69, 73, 125, 139, 142, 146, 151, 230, 238, 246, 266, 394; ELDERBERRY BERRIES, 267

ELM, 173–74, 121

ELM, 176–78, 28, 45, 139, 167, 173–74, 201, 260, 274, 322, 332, 343, 394. *See also* AMERICAN ELM

EMERALD'N GOLD, 152

EMPRESS TREE, 96, 86, 98–101

ENGLISH BROOM. See SCOTCH BROOM

ENGLISH ELM, 173–74

ENGLISH HAWTHORN, 105

ENGLISH HOLLY. See HOLLY

ENGLISH IVY, 152, 154

ENGLISH OAK. See OAK

ENGLISH WALNUT, 219

EUROPEAN ALDER. See ALDER

EUROPEAN ASPEN. See ASPEN

EUROPEAN BARBERRY. See COMMON BARBERRY

EUROPEAN BEECH. See BEECH

EUROPEAN BIRCH. See EUROPEAN WHITE BIRCH

EUROPEAN BIRD CHERRY, 82

EUROPEAN BLACK CURRANT, 137

EUROPEAN BLACK PINE. See AUSTRIAN PINE

EUROPEAN BLADDERNUT. See BLADDERNUT

EUROPEAN BROOM. See SCOTCH BROOM

EUROPEAN BUCKTHORN, 140. See also GLOSSY BUCKTHORN

EUROPEAN CHESTNUT, 170

EUROPEAN CRAB APPLE, 89

EUROPEAN CRANBERRY BUSH, 68

EUROPEAN ELDERBERRY. See ELDERBERRY

EUROPEAN FILBERT. See FILBERT

EUROPEAN FLY HONEYSUCKLE. See DWARF HONEYSUCKLE

EUROPEAN GOOSEBERRY, 137

EUROPEAN HIGHBUSH CRANBERRY. See EUROPEAN CRANBERRY BUSH

EUROPEAN HORNBEAM. See HORNBEAM

EUROPEAN HORSE CHESTNUT. *See HORSE CHESTNUT*
EUROPEAN LARCH. *See LARCH*
EUROPEAN MOUNTAIN ASH. *See MOUNTAIN ASH*
EUROPEAN PRIVET, 48
EUROPEAN RED CURRANT. *See CULTIVATED CURRANT*
EUROPEAN SPINDLETREE, 240
EUROPEAN SPRUCE. *See NORWAY SPRUCE*
EUROPEAN WHITE BIRCH, 320
EUROPEAN WILLOW. *See WHITE WILLOW*
Evolution, vii, xi, 2, 4, 5, 6, 57, 118, 212, 220, 227, 228, 259, 321, 383, 384

Fall cleanup, 227–28
FALSE CYPRESS, 324
FALSE-GRAPE. *See HEARTLEAF PEPPERVINE*
FALSE INDIGO BUSH, 132–33, 25, 137, 149–50, 230, 246, 334
FALSE SHAGBARK HICKORY. *See RED HICKORY*
FEBRUARY DAPHNE. *See DAPHNE*
FERNLEAF BUCKTHORN. *See GLOSSY BUCKTHORN*
FIELD MAPLE. *See HEDGE MAPLE*
FILBERT, 102, 311, 394
FIREBERRY HAWTHORN, 107
FIREBUSH. *See WINTERBERRY*
Fireflies, 12, 221, 227
FIVE LEAF AKEBIA, 152
FLAME AZALEA, 57–58, 128–29
FLOWERING ALMOND, 16. *See also FLOWERING PLUM*
FLOWERING ASH, 161
FLOWERING CHERRY. *See WINTER-FLOWERING CHERRY*
FLOWERING DOGWOOD, 94–95, 24, 51, 80, 84, 101, 114, 141, 187, 194, 246, 253, 260, 332
FLOWERING PLUM, 16
FLOWERING QUINCE, 31, 33
FLY HONEYSUCKLE, 37
FORSYTHIA, 34, 63–64, 141, 363
FORSYTHIA OF THE WILDS. *See SPICEBUSH*
FORT SHERIDAN HAWTHORN, 107
FORTUNE MEADOWSWEET. *See JAPANESE SPIREA*
FOTHERGILLA, 27, 14, 15, 16, 21, 33, 36, 39–40, 45, 52, 63–64, 75, 136–37, 142, 144, 234, 246, 309, 316

FOX GRAPE, 153
FRAGRANT ABELIA. *See ABELIA*
FRAGRANT HONEYSUCKLE. *See SWEET BREATH OF SPRING*
FRAGRANT SNOWBELL, 116
FRAGRANT SUMAC, 242–43, 7, 157, 248, 316, 377
FRAGRANT WINTERHAZEL. *See WINTER HAZEL*
FRANKLINIA. *See FRANKLIN TREE*
FRANKLIN TREE, 147, 81, 149, 181, 187, 216, 246, 253, 316
FRENCH HYDRANGEA, 142
FRENCH MULBERRY. *See AMERICAN BEAUTYBERRY*
FRENCH ROSE, 60
FRINGE TREE, 103, 21, 37
FRINGE TREE, 104–5, 15, 16, 21, 25, 33, 40, 45, 46, 52, 67, 80, 84, 109, 114, 129, 142, 144, 150, 181, 187, 194, 253, 259, 260; FRINGE TREE IN FALL, 283
Frogs, 132
FROSTED HAW. *See WAXY-FRUITED HAWTHORN*
FROST GRAPE, 153
FULL MOON MAPLE, 251
FUZZY PRIDE-OF-ROCHESTER, 25

GAIETY, 152
GINKGO, 178–79, 148, 210, 325, 372
GLOSSY BUCKTHORN, 140
GOAT WILLOW. *See PUSSY WILLOW*
GOLDEN CURRANT, 35, 23, 142, 151, 234, 248
GOLDEN LARCH, 189
GOLDEN RAIN TREE, 181
GOLDEN WILLOW, 118
GOOSEBERRIES, 36, 42
GRAPE, 153–54, 92, 105, 121, 394
GRAY ALDER. *See ALDER*
GRAYBARK GRAPE, 153
GRAY BIRCH, 320. *See also YELLOW BIRCH*
GRAY DOGWOOD, 49, 311; GRAY DOGWOOD IN FALL, 268
GRAYLEAF RED RASPBERRY, 139
GRAY POPLAR, 165
GREAT LAKES SANDCHERRY. *See SANDCHERRY*
GREAT LAUREL. *See ROSEBAY RHODODENDRON*
GREEN ALDER, 317
GREEN ASH, 161
GREEN HAWTHORN, 107, 80

GREENSTEM FORSYTHIA, 34
GROUNDCOVERS, VINES, 152
GUELDER ROSE. See EUROPEAN CRAN-
BERRY BUSH

HACKBERRY, 174–76, 159, 164, 167, 180, 192,
201, 260, 322, 332, 394; HACKBERRY IN
FALL, 284
HALBERD-LEAVED MALLOW, 146
HARDHACK. See STEEPLEBUSH
HARDY HIBISCUS. See ROSE OF
SHARON
HARDY HIBISCUS. See MALLOW
HARDY PECAN. See PECAN
Harper, Seth, 174, 194
HARRY LAUDER'S WALKING STICK, 311
HAWTHORN, 105–6, 325
HAWTHORN, 106–8, 23, 80, 91, 93, 114, 125,
142, 152, 179, 211, 246, 253, 260, 265, 324,
332, 354, 394; DOWNY HAWTHORN
BERRIES, 265; WASHINGTON
HAWTHORN BERRIES IN FALL,
299; WASHINGTON HAWTHORN
IN WINTER, 354
HAZEL. See FILBERT
HAZEL ALDER, 317, 248
HAZELNUT, 37
HAZELNUT, 102–3, 52, 55, 75, 105, 118, 142, 171,
183, 246, 260, 274, 312, 316, 332, 344, 394
HEARTLEAF PEPPERVINE, 153, 152
HEDGE MAPLE, 251
HEDGES, 140–41, 47, 125, 145, 169
HEDGES, 141–42, 13, 21, 47–48, 69, 127, 318. See
also BORDERS
HEMLOCK, 325
HEMLOCK, 325, 315
HICKORY, 221–23, 101, 121–22, 188, 198, 200,
212, 225, 259, 260, 294, 304, 332, 394;
SHAGBARK HICKORY IN FALL, 294
HIEDRA CREEPER. See WOODBINE
HIGHBUSH BLUEBERRY, 27–28, 139, 151
HIGHBUSH CRANBERRY. See AMERI-
CAN CRANBERRYBUSH
HILL'S OAK, 205; HILL'S OAK LEAVES
IN FALL, 273, 291
Hilty, John, ix, 30, 59, 83, 90, 108, 143, 244, 326,
328, 363, 365–70, 374, 377, 379–80, 391
HIMALAYAN BLACKBERRY, 151
HINOKI CYPRESS, 324
HOG PLUM. See HORTULAN PLUM
HOLLY, 313, 231, 249, 324
HOLLY, 237–38, 52, 72, 142, 234, 246, 248 260,
308, 316, 334, 394

HOLLYLEAVED BARBERRY. See
MAHONIA
HONEYBALLS. See BUTTONBUSH
HONEY-BUSH. See BUTTONBUSH
HONEY LOCUST, 163–64, 101, 159, 178–81,
187, 192, 194, 207, 257, 259–60, 332;
HONEY LOCUST TREE IN FALL,
285; HONEY LOCUST IN WINTER,
353
HONEYSUCKLE, 37, 3, 6, 141, 249
HONEYSUCKLE, 155, 38–39, 21, 23, 40, 41,
63–64, 116, 128, 136, 137, 144, 146, 151, 246,
248, 316, 394–95
HONEYSUCKLE AZALEA, 56
HOP HORNBEAM, 183, 81, 178, 185, 188, 212,
253, 260, 394
HOPTREE. See WAFER ASH
HORNBEAM, 182, 326
HORNBEAM, 182–84, 81, 178, 187, 188, 212,
253, 260, 275, 332, 394
HORSE CHESTNUT, 108, 184, 326
HORTULAN PLUM, 79
Host plants ranked by Lepidoptera (butterfly/
moth) species productivity: large native
trees; small native trees, shrubs, vines,
394–95; native herbaceous species, 395
HUCKLEBERRY, 28
HYBRID PLANE. See PLANE TREE
HYDRANGEA, 142, 39, 42, 153
HYDRANGEA, 143–44, 14, 21, 28, 39, 40, 42,
45, 52, 73, 74, 128, 132, 136, 137, 149, 153, 239,
246, 248, 309, 316, 334, 395; OAKLEAF
HYDRANGEA IN FALL, 269; OAK-
LEAF HYDRANGEA IN WINTER,
336

Ice Ages, 2, 87, 100, 118, 332
ILLINOIS ROSE. See CLIMBING ROSE
INDIAN BEAN. See CATALPA
INDIAN CHERRY. See CAROLINA
BUCKTHORN
INDIAN CURRANT. See CORALBERRY
INDIGO BUSH. See FALSE INDIGO
BUSH
INKBERRY, 308, 7, 142, 234, 238, 248, 314, 315,
394
INLAND SHADBLOW, 78
Insects
Andrena spp., 51
Andrenid bees, 91, 53, 91
Bee flies, 124
Bumblebees, 61, 198, 18, 39, 58, 88, 91, 98, 101,
138, 147, 154, 179, 191, 256

Flower flies, 125, 144, 154
Green leaf katydid, 211
Honeybee, 18, 30, 53, 88, 91, 179, 199, 244, 256
Leafcutting bee, 256
Leafhopper, 98, 108, 134, 211, 214, 361
Orchard mason bee, 58
Syrphid fly, 256
Tumbling flower beetle, 144
Invasive plants, vii, xi, xii, 3, 4, 7, 21, 25, 37, 39, 40, 41, 42, 43, 48, 52, 60, 63, 64, 68, 77, 82, 89, 96, 100–101, 121, 126, 127, 129, 137, 140, 145, 146, 147, 149, 151, 152, 155, 158, 165, 173, 174, 181, 194, 195, 200, 202, 225, 226, 227, 229, 231, 240, 241, 247, 251, 254, 258, 304, 314, 316, 327, 383, 384, 385, 386, 391–92
IOWA CRAB APPLE. See PRAIRIE CRAB APPLE
IRONWOOD. See HORNBEAM
IRONWOOD. See AMERICAN HORN-BEAM; HOP HORNBEAM

JACK OAK. See HILL'S OAK
JACK PINE, 312
JAPANESE ANGELICA TREE. See ANGELICA TREE
JAPANESE AZALEA, 56
JAPANESE BARBERRY, 231, 3, 225–26, 369, 376, 383
JAPANESE BLACK PINE, 327
JAPANESE BOXWOOD. See LITTLELEAF BOXWOOD
JAPANESE BUCKTHORN, 140
JAPANESE CATALPA. See CHINESE CATALPA
JAPANESE CEDAR. See CEDAR
JAPANESE CHESTNUT, 170
JAPANESE CORK TREE, 158
JAPANESE CORNEL DOGWOOD. See ASIATIC DOGWOOD
JAPANESE DOGWOOD. See DOGWOOD
JAPANESE FALSE CYPRESS. See FALSE CYPRESS
JAPANESE FLOWERING CHERRY, 81–82
JAPANESE FLOWERING CRAB APPLE, 89
JAPANESE FLOWERING QUINCE, 31
JAPANESE HEMLOCK, 325
JAPANESE HOLLY, 313
JAPANESE KERRIA. See KERRIA
JAPANESE LILAC, 42
JAPANESE LILAC TREE, 186, vii
JAPANESE MAGNOLIA. See LILY-FLOWERED MAGNOLIA

JAPANESE MAPLE, 251–52
JAPANESE MEADOWSWEET. See JAPANESE SPIREA
JAPANESE PAGODA TREE, 187
JAPANESE PRIVET, 48
JAPANESE RED PINE, 327
JAPANESE ROSE, 60. See also KERRIA; MULTIFLORA ROSE
JAPANESE SILVERBERRY. See AUTUMN OLIVE
JAPANESE SNOWBALL VIBURNUM, 68, 116
JAPANESE SPIREA, 126, 121, 67
JAPANESE STEWARTIA. See STEWARTIA
JAPANESE STRIPED-BARK MAPLE. See SNAKEBARK
JAPANESE TREE LILAC. See JAPANESE LILAC TREE
JAPANESE WHITE OAK, 201
JAPANESE WHITE PINE, 327
JAPANESE WINEBERRY. See WINEBERRY
JAPANESE WISTERIA, 43, 75
JAPANESE WITCH HAZEL, 74
JAPANESE YEW, 314
JAPANESE ZELKOVA. See ZELKOVA
JERSEY PINE. See VIRGINA PINE
JETBEAD, 40
JUNEBERRY. See SERVICEBERRY
JUNIPER, 326, 309, 314
JUNIPER, 306–7, 157, 246, 248, 314, 394

KALM'S ST. JOHN'S WORT, 145
KATSURA TREE, 188
Keeler, Harriet L., ix, 90, 99, 106–7, 111, 169, 208, 222, 244, 367–68, 371, 373–74, 377
KENTUCKY COFFEE TREE, 159–60, 92, 164, 178–79, 181, 187, 257, 259–60, 332, 394; KENTUCKY COFFEE TREE IN FALL, 286; KENTUCKY COFFEE TREE IN WINTER, 346
KENTUCKY YELLOWWOOD. See YELLOWWOOD
KERRIA, 41
Keystone Species, 122, 304
KINGNUT, 222, 374
KINNIKINNICK. See BEARBERRY
KOBUS MAGNOLIA, 109
KOREAN ABELIA. See ABELIA
KOREAN AZALEA, 56
KOREAN BARBERRY, 231
KOREAN BOXWOOD, 308
KOREAN EVODIA, 189

KOREAN MAPLE, 252
KOREAN MOUNTAIN ASH, 254
KOREAN RHODODENDRON, 56
KOREAN SPICE VIBURNUM, 68
KOUSA DOGWOOD. See DOGWOOD

LACE SHRUB. See CUTLEAF
STEPHANANDRA
Lady Bird Johnson Wildflower Center, ix, 22,
87, 209, 390, 391, 393
LANCELEAF BUCKTHORN, 141
LANTANAPHYLLUM VIBURNUM, 68
LARCH, 189
LARCH, 189, 173, 260, 394
LARGE FOTHERGILLA, 27
LARGE GRAY WILLOW, 52, 118
LARGE MAPLE. See MAPLE
LARGE-TOOTHED ASPEN. See BIG-
TOOTH ASPEN
LAUREL WILLOW, 52, 118
LAVALLE CORK TREE, 158
LEADPLANT, 133–34, 25, 149, 334
LEATHERLEAF ARROWWOOD, 68
LEATHERWOOD, 232–33, 23, 33, 36, 42, 63–
64, 139, 238, 253, 314, 395
LILAC, 42, vii, 136, 141, 186
LILAC CHASTE TREE. See CHASTE TREE
LILY-FLOWERED MAGNOLIA, 110
LILY OF THE VALLEY TREE. See
SOURWOOD
LIMBER HONEYSUCKLE, 155
LINDEN, 190, 108
LINDEN, 190–92, 81, 88, 101, 181, 187, 189, 255,
275, 394
LINGONBERRY. See MOUNTAIN
CRANBERRY
LITTLELEAF BOXWOOD, 308
LITTLELEAF LILAC, 42
LITTLELEAF LINDEN, 190
LOBLOLLY PINE, 328
LOMBARDY POPLAR. See BLACK
POPLAR
LONDON PLANE TREE. See PLANE
TREE
Lounsberry, Alice, ix, 11, 53, 77, 82–83, 86, 90,
92, 96, 99, 102, 164, 167–68, 170–71, 179,
184, 186, 191, 204, 207, 215, 220, 252, 256,
259, 321, 328, 362, 364, 371, 378–79
LOW BUSH HONEYSUCKLE. See
NORTHERN BUSH
HONEYSUCKLE
LOWBUSH BLUEBERRY. See
BLUEBERRY

LOWBUSH CRANBERRY. See
SQUASHBERRY
LOW ROSE. See PASTURE ROSE

MAACKIA, 109, 76
MAGNOLIA, 109–10, 46
MAGNOLIA, 110–12, 20, 83, 101, 179–80, 181,
187, 192, 194, 260, 394
MAHALEB CHERRY, 82
MAHONIA, 231, 376
MAIDENHAIR TREE. See GINKGO
MALLOW, 146–47, 136, 137, 142
MANCHURIAN CHOKECHERRY. See
AMUR CHERRY
MANCHURIAN CRAB APPLE. See SIBE-
RIAN CRAB APPLE
MANCHURIAN HONEYSUCKLE, 37
MANCHURIAN SNAKEBARK MAPLE,
252
MANY-FLOWERED COTONEASTER. See
RED COTONEASTER
MAPLE, 192, 194–95, 251, 76, 130, 149, 193,
251–53
MAPLE, 197–99, 252–53, 28, 81, 121, 122, 139,
149, 159, 164, 165, 168, 178, 180, 185, 187, 188,
192, 200, 202, 206, 208, 219, 260, 287–89,
323, 332, 334, 351, 394; MAPLE TREE IN
FALL, 287. See also BLACK MAPLE;
BOXELDER; MOUNTAIN MAPLE;
RED MAPLE; SILVER MAPLE;
STRIPED MAPLE; SUGAR MAPLE
MAPLELEAF VIBURNUM, 71, 73, 136–37,
334, 365
MARGARETT'S HAWTHORN, 107
MAZARD CHERRY. See SWEET CHERRY
MEADOW ROSE. See SMOOTH ROSE
MEADOW WILLOW, 53
MEMORIAL ROSE, 60
MENTOR BARBERRY, 231
MEXICAN PLUM, 79
MEYER LILAC, 42
MEZEREUM. See DAPHNE
MICHIGAN ROSE. See CLIMBING ROSE
Migration corridors for wildlife, viii
MIMOSA, 194
MISSOURI CURRANT. See GOLDEN
CURRANT
MISSOURI GOOSEBERRY, 138–39
MISSOURI RIVER WILLOW, 53
MIYABE MAPLE, 252
MOCKERNUT HICKORY, 222
MOCKORANGE, 46, 395
MONGOLIAN LINDEN, 190

MONGOLIAN OAK, 201
MOOSEWOOD. See STRIPED MAPLE
MOOSEWOOD VIBURNUM. See
    SQUASHBERRY
MORROW'S HONEYSUCKLE, 37
Morton Arboretum, The, xii, 27, 77, 96, 100–
    101, 138, 140, 161, 195, 218, 231, 235, 240, 241,
    251, 258, 316, 320, 327, 390, 392
Moths
    Azalea sphinx moth, 187, 218
    Cecropia moth, 18, 182, 191
    Columbia silkmoth, 18, 83, 127, 177, 189, 232,
        325, 332
    Great ash sphinx moth, 162, 167
    Hummingbird clearwing moth, 72, 18, 73
    Imperial moth, 329, 199, 211
    Io moth, 91, 54, 199, 223
    Locust underwing moth, 101
    Luna moth, 54, 182, 199, 216, 221, 223, 244,
        320, 322, 379
    Pandora sphinx moth, 155
    Polyphemus moth, 211, 51, 103, 182, 223, 322,
        384
    Promethea silkworm caterpillar, 22
    Rosy maple moth, 199
    Slender clearwing moth, 28, 58, 139, 146, 156,
        187
    Tulip tree silkmoth, 180
    White-lined sphinx moth, 108, 18
MOUNTAIN ALDER. See GREEN ALDER
MOUNTAIN ASH, 254
MOUNTAIN ASH, 255, 81, 125, 149, 159, 164,
    179, 181, 194, 226, 253, 255, 334, 357, 259,
    334, 394
MOUNTAIN AZALEA, 58
MOUNTAIN CAMELLIA. See
    STEWARTIA
MOUNTAIN CRANBERRY, 28, 157
MOUNTAIN FLY HONEYSUCKLE, 38,
    128
MOUNTAIN LAUREL, 58–59, 129, 142, 312,
    334
MOUNTAIN MAPLE, 252–53, 81, 149, 187,
    198, 200, 219, 334
MOUNTAIN STUARTIA. See
    STEWARTIA
MOUNTAIN WITCHALDER. See LARGE
    FOTHERGILLA
MUGO PINE, 315
MULAN MAGNOLIA. See LILY-FLOW-
    ERED MAGNOLIA
MULBERRY, 194
MULBERRY. See RED MULBERRY

MULTIFLORA ROSE, 60
MUSCLEWOOD. See AMERICAN
    HORNBEAM
MYROBALAN PLUM, 81–82

NANKING CHERRY, 17, 82
NANNYBERRY, 71, 81, 85, 93, 260
NARROW-LEAVED CRAB APPLE. See
    SOUTHERN CRAB APPLE
Nativars/cultivars, vii, xii, xiv, 3, 4, 5, 7, 8, 9, 12,
    16, 37, 44, 45, 47, 48, 56, 59, 65, 68, 77, 78,
    81, 89, 91, 93, 94, 101, 106, 107, 122, 126, 129,
    137, 140, 141, 142, 143, 145, 152, 158, 164, 164,
    176, 196, 228, 237, 242, 308, 311, 384
Native Americans, viii, 11, 33, 61, 78, 79, 83, 102,
    121, 177, 178, 179, 190, 195, 196, 197, 198, 210,
    213, 220, 223, 225, 226, 231, 237, 240, 242,
    245, 251, 252, 303, 308, 309, 311, 320, 326,
    330, 381, 384
Naturalized nonnative plants, xi, xii, 2, 3, 4, 15,
    16, 25, 31, 34, 42, 46, 48, 60, 63, 65, 67, 68,
    82, 85, 89, 106, 118, 123, 126, 129, 137, 140,
    145, 146, 148, 150, 151, 164, 165, 168, 170, 173,
    179, 181, 184, 187, 188, 189, 190, 192, 194, 195,
    196, 202, 219, 229, 231, 240, 249, 251, 252,
    254, 308, 311, 313, 314, 320, 327, 330, 331, 383,
    384, 392
NEW JERSEY TEA, 134–35, 25, 28, 40, 45, 122,
    128, 137, 139, 142, 144, 149, 157, 234, 246,
    248, 316, 394
NIKKO MAPLE, 252
NINEBARK, 44–45, 7, 14, 15, 31, 39, 40, 41, 46,
    47, 52, 63, 64, 67, 74, 136, 137, 142, 144, 146,
    230, 234, 246, 248, 316, 334, 364, 394;
    NINEBARK IN FALL, 268
NORTHERN ALDER. See GREEN ALDER
NORTHERN BAYBERRY. See BAYBERRY
NORTHERN BUSH HONEYSUCKLE, 38,
    33, 146, 248, 316
NORTHERN CATALPA. See CATALPA
NORTHERN DEWBERRY. See
    DEWBERRY
NORTHERN HACKBERRY. See
    HACKBERRY
NORTHERN MOUNTAIN ASH, 255
NORTHERN PIN OAK. See HILL'S OAK
NORTHERN RED OAK. See RED OAK
NORTHERN SPICEBUSH. See
    SPICEBUSH
NORTHERN WHITE CEDAR. See AMERI-
    CAN ARBORVITAE
NORWAY MAPLE, 196, 130, 192, 193 199, 200,
    372

NORWAY PINE. See RED PINE
NORWAY SPRUCE, 330–31
Nursery industry, 4, 226, 309

OAK, 201–2, 115
OAK, 202–12, 18, 24, 28, 53, 55, 80, 118, 121, 122,
    139, 142, 159, 164, 169, 170, 171, 178, 180, 181,
    185, 188, 192, 198, 199, 200, 218, 221, 226,
    236, 253, 260, 279, 281, 290, 291, 292, 293,
    295, 296, 304, 311, 312, 322, 332, 347, 350,
    394; BUR OAK LEAVES IN FALL,
    279; BUR OAK IN WINTER, 350;
    CHINKAPIN OAK IN FALL, 281;
    HILL'S OAK LEAVES IN FALL, 273,
    291; OAK SP. IN FALL, 290; OAK
    TREES IN WINTER, 347; RED OAK
    IN FALL, 292; SCARLET OAK IN
    FALL, 293; SHUMARD OAK LEAVES
    IN FALL, 295; SWAMP WHITE OAK
    IN FALL, 296
OAKLEAF HYDRANGEA, 144, 149, 239, 246,
    248, 309, 336; OAKLEAF HYDRAN-
    GEA IN FALL, 269; OAKLEAF HY-
    DRANGEA IN WINTER, 336
OCCIDENTAL PLANE. See AMERICAN
    SYCAMORE
OHIO BUCKEYE, 184–85, 33, 81, 99, 159, 171,
    187, 192, 257, 259–60, 332; OHIO BUCK-
    EYE IN FALL, 278
OLDFASHIONED WEIGELA, 74
OLD FIELD BIRCH. See GRAY BIRCH
OLDFIELD PINE. See LOBLOLLY PINE
ONESEED HAWTHORN, 106
ONTARIO HAWTHORN. See COPEN-
    HAGEN HAWTHORN
ORANGE-EYE BUTTERFLY BUSH. See
    BUTTERFLY BUSH
OREGON GRAPE-HOLLY. See MAHONIA
ORIENTAL ARBORVITAE. See
    ARBORVITAE
ORIENTAL CATALPA. See CHINESE
    CATALPA
ORIENTAL CHERRY. See JAPANESE
    FLOWERING CHERRY
ORIENTAL PHOTINIA, 47, 315
ORIENTAL SPRUCE, 330
ORIENTAL SWEETGUM. See
    SWEETGUM
ORIENTAL WHITE OAK. See JAPANESE
    WHITE OAK
OSAGE ORANGE, 259, 52, 113, 142, 164, 179,
    201, 334, 394
OSIER WILLOW, 118

OVERCUP OAK, 209
OZARK WITCH HAZEL, 75, 23, 24, 33, 36,
    45, 55, 63, 150, 246, 260, 312, 316, 334
O-ZUMI CRAB APPLE, 89

PACIFIC SERVICEBERRY. See INLAND
    SHADBLOW
PAGODA DOGWOOD. See ALTERNATE-
    LEAF DOGWOOD
PAINTED MAPLE, 252
PANICLED HYDRANGEA, 142
PAPERBARK MAPLE, 252
PAPER BIRCH. See CANOE BIRCH
PAPER MULBERRY, 195, 200
PARADISE APPLE, 89
PARASITIC IVY. See WINTERCREEPER
Parshall, David K., 54, 167, 211
PASTURE ROSE, 61, 248, 365
PAWPAW, 113–14, 80, 84, 101, 171, 179, 201, 253,
    260, 394
PEACH, 82, 16
PEACH LEAVED OAK. See WILLOW
    OAK
PEACH-LEAVED WILLOW, 118
PEAR HAWTHORN, 107
PECAN, 222–23, 260
PEE-GEE HYDRANGEA, 142
PEKING COTONEASTER, 246–47
Pemmican, 11, 384
PERSIAN LILAC, 42
PERSIMMON, 256, 101, 113, 171, 179, 201, 257,
    259, 394
Pesticides, 2, 12, 16, 59, 61, 221, 308, 384
PIEDMONT AZALEA. See MOUNTAIN
    AZALEA
PIGNUT HICKORY, 222
PIN CHERRY, 83–84, 19, 82, 260
PINE, 327, 315
PINE, 312, 328–29, 35, 122, 138, 142, 157, 178, 228,
    309, 330, 322, 394
PINK AZALEA, 58
PINKSHELL AZALEA, 58
PINK SPIREA. See STEEPLEBUSH
PIN OAK, 205, 200
PINXTERBLOOM AZALEA. See PINK
    AZALEA
Pippen, Jeffrey S. ix, xiii, 391
PITCH PINE, 329
PLANE TREE, 213, 330
PLUM. See CHERRY, PLUM, ALMOND
PLUM, 78, 114
PLUMLEAVED CRAB APPLE, 89
POPLAR, 215

PORCELAINBERRY VINE, 152
POSSUMHAW. See POSSUMHAW
    HOLLY; POSSUMHAW
    VIBURNUM
POSSUMHAW HOLLY, 237–38, 72, 142, 237,
    316, 334, 308, 314
POSSUMHAW VIBURNUM, 72, 237
POST OAK, 205
PRAIRIE CRAB APPLE, 90, 92, 367
PRAIRIE ROSE, 60, 91, 157; PRAIRIE ROSE
    LEAVES AND HIPS IN FALL, 269;
    PRAIRIE ROSE HIPS IN WINTER,
    339
PRAIRIE SHOESTRINGS. See
    LEADPLANT
PRAIRIE WILD ROSE. See PRAIRIE
    ROSE
PRAIRIE WILLOW, 53, 118, 150, 312, 334
PRICKLYASH, 124–25, 45, 63–64, 142, 230,
    250, 255, 395
PRICKLY GOOSEBERRY, 139
PRICKLY ROSE, 61
PRINCESSTREE. See EMPRESS TREE
PRIVET, 47–52, 141, 186, 364
PRIVET HEDGE. See PRIVET
PROVENCE ROSE. See CABBAGE ROSE
PURPLE BEAUTYBERRY, 234
PURPLE BLOOM MAPLE. See KOREAN
    MAPLE
PURPLE CHOKEBERRY, 14
PURPLEFLOWERING RASPBERRY, 62,
    139, 148, 151, 334
PURPLELEAF CHERRY, 17, 215
PURPLE-LEAF SANDCHERRY. See PUR-
    PLELEAF CHERRY
PURPLEOSIER WILLOW, 118
PUSSY WILLOW, 52, 118, 150
PUSSY WILLOW, 53, 118, 150

QUAKING ASPEN. See AMERICAN
    ASPEN

RACCOON GRAPE. See HEARTLEAF
    PEPPERVINE
RED BUCKEYE, 32–33, 21, 59, 81, 85, 93, 95,
    99, 101, 108, 115, 171, 181, 185, 194, 253, 312,
    316, 334
REDBUD, 115
REDBUD, 92, 21, 78, 80, 84, 88, 94, 95,
    101, 114–15, 142, 159, 188, 192, 194, 201,
    246, 253, 260, 332, 394; REDBUD IN
    FALL, 297; REDBUD IN WINTER,
    341, 355

RED CEDAR, 323–24, 52, 142, 207, 239, 307,
    309, 326, 332, 394
RED CHERRY. See PIN CHERRY
RED CHOKEBERRY, 13–14; RED CHOKE-
    BERRY IN FALL, 270
RED COTONEASTER, 247
RED CURRANT, 35
RED ELDERBERRY, 30
RED ELM. See SLIPPERY ELM
RED HAW. See DOWNY HAWTHORN
RED HICKORY, 222
RED HONEYSUCKLE. See LIMBER
    HONEYSUCKLE
REDLEAF ROSE, 60
RED MAPLE, 197, 81, 187, 206, 252; RED
    MAPLE IN WINTER, 351
RED MULBERRY, 195, 159, 167, 176, 322, 334,
    394
RED OAK, 205–6, 200, 202, 204, 207, 209, 211,
    384; RED OAK IN FALL, 292
REDOSIER DOGWOOD, 310–11, 28, 49–52,
    142, 151, 246
RED-PANICLED DOGWOOD. See GRAY
    DOGWOOD
RED PINE, 329
RED SPRUCE, 332
RED STEM DOGWOOD. See REDOSIER
    DOGWOOD
RED-STEMMED DOGWOODS. See
    DOGWOOD
RED-STEMMED DOGWOODS. See RE-
    DOSIER DOGWOOD; SILKY
    DOGWOOD.
REDTWIG DOGWOOD, 310
RED WILLOW. See REDOSIER
    DOGWOOD
REGAL PRIVET. See BORDER PRIVET
RHODODENDRON, 56, 15, 249
RHODODENDRON, 56–58, 14, 21, 25, 33, 41,
    45, 128–29, 139, 144, 246, 394
RHODODENDRON, AZALEA, 56, 15, 249
RHODODENDRON, AZALEA, 56–59, 14,
    21, 25, 33, 41, 45, 128–29, 139, 144, 246
RHODORA, 58
RIVERBANK GRAPE, 153
RIVER BIRCH, 320; RIVER BIRCH IN
    FALL, 297
RIVER COTTONWOOD. See SWAMP
    COTTONWOOD
ROCK ELM, 176
ROCKY MOUNTAIN DOUGLAS FIR. See
    DOUGLAS FIR
ROSE, 59–60, 68, 41, 37, 145

ROSE, 60–62, 4, 11, 14, 41, 79, 91, 106, 129, 139, 157, 239, 246, 248, 268, 303, 316, 339, 394, 395; PRAIRIE ROSE HIPS AND LEAVES IN FALL, 269; PRAIRIE ROSE HIPS IN WINTER, 339
ROSEBAY RHODODENDRON, 58, 129
ROSEMALLOW, 146–47, 136, 137. *See also* MALLOW
ROSEMARY PINE. *See* LOBLOLLY PINE
ROSE OF SHARON, 146, 141
ROSESHELL AZALEA. *See* EARLY AZALEA
ROUGHLEAF DOGWOOD, 49–50, 23, 36
ROUNDLEAF DOGWOOD, 50–51
ROYAL PAULOWNIA. See EMPRESS TREE
RUGOSE ROSE. See JAPANESE ROSE
RUM CHERRY. *See* BLACK CHERRY
RUNNING JUNEBERRY. *See* RUNNING SERVICEBERRY
RUNNING SERVICEBERRY, 21
RUNNING STRAWBERRY BUSH, 241, 157, 316
RUSSET BUFFALOBERRY, 230
RUSSIAN ARBORVITAE. See ARBORVITAE
RUSSIAN CYPRESS. See ARBORVITAE
RUSSIAN MULBERRY. See MULBERRY
RUSSIAN OLIVE, 229, 15, 76, 168, 250, 319
RUSTY BLACKHAW, 72, 81, 85, 93, 260

SAKHALIN CORK TREE, 158
SALT CEDAR. See TAMARISK
SANDBAR WILLOW, 53
SAND CHERRY, 17, 25, 28, 33, 79, 84, 146, 157, 246, 362
SAPPHIRE-BERRY, 148
SARGENT CHERRY, 82
SARGENT CRAB APPLE, 88
SASSAFRAS, 99, 23, 36, 45–46, 63, 80, 95, 179–80, 201, 246, 260, 332, 367, 394
SAUCER MAGNOLIA, 110, xii
SAWTOOTH OAK, 202
SCARLET ELDER. *See* RED ELDERBERRY
SCARLET FIRETHORN, 249, 315
SCARLET HAWTHORN. *See* COPENHAGEN HAWTHORN
SCARLET OAK, 206, 200, 226; SCARLET OAK IN FALL, 293
SCENTLESS MOCK ORANGE, 46, 15, 45, 47, 52, 67, 74, 144, 248, 312, 316
SCOTCH BROOM, 63
SCOTCH PINE, 327

SCOTCH ROSE, 60
SCOTS PINE. See SCOTCH PINE
SCRUB CHESTNUT OAK. *See* DWARF CHINKAPIN OAK
SCRUB PINE. *See* VIRGINIA PINE
SERBIAN SPRUCE, 330
SERVICEBERRY, 20–21, 77–78, 7, 11, 14, 15, 16, 24, 25, 28, 31, 36, 39, 40, 45, 46, 47, 52, 63, 67, 74, 84, 91, 93, 95, 101, 114, 139, 142, 157, 194, 199, 201, 246, 248, 253, 260, 312, 316, 332, 340, 394; SERVICEBERRY IN FALL, 271; SERVICEBERRY IN WINTER, 340
SEVEN-SON FLOWER, 148–49, 215
SHADBLOW SERVICEBERRY. *See* COMMON SERVICEBERRY
SHADBUSH. *See* SERVICEBERRY
SHAGBARK HICKORY, 222–23, 101, 188, 260, 304, 374; SHAGBARK HICKORY IN FALL, 294
SHELLBARK HICKORY. *See* KINGNUT
SHINGLE OAK, 207, 142
SHINING SUMAC, 243
SHINY COTONEASTER, 247
SHORTLEAF PINE, 329
SHOWY FLY HONEYSUCKLE, 37
SHOWY FORSYTHIA, 34
SHOWY MOUNTAIN ASH. *See* NORTHERN MOUNTAIN ASH
SHRUBBY CINQUEFOIL. *See* BUTTERFLY SHRUB
SHRUBBY LESPEDEZA, 149
SHRUBBY POTENTILLA. *See* BUTTERFLY SHRUB
SHRUBBY ST. JOHN'S WORT. *See* ST. JOHN'S WORT
SHUMARD OAK, 207; SHUMARD OAK LEAVES IN FALL, 295
SIBERIAN CRAB APPLE, 89
SIBERIAN CYPRESS. See ARBORVITAE
SIBERIAN DOGWOOD. See REDTWIG DOGWOOD
SIBERIAN ELM, 173–74
SIBERIAN PEASHRUB, 64
SIEBOLD'S ARROWWOOD, 68
SILK TREE. See MIMOSA
SILKWORM MULBERRY. See MULBERRY
SILKY DOGWOOD, 50, 142, 148, 311
SILKY WILLOW, 53, 150
SILVERBERRY, 229, 55, 64, 148, 234, 238, 250, 309
SILVER BIRCH. See EUROPEAN WHITE BIRCH

SILVER BUFFALOBERRY, 229–30, 23, 36, 42, 64, 108, 125, 312, 316, 334
SILVER-LEAVED LINDEN. See WHITE BASSWOOD
SILVER LINDEN, 190
SILVER MAPLE, 193, 165, 168, 198, 200, 252; SILVER MAPLE IN FALL, 288
SILVER POPLAR. See WHITE POPLAR
SINGLESEED HAWTHORN. See ONE-SEED HAWTHORN
SLENDER DEUTZIA, 25
SLENDER PRIDE OF ROCHESTER. See SLENDER DEUTZIA
SLIPPERY ELM, 176
SMOKE BUSH. See AMERICAN SMOKETREE
SMOKETREE, 65, 250
SMOKETREE. See AMERICAN SMOKETREE
SMOOTH ALDER. See HAZEL ALDER
SMOOTH AZALEA, 58
SMOOTH HAWTHORN. See HAWTHORN
SMOOTH HYDRANGEA. See WILD HYDRANGEA
SMOOTH ROSE, 61
SMOOTH SERVICEBERRY. See ALLEGHENY SERVICEBERRY
SMOOTH SUMAC, 243
Snags, 12, 55, 155, 227, 228, 305, 376
SNAKEBARK, 252
SNOWBELL, 116
SNOWBELL, 116–17, 16, 25, 31, 39, 42, 46, 67, 80, 84, 93, 105, 129, 144, 253, 260, 395
SNOWBERRY, 236–37, 155, 247, 309, 316, 377, 394–95
SNOWDROP TREE. See CAROLINA SILVERBELL
SORREL TREE. See SOURWOOD
SOURGUM. See BLACKGUM
SOURWOOD, 186–87, 28, 58, 81, 117, 122, 139, 181, 189, 194, 200, 219, 226, 246, 253, 260, 334, 394
SOUTHERN ARROWWOOD. See ARROWWOOD VIBURNUM
SOUTHERN BLACKHAW. See RUSTY BLACKHAW
SOUTHERN CATALPA, 85–86
SOUTHERN CRAB APPLE, 90
SOUTHERN HACKBERRY. See SUGARBERRY
SOUTHERN RED OAK, 209
SPANISH OAK, 209

SPECKLED ALDER. See ALDER
SPICEBUSH, 22, 25, 36, 39, 41, 45, 46, 47, 52, 63–64, 73, 99, 101, 136, 139, 142, 147, 181, 239, 246, 395
Spiders, 223, 325, 332
SPIRAEA VANHOUTTEI, 67
SPIREA, 67, 126–28, 394
SPREADING COTONEASTER, 247
Spring cleanup, 12, 228
SPRUCE, 330–31
SPRUCE, 331, 332, 333, 394
SPRUCE PINE. See SHORTLEAF PINE
SPURGE OLIVE. See DAPHNE
SQUASHBERRY, 72
STAGHORN SUMAC, 243, 312
STANDISH'S HONEYSUCKLE, 37
ST. ANDREW'S CROSS, 145, 157
STAR MAGNOLIA, 110
STEEPLEBUSH, 127–28, 122, 136–37, 150, 246
Sterile invasive nonnative plants, 226, 382
Sternberg, Guy, and Jim Wilson, 33, 50–51, 57, 92, 94, 105, 108, 142, 204, 214, 221, 233, 241–42, 331
STEWARTIA, 215
STEWARTIA, 215, 122, 144, 147, 187, 219, 253, 260
STIFF DOGWOOD. See SWAMP DOGWOOD
ST. JOHN'S WORT, 145, 36, 39; SHRUBBY ST. JOHN'S WORT IN WINTER, 339
STRIPED MAPLE, 252, 198, 200, 219, 323, 334
STUARTIA. See STEWARTIA
SUGARBERRY, 174
SUGAR MAPLE, 198, 226, 252, 373, 387; SUGAR MAPLE IN FALL, 289
SUMAC, 257
SUMAC, 242–44, 7, 28, 42, 52, 142, 157, 221, 226, 248, 250, 253, 259, 312, 314, 316, 334, 394; SUMAC SPP. IN FALL, 242, 272
SUMMER GRAPE, 153
SUMMERSWEET. See CLETHRA
SUNSHINE ROSE. See PRAIRIE ROSE
SWAMP AZALEA, 58, 129
SWAMP CHESTNUT OAK, 209
SWAMP COTTONWOOD, 167, 218
SWAMP DOGWOOD. See GRAY DOGWOOD
SWAMP HICKORY, 221
SWAMP MAGNOLIA, 112
SWAMP RED OAK, 207
SWAMP ROSE, 61, 129
SWAMP TUPELO. See WATER TUPELO

SWAMP WHITE OAK, 207–8, 118; SWAMP WHITE OAK IN FALL, 296
SWEET AZALEA. *See* SMOOTH AZALEA
SWEETBAY MAGNOLIA, 111, 83, 179, 180
SWEET BIRCH, 321–22
SWEET BREATH OF SPRING, 37
SWEETBRIAR ROSE, 60
SWEET BUCKEYE. *See* YELLOW BUCKEYE
SWEET CHERRY, 82
SWEET CRAB APPLE. *See* AMERICAN CRAB APPLE
SWEET-FERN, 157
SWEETGUM, 216
SWEETGUM, 216–17, 159, 194, 226, 260, 394; SWEETGUM TREE IN FALL, 298; SWEETGUM IN WINTER, 348
SWEET LOCUST. *See* HONEY LOCUST
SWEET MOCKORANGE. See MOCKORANGE
SWEETPEPPERBUSH. *See* CLETHRA
SWEET-SCENTED CRAB APPLE. *See* AMERICAN CRAB APPLE
SWEETSHRUB, 19, 25, 33, 74, 113, 129, 136–37, 144, 246, 395
SWISS STONE PINE, 327
SYCAMORE. *See* AMERICAN SYCAMORE
SYCAMORE MAPLE. See MAPLE

Tallamy, Douglas, vii–viii, xii, 5, 53, 57, 83, 95, 122, 129, 131, 154, 180–81, 202, 210–11, 216, 220–21, 226, 304, 322, 357, 359, 361–62, 367, 369, 372, 374, 384, 394–95
TALLHEDGE BUCKTHORN. See GLOSSY BUCKTHORN
TAMARACK. *See* AMERICAN LARCH
TAMARISK, 149–50, 370
TATARIAN DOGWOOD. See REDTWIG DOGWOOD
TATARIAN HONEYSUCKLE, 37
TATARIAN MAPLE, 252
Taylor, Patricia A., 9, 27, 58, 80, 109–11, 126, 133, 143, 146, 241–42, 310, 363, 365–66, 368–70, 377, 379, 388
THICKET CREEPER. *See* WOODBINE
THICKET SERVICEBERRY. *See* SERVICEBERRY
THIMBLEBERRY, 62, 139, 151
THORNLESS COCKSPUR HAWTHORN, 106
THORNLESS HONEY LOCUST, 164
THORNY LOCUST. *See* HONEY LOCUST
THORNY OLIVE, 229
THREE-FLOWER MAPLE, 252

TOOTHACHE TREE. *See* PRICKLYASH
TORINGO CRAB APPLE, 89
TREE HYDRANGEA. See PANICLED HYDRANGEA
TREE OF HEAVEN, 258
TREE RHODODENDRON, 56
TREMBLING ASPEN. *See* AMERICAN ASPEN
TRIDENT MAPLE, 252
TRUMPET CREEPER, 155
TRUMPET HONEYSUCKLE. *See* CORAL HONEYSUCKLE
TRUMPET VINE. *See* TRUMPET CREEPER
TULEPO, 218
TULIP MAGNOLIA. See LILY-FLOW-ERED MAGNOLIA
TULIP TREE, 179–80, 83, 88, 159, 185, 219, 255, 260, 334, 361, 394; TULIP TREE IN FALL, 299; TULIP TREE IN WIN-TER, 349
Turtles, 51, 54, 199
TWINBERRY HONEYSUCKLE, 38–40, 128

UMBRELLA MAGNOLIA. *See* UMBRELLA-TREE
UMBRELLA-TREE, 112
Unusual trees for specimen planting, xii, 33, 45, 70, 80, 105, 111, 113, 123, 141, 146, 182, 184, 186–187, 242, 321
USDA PLANTS, ix, xi–xii, xv, 2–4, 357–60, 383, 386, 392–93

VAN HOUTTE SPIREA. See SPIREA VANHOUTTEI
VERNAL WITCH HAZEL. *See* OZARK WITCH HAZEL
VIBURNUM, 68
VIBURNUM, 69–73, 21, 24, 28, 36, 39–41, 52, 63, 81, 85, 93, 95, 108, 114, 136–37, 142, 151, 230, 234, 237, 239, 246, 248, 260, 272, 394
VINES, GROUNDCOVERS, 152
VIRGINIA CREEPER, 154, 73, 394
VIRGINIA PINE, 329
VIRGINIA ROSE, 61
VIRGINIA SWEETSPIRE, 126–27, 121, 136–37, 142, 149–50, 234, 240, 246
VIRGINIA WILLOW. *See* VIRGINIA SWEETSPIRE

WAFER ASH, 45, 21, 28, 46, 52, 67, 85, 93, 95, 105, 114, 117, 125, 164, 181, 239, 246, 255, 260, 316, 334, 395
WAHOO. *See* AMERICAN STRAWBERRY BUSH; WINGED ELM

Walcott, Mary Vaux, ix
WALNUT, 219
WALNUT, 220–23, xii, 21, 22, 30, 39, 41, 43, 44,
    49, 50, 53, 62, 70, 72, 71, 72, 75, 78, 80, 83,
    84, 92, 94, 98, 99, 100, 102, 105, 108, 111, 114,
    122, 124, 125, 134, 143, 145, 153, 154, 155, 159,
    163, 164, 169, 170, 171, 176, 179, 180, 182, 185,
    193, 198, 200, 204, 206, 207, 208, 210, 212,
    214, 218, 241, 242, 245, 256, 258, 259, 260,
    306, 317, 318, 322, 324, 334, 394
WASHINGTON HAWTHORN, 107, 80, 114;
    WASHINGTON HAWTHORN BER-
    RIES IN FALL, 299; WASHINGTON
    HAWTHORN IN WINTER, 354
WATER BEECH. *See* AMERICAN
    HORNBEAM
WATER GUM. *See* WATER TUPELO
WATER OAK, 209, 211, 218
WATER TUPELO, 218
WAXY-FRUITED HAWTHORN, 107
WAYFARING TREE, 68
Weeks, Sally, Harmon P. Weeks Jr., and
    George R. Parker, 13, 20, 41, 49, 58, 71, 78,
    82, 96, 99, 102, 118, 126, 128, 138, 147, 152,
    231, 233, 236, 239, 362–65, 367, 369–70,
    373, 376–77, 379
WEEPING FLOWERING CHERRY, 82
WEEPING FORSYTHIA, 34
*WEEPING WHITE BIRCH. See EURO-
    PEAN WHITE BIRCH*
WEEPING WILLOW, 117
WEIGELA, 74
WHITE ASH, 161–62, 179, 300; WHITE ASH
    TREE IN FALL, 300
WHITE BARKED HIMALAYAN BIRCH,
    320
WHITE BASSWOOD, 191, 181
WHITE BIRCH, 320
*WHITE BLADDERNUT. See
    BLADDERNUT*
WHITE CEDAR. *See* AMERICAN
    ARBORVITAE
WHITE FRINGE TREE. *See* FRINGE
    TREE
WHITE LAUREL. *See* ROSEBAY
    RHODODENDRON
WHITE LINDEN. *See* WHITE
    BASSWOOD
WHITE MEADOWSWEET, 128, 122
WHITE MULBERRY. See MULBERRY
WHITE OAK, 208–9, 121, 170, 201–2, 204–5,
    211, 296, 373
WHITE PINE. *See* EASTERN WHITE
    PINE

WHITE POPLAR, 165
WHITE SPIREA. *See* WHITE
    MEADOWSWEET
WHITE SPRUCE, 331–33
WHITE WALNUT. *See* BUTTERNUT
WHITE WILLOW, 118
WILD BLACKBERRY. *See* COMMON
    BLACKBERRY
WILD BLACK CHERRY. *See* BLACK
    CHERRY
WILD BLACK CURRANT. *See* AMERI-
    CAN BLACK CURRANT
WILD CRAB APPLE. *See* AMERICAN
    CRAB APPLE
WILD GOOSEBERRY. *See* MISSOURI
    GOOSEBERRY
WILD HONEYSUCKLE. *See* LIMBER
    HONEYSUCKLE
WILD HYDRANGEA, 143–44, 334, 370
Wildlife tree, 220. *See also* Snags
WILD LILAC. *See* NEW JERSEY TEA
Wild Ones, xiv, 7
WILD RED PLUM. *See* AMERICAN PLUM
WILD SWEET CRAB APPLE. *See* PRAI-
    RIE CRAB APPLE
WILD YELLOW PLUM. *See* AMERICAN
    PLUM
WILLOW, 117–18, 52, 311, 74, 150, 223, 315
WILLOW, 118, 53–55, 28, 80, 119, 126, 128, 139,
    150, 167, 176, 178–79, 201, 209, 211, 228, 255,
    310, 312, 316, 317, 322, 334, 394
WILLOW OAK, 209, 118, 211
Wilson, Helen Van Pelt, and Léonie Bell, 29, 35,
    46, 61, 100, 105, 363–65, 367–68
WINEBERRY, 151
WINE RASPBERRY. *See* WINEBERRY
WINGED ELM, 176–77
*WINGED EUONYMUS. See BURNING
    BUSH*
WINGED SPINDLE TREE, 240
WINGED SUMAC. *See* SHINING SUMAC
WINGED WAHOO. *See* BURNING BUSH
WINTERBERRY, 237, 234, 245, 247, 250, 308,
    314, 316, 394
WINTERCREEPER, 152, vii, 248
WINTER-FLOWERING CHERRY, 82
WINTER GRAPE. *See* GRAYBARK
    GRAPE
WINTER HAZEL, 74
*WINTER HONEYSUCKLE. See SWEET
    BREATH OF SPRING*
WISCONSIN WEEPING WILLOW, 117
*WISTERIA. See CHINESE WISTERIA;
    JAPANESE WISTERIA*

WITCH HAZEL, 75, 244
WITHEROD, 73
WOODBINE, 154, 394
Woodpile, 12, 305
WOODS' ROSE, 61
WOODVAMP. *See* CLIMBING
    HYDRANGEA
WOODVINE. *See* VIRGINIA CREEPER

YELLOW AZALEA, 56
YELLOW BIRCH, 321–22
YELLOW BUCKEYE, 98, 33, 80, 85, 109, 164,
    171, 181, 185, 187, 192, 194, 260, 332
YELLOW CATALPA. See CHINESE
    CATALPA

YELLOW CHESTNUT OAK. *See*
    CHINKAPIN OAK
YELLOW HONEYSUCKLE, 155
YELLOW PINE. *See* SHORTLEAF PINE
YELLOW POPLAR. *See* TULIP TREE
YELLOWROOT, 157, 395
YELLOWWOOD, 96–97, 45, 80, 84, 109, 114,
    164, 171, 178, 181, 187, 189, 192, 194, 253,
    260, 332, 395; YELLOWWOOD IN
    FALL, 301; YELLOWWOOD IN
    WINTER, 354
YEW, 314
YEW, 314

ZELKOVA, 174